Loosening the Seams

Loosening the Seams:
Interpretations of Gerald Vizenor

edited by

A. Robert Lee

Bowling Green State University Popular Press
Bowling Green, OH 43403

Library of Congress Cataloging-in-Publication Data

Loosening the seams : interpretations of Gerald Vizenor / edited by A.
Robert Lee
     p. cm.
     Includes bibliographical references and index.
     ISBN 0-87972-801-9 -- ISBN 0-87972-802-7 (pbk.)
     1. Vizenor, Gerald Robert, 1934---Criticism and interpretation.
    2. Indians in literature. I. Lee, A. Robert, 1941-

PS3572.I9 Z76 2000
813'.54--dc 21
                                                    99-058862

CONTENTS

ACKNOWLEDGMENTS

In common with a number of the contributors to *Loosening the Seams* I have every reason to recognize a thousand personal kindnesses on Gerald Vizenor's part, a trickster friendship, a live colloquium, offered unreservedly. I once more thank him, and Laura Hall, his wife.

This collection has also had the benefit of encouragement and help from a number of colleagues and friends. I especially thank John G. Cawelti of the University of Kentucky, who has been simply stalwart in his support.

Louis Owens is a boon, and a necessity, in any concern with Native American literature: I have had the immense advantage of being able to draw on his advice.

I need, too, to acknowledge much personal support from David Murray, Arnold Krupat, Barry O'Connell, Richard Hutson, Kathleen Moran, Donald McQuade, Joe Rigert, Gary Strankman, and Linda Lizut Helstern.

Pat Browne at Popular Press has been the soul of cooperation and sound suggestion: she has made the passage of this book from manuscript to publication a pleasure. This volume owes any number of further editorial debts to Karen Wiechman and Alma MacDougall. Their care about the project has been a major bonus and I thank them both enormously.

As always, and throughout, I owe a continuing debt of life, and Spain, to Josefa Vivancos Hernández.

INTRODUCTION

A. Robert Lee

The tribal tricksters in their stories were compassionate, cross-
bloods, and they liberated the mind.
—Gerald Vizenor, "Thank You, George Raft," in *Interior
Landscapes: Autobiographical Myths and Metaphors* (1990)

The shadows and language of tribal poets and novelists could
be the new ghost dance literature, the shadow literature of liberation
that enlivens tribal survivance.
—Gerald Vizenor, "Shadow Survivance," in *Manifest
Manners: Postindian Warriors of Survivance* (1994)

I

If, since the 1960s, it has become general currency to speak of
a Native American Renaissance, then Gerald Vizenor, mixedblood
Chippewa/Ojibway—Anishinaabe—novelist, poet, essayist, autobiographer, dramatist, journalist, editor, professor, belongs utterly in its
making. Yet however tempting the notion of a "renaissance," a no doubt
well meant (albeit, arguably, late arriving and guilty) confirmation of
Native literary imagination, he would be among the first to point to any
number of vexing implications.

Did, somehow, no Native literature precede, whether as the sumptuous, linguistically diverse and ongoing oral legacy of the tribes or as the
written (including the "translated" in all its own vexation), and however
little previously given recognition in the American canon? How, as far as
the writings go, to account for an autobiography like *A Son of the Forest*
(1829) by the Pequot Christian mixedblood William Apess; or the first-
known Native novel, *The Life and Adventures of Joaquín Murieta, the
Celebrated California Bandit* (1854), by the half-Cherokee John Rollin
Ridge; or *Sundown* (1934) by John Joseph Mathews (Osage) with its
powerful fable of tribal disinheritance, Osage-white interface and Oklahoma oil politics; or a novel like *The Surrounded* (1936) by D'Arcy
McNickle (Cree-Metis, enrolled Salish) in which Native identity and
survival in the person of Archilde Leon, son of a Flathead mother and
Spanish father, is set within the Salish country of the Pacific Northwest?

These, and other earlier Native writing by names like George Copway (Chippewa), Sarah Winnemuca (Paiute), Alexander Posey (Creek) and Mourning Dove (Colville), give literary genealogy, a lineage of voice, to the generation of which Gerald Vizenor himself has been a part.[1]

Is it, too, to be assumed that a "renaissance," as in the case of that associated with Shakespeare and 17th-century England or with Emerson and 1840's-50's New England, has always to be scriptural, a feat only of print or page? How, indeed, to give due recognition to the sumptuous orality, the sheer diversity of spoken word and its performative accompaniments of tricksterism, ceremony, humor, irony, and even silence, within Native American legacy, Plains to Coastal, Woodland to Pueblo, and thereafter off-reservation and in the cities?

As simply the most published, the most prolific ever, of all Native authors, Vizenor has been a main player in the efflorescence usually dated from Scott Momaday's *House Made of Dawn* (1968), itself a massively landmark novel of self-loss, *cauchemar* and yet, in its own vision and narrative performance, also a healing. In the life and person of its damaged mixedblood protagonist, Abel, Momaday fuses Navajo, Pueblo and Kiowa story-telling into a "modern" Native American portrait set circularly in "Walatowa" (a fictionalization of Jemez Pueblo), World War II, a miasmic Los Angeles and, by eventual return, once more in the pueblo. Abel's slow, arduous recovery from every manner of self-division, even near anonymity, Momaday tells as a rite of spiritual as much as physical journey, the restitution of self through community.

Since then an ever gathering Native gallery of new voice would be undeniable. As, too, America moves towards the new millennium, the burgeoning fiction, poetry, autobiography, drama and essay work shows little abatement. How else to regard a literary roster which includes names, and authorings, by novelists like Leslie Marmon Silko (Laguna Pueblo), Louise Erdrich (Chippewa), James Welch (Blackfoot-Gros Ventre), Thomas King (Cherokee), Martin Cruz-Smith (Senecu del Sur/Yaqui), Sherman Alexie (Spokane-Coeur D'Alene), Janet Campbell Hale (Coeur d'Alene/Kootenai) or Betty Bell (Cherokee); by short story writers like Diane Glancy (Cherokee), Basil Johnston (Chippewa) or Michael Dorris (Modoc); by poets like Linda Hogan (Chickasaw), Simon Ortiz (Acoma), Joy Harjo (Creek), Wendy Rose (Hopi-Me-Wuk) or Duane Niatum (Klallam); by memoirists and essayists from Elizabeth Cook-Lynn (Sioux) to Vine Deloria (Sioux) to Ray A. Young Bear (Mesquakie); by dramatists like Vizenor himself and Hanay Geiogamah (Kiowa-Delaware); and by a critic like Louis Owens (Choctaw-Cherokee), novelist but also the author of quite some of the best analytical writing on Native literature, as borne out in his *Other Destinies: Under-*

standing the American Indian Novel (1992) and the newly issued *Mixed-blood Messages: Literature, Film, Family, Place* (1998)?

Even so, given the sheer abundance, and matching invention, of Vizenor's own fiction and stories, as in turn of his haiku and other poetry, essay work, autobiography and forays into screen writing and drama, any looker-on from either side of the Atlantic (or well beyond) might be forgiven for thinking him a Native American Renaissance virtually in his own right. It would be an irony, and a tribute, altogether in keeping.

"I believe we're all invented as Indians" runs an acclaimed Vizenor observation in the course of a 1981 interview. The point could not be more typical—companionable, wry, teasing, contrary, and a perfect reflexive pointer to his own tribal-cum-postmodern writerly tactics. For virtually all Vizenor's writings have been given over to the deinventing, and so at the same time the reinventing, of "the Indian." For him the panoramic travesty of Native America and its peoples reaches from Cotton Mather's "murderous wretches" to Rousseau's "Enfants du Paradis," from Twain's Injun Joe to the circus "redskin" warparties of Cody's Wild West shows, from Longfellow's ahistorically (and impossibly) conjoined Anishinaabe-Iroquois figure of Hiawatha to lexical residues in place names like Manhattan and Seattle, Connecticut and Tennessee, and from cars like Jeep Cherokee and Pontiac to sports teams uninhibitedly named the Atlanta Braves and the Washington Redskins. A further paradox, for him as for other Native writers, has been "The Indian" as at once Vanishing American yet also romanticized modern eco-messiah and forerunner of New Age religiosity.

These kinds of stopover have been as shrewdly well-chosen as voluminous, whether the 20 volumes of Edward S. Curtis's photographic stills (Vizenor calls them "preserved metasavages"), the "redface" travesties in early D. W. Griffith's movies like *The Redman and His Child* (1908) or *The Squaw's Love Story* (1911), or Korzak Ziolkowski's Black Hills rock sculpture of the Lakota Holy Man, Crazy Horse. Hollywood confections, however cinematically beguiling, have especially served. They include John Ford's *Fort Apache* (1948) and *Cheyenne Autumn* (1964), Eliot Silverstein's *A Man Called Horse* (1970), Arthur Penn's *Little Big Man* (1970) and, latterly, Kevin Costner's *Dances with Wolves* (1990), which, for all its use of the Sioux language and patent liberal good intent, still resorts to a white Cavalry hero, feathered tribespeople, an updated white-woman captivity drama and, once more, the "Vanishing American" ethos, and *Pocahontas* (1995), Disney's lavish cartoon fantasy as inventive in design as it is neglectful of any actual Powhatan history. To these Vizenor himself would add the latest imaging of "Indians" in Jonathan Wacks's *Powwow Highway* (1988), Michael Apted's *Thunderheart* (1992) and *Incident at Oglala* (1992), with the AIM figure of John Trudell at its center.

Other bearings are to be found in Vizenor's take, especially in *The Heirs of Columbus* (1991), on the High Admiral of America's 1992 quincentennary who, contradictorily, has doubled as both boldest Atlantic discoverer and yet the very icon of coloniality and the European (and in its wake Euro-American) will to dominate, if not frequently near erase, the New World's people of color. To make Columbus himself into a Native, a mixedblood, and so to subvert and contest any "oppression" he might be thought to represent, was a stroke as wonderfully mischievous as it was daring. Never one not to put the cat among the pigeons, Vizenor once more upsets cliché in refusing to believe himself "oppressed" by Columbus. Likewise he has borne down upon the media "Indian" who became Tonto in ABC's 1949-58 *The Lone Ranger* (and its 1930s forerunner of the Station WXYZ series), Jay Silverheels, as the perfect silhouette "faithful Indian companion," a latter-day Man Friday companion to Clayton Moore's masked hero and fantasy white lawman.

For Vizenor, as a first counterstrike, has always insisted that all Americans of tribal descent, past or present, be construed as anything but frozen in time, a species of immobile victimry ("the Indian stuff" as Holden Caulfield revealingly calls it in *The Catcher in the Rye*). Survival, and the tragic wisdom that it has engendered, the diverse human continuities of language, irony, humor, belief, and a deeply inward and necessary sense of history, for him remain dynamic not static, tokens of the Native living not dead. That, too, holds for the massive pluralities of tribal affiliation, whether his own Minnesota White Earth Anishinaabe, the Navajo to the Kwakiutl, the Laguna to the Mohawks, the Lakota to the Hopi and, for him as important as any, the "nation" of cross- or mixedbloods, the *métis* of French-Canadian encounter, the *mestizos* of the Cortés-Aztec legacy.

His own writing has so drawn attention always to the adaptability of the tribes through the time as much as the space of each American "historical" marker, be it the Trail of Tears in 1835 and all subsequent "removal" legislation, The General Allotment (or Dawes) Act of 1887, the Wounded Knee massacre at Pine Ridge, South Dakota, in 1890 and the spread of Ghost Dance revivalism across the Plains and beyond, Congress's granting of citizenship to "Indians" in 1924 or, latterly, the so-called "termination" policies of the 1950s with their aim of imposing local closure to land claims and the like, the Wounded Knee occupation in 1973, and the rise of the casino and lottery empires of the 1980s.

Who, too, more unabatingly, or with keener antic verve, has tackled "Indian" politics from the Bureau of Indian Affairs (BIA) to Tribal Councils to the American Indian Movement (AIM); or "Indian" health issues from alcoholism to joblessness both on the reservations and in the cities; or a latter-day Native America of contested self-governance, museum ownership of bones and artifacts, or cartoon, TV, film, press and other media imaging? Little wonder that one of Vizenor's key terms has been *postindian,* the notion that because Native lives have been so encrusted in myth and stereotype it becomes necessary to move on from, or leave behind, all fabricated versions of "the Indian."

His endeavor, at the same time, has been to recognize the ongoing-ness, or in one of his key coinings, the "survivance," of Native life in its all and every variety. That, paradoxically to some, has caused him to be as unbounded in his resort to the modern cultural theory of a Jabès, Barthes, Lyotard or Foucault (Jean Baudrillard's *Simulares et Simulation* [1981] and Umberto Eco's *Travels in Hyperreality* [1990] have been especially influential) as to the gallery of Native analysis.

The latter shows its own kind of range, to include, typically, a Sioux autobiographer like Luther Standing Bear, whose *My People the Sioux* (1928) records his life from reservation to Carlisle School to the movies to political activism; a lawyer and professor as fiercely polemical as Vine Deloria (Sioux) in books like *Custer Died for Your Sins: An Indian Manifesto* (1969); and a Native feminist/Gay Rights poet and novelist as spirited as Paula Gunn Allen (Laguna Pueblo) in writing like *The Sacred Hoop: Recovering the Feminine in American Indian Traditions* (1986).

This generous intellectual eclecticism underwrites almost all his assaults on the essentialist templates so often applied, and so distorting, to Native America. Once subjected to Euro-American gaze, politics, power, and language, Native peoples, he suggests, indeed became "oth-ered" *avant la lettre,* their lives and histories made over into chimerae, shadows, figures of fantasy in a whole diorama of invention. Nor would he anything but exempt the social sciences from these processes of reifi-cation: "Indians" made over into case study.

In consequence there has been no hesitation in taking on conven-tional pieties both non-Native *and* Native. Manifest Destiny or the Win-ning of the West loom large, but so, too, do arbitrary notions of Blood Quantum or Mother Earth. For all, too, of his own historic rootedness in *métissage,* and awareness of Native communalism, Vizenor has served no uncertain notice that he has been, and remains, equally possessed of his own play of viewpoint. Which is anything but to under-rate his bid to serve as "compassionate trickster," the communitarian and healer. His has been a literary art which shades the oral into written, a voice as often third person as first person, and in which ventriloquy and all manner of canny, invitational irony has been a hallmark from the outset.

The essays in *Loosening the Seams: Interpretations of Gerald Vizenor* seek to map, and for sure to analyze, this rare, exploratory, and always playful, force of imagination. More than almost any current Native writer Vizenor has positively relished reflexivity—Native storytelling as itself story, tricksterism about tricksterism, America's "Indians" if silhouettes or harlequins then answered back from inside a live "Indian" America.

Little wonder that Vizenor has long insisted on Native Americans as indeed postindian, mirror selves yet also actual selves, or in another of his greatly purposive coinings, "double others." Would not this be an apt designation for the heirship to the first peoples of the Americas whose inaugural encounters with the Euro-Americans, the British, Spanish and French above all, and then with a frontiering white America at large, made them into precisely some composite and binaried Other—be it as the "Indian," the "piel roja," or the "peau rouge"?

As to the author of these imaginings whose output now runs to more than thirty published titles, not to mention a huge body of magazine and review publication, and in anything but too hasty a spirit to conclude, each contributor could hardly avoid asking: who, indeed what, is Gerald Vizenor?

II

"Postindian mixedblood." The phrase recurs in Vizenor's self-chronicle, *Interior Landscapes: Autobiographical Myths and Metaphors* (1990). It acts as a summary, a kind of mnemonic, for a life whose trajectory evolves from the passed around child born in 1934 in Minneapolis through to the writer-professor currently tenured at Berkeley, and in like measure, for an *oeuvre,* already voluminous, which shows not the slightest sign of slowdown. Contrariety, a willingness to speak out or write against the grain whatever the controversialism, however, was always to be part of Vizenor's style.

One begins with his very name, Vézina (with a family variant as Vézinat), a French-Canadian or *métis* nomenclature as he explains in *Interior Landscapes,* and likely mistranscribed into Vizenor. This surname, born of the fusion of white fur trader and Chippewa-Ojibway origins, passes down through White Earth and its clans and dynasties into Depression-era Minneapolis. Vizenor himself saw light as the son of Clement Vizenor, his White Earth mixedblood father who had moved to the city and become a housepainter, and Laverne Lydia Peterson, his young and equally dispossessed third-generation Swedish-American mother, who would eventually pass more or less out of his life.

The brute, startling street murder of Clement (his son was a mere two years old), and his own subsequent abandonment by his mother, meant a hardscrub, near indigent upbringing. But if a city child forced largely to parent himself and early made familiar with fostering, welfare and frequent changes of residence, the young Vizenor, however obliquely at times, came also to know himself (not least through a feisty, singular grandmother like Alice Beaulieu) as heir to the history and cultural traditions of White Earth's woodland Anishinaabe people—a tribal name, as he explains in *Summer in the Spring* (1965), that signifies "the people of the woodland" who "drew pictures of their dream songs, visions, stories and ideas on birchbark."[2]

These, in due course, he would readily transcribe in works like *Escorts to White Earth, 1868-1968, 100 Years on a Reservation* (1968), *anishinabe adisokan: Tales of the People* (1970)—an earlier revision of *Summer in the Spring* (1965, 1981, re-issued 1993), *The Everlasting Sky: New Voices from the People Named the Chippewa* (1972) and *Tribal Scenes and Ceremonies* (1976, revised 1990), a volume made up of reprints of his journalism and magazine writing. Each of these bears witness to his interest in, and respect for, "the shadow stories," "the stories in the blood," of his Native origins.

It little surprises that a similar tribal sense of fabulation marks out his own youthful story inclinations, baroque, magic realist from the outset, and instinctively full of narrative reversals and wordplay. Such he would recall to perfection in a memoir typically and fantasizingly entitled "I know what you mean, Erdupps MacChurbbs" in *Growing Up in Minnesota: Ten Writers Remember Their Childhoods* (1976).

In life, as in word, Vizenor as contradancer could not have been more clearly indicated.

III

By suitably chance symmetry Vizenor made his literary bow at the beginning of the 1960s.[3] In March 1960, and in honor of Robert Vizenor, the son born to him and Judith Horns (they were married in 1959 and divorced in 1969) he produced *Born in the Wind,* ten pages of privately printed, intimate and celebratory, lyrics. *Two Wings the Butterfly: Haiku Poems in English* followed in 1962, 56 haiku given over to the four seasons with ink paintings to complete a text-and-image whole.[4]

Haiku as a form has occupied him across three decades. *Cranes Arise: Haiku Scenes* (1999), a recent collection which builds on a 1989 pamphlet, has just been completed—in part a reflection of his interest in Anishinaabe pictomyth and, more immediately, in the Japanese language and arts of calligraphy and silkscreen which he began to acquire during military service (he had been sent to Korea but, by chance, found himself required to disembark at Yokohama and then remain stationed in Japan).[5] *Two Wings the Butterfly* had the engaging, and further contrary, distinction of having been put together by the Printing Department of Minnesota State Reformatory. Vizenor's times, and the art to which they give rise, early made the customary into the uncustomary.

In 1950, resentful at high school, denied a coherent family life by death and abandonment, and in spirit if not in reality a dropout, the fifteen-year-old Vizenor lied about his age and entered the Minnesota National Guard. This, too, was the ex-Boy Scout who had been sent to camp on onetime Anishinaabe tribal grounds. Turning eighteen in October 1952, he enlisted in the Army, trained at Fort Knox, Kentucky, and by spring 1953 found himself on the troopship that, en route to Korea, would deposit him in Japan (for a sample of Vizenor's capacity for comedy at his own expense, his "July 1950: The Masturbation Papers" in *Interior Landscapes* takes some bettering). He also turned down a possible place at Officers' Candidate School with the pleasingly ingenuous words, "Well, Sir, I just want to be with the men." A near Catch-22 run of typical happenstance followed, not least on account of having a name at the end of the alphabet.

One unlikely role gave way to another: clerk, for which he trained in typing at the Army's correspondence school; tank commander, once in Japan, in the 70th Tank Battalion (his fellow combatants, replacement personnel like himself, were nearly all of Slavic background—names beginning with "v" or "w"); NCO trainee; soldier student in several high school equivalency correspondence courses; theater jack of all trades, director, and scriptwriter in an entertainment unit based near Camp Sendai; Army serviceman in civilian clothes whose love affair with Aiko Okada took him to Matsushima and other coastal venues; and, on discharge in August 1955, intending media specialist in Washington, D.C., at the Capital Engineering Institute. The worlds of Minneapolis, and White Earth beyond it, could not have seemed further behind.

Yet other twists lay to hand. Visiting with Army friends in New York City, he sat in on classes at NYU only to find himself, through 1955-56, and by a fudge of enrollment, a fulltime student. But cash was short, and from 1956 to 1960, he transferred to the University of Minnesota, majoring in Child Development and Asian Area Studies. On graduation, he married, and became a social worker in the Minnesota State Reformatory, whose printing press he would put to his own use (a county welfare job that included parts of the Leech Lake Reservation was denied him because as an "Indian" he had relatives on the client file); and, from 1962 to 1964, he returned to the university for graduate studies in Library Science and, again, Asian Studies. The early Kennedy-Johnson years, with Civil Rights, the War on Poverty, Community Action Programs, and Headstart, implicated him in another turning point. American "minority" status seemed destined for change, whether "Negro" as was and "Black" as was soon to be, "Hispanic" as was and "Latino" as was soon to be, or "Indian" itself with its pending alternative of "Native American."

First, he left the university, in part, ironically, because his own first serious "Indian" writing, a proposed graduate thesis on *The Progress,* the White Earth Reservation newspaper founded and edited by his own Beaulieu relatives, was not considered of "academic merit." He looks back on the decision as "institutional racism." Occasional journalistic pieces, however, had begun to find a home, the majority taken up with the plight of "urban Indians." The step into full-time activism followed readily enough.

From 1964 to 1968 he became a community organizer (which on more than a few occasions involved him in going against BIA policy decisions) and the hands-on, controversial director of The American Indian Employment Center in Minneapolis. Intentionally or not, he became notable enough to merit a visit from, and to become the frequent adviser of, then Senator Walter Mondale. But in the wake of this politics of "the street"—from welfare cases to tenancy problems, health or educations referrals to counseling of every stripe—another politics, this time explicitly of "the word," was to do its beckoning.

The transfer from one to the other came about mostly through his report on the trial and (later commuted) death sentence of Thomas James White Hawk. This South Dakota mixedblood Sioux, whom Vizenor has always believed suffered "cultural schizophrenia," obsessed him from the beginning. It led to "Thomas James White Hawk," an essay published in 1968, a specific case history that at the same time pointed to the far larger symptomology of the divided call on loyalties for most Native Americans. The White Hawk case together with that of Dane Michael White, a South Dakota tribal boy of thirteen who hanged himself in the Wilkin County Jail, Breckenridge, Minnesota, after being left mainly in isolation for six weeks for truancy, were to act as latest turning-points. They led him to become, from 1968 to 1970, a full-time reporter (Molly Ivins was a co-employee) for the *Minneapolis Tribune.*

His position on the *Tribune* also took different forms: general assignment staff writer initially, editorial writer with his own byline in 1974, and contributing editor from 1974 to 1976. He has had occasion to recall, and with not a little wryness, that his first assignment was a piece arguing in the light of Robert Kennedy's assassination that America, even so, did not amount to a violent society (" 'Violence' View Challenged" ran the headline). Not only, however, had the second Kennedy killing given him the opportunity of a career in journalism, a further irony offered itself in that RFK, as Chair of the Senate Subcommittee on Indian Education, had been spearheading an improvement in school and college opportunity for young Native Americans. Then, too, like other American newspapermen before him, most celebratedly Stephen Crane and Ernest Hemingway, he found that the regimen of matching word to experience edged him more and more toward the very literary vocation that would take him out of journalism.

Other markers were quick to show themselves. One came out of his assignment in 1972 for a seven-part editorial series on AIM, which led not only to his journalism but to an array of pastiches based on the Wounded Knee events of 1973 and the whole ensuing Banks-Means-Bellecourt and FBI imbroglio. Another could be seen in his growing output of poetry, haiku as ever but also a range of verse exhibiting its own Native reference and metaphor.

Most tellingly, he had also been seized by the emergence of new and soon to be landmark Native written texts, successors, for him, to the Thomas Wolfe, John Steinbeck, and Kahlil Gibran he had once found himself borrowing from the Camp Schimmelfennig Military Library in Japan, itself a name worthy of Vizenor's own best satiric devising. None, in this respect, more aroused his admiration or writerly sense of getting left behind than N. Scott Momaday's *House Made of Dawn* (1968). In Dee Brown's *Bury My Heart at Wounded Knee* (1970) Vizenor also warmed to history that challenged American "exceptionalist" self-congratulation and, whatever Brown's personal origins, sought a Native American perspective.

Yet another kind of marker arose out of his return to the academy and to a formal context of books and scholarship. When Lake Forest College, Illinois, asked him in 1970 to undertake a year's teaching, paradox again played its part. For the first time ever he was asked to "memorialize" his life in a Curriculum Vitae. The graduate student of a few years earlier had become the professor. His sponsor wanted to employ him for his haiku rather than any social science or other skill. And, for a reporter who had already seen his share of the cutting edge, he discovered himself not a little shocked, "distracted" he called it, at the campus drug scene.

Just as quickly, however, in 1970 he stepped into a federal Desegregation Program in Park Rapids School District, Minnesota; in 1971-72 became Director of Indian Studies at Bemidji State University, Minnesota; in 1973 was awarded a Bush Foundation Leadership grant and studied at Harvard; and, after his two-year stint as editorial writer for the *Tribune,* in 1976 accepted an appointment at Berkeley in Native American Studies, which he would alternate with teaching commitments at the University of Minnesota. In 1978 Minnesota made him their James J. Hill Professor. Vizenor's fellow Minnesotan novelist, Scott Fitzgerald, must have smiled down in amusement from his Jazz Heaven at a Chair so named: Hill, as railway magnate, serves as his ironic watchword in *The Great Gatsby* for one of the Gilded Age's most unregenerate robber barons.

Through his own Nodin Press ("nodin" means "wind" in Anishinaabe), which he sold after a year to the book distributor Norton Stillman, he published a series of handsomely bound and printed collections like *Seventeen Chirps: Haiku in English* (1964), *Raising the Moon Vines: Original Haiku in English* (1964), *Slight Abrasions: A Dialogue in Haiku* (1966), co-written with Jerome Downes, and *Empty Swings: Haiku in English* (1967). Other small presses and publishers, among them Callimachus, Four Winds New Rivers, and Crowell-Collier, would be involved in issuing his transcriptions of Anishinaabe tribal history, oral lore and myth. In 1974, however, his interests drew him to the genre that would do most to establish his reputation. He began the first of his novels, a pilgrim's progress or dream quest told in part as a book-within-a-book and in part as a satyricon, which initially he published in 1978 as *Darkness in Saint Louis Bearheart,* and then, in 1990, under the revised title of *Bearheart: The Heirship Chronicles.*

In June 1983, having two years earlier married Laura Hall, a Britisher of English and Chinese-Guyanese background who had been studying at Berkeley, he left Minnesota permanently. The call to other change had sounded. No small move, furthermore, was to be involved: Vizenor and Hall stepped at once west and east, to Tianjin University, and to a China still, if uncertainly, under Maoist political rules. In due course it would yield his second novel, *Griever: An American Monkey King in China* (1987), which weaves the "mind monkey" tricksterism of Chinese opera in the person of Sun Wu k'ung into Griever de Hocus as Anishinaabe counterpart. Vizenor takes well-aimed shies at both communism and capitalism, the politics of Chinese state puritanism and of American profligacy.

In spring 1984, after an interlude writing in Santa Fe, New Mexico, he returned to Berkeley, first half time and then full time, appointments he held for three years. In 1987 he then followed Highway 1 the 70 or so miles south to a senior professorship in literature at UC Santa Cruz, becoming Provost of Kresge College during 1989-90. Four years later, 1991-92, saw him in the David Burr Chair of Letters at the University of

Oklahoma, Norman, before accepting his present full-time position, once more in Ethnic Studies at Berkeley. His career, too, as leading Native American writer-professor has increasingly required that he play the inveterate panelist both in America and in different international forums, with a matching run of radio and TV spots. USIA lectures and reading tours have taken him in the last decade to Canada, Japan, Germany, Italy, Holland, and England, interspersed with research and other trips to Britain, Tanzania, Guyana, and Hong Kong.

The writing from this latter decade has amounted to a near flood, to which should be added frequently anthologized pieces like the haiku included in Louis Untermeyer's *The Pursuit of Poetry* (1970), "Bound Feet" and "Holosexual Clown," the two extracts selected by Ishmael Reed and his fellow editors for *The Before Columbus Foundation Fiction Anthology* (1992), the writings gathered in *Shadow Distance: A Gerald Vizenor Reader* (1994), and the literary choices which make up *Native American Literature: A Brief Introduction and Anthology* (1995) in the HarperCollins Literary Mosaic Series under the General Editorship of Ishmael Reed.

Wordarrows: Indians and Whites in the New Fur Trade (1978) threads seventeen sketches of "the urban reservation" into a single seam. *Earthdivers: Tribal Narratives on Mixed Descent* (1981) mixes story and reportage to locate yet other tribal experiences of the city. *Crossbloods: Bone Courts, Bingo, and Other Reports* (1990) shows the local acuity of his newspaper-trained eye, whether for the issue of museum-held tribal "remains," reservation lottery, AIM militancy, or the use of "Indian" names. *Landfill Meditation: Crossblood Stories* (1991) offers a play of word, voices and spoof in just measure for his own brand of magic-realist tribal storytelling. *Manifest Manners* (1994), in turn, cagily elides story into essay and vice versa to sustain his analysis of, and wholly unrepentant rebuke to, the processes severally responsible for all spurious "Indianness."

Vizenor has subsequently weighed in with his latest and full-length *discursus—Fugitive Poses: Native American Indian Scenes of Absence and Presence* (1998). If Native peoples have been deadeningly imaged, appropriated, in museum displays, captivity narratives, BIA and other "documentation," anthropology (which he insists should be called "anthropologetics"), New Age or other bogus shamanism, they have in fact, and in simply myriad "live" ways, *always* confuted so static a set of reductions. Initially addresses given in the name of the Great Emancipator, the Abraham Lincoln Lecture Series of 1997, at the University of Nebraska, *Fugitive Poses* represents Vizenor at strength, a rich, fierce, detailed anatomy of the "theaters" of contradiction which have held sway both about, and within, Native American culture. There can also now be added *Postindian Conversations* (1999) by Gerald Vizenor and A. Robert Lee, a full-length and broad-ranging volume of opinion and exchange.

Much of his work, too, has had an alternative life, as it were, not just in newspapers like the *Minneapolis Tribune* or *Twin Citian* but in Italian, French and German translations, and, to invoke the more prominent, in journals like *World Literature Today, Fiction International, Caliban, Before Columbus Review, Wicazo Sa Review, Native American Literature,* and *Zyzzyva.* Given so unceasing a creativity, it merely adds to the record that he established the first Native American Literature prize, while teaching at Santa Cruz, and in 1990 proposed, and then became the editor of, the University of Oklahoma Press's American Indian Literature and Critical Studies Series, acting in the process as mentor to a new generation of Native American writers like Kimberly Blaeser (Chippewa-Ojibway), whose *Gerald Vizenor: Writing in the Oral Tradition* (1996) marks the first full-length critical study of his work, Diane Glancy (Cherokee), Gordon Henry Jr. (Chippewa-Ojibway) and Betty Louise Bell (Cherokee).

No sense of Vizenor, man or writer, however, could be fully complete without reference to *Interior Landscapes: Autobiographical Myths and Metaphors* (1990), deservedly the winner of the PEN Oakland Josephine Miles Award. Like "Crows Written on Poplars: Autocritical Autobiographies," a soliloquy on tribal history and the creative vocation that he contributed to Arnold Krupat's *I Tell You Now: Autobiographical Essays by Native American Writers* (1987), it makes, too, a necessary context for his ongoing novels.

These, in the wake of *Bearheart* (1978, 1990) and *Griever* (1987), show an imagination as always and continuingly taken up with ancestry, memory, pastness, yet nothing if not modern into postmodern, full of reflexive turn and swerve. *The Trickster of Liberty: Tribal Heirs to a Wild Baronage* (1988) develops into a kind of antic detective story involving a Berkeley-style campus, purloined "Indian relics," anthropology and computers and which plays the habits and texts of academism against Native trickster lives and history. *The Heirs of Columbus* (1991) amounts to a teasing and about-face quincentennial "tribal story" of Columbus as Mayan, a transposition of Spain's Genoese discoverer of "The New World" into himself a Native mixedblood. His descendant, Stone Columbus, runs a bingo barge, the *Santa Maria Casino,* whose laser light show literally highlights against the night sky many of the key figures in the story of Native America: Naanabozho, Buffalo Bill Cody, the *métis* leader Louis Riel, Crazy Horse, Black Elk, along with Eleanor Roosevelt. Vizenor is able, thereby, simultaneously to deconstruct the

Columbus lore and, postindianly to a fault, then both deinvent, and reinvent, the very notion of "The Indian."

In *Dead Voices: Natural Agonies in the New World* (1992), Vizenor shadows Beckett terrain, though always from within his own Native play of myth. Told as a bear-woman transformation in the person of Bagese, and given the design of the seven-card Anishinaabe chance game *wanaki,* it yields a cycle of shamanistic stories in the mirror. A story as parabular, and elliptical, as any he has written, rarely has Vizenor managed a more challenging vision of Native identity.

Hotline Healers: An Almost Browne Novel (1997), teasingly a novel as story-cycle, situates its hero, Almost (the perfect trickster-mixedblood name), at the center of a whole family "barony" of White Earth tricksters. The upshot is Vizenor's pastiche of New Age and psychic phone services, the academy, a Nixon who wants "Indians" to invade Cuba, together with a marvellously funny-ingenious explanation of the 18-minute gap in the Watergate tapes.

Introducing *Narrative Chance: Postmodern Discourse on Native American Indian Literatures* (1989), an essay collection under his editorship given over to "translation and representation in tribal literature," he insists that "Native American Indian Stories are told and heard in motion." The point could as readily apply not only to his own writing but his own life. "Motion," or to put it another way, "chance," can be said to have been his one constant. "Chance and the contradictions of tribal and national identities," he observes, "would become my sources of inspiration as a creative writer."

IV

The essays in *Loosening the Seams: Interpretations of Gerald Vizenor,* by editorial design at least, are intended to take up both the span and the detail of Vizenor's writing. Thus in weighing the literary career overall they seek to develop context, cross-refer, adduce relevant theory, yet at the same time keep the imaginative specifics of each Vizenor text always sharply in view.

Four general accounts open the bidding. David Murray pursues the ventriloquy at work in Vizenor, his often fantastical subversion and appropriation in both fiction and non-fiction of stereotypical "Cowboys and Indians," nostalgic "Vanishing Americans." The emphasis falls upon Vizenor's storytelling forms and tropes, a disruptive circuit of language, namings and story as counterweight to each historic cliché about Native America. Elaine Jahner, relatedly, analyzes tricksterism as the determining "narrative dynamic" in Vizenor, the refusal of all totalizing schema with as "open" a run of texts as possible to match.

Barry O'Connell takes on the complex issue of "representation" in Vizenor's imagined worlds, his steadfast subversion of savagism, Noble or Daemonic, not to mention victim-mongering, the affrays of fullblood as against mixedblood credentials, and New Age religiosity with all its largely invented (and often comic) baggage. Vizenor's quest, he suggests, seeks history from out of myth, truth from out of category. If, given the wide view of Vizenor as one of America's ranking postmoderns, then why not a comparison with Afro-America's co-spirit in the form of Ishmael Reed? Amy J. Elias offers a full, scrupulous taxonomy of both, two complementary styles of syncretism—Native American and African American, in which, she suggests, both writers display a virtuoso hand in the turns of reflexive storytelling.

Two "life studies," to borrow Robert Lowell's phrase, follow. Richard Hutson identifies the subtle riffs of voice and texture in Vizenor's *Interior Landscapes: Autobiographical Myths and Metaphors,* his "contradictory identities" given their own matching "contradictory" first-person form. Joe Rigert, Vizenor's early and longtime colleague at the *Minneapolis Tribune,* offers a complementary memoir, an affectionate looking-back to the print journalist even at the outset as willing to tackle a self-publicizing AIM leadership as white establishment politicians.

Each subsequent essay centers more on specific writings by Vizenor. In her closely allusive reading of *Griever: An American Monkey King in China* Linda Lizut Helstern pursues the parallels between Anishinaabe and Sun Wu-k'ung tricksterism in Vizenor's "China" fable. She emphasizes the role of Chinese opera, folk myth, avian and transformational imagery in the shaping of the novel.

The Heirs of Columbus attracts two distinctive accounts. Elizabeth Blair subjects it to whodunnit or detective rules, a "Columbus text" which enfolds a far deeper historical-tribal mystery within its ostensibly conventional mystery format. Arnold Krupat examines the same novel for its implications of "nation and narrative" within the contextual ambiguity of America's 1992 quincentenary self-celebration. As to *Dead Voices: Natural Agonies in the New World,* that comes under a five-author collective scrutiny, a vision story both shamanistic in itself and about shamanism. The essay explores Vizenor's envisioning of the world (its setting is contemporary Oakland) as chance game, his use of "gaze," and play of voice, as simultaneously indebted to a tribal bear woman and Samuel Beckett. David Mogen, in comparing Vizenor's novels with Leslie Marmon Silko's novel-anthem to Laguna and other Native casualty in the drama of America's western settlement in *Almanac of the Dead* (1991), argues for a transformed, and transforming, Science Fiction perspective, Vizenor and Silko as writing "crossblood metaphysics."

Tom Lynch analyzes Vizenor's poetry, the successive collections of haiku and the longer verse, using the play of impermanence and permanence as a key dialectic in the language of what has been a lifetime's craft. James Ruppert treats Vizenor's *Harold of Orange* as trickster screenplay, "Indians," as it were, playing "Indians," and in a comedy whose implications defamiliarizingly point to a familiar, and longstanding, American drama of mistaken Native identity.

Louis Owens, mixedblood novelist in his own right who made his bow in *Wolfsong* (1991), a Native rite of passage story set against the North Cascades in Washington State and steeped in Salish landscape and history, examines the significance of the essay "Ishi Obscura" and the play *Ishi and the Wood Ducks* as coeval parts in Vizenor's campaign against "museum Indians." He argues for the Yahi survivor in Vizenor's imagining as at once the incarnation, and yet always not, of America's love-hate romanticization of its Native peoples.

For her part Juana María Rodríguez links Ishi to another figure who has long occupied Vizenor, namely Thomas White Hawk, the young Dakota Sioux crossblood sentenced in 1967 for the murder of James Yeado and the rape of his wife. Both Ishi and White Hawk, she argues, need to be situated within the context of America's internal colonialism, jurisprudence, and popular culture "myths of the Indian."

My own account of *Manifest Manners: Postindian Warriors of Survivance* seeks to locate how, in his untiring fascination with the "simulations" of Native America (with, again, Baudrillard a prime influence), he has played the textual shape-shifter—a "postindian" authoriality ingeniously at one with "postindian" Native life and experience. It offers a necessarily close reading, the examination of those stylings of language and argument which have been so intrinsic to Vizenor's postindian crossblood vision.

Latest Vizenor, the novel *Hotline Healers: An Almost Browne Novel* (1997) and his discursive *Fugitive Poses: Native American Indian Scenes of Absence and Presence* (1998), is taken up by Colin Samson. A social scientist himself by training, Samson looks into Vizenor's teasing of all social-scientific category: its frequent reduction of human "transmotion" to stasis, its keeping company with essentialists, be they Native or Non-Native.

Few who confront Vizenor's writing can be long in doubt of its virtuosity or its grounds for durability. He has been, and remains, a key shaping presence in all consideration of Native imaginative achievement—and as bold in the irony of his vision as in his wordplay. The present collection was conceived to evaluate him overall, a set of pathways into the achievement of one of Native America's, one of America's, out front inventive talents.

Gerald Vizenor may not find himself, nor may all his readers, wholly in accord with every interpretation offered in *Loosening the Seams*. That would be unlikely in quite any writer of consequence, and especially one whose vision has thriven on equivocation, tease, every kind of rare chance-taking in language or story. But neither he, nor they, and whether from inside or beyond Native America, will fail to discern an overall warmth of esteem, the readiest sense of his "postindian" challenge as a source not only of enlightenment but of pleasure.

Notes

1. William Apess, *A Son of the Forrest: The Experience of William Apess, a Native of the Forest, Comprising a Notice of the Pequot Tribe of Indians* (New York: Author, 1829); John Rollin Ridge, *The Life and Adventures of Joaquín Murieta, the Celebrated California Bandit* (1854; reprinted Norman: U of Oklahoma P, 1977); John Joseph Mathews, *Sundown* (New York: Longmans, Green, 1934); and D'Arcy McNickle, *The Surrounded* (New York: Dodd, Mead, 1936).

2. "I Know What You Mean, Erdupps MacChurbbs," in Chester Anderson, ed., *Growing Up in Minnesota: Ten Writers Remember Their Childhoods* (Minneapolis: U of Minnesota P, 1976).

3. This biographical section reworks materials which first appeared in my "Introduction" to *Shadow Distance: A Gerald Vizenor Reader* (Middletown, NH: Wesleyan UP, 1994).

4. Both these collections were privately printed in St. Cloud, MN.

5. The earlier collection is *Water Striders*, Porter Broadside Series (Santa Cruz, CA: Moving Parts P, 1989).

Works Cited

Allen, Paula Gunn. *The Sacred Hoop: Recovering the Feminine in American Indian Tradition.* Boston: Beacon P, 1986.

Apess, William. *A Son of the Forrest: The Experience of William Apess, a Native of the Forest, Comprising a Notice of the Pequot Tribe of Indians.* New York: Author, 1829.

Baudrillard, Jean. *Simulares et Simulation.* Paris: Galilée, 1981.

Blaeser, Kimberly. *Gerald Vizenor: Writing in the Oral Tradition.* Norman: U of Oklahoma P, 1996.

Brown, Dee. *Bury My Heart at Wounded Knee: An Indian History of the American West.* New York: Holt, 1971.

Deloria, Vine. *Custer Died for Your Sins: An Indian Manifesto.* Norman: U of Oklahoma P, 1969.

Eco, Umberto. *Travels in Hyperreality.* San Diego: Harcourt, Brace, Jovanovitch, 1990.

Mathews, John Joseph. *Sundown.* New York: Longmans, Green, 1934.

McNickle, D'Arcy. *The Surrounded.* New York: Dodd, Mead, 1936.

Momaday, N. Scott. *House Made of Dawn.* New York: Harper and Row, 1968.

Owens, Louis. *Mixedblood Messages: Literature, Film, Family, Place.* Norman: U of Oklahoma P, 1998.

——. *Other Destinies: Understanding the American Indian Novel.* Norman: U of Oklahoma P, 1992.

——. *Wolfsong.* Albuquerque: West End P, 1991.

Reed, Ishmael, Kathryn Trueblood, and Shawn Wong, eds. *The Before Columbus Foundation Fiction Anthology.* New York: Norton, 1992.

Ridge, John Rollin. *The Life and Adventures of Joaquín Murieta, the Celebrated California Bandit.* 1854. Norman: U of Oklahoma P, 1977.

Silko, Leslie Marmon. *Almanac of the Dead.* New York: Simon & Schuster, 1991.

Standing Bear, Luther (Ota K'te). *My People, the Sioux.* Brininstool, 1928; Lincoln: U of Nebraska P, 1975.

Swann, Brian, and Arnold Krupat, eds. *I Tell You Now: Autobiographical Essays by Native American Writers.* Lincoln: U of Nebraska P, 1987.

Untermeyer, Louis, ed. *The Pursuit of Poetry.* New York: Simon & Schuster, 1970.

Vizenor, Gerald. *anishinabe adisokan: Tales of the People.* Minneapolis: Nodin P, 1970.

——. *Bearheart: The Heirship Chronicles.* Minneapolis: U of Minnesota P, 1990.

——. *Crossbloods: Bone Courts, Bingo, and Other Reports.* Minneapolis: U of Minnesota P, 1990.

——. *Darkness in Saint Louis Bearheart.* Minneapolis: Truck P, 1978.

——. *Dead Voices: Natural Agonies in the New World.* Norman: U of Oklahoma P, 1992.

——. *Earthdivers: Tribal Narratives on Mixed Descent.* Minneapolis: U of Minnesota P, 1981.

——. *Empty Swings: Haiku in English.* Minneapolis: Nodin P, 1967.

——. *Escorts to White Earth, 1868-1968: 100 Years on a Reservation.* Minneapolis: Four Winds, 1968.

——. *The Everlasting Sky: New Voices from the People Named the Chippewa.* New York: Crowell-Collier P, 1972.

——. *Fugitive Poses: Native American Indian Scenes of Absence and Presence.* The Abraham Lincoln Series. Lincoln: U of Nebraska P, 1998.

——. *Griever: An American Monkey King in China.* Normal: Illinois State U and Fiction Collective, 1987. Reprinted Minneapolis: U of Minnesota P, 1990.

——. *The Heirs of Columbus.* Middletown, CT: Wesleyan UP, 1991.

——. *Hotline Healers: An Almost Browne Novel.* Hanover, NH: Wesleyan UP, UP of New England, 1997.

——. *Interior Landscapes: Autobiographical Myths and Metaphors.* Minneapolis: U of Minnesota P, 1990.

——. *Landfill Meditation: Crossblood Stories.* Hanover, NH: Wesleyan UP/UP of New England, 1991.

——. *Manifest Manners: Postindian Warriors of Survivance.* Hanover, NH: Wesleyan UP/UP of New England, 1994.

——. *Narrative Chance: Postmodern Discourse on Native American Indian Literatures.* Albuquerque: U of New Mexico P, 1989. Paperbound ed. Norman: U of Oklahoma P, 1993.

——. *Native American Literature: A Brief Introduction and Anthology.* New York: HarperCollins, 1995.

——. *Postindian Conversations* with A. Robert Lee. Lincoln: U of Nebraska P, 1999.

——. *Raising the Moon Vines: Original Haiku in English.* Minneapolis: Nodin P, 1964.

——. *Seventeen Chirps: Haiku in English.* Minneapolis: Nodin P, 1964.

——. *Shadow Distance: A Gerald Vizenor Reader.* Ed. A. Robert Lee. Hanover, NH: Wesleyan UP/UP of New England, 1994.

——. *Slight Abrasions: A Dialogue in Haiku,* with Jerome Downes. Minneapolis: Nodin P, 1996.

——. *Summer in the Spring: Anishinaabe Lyric Poems and Stories.* Norman: U of Oklahoma P, 1993.

——. *Tribal Scenes and Ceremonies.* Minneapolis: Nodin P, 1976

——. *Tribal Scenes and Ceremonies.* Rev. ed. Minneapolis: U of Minnesota P, 1990.

——. *The Trickster of Liberty: Tribal Heirs to a Wild Baronage.* Minneapolis: U of Minnesota P, 1988.

——. *Wordarrows: Indians and Whites in the New Fur Trade.* Minneapolis: U of Minnesota P, 1978.

1

CROSSBLOOD STRATEGIES
IN THE WRITINGS OF GERALD VIZENOR

David Murray

Over many centuries Indians have occupied a paradoxical and puz-
zling place in American life and thought, throwing into question the very
bases of the nation, and its claims to legitimacy. In claiming an absolute
priority and sovereignty which negates the moral and legal power of the
United States over them, they are different from all other racial or ethnic
groups, and constitute an implicit challenge to the ways in which issues
of ethnicity and multiculturalism are currently being reformulated. A further irony, though, is that this most ambiguous and paradoxical group
has been subject to an essentializing rhetoric, in which Indianness is constantly associated with purity or simplicity, rather than the complexities
and ambiguities of change and history.[1] The effects of this can still be
seen in much Indian as well as white writing, and Gerald Vizenor's writing, with its emphasis on the crossing of races, genres, conventions and
boundaries of all kinds offers one of the most powerful and extended
demystifications of this rhetoric of Indianness, wherever it is found.

Vizenor's witty and often surreal narratives move freely across the
genres of novel, autobiography, history, myth and fantasy. While some
of his work is more clearly fiction or reportage, the genres are always in
an unstable and often exhilarating relation, with the result that the reader
is never allowed to forget the complexity of any situation involving the
representation, including self-representation, of American Indians. Since
his first full-blown novel, *Darkness in Saint Louis Bearheart* (1978),
reissued as *Bearheart: The Heirship Chronicles* (1990), he has published
several series of linked stories, among them *The Trickster of Liberty*
(1988), *Landfill Meditation* (1991), and *Dead Voices: Natural Agonies in
the New World* (1992), collections of essays and reportage (*The People
Named the Chippewa* [1984], *Crossbloods* [1990] and *Manifest Manners: Postindian Warriors of Survivance* [1994]), as well as an autobiography, *Interior Landscapes* (1990), and poems and journalism. His 1991
book, *The Heirs of Columbus,* was a timely and characteristically witty
re-writing of the Columbus material which avoided the stale oppositions

of celebration and recrimination triggered off by the Quincentenary.

Because of the deliberate blurring of genres in Vizenor's work, but also because of a tendency to repeat material, only marginally changed or revised, from one book to another, some of the books are difficult to keep separate, and they can all be said to be addressing in different ways the same issue, of how to imagine and express a viable contemporary Indian identity. Straightaway, though, this must be qualified by saying that Vizenor avoids the word Indian, using the terms "tribal people" or, most crucially, "crossblood." These represent two important aspects of contemporary Indian identity, and in Vizenor's work they act in a relation of supplementarity. The crossblood acts as supplement, both in *adding to,* but also in *replacing* the idea of a pure tribal Indian identity based on blood and lineage, and it is this shifting and ultimately undecidable relation of the two terms which I think reflects Vizenor's enterprise.[2] As Vizenor insists, to be an Indian now usually is to be a mixedblood, both racially and culturally, even though the white cultural traditions in which Indians have been represented have always associated pure blood with authenticity and "half-breeds" or mixedbloods with degeneration. (His more recent use of the term "postindian" is a typically ambiguous formulation, referring to the strategic claiming of Indian status and made possible precisely by the absence of the real thing, what he calls the "sensation of a new tribal presence in the very ruins of the representation of invented Indians.")[3]

By insisting on the term crossblood and focusing as much on the urban as on the reservation dimensions of contemporary Indian life, Vizenor is dissociating himself from a well-worn stance which tries to recapture, in writing if not in life, a purer past. For most Indian writers this relation to the past has been crucial, if only in that, as for any ethnic identity, this is at least the starting point for identifying what constitutes one's ethnic specificity and difference. For Indians, though, this past is so overlaid with distortions and misconceptions as to be well-nigh unrecoverable, and yet the contemporary versions of Indianness on offer seem to be profoundly bound up in this history, or in the circulation of images which seems to constitute history for most Americans. Umberto Eco uses the term hyperreality to describe the product of the process whereby "the American imagination demands the real thing and, to attain it, must fabricate the absolute fake; where the boundaries between game and illusion are blurred."[4] For Indians this is not just confined to such obvious cases of prepackaging and historical consumerism as Disney World, but has permeated all representations, from the scientific to the popular. "Tribal peoples, in this sense, have been invented as 'absolute fakes' in social science models, cinema and popular media" (*Crossbloods* 55).

For Vizenor the epitome of this transformation of living cultures into frozen tableaux, to be used for instruction or entertainment, is the case of Ishi. During the 1920s, as the sole remaining member of his small tribe, Ishi actually lived in a museum at Berkeley for the last part of his life, where he could be viewed making tools and acting out the role of wild Indian. Vizenor picks up the fact that Ishi's tribal name was never divulged, as there was no tribe to share it with, and insists that "Ishi was never his real name. Ishi is a simulation, the absence of his tribal names" (*Manifest Manners* 126). He is a perfect example for Vizenor, in that he embodies literally and concretely that process of objectification which takes place more generally but metaphorically, and which has been the subject of so much self-scrutiny in anthropology.[5] He is also interesting, though, for the way his case reveals the limits of such a process, even for those carrying it out. When Ishi died his friend and guardian Alfred Kroeber refused to allow his remains to be used for scientific purposes, declaring in a ringing phrase that science could go to hell.[6]

Together with Ishi's treatment Vizenor puts the widespread "capturing" of the images of Indians in settings and poses which fix and limit them as "vanishing Americans."[7] He singles out a photograph by Edward Curtis, from whose huge collection many of the iconic images of Indians we have inherited have been taken. Vizenor points out that an alarm clock has been erased from the photograph, because it jarred with the desired mood in suggesting change and adaptation rather than doomed stasis. In one of his best pieces, Vizenor has one of his trickster characters, Tune Browne, stand in an election, only to find his image captured and distorted by his opponents: "Who *was* that stranger in the image?" (*Crossbloods* 89) the text asks, with clear echoes of another racist scenario. At the first international conference on "socioacupuncture and tribal identities" Browne has Curtis responsible for the present distortions of his image. "We were consumed in camera time, we lost the election and became prisoners in his negatives."[8]

The antidote for Vizenor's characters is what he calls socioacupuncture, a cultural striptease which "reverses the documents, deflates data, dissolves historical time, releases the pressure in captured images and exposes the pale inventors of the tribes" (*Crossbloods* 91), and while his characters literally act this out, it is also a good description of Vizenor's own literary strategies. It is important to see that such a "striptease in mythic satire" is different from a mere correction of stereotypes or a call for historical accuracy. What appeals to Vizenor about striptease is its contradictory quality, and the fact that it provokes what Roland Barthes calls a "pretense of fear, as if eroticism here went no further than a sort of delicious terror" (qtd. in *Crossbloods* 83). The paradox is that the

eroticism is in the clothes and in the tease, rather than the final nakedness, and Vizenor draws a parallel with the putting on and off of images.
If "tribal cultures are colonised in a reversal of the striptease," then they
can be freed not with a nakedness which is a lack of any identity but a
creative and teasing play with costume and imposture. As he observes:

We lost the election in leathers and feathers, failed and fixed in history, but
through mythic satire we reverse the inventions, and during our ritual striptease
the inventions vanish. (*Crossbloods* 92)

One such performance is staged when, as Tune Browne relates it, he and
Ishi are given honorary degrees by the anthropologists of the University
of California, where Ishi was a living exhibit. Browne is dismissive of
academia, referring to degrees as merely "uniforms in the word wars . . .
not much better than being elected to the plastic flower growers association hall of fame" (93), but Vizenor is also prepared at least to float the
possibility that such a belated recognition would signify some important
change. He quotes the sociologist Robert Bellah to the effect that "the
transvaluation of roles that turns the despised and oppressed into symbols
of salvation and rebirth is nothing new in the history of human culture,
but when it occurs it is an indication of new cultural directions, perhaps
of a deep cultural revolution" (*Trickster of Liberty* 49-50). In his description of the ceremony Vizenor combines a reference to this passage, Ishi's
first recorded English words ("evelybody hoppy?") and an allusion to
Barthes on striptease to create a typically complex and comic scene.

Tune and Ishi paraded down the aisles in the amphitheater, dressed in their
breechcloths and academic sashes with animals and tribal spirits under the red-
wood trees. The two graduates circled the dais and then rendered a ritual
striptease deep in a cultural revolution
    "Evelybody hoppy?" asked Doctor Ishi.
    "What delicious terrors," said Doctor Tune Browne.
    "Strip the anthropologists."
    "Strip their words," someone shouted.
    "Evelybody strip," three tribal women mocked from the back of the
amphitheater, "that would make us very hoppy." They unbuttoned their blouses
and trousers as they moved down the aisle.
    "Evelybody hoppy?" asked Doctor Ishi.
    "Evelybody hoppy," mocked the trickster. (50)

For Vizenor, the most effective response to false images is not just
more accuracy, better history, but a creative awareness, using humor,

myth and dream, of how such images have to be deconstructed and used rather than ignored and dismissed. His defense of satire corresponds to this, in that rather than operating, as satire traditionally has, from a firm moral standpoint, or a position of more knowledge, his method works from "magical connections with the oral tradition." He wants "mythic satire, not as a moral lesson, but a dream voice out of time like a striptease in the middle of the word wars" (*Crossbloods* 91). In developing such satire, too, Vizenor is careful not to claim too privileged a standpoint based on his own Indian identity or lineage. He takes too seriously the deconstructive postmodern theorists he quotes, to believe that anyone can just step outside this circulation of mutually reinforcing images and ideologies, particularly by recourse to such an ideologically overdetermined term as blood or race.

Though he opens his most autobiographical book, *Interior Landscapes,* with an invocation of mythic time "when the earth was new" and identifies his Indian ancestors, his grandmother and father, with their totemic animal, the crane, and though his avowed aim is to celebrate "that succession over a wild background of cedar and concrete, shamans and colonial assassins," he is at pains not to idealize that succession. "My grandmother did not hear the beat of a crane in the cities. . . . My father died in a place no crane would choose to dance, at a time no tribal totem would endure."[9] The picture that emerges of him as he grows up is of someone rather mystified by the Indian connections. He describes, for instance, how, as a Boy Scout, having been brought up in the urban environment of Minneapolis, he goes to a summer camp which, to his surprise, is on the White Earth reservation of his ancestors. The white Scout leaders enact a mock Indian ceremony, the Order of the Arrow, to initiate older Scouts. Later he is able to describe it as "an adventitious comic opera with racialism" (60), but this is because he has been able to make meaningful connections with his personal and tribal past, largely through reading and writing, not through any unmediated sense of Indianness.

In *The People Named the Chippewa,* though he may begin with tribal origins, it is entirely characteristic of Vizenor that the key moment he chooses to concentrate on in tribal history is the point at which his mixedblood ancestors, from a marriage between a Chippewa woman and a French fur trader called Beaulieu, published a newspaper on the White Earth reservation, to which they had been moved. The agent's attempts to suppress it as a mischievous challenge to his authority were defeated in a court case, an incident described at length in the book.[10] As well as, or perhaps instead of, a full-blood tribal ancestor, then, Vizenor is setting up a mixedblood writer and polemicist, and he stresses the mixed nature of reservations like White Earth which have been "virtual bicultural centers for intermarriage and cultural diffusion."[11] He also points out that some reservations have a mixture of black as well as white roots, something often ignored, and criticizes the appeals to racial purity. "Crossbloods who hate white and black must hate that place and time in themselves" (*Landfill Meditation* 149).

His use of the reservation in his fiction reflects this fluidity, and sees the imaginative creation of a changing community and identity in positive terms. In a story based on White Earth history, a new missionary is warned of the difficulty of categorizing the reservation.

This place must be a collection of every changing trickster story, and the longer I am here, the more we seem to change each time a story is told. White Earth may be one of those transitional places on the earth where the past is never the same in the memories of the people who lived here. This reservation is a collection of crossblood stories. (*Landfill Meditation* 79)

Vizenor's grandmother was allotted land under the provisions of the Dawes Act, which divided land amongst tribal members. While the avowed aim of the Act was to create independent landowning farmers, the more common result, as in the case of Alice Beaulieu, was that, out of ignorance and poverty, the Indians were forced to sell their land, or were swindled out of it. Vizenor takes the allotment episode, even quoting the exact language of his grandmother's deed of title, but he gives it a fictional, and altogether more comic twist. In *Trickster of Liberty,* in a parodic echo of American myths of foundation and origin, he creates an entire territory complete with trickster founder, but this founder is himself already not "pure" or "original." Luster Browne, "a mixedblood at the scratchline," is given an allotment of land wrongly believed by the government agent to be worthless, and as a condescending joke given the title of Baron of Patronia. From him come the diverse line of trickster figures who populate Vizenor's work.

Vizenor does not use this fictional line to *efface* or obscure his actual ancestry, or idealize his past, unlike some self-appointed Indian spokesmen who, he suggests, inflate their tribal and traditional origins. Indeed he provides a powerful, harrowing and entirely unsentimental account of his own abandonment and subsequent fosterings and is in no doubt about real conditions on reservations and in cities. Nevertheless the idea of Patronia, like the idea in *The Heirs of Columbus,* that his trickster figures can be traced, through the latest genetic fingerprinting, to Columbus, who was himself "an obscure crossblood who bore the tribal signature of survivance,"[12] exemplifies his use of myth and humor as a sort of utopian dimension, not as a way of escaping from the actual, or from history, but of presenting an alternative view, as part of the grounds for critique.

So far I have emphasized Vizenor's treatment of the reservation, but one of the most distinctive things in his writing is the mix of the city and the reservation. He coins phrases like the "urban fur trade," and "urban reservations" to emphasize the continuation of cultural and economic power relations and negotiations in a new mode. In *Dead Voices,* for the animals and tricksters "the cities became our sanctuaries, and we were closer to the natural world in our stories."[13] For them the choice is "between the chance of tricksters and the drone of cultural pride on reservations" (136). Vizenor has worked politically to have urban Indians, who now account for more than half of the Indian population, fully recognized and eligible for the same government services as if they remained on a reservation, and this appears in his writing as part of a more general insistence that to be a mixedblood or crossblood is not to be just part Indian, which would imply that Indianness was defined exclusively by blood.[14] Instead he makes the crossblood the symbol of Indian survival.

The crossblood, or mixedblood, is a new metaphor, a transitive contradancer between communal tribal cultures and those material and urban pretensions that counter conservative traditions. The crossblood wavers in myths and autobiographies; we move between reservations and cities, the stories of the crane with a trickster signature. (*Interior Landscapes* 263)

The figure of the crossblood or the trickster (the terms become almost synonymous) flickers or "wavers'" through Vizenor's own complex mix of "myths and autobiographies." In *Wordarrows,* for instance, and elsewhere, he uses a character, Clement Beaulieu, who is an invented name, drawn from various ancestors, for the figure of the author in the text, so that he "avoids the first-person grammatical limitations in narrative perspective,"[15] and throughout his writings there is a marked ambiguity or elusiveness about his own narrative position. Even in *Interior Landscapes,* his most directly and most harrowingly autobiographical book, the subtitle talks of autobiographical "myths and metaphors" so that like the rest of his work it works by obliquities and in fragments, rather than, like most autobiography, within the narrative conventions of realist fiction. To invoke a fixed or consistent "I" or "we" is to risk being fixed in one of the many ready-made Indian identities, and become an "invented Indian." In one of Vizenor's most complex blendings, "Four Skin Documents," the first-person narrator, a writer, expresses many of Vizenor's concerns transposed into a comic fictional world. A research student at Berkeley, the narrator is also simultaneously an informer for an intelligence firm and a novelist, and thus connected with two independent computer editors. Both the publishing house and the intelligence firm use his stories for their own purposes, reflecting the seamless nature of modern communication systems, and their circulation of information, and perhaps Vizenor's postmodern awareness of the ease with which even the most subversive ideas can be commodified. Through the computer, though, within the timeless present of paranoid connections, he can get beyond the normal realms of politics and fiction. "The open world of fiction is political, but the secret world, the world of the informer, is a mythic connection to the sacred and a real event for me. I am the new tribal memories in the computers" (*Landfill Meditation* 164).

If, once language is used in the public or political world, it is co-opted and corrupted, then the computer may offer something else altogether, an almost mystical dimension, in the silence of its inner recesses of memory.

Silence is not an invention; there are no beaded thunderbirds, material separations, chicken feathers or plastic claws in the computer. . . . Urban skins know about the magic of telephones and televisions, microwaves and tape decks, but not enough about visions and dreams and silence. Silence. Secrets and silence . . . Shamans hold secrets and silence in remembered stories; mine are in the computer. (*Landfill Meditation* 178)

The narrator admits his susceptibility to this, in terms indistinguishable from Vizenor's own statements elsewhere. "For me, separated from the sacred, but skeptical about tribal fundamentalism, terminal creeds, and political spiritualism, personal power lurked in secrets and trickeries. Secrets became mythic connections" (170). When we ask, though, what sort of personal power this is, and what mythic means here, we come up against a key question raised by Vizenor's fusion of postmodernism and the tribal past. If we are to take the area of freedom and personal power found in the computer as an invoking of spiritual presence and transcendence equivalent to the spiritual presence expressed in traditional visions and myths, then this reveals an aspect of Vizenor difficult to reconcile with his postmodern and deconstructive skepticism. True, we could find other passages which might be seen as celebrating a transcendence. At the end of *Bearheart,* for instance, the crossblood pilgrims end their epic journey across an America of the future, where oil has run out and chaos reigns, in the Southwest, at one of the oldest Indian sites, Chaco Canyon. There Proude Cedarfair passes through a vision window into a fourth world.[16]

The question is whether the silence and freedom offered through the computer screen is the same as that offered by the vision window, or whether it is an illusory sense of power and freedom, a narcissistic postmodern free-play, its freedom guaranteed only by its irrelevance.[17] The other possibility would be to see the silence offered by the computer as an empty rather than a "full" or spiritual silence, which would imply a William Burroughs-like nihilism, a recourse to silence to defeat the virus which is language. To put the question in terms of Vizenor's larger enterprise, what is the relation between his celebration of the trickster crossbloods, inhabiting an imaginary world, which fuses the mythical and the historical, and the actual political and historical situation of Indians? Is he vulnerable to the charge of a playful and apolitical postmodernism? He is himself clearly aware of this issue, and defends his mode of writing as a stratagem for combatting the distortions and lies of language and image, and in "Four Skin Documents" the narrator's own writing exemplifies this: "Our languages and mood of encounters and learning are still open to the world, the tart tongues of satire and trickeries on computer screens" (*Landfill Meditation* 166). One of the narrator's own fictional characters introduces himself in terms which highlight the stratagems required.

Cedarbird is the name, sir, *cedar* and *bird,* the whole name, first and last name, *cedarbird, cedarbird,* metamask and metaphor, sacred and secular, in one unsevered avian word. (*Bearheart* 162)

Vizenor peppers his books with a range of wonderful names, among them Erdupps MacChurbbs, Scintilla Shruggles, Pure Gumption, Little Big Mouse, Monsignor Lusitania Missalwait, Griever de Hocus, Mouse Proof Martin, Nose Charmer and Belladonna Winter Catcher. Identities, like names, can be renewed and changed, and at The Last Lecture, which he describes as "a tavern and sermon center" built on the edge of a cliff, people can opt to "choose a new name and walk over the edge" (*Bearheart* 67). In the case of Cedarbird, though, it is the conjunction of dissimilar elements which Vizenor uses as a grammatical reflection of the political condition of being a mixedblood. In another of his stories one of the characters, talking of dogs, refers to "the best mongrels." Told that this phrase is an oxymoron, he retorts that "reservation's an oxymoron, pure mongrels, tribal dances on the Fourth of July, how about that." He talks of a girl who "won the annual White Earth Oxymora Competition twice in a row with 'warm winter' and 'treaty rights' but 'white blood' and 'indian time' are her best ones" (*Landfill Meditation* 40).

To be able to negotiate a way through such contradictions, paradoxes and conflicts requires one to be, in Vizenor's words quoted above, "a transitive contradancer" if one is not to be destroyed by the contradictions of being an Indian in America. As a reporter and activist Vizenor testified at the trial of a young Indian, Thomas White Hawk, charged with an apparently motiveless murder and rape, and he argued for the need for awareness of what he called cultural schizophrenia. Describing a classic double bind, he argued that "the very society which created the sickness in which Indians have had to live . . . is the very society which every day becomes the doctor" (*Wordarrows* 54).

While Vizenor is keenly aware of the disadvantages suffered by Indians, he is skeptical about any oppositional stance or action which reduces the necessary and productive tension found in the metaphor of the mixedblood position. In "Four Skin Documents," the author-narrator and his character Cedarbird are contrasted with the fashionable political positions taken up by the "San Francisco Sun Dancers," "a pride of urbanescent warriors with new descriptive names and new tribal ceremonies, and medicine bundles filled with vitamins and urban artifacts" (*Landfill Meditation* 175). Vizenor's relation to contemporary radical Indian movements, in particular AIM or the American Indian Movement, has been a difficult one. His outspokenness even led at one point, apparently, to threats to his life. His main criticism is that they are just as involved as the whites they attack, in the perpetuation of false images of Indians, and he is scathing about what he sees as the careerism and opportunism of some of the leaders. "The American Indian Movement was a radical urban organization whose members tried from time to time to return to reservations as warrior heroes" (*Crossbloods* 47). The juxtaposition in *Crossbloods,* on facing pages, of photographs of Hubert Humphrey and his wife Muriel dressed up as comic Indians, and a leading activist Dennis Banks and his bride sporting Indian ornaments is hardly coincidental, and reflects Vizenor's scorn for any easy or sentimental invocation of an Indian identity.

The particular focus on Dennis Banks, who is subjected to stinging attacks throughout Vizenor's work, presumably stems from the fact that like Vizenor he is a mixedblood Chippewa, but in Vizenor's terms he blunts the cutting edge of such a position by exploiting and re-circulating prepackaged images of Indianness. For a court appearance, for instance, Dennis Banks is described, in an acid phrase, as wearing "beads, bones, leathers, ribbons and a wide cultural frown" (46). The problem is not merely one of style, though, since this easy appeal to Indianness also carries with it a claim to be *representatively* Indian. In fact, though, most radicals had no clear constituency on the reservations, and were dismissive of the machineries of tribal government, and Vizenor is critical of their rhetorical and uncompromising positions.

Unlike Vernon Bellecourt, who was equally radical but returned to the White Earth reservation to serve as elected representative, "Dennis of Wounded Knee" continued on a media spree. "At the same time the new racial conciliation board was negotiating in Rapid City, Banks was riding a horse around Wounded Knee for photographers" (173).

In a manner characteristic of the blend of fact and fiction in Vizenor's work, and also of the swirls of repetition, where individual phrases reappear continually, there is a character in *The Trickster of Liberty,* Coke de Fountain, who

was an urban pantribal radical and dealer in cocaine. His tribal career unfolded in prison, where he studied tribal philosophies and blossomed when he was paroled in braids and a bone choker. He bore a dark cultural frown, posed as a new colonial victim, and learned his racial diatribes in church basements; radical and stoical postures were tied to federal programs. The race to represent the poor started with loose money and ran down to end with loose power. (111)

Similarly, the figure of Matchi Makwa, also known as Mother Earth Man, in *Wordarrows* seems to be based on Banks.

One of the easy rhetorical appeals Vizenor singles out for attack is to Mother Earth, and to an Indian purity that comes from proximity. In *Landfill Meditation* Belladonna Winter Catcher is ridiculed when in a lecture she insists that "my blood moves in the circles of mother earth and through dreams without time, and my tribal blood is timeless, it gives me strength to live and deal with evil in the world" (112). When her audience skeptically challenges her to explain key words like tribal, and blood, and to demonstrate the difference between Indians and whites, she is driven to insist merely that "Indian blood is not white blood." Such static oppositions are a sure sign, in Vizenor, of a dead-end, and here the audience, following the sign on the wall announcing that "Terminal Creeds are Terminal Diseases," quite literally terminate her by giving her a poison dessert cookie. As she dies she appropriately goes into reverse, "walking and talking backward down the road."

Any high seriousness or monolithic point of view, then, is attacked, but more often than the destruction and death used here, Vizenor uses humor, particularly the unsettling and debunking humor of the trickster, who has a special significance for Vizenor and for Indian cultures in general. His most succinct but perhaps most fundamental criticism of AIM was that "the radicals never seemed to smile, there were no tricksters, no humor; an incautious throwback to the stoical tribal visage of slower camera shutters" (a reference to the noble but ahistoric Indian presented in early photographs) (*Crossbloods* 48).

Characteristic of his comic method, for instance, is the way he uses the character of Martin Bear Charme and his practice of "landfill meditation" to mount an attack on notions of purity and geopiety, in which the earth and Nature are used as sources of spiritual value uniquely accessible to Indians. Charme has created a new reservation, and a fortune, from filling wetlands near San Francisco with waste, and erecting this into a useful symbol of the necessary stance of contemporary Indians.

On the old reservations the tribes were the refuse. We were the waste, solid and swill on the run, telling stories from a discarded culture to amuse the colonial refusers. Over here now, on the other end of the wasted world, we meditate in peace on this landfill reservation. (101)

He develops this into an attack on idealist and transcendent philosophies, urging people to come and

focus on waste and transcend the ideal worlds, clean talk and terminal creeds, and the disunion between the mind and the earth. Come meditate on trash and swill odors and become the waste that connects us to the earth. (105)

Landfill meditation therefore "restores the tribal connections between refuse and the refusers" (99) but as always with Vizenor it would be dangerous to try to locate a fixed position, let alone Vizenor's own, in one of his huge cast of characters. This is partly because his more significant characters are themselves tricksters who by definition refuse definition, and are sworn enemies of consistency or logic, and partly because the swirling plots and mixture of genres mean we are constantly off-balance and discomfited. In other words, and in true postmodern fashion, Vizenor is trying to find a form which is both encouraging us to form patterns, to draw conclusions and yet preventing us from building on them, either in narrative or in more abstract or structural ways.[18] His use of academic studies of the trickster in the prologue to *Trickster of Liberty* is a good example of this. Here we have a fictional framework, an anthropologist, Eastman Shicer, struggling to identify and understand what he thinks is a trickster code in the language of an Indian informant. Shicer is a figure of some ridicule, for whom "academic evidence was a euphemism for linguistic colonization of tribal memories and trickster narratives" and who is constantly fending off the trickster's dog, who (like Trickster himself in so many traditional stories), "ravished with priapism, mounts and humps whatever is upright and pretentious" (xvi). Even here, though, it is not a clearcut opposition between white learning and logic and Indian essence. The Indian, Sergeant Alexina

Hobraiser, "a woman warrior, a decorated and disabled veteran who told trickster stories" and is known as Alex, is hardly a traditional figure, and even the anthropologist's name may combine a reference to the Sioux writer Charles Eastman[19] and, according to Arnold Krupat, the anthropologist Edward Spicer, as well as its more obvious connotations, so the identities are not clearcut. The two swap a wide range of quotations from scholarly authorities, which are tested for their provisional usefulness, rather than just dismissed, and this reflects Vizenor's general way of working, through a bricolage structure of quotations, argument and assertion. For Vizenor the key thing about the trickster is that he/she is not a person so much as a sign, a function of difference between two qualities. Like the rainbow, the trickster, or trickster-effect, can be recognized but not pinned down. As the sergeant says:

> "[W]e are never seen in the places we see, or what we see is never what we choose to see, and the trickster is a lure beyond our gaze."
> "Anamorphosis" said the anthropologist.
> "Jouissance," she responded.
> "Shit and clever delights," he retorted.
> "Shicer, you're a sign consumer, but you got the first word on my list. . . ."
> "Shit or the sign?" (xviii)

In this particular exchange the truth resides, if anywhere, flickeringly in the dialogue between the two sides, rather than being locatable in a single character, and one of Vizenor's criticisms of earlier accounts of the trickster is that they see "him" as a single person, like a character in a realist novel. Since for Vizenor the trickster is "not a presence or a real person but a semiotic sign in a language game, in a comic narrative that denies presence" (*Narrative Chance* 204), the presentation of such a figure in his writing needs to break with the character-conventions of realist fiction.

A modern image for the particular relational and virtual existence of the trickster is that of the hologram, and one of his characters, Almost Browne ("almost" because he was born in a car almost on the White Earth reservation), uses lasers to create another reality in the city. A classical crossblood trickster, Browne "resisted institutions and honored chance, but never conclusions or termination. His imagination overcame last words in education; he never missed a turn at machines" (*Landfill Meditation* 12). Using lasers he recreates communal memories and dreams; Christopher Columbus, presidents, but also the wilderness in the cities. "Hologrammic warriors and wild animals over urban ponds were natural amusements, but when the trickster chased a bear and three moose over a rise on the interstate, no one on the road was pleased" (17). In the ensuing court case the judge rules in favor of "light rights," describing the laser as "a tribal pen, a light brush in the wild air" and the hologram warriors as "new creations, an interior landscape, memories to be sure, an instance of communal rights and free expression" (21).

The key word here is perhaps communal, in that Vizenor's determination to rescue the trickster from individual angst and depth psychology is part of a larger opposition in his writing between the comic and communal and the individual and tragic. Vizenor makes an interesting distinction between modernist and postmodernist approaches, whereby "the trickster in modernist literature was invented to be an individual, or at least the metaphor of individualism; this image supported the notion of vanishing tribes" (*Narrative Chance* 193). That is, just as politically the Indians were supposed to survive as individuals or not at all, so anything valuable or salvageable from their cultures would be seen in individual rather than communal terms, and in order to be useful or valuable the trickster would have to be seen to enact a process of individuation, as in Paul Radin's presentation of a Winnebago *cycle* of myths with a definite shape and progression toward a sort of individual selfhood. Vizenor's use of the crossblood as the focus of his writing is diametrically opposed to the use of the tragic halfbreed or mulatto, stranded between cultures and forced into an alienated existence. Rather,

[C]rossbloods are a postmodern bloodline, an encounter with racialism, colonial duplicities, sentimental monogenism, and generic cultures. The encounters are comic and communal, rather than tragic and sacrificial; comedies and trickster signatures are liberations; tragedies are simulations, an invented cultural isolation. Crossbloods are communal and their stories are splendid considerations of survivance. (*Crossbloods* viii)

For Vizenor it is the social and communal dimensions of language which are crucial.

We are touched into tribal being with words, made whole in the world with words and oratorical gestures. Tribal families created the earth, birds and animals, shadows and smoke, time and dreams, with their words and sacred memories. (*Wordarrows* vii)

In isolation this passage could sound very close to the idealizing of the mythic and the natural Indian as "other" which Vizenor has criticized so relentlessly, but I think we have to see the "we" invoked here, and the word "tribal," as not exclusively referring to traditional Indians, or even exclusively to mixedbloods, since it is identifying a fundamental way of creating the world in language and in narrative. This active role of language, and the work being done by the first person pronoun, is underlined in one of Vizenor's recent neologisms:

The *pronounance* combines the sense of the words *pronoun* and *pronounce* with the actions and conditions of survivance in tribal memories and stories. The *trickster pronounance* has a shadow with no numbered person; in the absence of the heard the trickster is the shadow of the name, the sound, the noun, the person, the *pronounance.*[21]

Like many other writers and commentators he returns to N. Scott Momaday's remark that "We are what we imagine. Our very existence consists in the imagination of ourselves . . . The greatest tragedy that can befall us is to go unimagined" (qtd. in *Wordarrows* vi), and here too the "we" is not restricted to Indians but an inclusive usage. This imagining stems out of the past, and uses it, but it is not determined by it, and this is why Vizenor is able to see it as ultimately comic rather than tragic.

To invoke an inclusive "we" at all, though, might seem to run counter to Vizenor's approving use of postmodernist ideas, and returns us to the problematic relation between ethnicity and the idea of an overarching community beyond any particular ethnic group. Vizenor picks up and uses particularly the correspondence between the postmodernist rejection of the metanarratives and "grand recits" of earlier systems found in Lyotard and elsewhere and his own rejection of "terminal creeds." As with other oppressed or underheard groups, the undermining and decentering of the legitimating narratives of colonialism and white racism have allowed room for local narratives to be heard, but in taking postmodern ideas seriously Vizenor is also then committed to rejecting any view of traditional Indian cultures as fundamentally centered and fixed. This distinguishes him from those Indian writers who see postmodernism as symptomatic of the rootless and hopeless condition of modern secular society, as opposed to Indian spiritual values. Rather, Vizenor takes a positive view of the prospect of a multiplicity of smaller stories which cannot be totalized or fitted into one universalizing system, seeing the process as already existing within tribal cultures, and epitomized in the figure of the trickster. The idea of identity, whether group and individual, as something invented and sustained in narrative is, for Vizenor, not so much the product of late capitalism or shopping mall culture as something already existing, and endlessly recreated in tribal and mixedblood cultures. To this extent postmodernism merely allows a cultural alignment that "liberates imagination and widens the audiences for tribal literatures; this new criticism rouses a comic world view, narrative discourse and language games on the past" (*Narrative Chance* 6).

The risk in aligning the tribal and the postmodern like this, as Vizenor is well aware, is of creating and presenting another white invention, rather than creatively imagining a new identity, whether personal or tribal. The remark of the unnamed protagonist at the end of Ralph Ellison's *Invisible Man* (a novel with its share of trickster figures and stratagems), "Who knows but that, on the lower frequencies, I speak for you?"[22] invoked a larger, presumably white audience, for whom in his alienation and impotence the invisible man could speak, and some readers felt that Ellison was straining for an unnecessary and politically inappropriate universality. Any too easy identification between the mixedblood urban trickster and the postmodern condition in general could just create one more "white man's Indian" whose subversive possibilities would be lost. Perhaps, like the fleas in *Dead Voices,* the way to survive distinct is to take just what you need, and no more. "So, we ride on the neck of a sparrow in our stories, mock our natural enemies, and suck just enough blood not to crash land" (*Dead Voices* 44). It is to avoid too easy identification or allegorization that Vizenor has developed his restless shifts in tone and standpoint, and his particular mix of history and imagination. "The trick," he tells us, "in seven words is to *elude historicism, racial representations, and remain historical*" (*Trickster of Liberty* xi).

Notes

1. The best general account of the way Indians have been conceptualized and represented by whites is to be found in Robert Berkhofer, *The White Man's Indian* (New York: Vintage, 1970). The tangle of paradoxes surrounding Indians is reflected in the difficulties of naming. I have chosen to stick to "Indians," problematic though it is, as it is still more generally used than Native Americans or native or aboriginal peoples, which all also involve assumptions which Vizenor is at pains to challenge.

An earlier version of this essay appeared in *Yearbook of English Studies.* We are grateful for permission to use it in this collection.

2. See Derrida, *Of Grammatology* (Baltimore and London: Johns Hopkins UP, 1976), 141-64.

3. *Manifest Manners: Postindian Warriors of Survivance* (Hanover and London: Wesleyan UP, 1994), 3. Postindian seems often interchangeable for Vizenor with postmodern. See, for instance, the changes in the first paragraph of the essay "The Ruins of Representation: Shadow Survivance and the Literature

of Dominance," *American Indian Quarterly* 17.1 (1993): 7, on its way to becoming the opening of the chapter "Shadow Survivance" in *Manifest Manners*.

4. Quoted in *Crossbloods: Bone Courts, Bingo and Other Reports* (Minneapolis: U of Minnesota P, 1990), 55.

5. See, for instance, James Clifford and George Marcus, *Writing Culture: The Poetics and Politics of Ethnography* (Berkeley: U of California P, 1986), James Clifford, *The Predicament of Culture: Ethnography, Literature and Art* (Cambridge, MA: Harvard UP, 1988), and David Murray, *Forked Tongues: Speech, Writing and Representation in North American Indian Texts* (Bloomington: Indiana UP, 1991).

6. This echoes one of Vizenor's journalistic campaigns to set up what he calls "bone courts" to determine the rights of Indian bones being exhumed by students in the name of science. To buttress his argument he invokes an array of recent theorists in favor of dialogue and rights rather than monologue and scientific hegemony, but while he is clearly in earnest the essay almost works better as a parody of the language of the liberal argument of rights than it does as polemic for the human rights of bones. See *Crossbloods* 62-82. A further parody of the language of rights is found when Martin the trickster in *Dead Voices* tells the fleas that "rights come not with manners but with power and violence. . . . the right to mount, ride, and suck on bird and beast is aboriginal" (47). The male mantises, too, get in on the act, in objecting to being eaten after sex on the grounds that "not to be eaten overnight is a basic mantis right . . . you deserve more out of sex than sudden death" (74).

7. Vizenor contributed an essay on a single photograph of Ishi to Lucy R. Lippard's collection of essays on Indian photographs, *Partial Recall* (New York: New P, 1992). A revised version of this appears as the chapter "Ishi Obscura" in *Manifest Manners*.

8. *The Trickster of Liberty: Tribal Heirs to a Wild Baronage* (Minneapolis: U of Minnesota P, 1998), 45.

9. *Interior Landscapes: Autobiographical Myths and Metaphors* (Minneapolis: U of Minnesota P, 1990), 4.

10. *The People Named the Chippewa: Narrative Histories* (Minneapolis: U of Minnesota P, 1984), 78-92.

11. *Landfill Meditation: Crossblood Stories* (Hanover and London: Wesleyan UP, 1991), 149.

12. *The Heirs of Columbus* (Hanover and London: Wesleyan UP, 1991), 3.

13. *Dead Voices: Natural Agonies in the New World* (Norman and London: Oklahoma UP, 1992), 133.

14. In a typical seriocomic episode, in a story based on the controversies over the economic importance to reservations of running bingo halls for whites on their land, Vizenor has a character change the name of the game from "bingo" to "tribe." "Tribe is the same game as bingo" the character explains,

"but when bingo drew too much attention, I sold out and changed the name to tribe, which is still a game of chance in some reservation communities" (*Trickster of Liberty* 122-23).

15. *Wordarrows: Indians and Whites in the New Fur Trade* (Minneapolis: U of Minnesota P, 1978), x.

16. *Bearheart: The Heirship Chronicles* (Minneapolis: U of Minnesota P, 1990), 243.

17. Arnold Krupat has an interesting and skeptical discussion of Vizenor's use of postmodernism in *Ethnocriticism: Ethnography, History and Literature* (Berkeley: U of California P, 1992), 182ff. Krupat's work, here and in his earlier work on Indian autobiography, contains some of the most important explorations of many of the issues raised in this essay.

18. Kimberly M. Blaeser has shown that this concern to create open texts, requiring an active reading, can be found in Vizenor's earlier work with the haiku, and his characteristic "crossbreed" combination of Japanese forms and Chippewa materials in "a text that advertises its absences and requires the response of the reader to bring it to fruition . . . in the process of 'unfixing' the text." "The Multiple Traditions of Gerald Vizenor's Haiku Poetry" in *New Voices in Native American Literary Criticism,* ed. Arnold Krupat (Washington and London: Smithsonian Institution P, 1993), 348.

19. In his stratagems, both as writer and Indian activist, for coming to terms earlier in the century with an Indian legacy in a white world, Charles Eastman offers fascinating contrasts with Vizenor, as do many of his contemporaries. See, for a useful account of earlier attempts to forge an Indian identity, Hazel Hertzberg, *The Search for an American Indian Identity: Modern Pan-Indian Movements* (Syracuse: Syracuse UP, 1972).

20. Both structuralist and psychoanalytic approaches tend to define the trickster figure through oppositions and fixed qualities, whereas for Vizenor it "is not a structural opposite or an element in a tragic model; the trickster is a comic sign, neither a real person nor a character with 'aesthetic presence'" (*Narrative Chance: Postmodern Discourse on Native American Indian Literatures,* ed. Gerald Vizenor [Albuquerque: New Mexico UP, 1989], 207). It is typical of Vizenor, though, that Radin, Jung, Barnouw and many other standard accounts of the trickster are used and quoted in his work because he plays off the limitations of scholarship and criticism rather than rejecting it in the name of an unmediated Indianness. Andrew Wiget's succinct review of Vizenor's collection raises some difficult questions about his eclectic use of different theoretical approaches, and his particular use of the trickster, in *Modern Philology* 88 (1991): 474-79.

21. "The Ruins of Representation: Shadow Survivance and the Literature of Dominance" in *American Indian Quarterly* 17.1 (1993): 23-24.

22. Ralph Ellison, *Invisible Man* (Harmondsworth: Penguin, 1965), 469.

2

TRICKSTER DISCOURSE AND POSTMODERN STRATEGIES

Elaine A. Jahner

Gerald Vizenor, the self-styled postmodern Ojibway Trickster strategist, goes on writing book after book reminding everyone that post-modernism, American Indian style, has come a long ways from anything Jean-François Lyotard or Fredric Jameson could possibly have imagined in the late 1970s when *The Postmodern Condition* proved that modernist thinking had generated enough reflexive resonance to provoke the prefix of "post." In fact, Vizenor's postmodernism has come so far that asking where his ideas converge with current European thinking about "the post-modern condition" is a useful exercise that can shed light on several of Vizenor's favored strategies at the same time as it sets up a whole range of comparisons among various writers and cultures. Ever since Jameson wrote his introduction to the English translation of Lyotard's book and used that occasion to challenge rather than blandly support Lyotard's characterization of postmodernism, we have had in place the basic terms for debating the philosophical and political questions shaping an intellectual community that now uses the label "postmodern" like a coin whose flip will determine the proceedings of the day.[1] Vizenor explicitly joined these debates when he labeled certain of his ongoing narrative strategies as constitutive elements of "Trickster discourse." With that move, he assumed his own place in the postmodern language games and he has been using his rather surprising position as a base from which to recruit other players from a range of different cultures ordinarily deemed outside the theoretical arenas of postmodern debates.

Looking at some of the terms of postmodern inclusion and exclusion as these apply to different cultures and then examining Vizenor's strategies for bringing the excluded explicitly into the global games sets up the series of descriptive moves that organize this critical narrative about postmodernism. Of course, the force of the preposition "about" means that this critical essay is a decidedly modern academic exercise, balanced precisely on the crucial distinction between modern and post-modern that Lyotard identified in a footnote for *Just Gaming,* a pub-lished dialogue in which he mentions American Indians as exemplary

players of the "narrative game" (53). On that occasion he characterized
as modern that which has a definite addressee and a regulating ideal. As
he sees it, the modern generates certain pragmatic conditions that, in
their turn, give rise to the postmodern condition. Any effort to compare
French postmodernism with Vizenor's endeavor has to forefront the critical force of Lyotard's understanding of the pragmatic implications of
postmodern thought. His crucial distinction between modern and postmodern is achieved by way of pragmatic conditions for, as he claims:

Postmodern (or pagan) would be the condition of the literatures and arts that
have no assigned addressee and no regulating ideal, yet in which value is regularly measured on the stick of experimentation. Or to put it dramatically, in
which it is measured by the distortion that is inflicted on the materials, the
forms and structures of sensibility and thought. Postmodern is not to be taken in
a periodizing sense. (16)

Setting the notion of the postmodern free from historical periodiza-
tion and linking it to "pagan" would seem to be a grandly inclusive gesture and Vizenor has made the most of that seeming. But it was not an
inevitable development nor have most intellectuals yet grown accustomed to addressing the range of assumptions implicit in that inaugural
move. From the very beginning of the debates about postmodernism,
exclusive distinctions have been in place even if they have been barely
in evidence, have, in fact, often been repressed. In one of the most
telling statements of his consistently trenchant and now famous critical
introduction to *The Postmodern Condition,* Jameson pinpointed the
dilemmas of postmodernism as distrustful ambivalence on the part of
"First World intellectuals today" toward master narratives of any kind.
The specification of intellectuals as "First World" seemed to imply his
early recognition that Third World intellectuals are likely to interpret
somewhat differently the dangers of growing First World confusion over
how to steer clear of the quicksands of relativism, dodge the imperialis-
tic impulses of master narratives and still maintain some workable form
of teleological vision to avoid the "crisis of legitimation" that defines
postmodernism as effectively as any other criterion.[2]

Jameson's distinction is becoming more important as time passes.
The distances between First and Third World positions change without
diminishing and these distances are increasingly calibrated in terms of
control over information technology which, in turn, drives global economic machines. Postmodern theorists now talk less about master narratives and more about virtual reality. Theory suggests ways to avoid the
trap of believing in "the perfect crime," to use the title of Jean Bau-

drillard's recent book on appearances in a world of virtual reality for which the Hubble Telescope provides a source of metaphors as well as scientific data as it moves through space, "viewing" the cosmos through corrective lenses in order to send images to earth for decoding and interpretation.[3] As metaphor, the Hubble Telescope reminds us that it is a lot harder to conceive of the corrective lenses that would allow us to adjust for the distortions imposed by various information media upon our view of changing sociological factors. New, or changing, sociological entities are emerging with a force that seems to surge from previously unrecognized or undervalued historical origins whose renewed energy now surprises everyone. Theories, governments and currencies collapse, singly or together in a world linked by a few major airlines, a few mainframe megacomputers, a few satellite signal transmitters and a great many individual credit cards. Individual speech gets reduced to sound-bytes; ethics to politics; theories to the length of an academic paper and the distortions imposed by oversimplification leave a lot of people feeling like outsiders. They wait, often alertly, seeking the moment and the means to gain acccess to the technological resources that keep so-called First World powers in confident charge of the virtual reality we all see and hear. And, every once in a while, someone comes along who manages to express the significance of this waiting game, someone who gives a definite sense of how to make it the opportunity of a culture's lifetime.

Enter Vizenor and "trickster discourse," based on a thoroughly pragmatic set of assumptions about language and political power.[4] The distances between subject and object, between cultures, between theory and practice, or, for that matter, any distance between any real or virtual element, become a performance arena for Trickster, the original and traditional exponent of chaos theory who is a reasonably well-recognized, if not necessarily well-understood, world class mythic figure. Trickster does not just talk; he acts; he is the ultimate agent, sometimes a secret agent working within cultural, psychological and/or political repressions. "Trickster *discourse,*" though, implies a speculative focus on what Trickster does and on the language games deriving from his activity; it is a thoroughly contemporary practice at work in the postmodern condition within which Trickster is a natural performer. "Discourse," of course, implies a sender and a receiver and pragmatic conditions controlling the communicative action. Trickster explicitly playing with discursive conventions makes sure the rules don't put the damper on the communicative action and, in the process, his dramatics reveal that rules are the stuff of cultural creation. But to call the rules arbitrary conventions is not to deny any of their pragmatic force. It is simply to recognize that, like any other conventions, they adjust to the very action they guide; and if people try to repress this responsiveness, the effect is to initiate another sphere of action with less recognizable relations to social structures. To miss this reciprocity is to miss the life of culture as Trickster never does. Trickster's shenanigans enact this creative and occasionally even frightening vitality within culture; and they are every culture's fail-safe option for keeping language in line with life. "Trickster discourse," obviously, has a deliberate and appropriately deconstructive pretentiousness about it. In a postmodern context, the time has come for Trickster to don academic regalia in order to get some attention for his particular style of self-conscious action within language. Trickster's action is, to return to Lyotard's characterization of the postmodern, always "measured on the stick of experimentation."

Well-equipped with the self-styled "wild" difference of "an urban mixedblood," Vizenor takes theory's instrumental possibilities as an irresistibly fascinating invitation to experiment with what will hold up in the diversity of the tribal world. Postmodern ideas transplanted there either wither and die or adapt into hardy variations. As Vizenor sees it, "the postmodern idea opened in tribal imagination: oral cultures have never been without a postmodern that enlivens stories and ceremonies, or without trickster signatures and discourse on narrative chance" (Research Statement and Proposal).

Vizenor learned a lot about technique from postmodern writers and theorists whom he reads as though they were novelists. He has taken their strategic emphasis on performance and game theory and set it in productive relation to the performance contexts of traditional storytelling which keep any given culture's cognitive style alive. He has even given the resulting insights an international twist by translating the entire process from the Americas to China in order to prove that, as a repertoire of artistic and interpretive devices, postmodernism American Indian style can undermine the colonial or neo-colonial project of maintaining all the discursive supports that represent difference as radical otherness.

Steven Connor's description of postmodern language strategies can give us some of the contextualizing information we need to see why Vizenor can approach these same strategies as opportunities for staging traditional performance practices in modern costume. After analyzing Lyotard, Jameson and Baudrillard as the central postmodern theorists, Connor writes,

[F]or all these writers postmodernity may be defined as those plural conditions in which the social and the cultural become indistinguishable. Although Baudrillard goes further than the others in collapsing the distinction between theory and its object, all three of the theorists of the postmodern discussed in this section arrive at the difficult question of the hermeneutic entanglement of theory with the social reality that it describes. This is to say that postmodernity must be considered partially in terms of the difficulty of describing 'it'; or rather, in terms of the difficulty of specifying the 'it' which is postmodernity after the drawing of knowledge and theory into the sphere of culture, even as culture itself alters its scope and coordination.[5]

The dispassionate distance between object and theory, the social and the cultural, which allows for the pose of objective judgement and categorization is what postmodernism has rejected. But what is left and what does this have to do with Trickster discourse? Postmodern intellectuals may deny the validity of conclusions based on prejudice masquerading as analytic objectivity, and they may calmly acknowledge the negative political consequences of slanted historical judgements about the relative merits of cultures and societies, but the problem with our current innocence regained is that even intelligently articulated recognition does not in and of itself solve any of the disparities in power. There is a stubbornly institutionalized durability to the beliefs that so many intellectuals now disclaim and then ignore instead of doing something to defuse these time bombs. And, according to Vizenor, reminding everyone of a job only half done is a postmodern task made to order for Trickster whose cultural role has always been to remind people to watch out for the consequences of any language game. The Trickster role, dramatized for the contemporary postcolonial task, draws definite attention to the pragmatic consequences of rhetoric, and he is especially effective when forcing people to see the concretely dramatized effects of what people would like to repress. He reveals the operation of desire and enables its postcolonial critique, a point that I will expand upon in the section of the essay which refers to specifics within the Vizenor opus.

Postmodernism alters the modernist relationship between philosophical precept and social action. Lyotard, always alert to the political implications of any philosophy, managed to frame this aspect of the postmodern struggle with the metaphor of gaming in the book *Just Gaming* where we find lines that can serve as a superb epigraph for Vizenor's work. "And so, when the question of what justice consists in is raised, the answer is: 'it remains to be *seen* in each case,' and always in humor, but also in worry, because one is never certain that one has been just, or that one can ever be just" [emphasis added].[6] With his reference to seeing, to the operation of immediate assessment, Lyotard is reapportioning modernist ethical emphasis on the prescriptive, giving more attention to the descriptive. His precise moves are important to note if Vizenor's relationship to postmodernism is to be specified. Lyotard claims that exact description of the pragmatic context of any given language game leads to the emergence of the "idea" of a multiplicity of "small narratives" which ought to be maximized. He then proposes a move that corresponds to Trickster's time-honored role, namely extending as far as possible whatever significance is contained in a description. His use of the term "ought" is a philosophical instruction that marks the postmodern relation between prescription and description.

Now this "ought" does not signal that a field of prescriptions is opening up; it marks a transit point from a descriptive game whose goal is knowledge of the given, to a descriptive game (by Ideas) of the exploration of the possible. The transit point is marked by the prescriptive. (59)

Lyotard's emphasis on the descriptive, bound to the visual in his statement "it remains to be seen in each case and always in humor" can appropriately be juxtaposed to Vizenor's constant references to the visual and to humor which is Trickster's modus operandi. To understand how and why Vizenor privileges the visual and makes it the basis for his versions of postmodern games, we have to trace the development of his emphasis in relation to his awareness of his own Ojibway traditions and the way in which they set up a cross-cultural perspective based on a philosophy of wait-and-see, then call it exactly as you see it.

Vizenor has on several occasions stated that "the oral tradition is a visual event." Like other of his one-liners, this statement disorients attentive readers because it requires an unexpected shift from auditory to visual emphasis. Vizenor is not just having fun. On the contrary. With this one-liner he gives basic clues to his enormously sophisticated ideas about the nature of language, whether oral or written. All his beliefs about language are founded on the way he valorises visual perception.

As he claims in another context, his most effective and powerful narratives are always "written in double visions, peeled from visual experiences near the spacious treeline" (*Earthdivers* 166) of human understanding. "Written" in this context, is primarily a reference to the pragmatic structure that sustains any textuality rather than to a particular mode of transcribed presentation. For Vizenor, all experience of textuality is a way of actively tracking presence. Belief in that now-absent presence which has made the "footprints" leads listeners/readers/trackers onwards. The tracking that any text instrumentalizes is an adventure that is always immediate, happening now, registering the dynamics of belief. All of this gets us a bit closer to Vizenor's literary agendas when we note that his style of textual tracking is no solitary business—the quest brings together people who talk and wonder about what it is they are looking for. Textuality can provoke communal meditation and, in the spirit of Lyotard's "ought," Vizenor would say that such meditation ought to mark the transition from knowledge of the given to knowledge of the possible. Vizenor's narrative game is a pilgrim's progress. Or as he says in another quotable one-liner, "Interior glories from oral traditions burst in conversations and from old footprints on the trail" (*Earthdivers* 165).

Footprints work to establish basic Vizenor figurations. As mere traces, footprints obviously cannot be captured or controlled by repressive institutions. They always lead trackers onward toward evidence of the continuing vitality of oral traditions. The new, the effect of "interior glories" bursting like the sun from behind clouds into conversations, is aligned with the traditional and judged by it through the perceptual constancy that visual phenomenality produces. Vizenor sees this creative dynamic of following the "footprints" of being as one which has always animated tribal myth; and therein lies the basis for his assertion that there has always been a postmodern in the tribal imagination. Even the famous earthdiver episode from Ojibway creation tales becomes part of this dynamic and gets bound to his theories about language and the role of the visual imagination in keeping language "on track," migrating in time and in space through textuality "The tribes migrate on their voices from creation. . . . The tribal voice migrates in visions from creation. . . . We are earthdivers in our dreams, not mere word-mongers" (82). And, for purposes of this essay's argument, we might blandly paraphrase the last statement to read: we are postmodern in our dreams, not mere modernists.

Migrating "on their voices" the tribes travel through time and space "in visions." Vizenor is not referring exclusively to the interiority of meditative vision; he extends this notion of migration to the ordinariness of literal, daily attention to what is really happening in a given place. His notion of how cultural creation must be an ongoing metaphorical process is dependent on one basic pragmatic requirement. Tellers and listeners or writers and readers together must look at, truly visualize, the events narrated in texts in terms of definite historical settings. Today, of course, most people live in urban settings. This means that the metaphor of footprints needs some added speculative detailing. Footprints can be far harder to discern on concrete than they are in the impressionable soil near treelines. Nevertheless, Vizenor, whose own childhood home was on a site now covered by an interstate highway, insists that urban settings can and must be imaginatively envisioned as the pragmatic "soil" across which narrative presence moves and narrative audiences "track" meaning. Individual visual attention to immediate action means that mediation (and hence distortion) is an effect of one's own place in time and space and therefore the pragmatic adjustments that depend on communal recognitions and negotiations in which individuals jointly speculate on how Trickster and his avatars enact the fall-out of inevitable distortions that loners fall into as they interpret things.

Vizenor's beliefs about language and the Trickster elements within linguistic pragmatics have been translated directly into the experimental narrative strategies that have become Vizenor trademarks. Given his persistent and central emphasis on the visual, those of his experiments resulting in "word cinemas" have a certain felicitous appropriateness. The word cinemas in his mythically telling book *Earthdivers* give us several takes on why attention to the visual is a basic strategy for maintaining the human capacity to make ethical judgements in a postmodern world. Indulging as he so often does in the purposefully outrageous, Vizenor writes a word cinema in which Trickster takes the name of Martin Bear Charme, founder of the Landfill Meditation Reservation and teacher of a seminar with the same name. Bear Charme, like other of Vizenor's characters, recognizes that we become "victims of what we remember and avoid" (168). Therefore, responsible cognition involves a process of visualizing connections with what is absent or has been discarded and will have to be discarded again as soon as it is perceived. With all its varied and repulsive possibilities, Landfill Meditation is designed to keep its practitioners alert to the dangers of repressions and the word cinema ends with Bear Charme getting beyond the sights and smells of a city dump and dancing in flower-scented fresh air and sun. Visualizing connections helps maintain awareness of the vital bonds between the réfuse and refúsers. And Bear Charme, like Freud, sees that bond as constitutive of human subjectivity. Bear Charme, though, is rather more traditional than Freud although both share the emphasis on looking beyond words to action for the symptom that counts. Bear Charme explains,

[W]e are rituals, not perfect words; we are the ceremonies, not the witnesses, that connect us to the earth. We are the earth dreamers, the holistic waste, not the detached nose-pinchers between the réfuse and the refúsers. (182)

Bear Charme, a truly irksome Vizenor character, has to offend our sensibilities before he can make us reflect on why we react as intensely as we do when we read about life and thinking on the landfill. The sensual immediacy invoked by the language of this word cinema is more than we anticipate from words on a page. We react. The word cinema, the descriptive act par excellence, jolts us into responsiveness, individual knowing and awareness of vanished presence. As a result, Vizenor's stories, as he himself says, "take place in a house of word mirrors, with the dénouement being little more than the return of the narrator to our interior space" (174). The dynamics of exclusion and inclusion, of refusal and acceptance have to be visualized in their actual, precise corporeal immediacy. The visualized immediacy brings into play other remembered sensual responses and meditative perception creates a space of interiority which is, indeed, a distance within which Trickster can perform. But it is not the distance between object and theory. It is not dispassionate. Meditation sorts out crucial pragmatic effects of mediation. It reconnects what has been severed, brings back what has been excluded. Since politics is always the institutionalized act of creating boundaries for exclusion and inclusion, Landfill Meditation is an interior speculative game in which the human effects of political games are constantly revaluated. "Landfill meditation" and "Griever meditation" are two sides of the same coin, both are precursors of "trickster discourse." Memory, dreams and naive common sense come together in the meditation that generates trickster discourse.

Such a conjunction is ordinary enough; but Vizenor has his own quite unique ways of bringing it into the contemporary international arena. Memory reconstructs the scenes which show how dreams (visions) with their prelinguistic instinctual energies have reshaped traditional interpretations in the past to make sure that "possessive energies" (*Bearheart* 22) do not destroy the energies of seeing. Dreams inform "personal voices" ("personal" should be glossed as the contrary of "possessive"). Dreams, interpreted in the manner prescribed by traditional customs, keep personal and individual voices in touch with the life of a tradition even when actions which follow from a dream would seem to be wildly divergent from what we think we know about any given traditional culture. We can see how this eminently traditional approach operates in a modern, international setting by looking at how one Vizenor character manages to make Griever meditation into a cross-cultural communication strategy with more political implications that most people want to imagine.

Vizenor wrote *Griever: An American Monkey King in China* before the massacre in Tiananmen Square and he imaginatively anticipated that event. Obviously he was an acute observer who grasped the significance of details that other observers either ignored or underestimated. As Maria Hsia Chang wrote in *Global Affairs:* "Recent events in China demonstrate once again the inadequacy of mainstream Sinology in this country. Before the massacre at Tiananmen Square on June 4, none of the specialists whose expertise had been eagerly sought by the media predicted that the regime in Beijing would find it necessary to respond to the pro-democracy movement with such ruthlessness and brutality." She claims that western blindness derived in part from "the disposition of experts to provide descriptive or narrative accounts of their subject, rather than employ a more systematic approach that would make China a member of a class of political systems with discernible traits in common."[7]

Chang's use of the term "descriptive" is not equivalent to Lyotard's. He advocates description of pragmatic conditions—exactly what she calls "a systematic approach." Vizenor's narrative is creative play rather than social scientific commentary so he could depict concretely just those "discernible traits" that social scientists so often have to bypass in their hurry to make an objective point. The concreteness of a novelist's attentiveness and pragmatic awareness gleaned from his study of the American Indian past from a postcolonial perspective allowed Vizenor to sense and describe those subtle "inventions" of justificatory theory that signal any political system in danger. In Vizenor's lexicon, American Indian reservations are the "inventions" of colonialism and, as *Darkness* shows, he does not hesitate to extend the term "reservation" and use it to create a dynamic model of colonial circumstances. Any culture that has experienced colonization and its neocolonial reverberations is a reservation in his lexicon. The hero of his novel quickly observes about China: "This is an enormous reservation" (13). As a member of a repressed culture himself, Vizenor responds to social danger signals the way an acute allergy sufferer responds to allergens in the air; so he knew what he was seeing when he watched alert Chinese reach the do-or-die point in their relations with a bureaucracy determined to keep the lid on creative political aspirations. His main character Griever makes forays into bureaucratic strongholds that uncover the smoldering dreams and images of creative freedom which are China's heritage from the Monkey King, the Chinese Trickster.

Vizenor imaginatively worked out comparisons between the American Indian trickster figure and the Chinese Monkey King while he was in China. Any of Vizenor's regular readers can see the enormous appeal of a figure like Monkey, to whom the Buddha gives a name that means "Discoverer of Secrets." The traditional Chinese characteristics of Monkey invite comparison with the American Indian Trickster. Monkey can change into seventy-two different forms and he is known as a disturber of heavenly peace. He also has a remarkable capacity to understand secret signs. In a word, he is perfect for Vizenor's purposes.[8]

The plot of *Griever* is about as straightforward as Vizenor ever gets. An American Indian named Griever goes to China as an English teacher. (Apart from the name, this much is autobiographical.) He acts out his dreams of freedom by engaging in outrageous clowning. Some of the Chinese understand the clowning as part of the social role of their traditional Monkey King and they begin to reveal who they really are as they dodge official notice of their determined, creative enactments of Chinese traditions. Bit by bit, Griever uncovers evidence of a cadre of people who carry forward the freedom and vision exemplified by the Monkey King. Many of the episodes narrate Griever's discovery of this underground dimension of China, much as the Monkey King story cycle narrates Monkey's discoveries about Chinese character. As Griever meets the modern exemplars of traditional roles, he discovers that his dreams about China during his air flight there were prophetic. Then, on a government sponsored trip to a resort, he encounters a translater whose renditions of his stories prove that her imagination is powerful enough to make her a co-creator of the tales she translates. Delighted with their collaboration, they work both sides of the culture line discovering unities in their contrasting stories as their retellings and adaptations reveal the modern possibilities of traditional plots. Later in the novel, we learn that they also become co-creators of a child, a girl. China, though, is a nation where imaginative creation and physical procreation are both rigidly controlled in the interest of maintaining an efficient national apparatus. The young mother and her unborn child are murdered. Griever disappears into the sky in an ultralight plane.

I have a feel of the air now, and this view of the nation, this world of peasants, is very peaceful, like those brush strokes in an ink painting. Those artists must have been flying in their heads, but not with the roar of an engine. Now, for the first time, I can see from the air what they must have seen to paint their pictures. (232)

The frame surrounding this plot encircles it with an air of mystery that draws attention to its inner side, the seam where frolicking, sharply satiric high jinks merge into a mystical pattern that links the Americas and China finally bringing us back to the epistemological and political significance of Vizenor's emphasis on the visual. The first chapter is a letter written to his friend China Browne, named for her love of China. In it Griever tells about his dreams and meditations and we begin to understand the significance of the fact that he has more than one way of seeing. There is the literal level of a tourist's descriptions of a landscape encountered for the first time; and there is a seeing that is the taproot of memory sinking deep into the water of visionary dreams. He tells China about a dream in which bear shamans show him manuscripts about the history of China and, to his astonishment, he finds that the markings on the manuscript are the same as those on the tribal medicine scrolls from the reservation. . . . The fire bear told me some of the stories on the scroll, the histories of this nation, from the monkey origins to the revolutions, even the persecution of scholars, and the new capitalism, it was all there. But the future stories, what would become of this nation, she told me to read later. (18)

The next chapter presents China in China looking for the missing Griever and trying to reconstruct what has happened to him. She meets the warrior clown Wu Chou who had been an opera actor playing the Monkey King. Like Griever, he too "sees stories" (61). Wu Chou tells China that "Tianjin is a broken window. . . . Dreams retreat to the corners like insects, and there we remember our past in lost letters and colonial maps, the remains of foreign concessions" (22). What she learns from Wu Chou and in her letters from Griever sends the character China on a quest whose outcome remains unsettled at the book's end. We, like China, begin to understand what Griever meant in his letter when he described himself as "alone on the line." He stands on a boundary, not so much between cultures and countries as between ways of looking at the world. "On one side there are the teachers, the decadent missionaries of this generation, and on the other side, invented traditions, broken rituals, wandering lights, ear readers, and headless ghosts on the dark roads" (13). All of this could have been written about an American Indian reservation and Vizenor recognizes as much. "This is an enormous reservation with a fifty watter over the main street, but as Marco Polo said, 'I have not told the half of what I saw'" (13).

Griever meditation never loses touch with the workaday world. Good sense is the privileged interpretive technique taught by this peculiar meditative practice whose origins are ascribed to a gypsy clown who came to the White Earth Reservation and stayed just long enough to become the father of Griever the hero of the novel.

Besides the son, the gypsy left his Ojibway lover an instruction book entitled "How to Be Sad and Downcast and Still Live in Better Health Than People Who Pretend to Be So Happy." The title says it all. The chapter in the novel entitled "Griever Meditation" is a digression in which Griever, named for his father's meditative practice, remembers a grade school science class dissection lesson. Griever steals the frogs and liberates them after a teacher, in an effort to direct his high spirited disruptiveness, proclaims him "king of the frogs." He takes his role literally and sets his "subjects" free. Then he can actually see the results of his imagined status. Knowing by seeing turns out to have an active dimension. The Trickster acts so that he can see what will happen and know what lies beneath the surfaces of manners, conventions and apparent conformity. Griever draws what he sees, keeping his visual memories with him in a notebook in a holster.

> The lines and curves in his pictures are dance, meditation moves, those silent gestures in an opera scene . . . but there is much more to this trickster than mere transcendence. Griever discovers events, an active opera and an audience, all at once on rough paper. He paints the comic resolutions back into tragic dances . . . (34)

Griever in China has changed little from the kid who frees the frogs. The first time he goes to a market, he buys all the chickens and sets them free except for one cock who gets dubbed Matteo Ricci and becomes a companion and pet guaranteed to irritate all the other teachers and to remind traditional Chinese that the Monkey King traveled with companions. Griever definitely gets the attention of his audience and he makes the people laugh. As their laughter dissipates suspicion, he learns that he is not alone on the line; many of the Chinese people stand with him between power mongers on the one side, and invented traditions on the other.

Griever's dreams on the way to China bring the image of a child into this book as the visionary counterpoint to the episodes of outrageous clowning. A child returns again and again in Vizenor's writing. Vizenor remembers. The image of the child encompasses a realm of experience and a way of knowing that we enter with him as he and we gradually come to understand more and more about its place in our world. Through the figure of the child, memory binds the collective losses to the fragile self still moving back and forth through dreams across the threshold of the symbolic which the child is perpetually crossing even within the mature adult psyche.[9] In a dream Griever encounters a child whose existence is more than just a transitory realization of his nocturnal imaging. He is told that the child is "from old stories before liberation" (61). Vizenor's initial description of the child is a vulnerably lyrical summons that anticipates the novel's inward turn to emotions and understandings that can never be defended against what destroys tender beginnings.

> We were both mute on either side of the screen. I was perched inside on the wide wooden sill, and he stood near the door with one arm down, a slight stoop to the side, while mosquitoes held a spiral pattern above his head. We seemed to move at the same time, wavered together through the screen, and then it happened.
>
> There was a pale blue light around his head and chest, and then, much to my surprise, he grew taller right there in place. The air smelled of charcoal smoke. Crickets sounded in the room. The telephone rang and shattered the

silence. The blue light burst from his head and shot from his face and arms through the screen, right through me to the telephone, like lightning to a streamer. When the light passed through me, I became the child, we became each other, and then we raised the receiver to our ear. (59)

A mute child knows language in all its disturbing materiality as that which must be transformed in order to be used. Blue, the sky color, mystically charged with expansiveness and peace, surcharges the themes of transformation. The child merges with the adult and "we" respond. Only at the end of the novel, though, do we learn the meaning of the child's drawing depicting "a man with small blue bones in his hands" (62). The bones belong to children drowned in the same pond as Hester Hua Dan and her unborn child. The visionary child returns once more to Griever to reveal Hester's burial place.

The blue light was a court to a secret place, a shared dream that carries voices over a cataract. The dread was intense; the water drained lower and the stone man waded closer to the light at the bottom of the pond.
   Shitou raised the bones of babies from the blue muck. . . . The dead water had been a burial place, a killing pond, for unwanted children. (225)

Hester's name inevitably links her to Hawthorne's character in *The Scarlet Letter,* who also conceives a child in an act of passion that the public domain can not abide. Hawthorne's novel shows us a Hester whose fate is to know what it means to move back and forth across the boundary between public and private, belonging and ostracism, depending on how the community narrates different interpretations of who and what she is. Hester Prynne's life on the line eventually grants her independence and insight beyond that of the immature society that ostracized her. Through Hawthorne's writing, everything about her gets pulled into the resurgent life of narrative existence. Even the novel is redirected and sent forward in time by the narrative that frames it. "The Custom House" section assumes an autobiographical narrative stance that distances the teller from the tale and enhances the emphasis on shifting narrative dynamics rather than on direct mimetic representation. Vizenor, like Hawthorne, insists that to forget or to lie about the fact that all representation is humanly mediated through narrative is to endanger human life itself.
   Hester Hua Dan is in China and the difference in locale alters her fate and that of her story. She does not live long enough to experience the changing communal narratives surrounding and interpreting her. Unquestioning loyalty to franchised bureaucracy motivates the man who

kills her and tries to bury her story, end its power to upset official stories. Where there is frightened awareness that control is slipping, there must be no resurgence of the unsanctioned whether in or out of narrative deed. Such prohibition kills and gives rise to monstrous social conditions. "Shitou, the old stone man, said, 'Drown a girl, give birth to a monster,' when we carried Hester Hua Dan from the pond" (233). The fact of death throws everything into a conditional mode that reveals the terror within certain forms of postmodern conditionality. The Tiananmen Square massacres followed the publication of Vizenor's novel by less than two years.

Griever takes to the air. "No more panic holes for me because the air has become the place to release my rage. I roar at the dawn, I roar at the wind, I roar at nothing . . ." (233). Two sources provide appropriate commentary and glossing for the enigmatic ending of *Griever.* One is the ending of Arthur Waley's translation of *Monkey.* The other is the ending of Lyotard and Thebaud's *Just Gaming.*

At the end of the first cycle of Monkey stories, Monkey volunteers to go to India to Buddha and take the scriptures back to China. These scriptures "nurture our humors and hide our magic." Buddha tells Kuan-yin to help Monkey.

"I want you," said Buddha, "to make a thorough study of the air at a fairly low altitude, not up among the stars. Keep an eye on the mountains and rivers, and make careful note of the distances and traveling stages, so that you may assist the scripture seeker. But it is going to be a very difficult journey for him."[10]

In a postmodern setting, Buddha's advice still rings true. Visualizing distances still works as a strategy and traveling between cultures has lost none of its difficulty or necessity for thorough study. Vizenor's Griever gets back home by flying at low altitude across China in an ultralight airplane designed by an Ojibway relative who had graduated from Dartmouth College with honors in economics and enough insight into capitalism to play its games to the fullest. This character, Slyboots Browne, learned quickly to survey life from a safe distance, but always at low altitude, never flying too high to see what is happening in real towns down below, never depending too much on high tech instrumental mediation that minimizes the human perspective. Slyboots is, of course, another one of Vizenor's trickster figures whose inspired but practical low-technology enables Griever to release his rage at the same time as he gathers immediate knowledge about a reality he needs to understand. With his ultralight plane, Griever gathers his own impressions, noting them all carefully. He does not inhabit the manipulated world of virtual reality where everything is instantaneous. Griever will take whatever time is required to "see" what conditions will finally signal a just course of action. The ending of the novel leaves Griever in the air, waiting, watching. The novelistic frame does not tell us how Griever will resolve the paradoxes that his aerial reconnaissance enables him to see. We remain up in the air with him taking a new look at society, learning that waiting and watching are a postmodern necessity even if, or precisely because, most postmodern thinking denies just this necessity. Griever waits with rage but also with humor. Repression has taught him that humor and rage should not, must not cancel each other out. Humor is the affective evidence of continuing freedom. Nourished through Griever meditation, it can and must be artistically recast as the energy that enacts what is seen, what is so precisely visualized that its performance can provoke rage even as it hides the magic of humor conjoined with rage. Griever has devised strategies based on careful visualization and study that allow him to discern the signs of hope in the very process of revealing the dynamics of oppression and we, along with him, have to continue to watch. Set against this active inconclusiveness of the novel on China, Vizenor's early reworkings of Ojibway traditional lyrics take on contemporary significance. All this complex process of seeing and acting is captured in a translation of an Ojibway song that also gave Vizenor a title for a book of translations.

> as my eyes
> look across the prairie
> I feel the summer
> in the spring

Lyotard's final comments bring us back to the relationships between violence, terror and postmodern thinking. Like Vizenor, he has given a place in his writing and thinking to the fact that terror and violence have accompanied most of our moves toward cultural pluralism to date and he has made crucially important distinctions between conditions that lead to violence and those that lead to terrorism. His distinctions are disturbing, becoming more so as we see how he seems to have foreseen possibilities we read about every day in our newspapers.

[I]f a language game owes its efficacy, I would not say only, but also, to the fear of death, even if it is a minority game, it is unjust. Majority does not mean large number, it means great fear. Hence my second question: In order to become a majority, is it necessary to violate the boundaries of the language game concerned? Isn't there, in the pretension to regulate other language games, something like terror? (99-100)

Lyotard answers his own questions in the affirmative. The one pre-scriptive of universal value that he recognizes is that which

> prescribes the observance of the singular justice of each game such as it has just been situated: formalism of the rules and imagination in the moves. It authorizes the "violence" that accompanies the work of the imagination. It prohibits terror, that is, the blackmail of death toward one's partners, the blackmail that a pre-scriptive system does not fail to make us of in order to become the majority in most of the games and over most of their pragmatic positions. (100)

The crucial words "such as it has been situated" in the previous quotation place great, possibly too great, trust in the likelihood of cultures to work toward justice following socio-political norms that have been tested over the years and Lyotard recognized that fact. As he sees it, terrorism is the greatest danger that exists whenever someone is put out of social play. And terrorism, postmodern style, is a quite different matter from what we occasionally read about under that label in our newspapers. Lyotard recognizes a daily, ordinary terrorism in all of our postmodern institutions through which people lose their capacity to function because they are eliminated for reasons and through means beyond their cognitive reach. To go back to game imagery, we recognize that they are put out of play, not for reasons which have to do with their own playing or even with the rules of the game they think they are playing. They are eliminated for reasons that have to do with a game they can not even imagine. If we were to bring back the concept of justice implied by "Just Gam-ing," we would have bring individuals back into just play by letting them know the name of the games and the rules of the multiple games implied by multiple narratives. The postmodern ethical journey begins with a cognitive imperative.

Vizenor, with his Trickster discourse and word cinemas is mapping the cognitive terrain and he is revealing the strategies for multiple mappings. His strategies balance between the known and the emergent, the conscious and the unconscious, the modern and the postmodern. He is in touch with an all-important fail-safe option in the language game model of cultural pluralism when he points to the epistemological and practical complexity of knowing by dependence on his Trickster balancing act.

> My answer is this: . . . we seek to balance incompetence with the opposite . . . Contraries are the differences and nothing but the differences that balance the world. . . . Balance is not balance, no idea or event *is* what is named, there are no places that are known but through the opposites, nothing is sacred but what is not sacred. . . . No thing is in balance but what is confused and in discor-

dance. . . . The trickster seeks the balance in contraries and the contraries in balance; shaman tricksters avoid the extremes but not with extreme humor or intense manners. (*Earthdivers* 17)

Within any language game, Trickster as an avatar of the human enacts the contraries of propositions which are also instantiations of alternative outcomes to semantic potentials (the "Idea" that Lyotard takes from Kant). Trickster enacts the fact that human knowing is always mediated by all the distortions that follow from the simple fact of human corporeality (the Idea of desire). Trickster's enactments are concrete, visual reminders of the margin of error which is always part of the human condition. Trickster reminds people that there is no "perfect crime," no absolute conjunction between knowing and seeing and presence. Trickster's avatars all know why Baudrillard proclaims that the impossibility of "the perfect crime" is the happy ontological fault, the necessary condition of human existence. Like Baudrillard, Trickster's avatars believe that the closer we come to collapsing the human spaces of perception (and declaring them objective is one form of collapse), the closer we come to ending the human adventure. The perfect crime is also the totalizing terrorist act.

Vizenor has various figurations to represent his balancing act. In the preface to his book *Matsushima,* Vizenor has given a self-description that shifts the dynamics informing all his writing into another set of action metaphors.

The soul dancer in me celebrates transformations and intuitive connections between our bodies and the earth, animals, birds, ocean, creation; the street dancer in me is the trickster, the picaresque survivor in the wordwars at common human intersections, in a classroom, at a supermarket, on a bus; the word dancer is the imaginative performance, the mask bearer, shield holder, the teller in mythic stories at the treeline; and the last dancer who practices alone, in silence, to remember the manners of the street, the gestures of the soul, and the words beneath the earth. (6-7)

The progression in this quote sets up a paradigm for postmodern action that begins with visualizing connections (or disconnections), inclusion and exclusion. Next comes the necessity to enact, to publicly perform the meanings of connections and the relationships between réfuse and refúsers; next comes the formalized telling that is dependent upon the newly performed, sociologically immediate and exact enactment of human knowing and finally we find the meditative distance that keeps the dances going; that brings postmodern knowing full circle in time and space. Instantiation requires pragmatic response. It requires dance. Stillness is transition between steps (balance). The postmodern condition may arise in tribal imaginations but it is still being choreographed with intent to exclude tribal dances. Postmodern theorists need some time out to meditate on an inter-tribal pow-wow.

Notes

1. Jameson differs from Lyotard most explicitly on the question of the continuing productivity of a Modernist stage of culture. Using examples from architectural stylistic experimentation to make his point about more general tendencies in postmodernism, Jameson notes that architects of the International Style—Le Corbusier, Frank Lloyd Wright—were revolutionaries but they also generated imitators who could not maintain that revolutionary potential.

[T]he new buildings of Le Corbusier and Wright did not finally change the world, not even modify the junk space of late capitalism, while the Mallarmean "zero degree" of Mies's towers quite unexpectedly began to generate a whole overpopulation of the shoddiest glass boxes in all the major urban centers of the world. This is the sense in which high modernism can be definitively certified as dead and a thing of the past: its Utopian ambitions were unrealizable and its formal innovations exhausted. This is, however, not at all the conclusion that Habermas and Lyotard draw from what they think of in their different ways as the postmodernist movement; for both of them a return to the older critical high modernism is still possible, just as (equally anachronistically) for Lukács writing in the thick of the high modernist period, a return to some older premodernist realism was still possible. (*The Postmodern Condition* [Minneapolis: U of Minnesota P, 1979], xvii)

2. Jameson's context includes reference to the nature of master-narratives.

The great master-narratives here are those that suggest that something beyond capitalism is possible, something radically different; and they also 'legitimate' the praxis whereby political militants seek to bring that radically different future social order into being. Yet both master-narratives of science have become peculiarly repugnant or embarrassing to First World intellectuals today: the rhetoric of liberation has for example been denounced with passionate ambivalence by Michel Foucault in the first volume of *The History of Sexuality;* while the rhetoric of totality and totalization that derived from what I have called the Germanic or Hegelian tradition is the object of a kind of instinctive or automatic denunication by just about everybody. (xix)

3. It may be worth noting that, in 1977, Jean Baudrillard published the book *Oublier Foucault*. His most recent book (Editions Galilee, 1995) is also his most stylistically daring and polished. Several key passages bear intriguing parallels with Vizenor's published ideas about language. The following comparison is one of many possible ones:

Pour retrouver la trace du rien, de l'inachèvement, de l'imperfection du crime, il faut donc ôter à la réalité du monde. Pour retrouver la constellation du secret, il faut ôter à l'accumulation de réalité et de langage. Il faut ôter un à un les mots du langage, ôter une à une les choses de la réalité, arracher le même au meme. Il faut que, derrière chaque fragment de réalité, quelque chose ait disparu, pour assurer la continuité du rien - sans cependant céder à la tentation de l'anéantissement, car il faut que la disparition reste vivante, que la trace du crime reste vivante. (Baudrillard 16)

Vizenor has written

We should pull these words down, beat them on the altars until the truth is revealed, beat the sweet phrases from the institutions that have disguised the horrors of racism . . . drive the word pains and agonies from the heart into the cold . . . We are the victims of these words used to cover the political violence and white horrors in the memories of the tribes. Hear those primal screams, the tribes scream with the trees and rivers, from diseases, the massacres and mutilations of the heart . . . racist isolation and the repression of the heart in white schools and institutions . . . Break down the white word walls and dance free from isolation . . . dance in the sun. (*Earthdivers* 37)

4. See *Narrative Chance* (U of New Mexico P, 1989). In his introduction to that edition of critical essays, Vizenor expands upon his notions of Trickster discourse.

5. Steven Connor, *Postmodernist Culture* (New York: Basil Blackwell, 1989) 6.

6. See p. 99. In the "Afterword" of *Just Gaming*, Sam Weber engages in some critical gaming that suggest why Trickster discourse is so appropriately set in relation to the postmodern exercise exemplified in *Just Gaming*. His plays with notions of inside and outside should also be placed in referential comparison to Vizenor's ending to his novel about China where Griever floats above China in an ultralight plane.

But if in dreams as in popular narratives, "there is no place one can go to photograph the whole scene," it is not because, as we read in *Just Gaming*, "there is no exteriority" but because in a certain sense, there is only that; as soon as the unconscious is in play; we are dealing with an exteriority that tries to exclude itself, in other words to internalize, incorporate, appropriate itself, without ever managing to do it. But if we can never succeed in this impossible effort, neither can we renounce it, and it is precisely this double impossibility that makes the game of the unconscious both imprecise (because it is never completely determinable) and ambivalent (because it is always in the process of arresting itself, of revolving around a "fixation"). (111)

7. "The Meaning of the Tienanmen Incident" *Global Affairs* (Fall 1989): 12-13.
8. See E. T. C. Werner, *Myths and Legends of China* (Singapore: Graham Brash (PTE) Ltd., 1922), 325-69.
9. See the episode entitled "Sand Creek Survivors" in *Earthdivers.*

Remember this child, turned in his mind over and over like a phrase that never found a place to fit in time. *When is the best time to remember?* Trained to be dutiful scribe, at least as a reporter, he scratched into his notebook the practiced gentle words of the priest, but he resisted the words, his hand seemed to avoid the words, he hated the words. The sounds burst in his ears and shot down his arm, nothing smooth or soothing, nothing from forgiveness, no calm, no peace from tribal suicide. How can his words be so soft, so restrained, Beaulieu wrote in his notes. Dane knows no pleasure in the words of the white world; he was trapped and executed in a white institution. (36)

10. Arthur Waley, trans., *Monkey by Wu Ch'ang'en* (London: G. Allen, Unwin Lt., 1942), 139-40.

Works Cited

Baudrillard, Jean. *Le Crime Parfait.* Paris: Editions Galilee, 1995.
Chang, Maria. "The Meaning of the Tienanmen Incident." *Global Affairs* Fall 1989.
Connor, Steven. *Postmodern Culture.* New York: Basil Blackwell, 1989.
Lyotard, Jean-François. *Just Gaming.* Minneapolis: U of Minnesota P, 1985.
——. *The Postmodern Condition.* Minneapolis: U of Minnesota P, 1979.
Vizenor, Gerald. *Earthdivers.* Minneapolis: U of Minnesota P, 1981.
——. *Griever: An American Monkey King in China.* Minneapolis: U of Minnesota P, 1990.
——. *Matsushima.* Minneapolis: Nodin P, 1984.
——. *Narrative Chance.* Albuquerque: U of New Mexico P, 1989.
Waley, Arthur. *Monkey by Wu Ch'ang'en.* London: G. Allen Unwin Lt., 1942.
Werner, E. T. C. *Myths and Legends of China.* Singapore: Graham Brash Lt., 1922.

3

GERALD VIZENOR'S "DELICIOUS DANCING WITH TIME":
TRICKING HISTORY FROM IDEOLOGY[1]

Barry O'Connell

> The world comes together all at once . . . when time is turned loose
> like an animal in the mind park.
> —*Earthdivers: Tribal Narratives on Mixed Descent*

> The trick, in seven words, is to *elude historicism, racial representa-*
> *tions, and remain historical.* The author cedes the landscape to the
> reader and then dies, the narrators bear the schemes, bodies are wild,
> and the trickster liberates the mind in comic discourse.
> —*The Trickster of Liberty*

These words spin, escape ready sense, play around, and yet seem to
have meanings about which at least their author is clear. The only difference between a novice and a veteran reader of Vizenor, here, is that the
veteran may sooner relax into a more patient puzzlement, or, foolishly,
too quickly think he understands. The first sentence in the second epigraph is perhaps the easiest to gloss and the most immediately pertinent
to my essay. Its meanings depend on the technical term "historicism"
and working out what the connections between it and "racial representations" might be.

For now I want to take "historicism" simply as referring to most of
American history as it has been written: a narrative form which assumes
a coherent story with a distinct beginning, a middle which, however
muddled, becomes clear in a conclusive end. In this narrative, regardless
of its particular details, American history is a progressive tale. It begins
with European discovery and tells about the development of civilization
in a new setting, the overcoming of wilderness, the emergence and triumph of democracy (albeit with setbacks and contradictions). Vizenor's
own concept of "historicism" may also imply that those who practice it
assume the past as discoverable, knowable, a set of events and meanings
which careful empirical research can establish, always subject, of course,
to revision.[2]

"Racial representations" appear to be virtually corollary to "historicism," and so I believe they are in Vizenor's reading of written European and American history. Racial identities, indeed representations, are not only integral, but constitutive of the narrative structure I have been characterizing. In it, those who embody progress and civilization turn out to be always "white," the settlers of the continent; "red" people or Indians belong to the wilderness which must be subdued or domesticated, cultivated and civilized. Or, as Richard Drinnon puts it in a passage from *Facing West* which Vizenor quotes in *Earthdivers*:

In the national experience race has always been of greater importance than class. . . . Racism defined natives as nonpersons within the settlement culture and was in a real sense the enabling experience of the rising American empire: Indian-hating identified the dark others that white settlers were not and must not under any circumstances become, and it helped them wrest a continent and more from the hands of these native caretakers of the lands. (33)

Indians, like the wilderness, must inevitably be diminished and if they survive at all, only in reserves—less scenic counterparts to the National Park system.[3] "Black" people, slaves or former slaves, like the Indians, may be objects of white people's intentions, benevolent or not, but they, too, can never be quite "American," subjects and actors in the narrative, though in some versions they may, with enough hard work and education, become more like white people, thus more American.

In the nineteenth century, when the first great classics of American history were written and when, near its end, American history as an academic discipline was established, the place of Indians in American historical narratives was explicit and unqualified. They were a people fated to give way before the superior civilization of Anglo Europe. Occasionally an elegiac note might be sounded about the passage of a noble people, but the inevitability of their decline, if not their disappearance, was axiomatic. In such a climate little could be conceived that would genuinely be attentive to any aspect of the actual and continuing histories of some or all of the Native American cultures in North America. They were but figures in a Euro-American plot, confirmations of an already assumed teleology.

What narrative form should, in the late twentieth century, shape a history or histories of Native Americans? The question is not whether such histories exist, for, to the extent Native Americans have persisted with a distinctive sense of themselves as a peoples, there must be histories, but what are the markers, the chronologies, the plots, even the location of them? How much might they primarily consist not of external, public events but of what Vizenor calls "interior landscapes"? Or of events and experiences interior to Native American families and communities, kept from the oversight of a colonizing culture? How write histories of a people so falsely and yet powerfully represented in Eurocentric historiography, itself both a source and a result of equally powerful assumptions about the nature of Indians in the vernacular culture of most Americans and in the media? To invoke "Indians" is immediately to bring into play ideas and images which obliterate the actual histories of Native Americans. "Indians" are always and forever in "cowboys and Indians," in "vanishing Indians," as "noble savages," or the agents of "massacres"—in the nineteenth century—or as nothing but the victims of them in the late twentieth. The genre required is either melodrama or tragedy and in neither can one find any dependable history.

The ground could neither be slipperier nor more difficult to establish. Any conceptual stability recedes further when we remember that the concept of history itself may not be extricable from the very history of Euro-American conquest and domination of Native Americans. Most "records" of Native American histories are entirely within the conceptual and documentary frameworks of the conquest: in treaties virtually always translated into the European languages of the conquerors, Spanish, French, Dutch, or English; as reports by and to Europeans motivated by commercial or military ambitions; or as accounts of native "ways of life" intended to further the prospects of religious and/or cultural conversion. Or there are the investigations of anthropologists—resolutely ahistorical for much of the history of that field and thus, if not the origin, a critical reinforcement of monolithic notions of "Indian" ways and practices as fundamentally static and of a concept of tradition as itself so stable as to be essentially unchanging. The production of "Indians" has, in short, been a central cultural industry in Europe and the United States from the first encounter. Native Americans have been resolutely encased simultaneously within someone else's history and as irrecoverably outside and apart from History itself.

In the twentieth century the most publicized aspects of Native Americans' lives both elaborate the embedded images and rehearse a now very old ritual of regret and guilt among many white Americans. Native Americans are economically the most impoverished group in the United States. Life expectancy for native men and women is substantially lower than for any other group in the population, suicide and alcoholism rates higher. These "facts," for such they are, almost automatically reconstitute a notion of Native Americans as but a footnote to another people's history, a version of the disappearing Indian, of a doomed people. And they simultaneously invite particular members of the white world, in the guise of sympathy only or advocacy, to play the well-worn roles of representing Indians as victims so as to lament the losses and failures caused by the progress of civilization. Nostalgia thus works its common and strange illusion of appearing critical while soulfully affirming the goodness of members of the dominant culture because they "feel" the losses.

If these barriers to the writing of Native American histories were not sufficiently overwhelming, there are yet others. It would be sentimentality of another kind to diminish how much of Native American cultures has been lost or to pretend that each of them has not profoundly reshaped itself as part of a necessary process of accommodation, adaptation, and resistance to white culture. For most Native Americans English is now their first and only language. A large majority of Native Americans do not live on reservations. They share with all other Americans a body of common experiences (but it is not to be assumed that they make the same meanings from them) through the popular media, educational and political institutions, and in cities and towns and workplaces. The ways in which Native Americans are full and integral members of whatever can be understood as "American" culture are various and beyond capture by any conceptual means, as are the ways they inhabit identities which distinguish them. Commonplace and theoretical ideas about the nature of culture and identity are both inadequate to these complex experiences and histories, and powerful barriers to imagining, examining, or uncovering them.

Native Americans are the only members of American culture who have no choice but to struggle with all these matters, to be, that is, regularly engaged with issues about what constitutes their own history and struggling to extricate it from the thick web of white projections, media images, and other powerful expressions of the narratives which define "Indians." Were this not torturously complex enough, most Euro-Americans and their institutions only accept Native Americans as "Indians" if they conform to these narrative constructions: one cannot be an "Indian" unless one "looks like one," or acts according to prescribed expectations, or, for governmental or legal purposes, can establish possession of the required quantum of "Indian" blood. Thus every dominant cultural and political institution solicits Native Americans to masquerade in one or another stereotypical identity. Psychic, as well as economic, survival has often required many Native Americans to take up these masquerades. Some have done so with deliberate opportunism, but for many only confusion, a kind of cultural schizophrenia, has been the result. What belongs to being a Native American? What has been imposed? What, in being imposed, has been adapted and become an integral part of a culture's being? Vizenor's own account runs as follows:

Today few young people speak the *anishinabe* language. The culture of the *anishinabe* past has been homogenized by the dominant society for use in patent educational curriculum units. In classrooms today *oshki anishinabe* children are summoned to be proud of their invented *indian* and *chippewa* heritage. When a young *oshki anishinabe* is expected to know several thousand years of his history only in the superior language and superior cultural values of the dominant society his identity is a dangerous burden.

The cultural and political histories of the *anishinabe* were written in the language of those who invented the indian, renamed the tribes, allotted the land, divided ancestry by geometric degrees—the federal government identifies the *anishinabe* by degrees of indian blood—and categorized identity by the geography of colonial reservations. The inventions of the dominant society have nothing to do with the heart of the people. (*The Everlasting Sky* 12-13)

Some trick, indeed, to elude all of this. In the absence of any language or terminology free of history, our very means of thinking and telling tend readily to re-enact what Vizenor refers to as historicism and racial representations. Because actual history consists of our representations of what is beyond these, unfigured, the unspoken or the marginalized can become the means to new sight.

That one short sentence requires so extended an explication suggests the difficulty of Vizenor's proposed trick of remaining historical, of navigating within the shoals of our language, our embedded ideas, our very notions of our cultural identities, each of which has altogether been forged in the cauldron of "historicism, racial representations, and [the] historical." What, in practice, might a history, or histories, written with this awareness, look like and how might it be written? Or, in another equally difficult relationship, how help its readers engage such elusive and potentially shattering matters?

Exploring these questions is the task of this essay. My means, the very provocation of what perception and imagination I bring to the subject, is Vizenor's own writing.[4] I intend to argue that these questions, or something close to them, or—better—the project they imply, are at the heart of virtually everything he has written.[5] I do not mean, therefore, to claim that Vizenor is primarily an historian. He has worked across too great a range of genres, and mischievously muddled too many, for his writing to be reduced to a single form. Yet his imaginative enterprises recurrently evoke histories, question received historical narratives and conventions, and construct alternative histories. Historians are less routinely bashed than anthropologists—who "get it" in almost every piece Vizenor writes, but his general indictment covers them fully:

Cultural *anthropologies* are monologues with science; moreover, social science subdues imagination and the wild trickster in comic narratives. These anthropologies are at last causal methodologies and expiries, not studies of anthropos, human beings or even natural phenomena; rather, anthropologies are remains, reductions of humans and imagination to models and comparable cultural patterns—social science is institutional power, a tragic monologue in isolation. ("Trickster Discourse: Comic Holotropes and Language Games" in *Narrative Chance,* 187)

American history, and what I take him to mean by historicism, is, then, implicated everywhere in his books and essays, each of which seeks to move beyond boundaries, none more so than those induced by the specific concepts of nationality and identity pervasive throughout American history. And some of his books can not only be read as histories, they also present themselves as at least partially histories, most evidently *The Everlasting Sky: New Voices from the People Named the Chippewa* (1972), his first extended work in prose; *The People Named the Chippewa: Narrative Histories* (1984); and *Interior Landscapes: Autobiographical Myths and Metaphors* (1990). *Wordarrows: Indians and Whites in the New Fur Trade* (1978) and *Earthdivers: Tribal Narratives on Mixed Descent* (1981) are generically anomalous, an unnameable mixture of history, comedy, fiction, essay, and polemic, but both might well be considered as essential experiments moving toward the formal and textual assurance of *The People Named the Chippewa.* His important anthology, *Touchwood: A Collection of Ojibway Prose* (1987) is a historical collection of Anishinaabeg writers, almost half of which is devoted to the first Anishinaabeg historians. *The Heirs of Columbus* (1991), that exuberantly irreverent book of reversals, need not be classified, but its play on history, indeed the whole Columbian historical and cultural industry, is obvious.

The history Vizenor practices, typically, violates and mixes genres. As with all of his writing, one might call him an experimentalist. His experiments as a historian are driven less by any intrigue with novelty for its own sake, than by two intimately linked understandings at the heart of everything he has written. One rests on the conviction that the project of colonizing the world has been central in the development of "the modern," of Europe itself, and of its major outposts, among which the United States developed its own imperial culture, at once autonomous and new, and a continuation of the European. Native Americans were among the first peoples against whom colonization was directed and on whose bodies and lands the many forms of Europe articulated themselves. "History" or "literature" cannot, therefore, be universal categories of meaning. To write history conventionally, or fiction, would be to perpetuate the structures of colonialism and, either the erasure of native peoples' history or, what is erasure by other means, its distortion and falsification.

The comic best names the other understanding which continually informs Vizenor's ideas and writing. The comic in his work represents a deliberate commitment as much or more than it reflects some simple temperamental affinity or gift. It also provides an additional ground for resistance. Seeing his comedy as deliberate risks sobering it up, but his conscious refusal of any tragic or victimized reading of Native American experience should be acknowledged—for the wit, the struggle, and the discipline it requires. It also keeps him equally vigilant against allegiance to any ideas of essential Indian identities. The bond between the comic and the experimentalist in Vizenor generates his pleasure in subversion, anarchy, and pastiche, the crucial elements in his "trickster discourse."

Experiment, like the effort to be comic, does not always work. And if one rejects, as Vizenor so explicitly has, the impulse toward any absolute, then there cannot be any single alternative form towards which one works. Indeed any repertoire of "anti-colonial" forms would be false precisely to the degree of its predictability and subject to the charge of only mirroring the exercises of power which moved it. One could be an absurdist, as are many literary theorists who pose as "political" and read all literary and political acts as only texts of repetition or recurrence. For an absurdist, experiment might be desirable for the sake of variety, as a game which will inevitably be an endgame. Vizenor is not a writer of elegant despair, though the creative space he makes and lives in is precarious, elusive, because slippery, fragile, for nothing can be assumed in it. It does not make nor would it sustain large claims to truth. And so experiment must be unending, some more expressive and finished than others.

There is a kind of unsystematic method in Vizenor's extensive and varied body of work.[6] Those familiar with it are accustomed to characters reappearing, or their cousins, the repetition—sometimes with a difference and sometimes not—of particular stories, the recurrence of particular historical situations or actors, the slow elaboration over time of a body of special terminologies, a peculiarly Vizenorian vocabulary: "trickster discourse," "terminal creeds," "mythic time," "existential shaman," "ecstatic strategies," or "manifest manners." Neologisms abound so that reading Vizenor can feel at times like entering an idiosyncratic world, tantalizingly almost comprehensible, in which one wishes for explicit instruction which almost never is granted.

Repetition, recurrence, the elaboration of his own vocabulary are all part of Vizenor's experimentation, his constant trying out. His writing circles about on itself. A piece which appeared originally in a newspaper will surface later partly, or wholly, fictionalized in a short story, a novel, or a comic sketch. Whole books get rewritten and appear in new formats, new mixtures of genre: autobiography melds into fiction, history into mythology. This movement is rarely in one direction; in the most accomplished of his writing a reader must become accustomed to moving in and out of the recognizably fictional, barely disguised reportage, humor as fact, fact as fanciful, the sociological, and the metaphorical. His own narrative persona is deflected, muted, very much reserved. A reader hears or senses the presence of some guide, one with a reassuringly gentle and unjudgmental tone. The voice moves a reader without directing him or her. To read Vizenor often requires an unusual act of faith, resigning oneself not to an omniscient narrator, or to an anarchic narrative, but to something like the flow of experience beginning to take shape. This experimentalist is willing to hold in his mind, and to try out in his writing, ideas and experiences which he knows do not yet make a whole. He projects or invites a reader ready to contemplate, turn over, and sustain images, ideas, harsh and painful portions of actuality like Thomas White Hawk's sudden act of murder, or Vizenor's own father's unsolved murder when Vizenor was only two, or the social phenomenon of Native American alcoholism.[7] In all cases, resisting closure is essential. By doing so, Vizenor, the writer, keeps himself and his readers alive to the unexpected, the unseen, to the myriad of uncertain and unpredictable possibilities which hide in even the grimmest of life experiences.

II

The People Named the Chippewa: Narrative Histories exemplifies all these qualities. It will be my primary focus for examining Vizenor's play with and in history so central in everything he has written. The book is demonstrably the result of years of experiment and, to my mind, with *Interior Landscapes: Autobiographical Myths and Metaphors* (1990) and *Dead Voices* (1992), the most fully realized and sustained work Vizenor has so far published. I am tempted to claim it as a model for the writing of American history itself, although most scholars would take it to be more directly a book of, or about, Native American history. Vizenor himself, by the choice of title, might appear to limit its range yet further to the history of one particular Native American nation—the Chippewa, or the Ojibwa, or, in the name they themselves use, the Anishinaabeg. No better primer exists for anyone beginning to think about any Native American culture. His very deliberately restrictive specificity challenges Americans' habitual elision of any Native American culture into the generically "Indian."

Setting up *The People Named the Chippewa* as a model would mistake the book and the nature of its creator's artistry. Any model risks being monolithic. Vizenor's book is more an interrogation of how the history of the Anishinaabeg has been written, and thus, too, of the writing of American history, than a history itself. But it also tells histories, the plural is key, for what the text enacts, again and again, is multiplicity. By resisting any single narrative structure, it can perform many functions. It can be critical—of anthropology, sociology, and history, for example—without simply mirroring its object. It can be an anthology or review—of social science data on alcoholism, or of the early histories of the Anishinaabeg written by members of the nation (William Whipple Warren, Peter Jones, and George Copway). And it is filled with stories of many kinds: origin accounts in the oral tradition, the tales of old mixed-blood men around the stove in a store, the simulations of "Indianness" by members of AIM, or magically imaginative movements with two characters named Margaret Cadotte and Angelick Fronswa—perhaps actual historical persons who, nonetheless, in Vizenor's rendering violate the laws of time and space.

The multiplicities of *The People Named the Chippewa* begin in the title which challenges the most stubborn, perhaps the foundational, ideological construction of Indians. Whatever else, Indians turn out, in a dazzling range of guises, images, and articulations created by whites, to be all "essence": static and thus without or outside of history; stably one-dimensional, that is, all innocence or all savagery, feathered and brave, or drunk and decadent. They are without motive, or have only simple ones, never autonomous actors with plots and ideas of their own. They are rarely multiple and diverse, complex or mysterious.

Writing about one Native American group risks only reinforcing such monolithic conceptions, the very particularity of focus inviting most readers to assume that now we are being given *the* Chippewa. The risk is, ironically, heightened if the writer is himself Indian and identified with the specified group. Who would have better access to the "authentic" story, the "essence" of being—in this case—"Chippewa"? The very title, *The People Named the Chippewa,* immediately resists this in its ambiguity. It asks that we notice the provisionality and historicity of the very names themselves through which we identify others. What seemed substantial—the Chippewa, the Navajo, the Sioux—becomes shadowy, to use one of Vizenor's favored metaphors. The title makes an historical claim, one that plays with, as it resists, any Manichean oppositions. It proposes Chippewa as a name that cannot but be a part of any historical rendering of the people so-called, but also, implicitly, that it is but one name, expressive of some particular historical relationship between those who did the naming and those denominated. Its ambiguity denies us any sure knowledge of the namers or the named. The title does suggest an identity, a peoplehood, but makes it undecidable: these people, whoever they are, is the question the title floats and cannot answer.

The book does not ever answer this question. One might say that is precisely its point. Deciding who the Chippewas, or Ojibwas, or Indians (or, any other "strange" group colonizing Europeans have had to deal with) are is the professional raison d'etre, the obsession of, much of anthropology; the justification for sociologists and social workers supported by grants to help Indians; and, generally, the compulsion of Euro-Americans in the face of strangers whom they can racialize. This concern with defining Indians also marks an important body of American law because of its centrality to issues of ownership of the land. And every form of federal trusteeship, treaty, and program involving Indians requires such definition.

Were this all the book accomplished, it would be, finally, trivial, merely playing games. Though Vizenor has amply demonstrated his sympathy with postmodern theory, he is not content in *The People Named the Chippewa* with only exposing the several metanarratives entailed in most accounts of Native Americans.[8] A people named the Chippewa exist. By never providing a single answer to the question of who they are, or any assemblage of answers, the text keeps its readers in motion and, to the extent it succeeds in this endeavor, its subjects—the Anishinaabeg—themselves remain in motion, as alive as human beings and cultures can be and, in actuality, always are. Undecidability becomes not a theoretical flourish, but a narrative motive to keep the text and its readers considering, reconsidering, questioning, and all the while, as in a sustained relationship between persons, learning more about individual Anishinaabe, about Anishinaabeg history, and about many of its collectors, interpreters, and commentators. This, from *Griever: An American Monkey King in China* (1987), aptly speaks the temperament shaping such a narrative of continuous recognitions: "He was driven to be immortal because nothing bored him more than the idea of an end; narrative conclusions were unnatural, he would never utter the last word, breathe the last breath, he would never pick flowers, the end was never his end" (128).

No chapter in the book better illustrates this avoidance of conclusion than "Firewater Labels and Methodologies." It comes quite late in the text, in part because it requires a reader who has become accustomed to being suspended, able to tolerate, if not be quite comfortable with, a state of experience beyond ambiguity. Its subject one might say, ignoring the chapter title for now, is alcoholism or, bluntly, "the drunken Indian," one of the hoariest of stereotypes. The literal chapter title indicates Vizenor's more sophisticated sense of the subject and a good deal about his project as a writer. A subject cannot be divorced from the ways and practices by which it has been named. To make Indian alcoholism the subject already capitulates to the stereotype. How might we acknowledge Native Americans, beyond stereotype, who drink, may drink, drink a great deal, sometimes drink, never drink? What follows in the chapter marks an attempt to write histories of Native Americans attuned to their ideological representations.

An examination of "labels and methodologies" must be intrinsic to any such history. Doing so, however, can re-enact the madness it seeks to grasp and to escape. Rehearsing horrors readily becomes only a repetition with a difference, a vicariousness that is pornographic. An excursus into labels and methodologies could follow a possibly safer course—into theory or some other highly abstracted discourse. With either choice, the finally elusive variety of any body of human subjects gets lost—yet it is naive and sentimental to imagine that any discourse, artistic or analytical, can have direct access to this variety. I know of no other writer who so fully and richly engages these interpretative dilemmas, intrinsic to the human sciences. An examination of how he does so can illustrate some of the diverse and extraordinarily imaginative work the whole book performs.

The chapter begins with an epigraph, as does every chapter in the book. Vizenor often uses this compositional device.[9] Commonly he draws from a wide range of academic sources—historians, theorists like Derrida or Foucault or Eliade, sociologists. The device is itself an academic one, a gesture which, whatever else, usually indicates a writer's sense of inadequacy, her or his need to lean upon some authority just to get started. Rarely does it work as a substantial compositional motif, but in *The People Named the Chippewa* the epigraphs, like the title itself, are integral to the way the entire text works. Almost all the students in my classes initially read the epigraphs reflexively, almost unconsciously. A few peruse them closely, either at the beginning of their reading, or return to them in the hope of rescue from the bewilderments of a text that will not tell them what to think. Both groups assume them to be stand-ins for the author's ideas or interpretations.

The epigraph to "Firewater Labels and Methodologies" offers a resolution to the issues of the chapter to come even before we have gotten into them. Many non-Indian readers find it articulates, and gives a pleasingly sensitive answer to a question they often have carried subconsciously until this encounter—why do Indians drink? Here are Norman Jacobsen's words from *Pride and Solace: The Functions and Limits of Political Theory* (1978) which, in Vizenor's artful selection and context, reflect the question and seem to satisfy it all at once:

To be human means to stand in need of solace, of comfort in our grief or loss or in the painful throes of anxiety . . . to experience the pain in concert with our fellows, and to share our perceptions of meaning, however fleeting or partial, amidst confusion and despair is to be solaced, and at a price which, unbearable as it might seem, saves us from resigning our powers of decision to others. (113)

Drinking becomes understandable as solace, a response to the human condition, an act which an individual can feel is his or her own, and, when done in the company of others, all the more comforting.

"We" all know that Indians have suffered great losses. In this context, the Jacobsen quotation, wise and kindly, encourages a compassionate sigh about the tragedy of Indian history, tickles into consciousness the familiar narrative of the demise of a once proud and noble people. This belongs to the liberal version of American Indian history. Integral to the seductiveness of its self-satisfying sensitivities, here, at this turn in the national American narrative, is the actuality of what Native Americans have suffered. No other population in the Americas has been targeted for obliteration, cultural and/or physical, so persistently. Vizenor gives especially powerful voice to the pain in a meditation from *Earthdivers* called "Sand Creek Survivors":[10]

We should . . . beat the sweet phrases from the institutions that have disguised the horrors of racism . . . drive the word pains and agonies from the heat into the cold . . . We are the victims of these words used to cover the political violence and white horrors in the memories of the tribes.

Hear these primal screams, the tribes scream with the trees and rivers, from diseases, the massacres and mutilations of the heart in white schools and institutions. . . . Break down the white word wall and dance free from isolation . . . dance in the sun. (37)

Several truths rest, then, somewhere in the place Jacobsen's quoted words might take a reader, including the one that white people's pity is an important part of the history of Indian/white relations. Native Americans' suffering and losses are truths which can easily become falsities if transformed into commodities for Euro-American consumption, or, into self-pity. Whose pity, whose sympathy, whose solace and pride, all become, on reflection, consequential in making use of Jacobsen to grasp anything about why Native Americans might, among other ways of handling pain and loss, drink. The epigrammatic will not, then, work in this text as a reliable formulaic grid to elucidate all the mysteries. In Vizenor's hands, it explores and elaborates them.

The text moves abruptly from the Jacobsen epigraph into an entirely different rhetorical register. Jacobsen's therapeutically philosophical manner gives way to "Plain Johnson, deep in cigarette smoke, hunkers over the wads of paper labels he peeled from seven bottles of cheap beer at the back of the bar" (113). This could be the language of a sensitive social work or sociological case study playing to the sense, so persuasive to Americans, that only recognizable personal experience, something individual, can really be trusted. Examining "Plain Johnson," listening to his life story, may well entice other kinds of readers, those not attuned to the Jacobsen or inclined to skip over epigraphs, to think he will be the key to understanding Indian drinking. For a bit of the chapter, one might believe this to be Vizenor's intention, too, for he tells us what, once again, seems to be another twice-told tale, a narrative so familiar as to need only a few sentences for most readers to complete it on their own. Taken away at age nine from his mother when she is "accused" of being alcoholic, and separated from his siblings, Plain lives with seven white foster families in six years. In adulthood he refuses to give his tribal name in public, using instead a foster nickname "a name he claims he will bear until his mother returns and he locates his sisters" (114). His mother's story, naturally important for him, is part of this narrative.[11] Flooded out of her reservation home by an Army Corps of Engineers' dam, she moves to the cities, marries an abusive white man, has three mixedblood children, and becomes a barfly—a woman nearly obliterated by the exactions of racism and her pain.

The stark simplicity of Vizenor's portrait of Marleen American Horse makes her experience, and her suffering, so much her own that the urge for explanation begins to feel blunt, obtuse, dismissive. And the first use of a refrain Vizenor repeats periodically through the rest of the chapter nags at any alert reader. It comes immediately after the concluding sentence to Marleen American Horse's story. The sentence is discordant with the restraint of the rest of the telling in its soap operatic finality: "She wanted little more than to be loved in a cold and insensitive world" (114). And then, in a paragraph all to itself: "Plain peels another label."

The perplexities increase, especially if a reader by this point still expects sustainable generalizations about Indians. The narrator tells us that Plain's tribal friends find humorous any serious presentation of his past by social investigators (because it is so unremarkable, or idiosyncratic, or because writers and social scientists are, in their view, always trying to make much from little?). We are also told that Plain is as much separated from his tribal friends at the bar as from the values of the white foster families. This one Indian won't yield insight into all Indians, that much is clear. Later in the chapter, several other Indian habitues at the same bar are presented in equally vivid character sketches: Samuel gets drunk on cheap beer, tells good stories, and is an admired teacher at a small college; Cecelia has four children—all in foster care, is mixedblood, sustains her alcoholism on vodka and fruit juices but she finds a home in the bar with her friends; Ramon is a doctor, the first from his tribe, and an alcoholic; Harmon is a veteran who turned to drink after losing his right arm in battle; and Charles was an old man, a mixedblood trapper who journeyed between city and reservation until he froze to death in a snowstorm a few feet from his cabin. None provide much ground for ready generalization on the causes of Indian alcoholism, though we can see a good deal of the consequences for these six people.

Between the introduction to Plain and the sketches of the others at the neighborhood bar, Vizenor adds a third rhetorical mode. Call it expert testimony, or "a review of the literature," a dazzling array, and seductive—because each sounds utterly knowledgeable though none quite agrees with any other. In four pages nine experts weigh in, including the N.I.H. Most readers respond to such a superfluity of the authoritative by searching ardently for some indication of the narrator's stance, a guide, be it a revelatory ironic juxtaposition of quotations, or the unambiguous taking of a position with which, of course, one might then disagree. Vizenor's artfulness is especially evident in this selection. In all of his writing he loves quotation, an abundance of it. At times it can seem hasty or excessive; the discipline of his quotation in this chapter is almost lyrical in its compression and rightness.

His scholars not only all sound reasonable and intelligent, they are demonstrably so. One explicitly takes on the twin myths of the drunken Indian and of alcoholism as a particularly Indian problem, all seem sensibly aware of the play of power and inequality in the history of alcohol use and its introduction among Native Americans, and none can readily be characterized as patronizing or paternalistic. Each quotation is effective, pointed, interesting, and persuasive. Even with the disagreements among them, these scholars are good enough for readers to feel plausibly that, together, they might yield something like sufficient description and explanation. Were this possible, however, we still have Plain peeling another label, another set of names, not bad names in most cases, and

Vizenor bringing us back to the bar and the irreducible particularity of each of his mixedblood characters.

The chapter ends with a section which moves back and forth among three narrative presences: an impersonal and apparently objective narration; another and large selection of expert testimony, much of it from new voices which themselves review the literature on alcoholism from one field or another; and Plain and the others at the bar. Some of the experts portray the use of alcohol among native peoples in a positive light, others darkly remind us of just how devastating alcoholism can be, such as this observation from George Vaillant, the author of *The Natural History of Alcoholism:* "'Outside of residence in a concentration camp, there are very few sustained human experiences that make one the recipient of as much sadism as does being a close family member of an alcoholic'" (119). And many of the commentators make a point of challenging the racial assumption in the very articulation of "Indian alcoholism" as a problem by indicating how different the patterns of use are from one Native American culture to another.

My commentary cannot reproduce the powerful experience of reading this chapter. For some readers the effect is overwhelming. It leaves them literally not knowing what to think. One of my students said, flatly, that it gave him a headache. The chapter does a great deal of complex work. The different narrative structures Vizenor uses function to reveal what insight each can give, but also the ideological grounds upon which each rests. We thus get something much more valuable than a catalog, or a history, of different perceptions of native peoples, in this instance organized through the issue of alcohol. Even without a deliberate analysis of the chapter, many readers experience how a narrative form itself already establishes how and what we can understand of any phenomenon.

Some critics, not readily sympathetic with Vizenor, might propose that the juxtaposition of expert quotation becomes a nonsensical jumble enacting, or inviting, a profoundly anti-intellectual stance against any sustained inquiry. Or that Vizenor's expert use of pastiche moves toward the worst kind of fashionable postmodern despair about the prospect of effecting any change in human practices or institutions. As my most impatiently practical-minded students put it: "okay, but now what is to be done about alcoholics and the harm they inflict on themselves and others?" In a different style, others might, quietly or indignantly, denounce this chapter as finally an irresponsibly aesthetic exercise given the undeniably destructive impact of alcoholism in many Native American communities.

The text moves toward quite another place and can shape a different range of readerly responses. Formally it may not be entirely new; but I can think of no other text quite like it. It displays the results of his different writing apprenticeships: the straightforward, almost flat, descriptiveness journalists use to project objectivity; the journalistic manipulation of quotation to express a point of view without having to avow it; the fiction writer's ability to sketch a scene or give a sense of a character economically; his engagement as a disciplined student of contemporary literary theory; and his steady commitment to bringing the voices of many different Native Americans onto the page evident from *The Everlasting Sky* (1972) to the present.

The chapter achieves a remarkable comprehensiveness about its subjects while it avoids any pretense of absolutism or of a totality. Its readers are asked to listen to an extensive range of voices reflecting on what might constitute an adequate naming of the subject or subjects. Something coheres and yet much remains open, unsettled. To move forward through the chapter readers must achieve an engaged suspension: turning over every statement, holding it, letting it be qualified by another, or by a form of experience, seeing it contradicted but not refuted, and coming to accept that this process will not come to an end or enable them to become final arbiters. All of this depends on a narration that itself eludes characterization. Vizenor's prose in "Firewater Labels and Methodologies" does not pretend to neutrality. The narrator is not an inaudible presence. The chapter has too discernible a shape, and its sharply different rhetorical modes remind us that there is a composing hand and mind. In reading the chapter, the few moments when the narrator comes forward explicitly do not give the definitive effect that extracting them in quotation suggests—nonetheless, a point of view gets firmly spoken:

Tribal cultures are burdened with statistical summaries, romantic preoccupations, cultural inventions, social expectations, adverse public attitudes, in both tribal and urban white worlds. The view that tribal people drink to relume their past memories as warriors will neither explain nor mend the broken figures who blunder drunk and backslide through cigarette smoke from one generation to the next. Separations from tribal traditions through marriage or acculturation do not explain the behavior associated with drunkenness. Tribal cultures are diverse and those individuals who are studied at the bar, or on the streets, are unique, alive, troubled, not static entities from museums or the notebooks of culture cultists. There is some humor over the adversities tribal people bear in racist societies, but there is not much to laugh about in the families of alcoholics. (119)

Strong writing, this. It does not preach, but it unmistakably renders judgments. Like the movement of the chapter as a whole, however, it discriminates while it refuses conclusion and any singular point of view. And, like the many other strong viewpoints anthologized in the chapter, it is subject to the refrain which repeats throughout and, somewhat altered, brings the whole to a close: "Plain peels the last label for the night" (123).

Theory, analysis, generalization, characterization, explanation are all forms of human imagination and, as such, ever finite. Each, depending on how it is practiced, may produce valid insight so long as neither the mode nor its insights create closure. Vizenor, in this regard, might best be seen as a beautiful skeptic—trying, testing, unafraid of exposing the false, and never lending any formulation about human beings, including his own, final credence. He might prefer another term, as do I. "Firewater Labels and Methodologies," among its other achievements, finely exemplifies what Vizenor means by the comic—that to be human, as Emerson has it, is to be mistaken (or, as he says earlier in *Experience,* "a golden mistake"). The wit and the triumph is in the going on. If this chapter teaches anything, it is a quality of mind and heart far from despair or resignation: that we must continue to try to meet our needs and those of our fellows; we will best be able to persist in the venture to the extent we withhold allegiance from any single method, narrative, solution, treatment, attitude, or understanding. To do otherwise is to diminish ourselves and others.

The innovations and enterprise of *The People Named the Chippewa* are not limited to, or sufficiently illustrated by "Firewater Labels and Methodologies," or by any one of its other chapters. Each chapter substantially proceeds in a different manner, takes up and exposes, gently or angrily supplants, weaves new stories in and around the narratives of American culture which represent their projections of native identities and histories as actual and exclusive. To liberate ourselves from them requires being insistently historical by keeping as close to concrete and individual experience as possible while exposing the structures through which such "facts" have been conventionally mediated. So Vizenor must move variously in *The People Named the Chippewa* while always situating the conventional mediations in relation to specific Native American voices and histories.

Two chapters, "Shadows at La Pointe," early in the book, and "The Shaman and Terminal Creeds," its last, illustrate some of the complex range of formal innovation in the book. "Shadows at La Pointe" is the most lyrical chapter in the book, celebratory, optimistic, and yet unsentimental. Its opening gives one an immediate sense of these qualities and of Vizenor's stylistic reach:

This morning the lake is clear and calm.

Last night a cold wind washed slivers of ice clear over the beach, the end of a winter to remember. Now, the pale green becomes blue on the horizon. Spring opens in the birch, a meadow moves in the wind. The trees thicken down to the water, an invitation to follow the sun over the old fur trade post to a new world of adventures. (37)

We move through the chapter in the company of two young girls whose names we learn from their printing them in the sand by a dock on Madeline Island, the place where the world began (and begins) in Anishinaabeg accounts:

MARGARETCADOTTE
ANGELICKFRONSWA

I don't want to go by these wondrous inscriptions too quickly, though much comment may ruin their beautiful simplicity. These two young girls come into being in the narrative voice which opens the chapter and they seem almost palpable in these letters, the paradoxical magic of representational illusion, the sense of real presence, all through flat markings on a white page, letters little different than theirs on the sand.

As so often in Vizenor's writing, and in this book, these are both real and fictional, persons and characters. The girls move in real time and space and also, magically, transcend these barriers. They physically shrink small enough to ride in a trunk together on the steamer that goes between the island and the mainland. Their journey is local and historical, grounded in place, itself richly figured. They are joined by other characters, each himself or herself at once real and imagined: Eliza Morrison, mixedblood wife of a trader and hunter; old mixedblood and tribal men gathered around the stove at the American Fur Company store, telling stories; Abigail or Abba Spooner, a teacher at the first mission school on Madeline Island; Sherman Hall, its superintendent, a Presbyterian missionary; and we hear stories about Henry Rowe Schoolcraft, Lewis Cass, and Thomas McKenney, each an important Anglo-American in the post-contact history of the Anishinaabeg as well as creators of influential containments of Indians in treaty, anthropological, folkloric, and political narratives.

The narrative line of the chapter reads straightforwardly, pleasurably, unlike the knotty movement of "Firewater Labels." Quotations are used as pervasively—from historical documents, oral lore, and occasionally from secondary sources—but they do not turn on each other. One almost need not notice that they are quoted, so seamless is the movement forward. A history is being constructed of the Anishinaabeg in the nineteenth century, localized at Madeline Island, accenting and blending mixedblood and what Vizenor here calls "tribal people" as sources. This history, like mixedbloods, is a compound, both old and new. By making McKenney, Schoolcraft, and Cass, subjects in the story, Vizenor subtly exposes the invisible and compulsory authority they have in conventional histories for which their inventions, accepted as documents, have been the primary sources. They grow and shrink, though mostly shrink, just as they do in the marvelous stories about Schoolcraft told by the "third old mixedblood at the American Fur Company store" (41). The oral and the literate jostle each other nicely throughout the chapter, yet another mixture, call it a miscegenation, of forms. Vizenor as deftly and quietly shapes another such mixture: two young girls begin this chapter's journey, it coheres around them; the first document quoted is Eliza Morrison's letter. Gender does not become unimportant, thus, or erased, but hierarchy is displaced, within Native American and white communities and between them. Women simply have narrative authority here, a speaking presence.

Throughout the chapter bloods mix, as do genders. Time and place do not observe conventional boundaries. Catholic and Protestant quarrel over Anishinaabeg bodies and souls as they busily imagine them in the forms most compatible with missionary and cultural desires. At the same time the mixedbloods and the Anishinaabeg make various uses of what each dogmatic community offers—for some it is an affliction, for others an opportunity, or just a part of what exists. Nothing is cleanly or purely separate, cultural exchange happens everywhere—unconsciously, beneficially, oppressively, sometimes mutually, no form of it in this chapter's presentation is unmixed, one-directional. The chapter's end returns to Margaret's and Angelick's voices, but their "we" resonates in and with more than their two identities. They are both themselves and speakers of, spoken into being by, a body of history. That body cannot be fully articulated—for it is always changing and multiple beyond the ability of language to hold. If it is ineffable, it is only so in this sense, not as some mystical peoplehood, but as something which must ever be imagined and re-imagined, located in time and place yet transportable:

The steamboat whistle sounded several times, breathless at the dock, the last invitation to those still on the shore. The sound of the steam whistle was muffled inside the trunks, and each sound was a new port, a new dock, new faces, places on our dream maps. We walked down each dock beneath new parasols, our shadows traveled across the earth.

The steamboat moved from the dock. We could hear conversations on the side of the deck and we could imagine from the dark interior of the trunks all the people on the dock. Our friends from school were there, the old mixed-bloods who would tell stories about us in the store, the little priest, all waving to us as we leave the island for the first time. Our names held back the flood at the first place we knew on the earth. We will be remembered forever. (54-55)

Here is history, here imagination also, shadows and dreams walk about and move through the sound of a steamboat whistle, the twirl of a parasol, all that an old trunk evokes.

The People Named the Chippewa begins in a telling of a "traditional" origin story. Midway through the book Vizenor creates this new origin tale with first places and floods and the promise of life and immortality. The new and the old mix. Like the swirl of the waters at the dock, they can threaten the girls' inscribed names in the sand; engaged and imagined deeply enough, they may keep renewing each other forever.

"The Shaman and Terminal Creeds," Vizenor's final chapter, is also the most difficult in the historical, conceptual, and human issues it raises. The general subject, Native American spiritual beliefs and practices, has as long and contentious a history in Indian/white relations as does the struggle over land. Euro-Americans have been as intrusive and expropriative in matters of the soul as in those of the body. Initially, Europeans denied that Native Americans had any spiritual beliefs—let alone that there were sophisticated and diverse spiritual systems in each of the many Native American cultures. Then these beliefs were regarded as merely superstition, or evidence that Satan had Indians in his grasp. By the nineteenth century Native Americans became the object of a whole missionary machine dedicated to converting them to one or another Christian church. Missionaries ran most of the schools on the reservations and had power virtually equal to that of the government agents, a power which remained essentially unmodified until the mid-twentieth century and which was exerted, in part, to suppress all indigenous spiritual rituals.

Colonizing any peoples entails multiple interventions in and disruptions of their cultures, the most insidious of which are those which reach inside people's minds and spirits to alter their ways of making meaning, of locating themselves in the world and in the spiritual. In no Native American nation were people able to protect their belief systems, and the rituals which expressed and renewed them, from the impact of European policies, especially, of course, those of the many Christianizers. The rich body of spiritual knowledge and practice did not entirely disappear, but it had to change and in a myriad of ways—in many instances by absorbing particular Christian ideas or symbolic patterns, in others by trying to preserve older forms by keeping them in stasis, a mode of resistance itself a distortion and an effect of colonization.

Repression and extermination are indispensable tools in the colonial arsenal and under these headings one can assemble many of the governmental and Christian missionary efforts to reshape spiritual life in Indian country. But collecting, translating, and studying forms of expression are equally indispensable, though less obvious exercises of power:

Tribal cultures reveal supernatural events and remember the past in oral traditional stories. The tellers of these stories were the verbal artists of the time, those who imagined in their visual memories sacred and secular events. The stories that have been recorded, translated, and printed as scripture, however, have altered tribal religious experiences. Published stories have become the standardized versions, the secular work of methodological academics; the artistic imagination has been polarized in print, and the relationships between tellers of stories and the listeners . . . are lost in translation. The formal descriptions of tribal events by outsiders, such as missionaries, explorers, and anthropologists, reveal more about the cultural values of the observers than the imaginative power of spiritual tribal people. (139-40)

Native spiritual ideas and rituals became objects of fascination for Europeans and Euro-Americans almost as early as they became objects of contempt and control. Fear or fascination both disable the complex process of seeking to understand another culture.

Vizenor's own exploration in this chapter seeks to describe the distance between tribal cultures and the white world, but also the consequences of the confused ways bits and pieces of the different spiritual worlds come together within the psyches of some Native Americans. Two life stories are set side by side: John Ka Ka Geesick, a shaman and healer, born in 1844, who dies at the age of 124; and Cora Katherine Sheppo, a mixedblood woman, forty-two years old, who at times is filled with dread and, at others, feels moved by vague forces beyond her. Convinced, during one of these moments, that her twenty-month-old grandchild had been "'spawned by the devil,'" she smothers him to death.

Each life story represents something of the constant and often exhausting negotiations Native Americans conduct to locate themselves in multiple and mixed cultural histories. These take place in a society whose dominant members are fixated by concepts of Indian identity so powerful that they necessarily become one of the most powerful forces with which Native Americans must deal.

In Warroad, Minnesota, where John Ka Ka Geesick lived, he partly made his living through white people's fixations. He posed for a photograph used on postcards sold to tourists. In the image he wears a blanket and a turkey feather headdress: "the feathered visage encouraged the romantic expectations of tourists." Unlike Cora Sheppo, however, he somehow occupies an assured center. Vizenor does not explain how Geesick achieved this other than to offer these declarative descriptions:

Ka Ka Geesick was a man of visions and dreams; his music and world view connected him to a tribal place on the earth. He was secure at the center of his imagination and memories; in a sense, he was in a spiritual balance, blessed to live so long. The world around him, however, invented his culture and advertised his images on picture postcards. (143)

His balance is perceptible, just as are the disjunctions which his funeral rites reveal. When he dies the white citizens of the town plan a ceremonial public funeral in the local school gymnasium. A white mortician dresses him in a standard blue suit, white shirt, and tie, no more his dress in life than the blanket and feather headdress. His own people were not asked to plan the public celebration, but they did, nonetheless, call on a shaman to conduct a traditional burial ceremony in advance of the white-planned event. Though invited, the white people of the town chose to stay outside, peeking in, wondering at the medicine bundle, the Anishinaabeg language, the use of tobacco as an integral part of a sacred rite, the sound of the rattle. Then comes the white ceremony. An organ and Christian hymns, no tribal music, and a eulogy delivered by a white evangelist into whose church Geesick had never entered: two worlds stand next to each other, the members of one mostly uncomprehending even of the existence of the other; the members of the other continuously moving across a terrain on which they are sometimes invisible, at others like manufactured objects on a postcard, sorting, handling as best they can multiple translations, a colonized people who to survive need to be fluent in many discourses and histories.

Such fluency isn't guaranteed. Vizenor knows that whatever afflicts Cora Katherine Sheppo, that moves her to believe she must murder her own grandchild, is implicated in the unholy burden entailed in the need for such fluency and that many Native Americans cannot fully sustain it. Throughout the section on Cora Sheppo, Vizenor works two elusive terms: shamanism and schizophrenia. They belong to different histories, both speak to the psyche, and both are so clinically and culturally loaded, as to defy dependable definition. And so either one can be used to create an illusion of knowledge and understanding, to label and to dispense. Vizenor's use of the clinical psychiatric term is, on one hand, fully contextual, for schizophrenia is the name the court-appointed psy-

chiatrists used to characterize Cora Sheppo's mental state and which the
court accepted in deciding she could not stand trial and had instead to be
hospitalized. It also resonates with a piece of Vine Deloria, Jr.'s writing
which Vizenor used prominently in *Earthdivers* some twelve years earlier:

No matter how well educated an Indian may become, he or she always suspects
that Western culture is not an adequate representation of reality. Life therefore
becomes a schizophrenic balancing act wherein one holds that the creation,
migration, and ceremonial stories of the tribe are true and that the Western
European view of the world is also true . . . the trick is somehow to relate what
one feels to what one is taught to think. (viii)

Perhaps Vizenor chose not to recall Deloria's words in "Shamans
and Terminal Creeds" because their sensible tone simply cannot convey
what schizophrenic balancing acts are like in felt experience. At best,
Deloria's insight can take one only to the edge of the darkness of Cora
Sheppo's act, and the struggles of mind and soul out of which it came.
Bits of Christianity from her Catholic upbringing, shards of various
Native American spiritual practices—peyote ceremonies, sweat lodge
purifications, elements from the Sun Dance, experiences of culture
revivalism like The Longest Walk—mix with her hearing voices, seeing
visions. She is a soul in fragments.

The chapter is more sheerly descriptive in its narration than any of
the others in *The People Named the Chippewa*. It moves somberly in a
disciplined contemplation of two lives, of cultures, and spiritual ideas
and histories which it does not pretend to explain. It comes to no conclusion, ending in quotation and elision. It reads, for much of its length,
almost like a transcript, or a dispassionate and full newspaper account.
Vizenor does not venture, nor does he in any way invite readers to any
fancy theories about Cora Sheppo and her act. He bluntly blocks those
who might read her as a thwarted shaman and healer herself:

Cora Sheppo was not a shaman, she was not a healer, but her experiences . . .
have been diagnosed as schizophrenia and seem to be similar to those experiences associated with traditional tribal shamans. She confronted evil forces, she
heard voices out of familiar time. . . . Cora Sheppo needed a shaman to rescue
her soul and save her grandchild. (148)

In the face of such pain where might we who read move? where
those who write of it? those whose experience it is? The only hint of an
answer is in the second part of the chapter title. However incoherent her

beliefs, they became for Cora Sheppo "terminal creeds"—the frustration of her own ability to live in the world, the motive for the murder of her grandson.

Isn't Vizenor himself at risk of appearing to endorse another kind of terminal creed by ending *The People Named the Chippewa* with such a chapter? Might it seem to leave no alternative but an acquiescence in the judgment of an anthropologist like Harold Hickerson, whom Vizenor quotes and dissents from early in the chapter: "'Chippewa culture is a shambles . . .'" (143)? Or to further reinforce the cultural reflex of seeing Indians as victims, the course of their history as tragedy—a reflex Vizenor mocks, assails, and refuses throughout everything else he has written? These questions are substantial, not merely rhetorical. For me they suggest how much is at stake for Vizenor in this book, how bound to truth it is, how much he must dare. To end with this chapter seems a deliberate test of his and his readers' capacity to contemplate horror and pain without the comfort of any system of explication, not to blink the worst, and—to go on. He depends upon something akin to Simone Weil's conviction that real hope, truly a virtue, depends upon the experience—and then the refusal—of despair.

It is an act of faith Vizenor makes, and which those who read him may choose, to live in that difficult place which moves toward the fullness of history, nothing less than all of human experience itself, with only the resources of language and category, and in full acceptance that one will never reach its end. To affirm the insufficiency of language and category as one with the fallacies of human being itself, to keep inventing and trying language, to take pleasure in persistence, to be as open-eyed as possible, ready for surprise and compassionate when the human disappoints—this is to be comic. Only a comic should be trusted to write our histories. Let us salute a master comedian.

Notes

1. This essay has been long in the making. Nor am I near to being finished with the issues it seeks to raise and to explore. My wish, then, is to see this as a work-in-progress which will prove to be, I hope, more than a devious rationalization for its shortcomings. My acknowledgments must be shorter than my debts: to Gerald Vizenor, for teaching me, first through his books, and then in friendship, all I think I understand of the complexity of writing about Native Americans. Arnold Krupat's generous and extensive scholarship on Native American literature continues to inspire and instruct my own. Although I do not specifically cite them in this essay, I could not have written about Vizenor, with-

out the help of three scholars' previous work on him. Not for the first time, I found reading Louis Owens, *Other Destinies: Understanding the American Indian Novel* (Norman: U of Oklahoma P, 1992) got my thinking started. I suspect that there is nothing here he has not already said better in his fine chapter on Vizenor. Elaine Jahner, "Cultural Shrines Revisited," *American Indian Quarterly* IX:1 (Winter 1985): 23-30, is as brilliant as it is concise. Betty Louise Bell, "Almost the Whole Truth: Gerald Vizenor's Shadow-Working and Native American Autobiography," *Auto/Biography Studies* VII: 2 (Fall 1992): 180-95, shares many of my concerns and questions and superbly focuses them theoretically.

2. The revisability of the "known" is a necessary assumption in any progressive understanding of history, for essential to progress is the belief that "we" become more enlightened, rational, comprehensive and comprehending—in part by seeing around or through the errors of our predecessors.

3. The creation of the first reservations and of the beginnings of the national parks are not simply coincidental. Both are moved by a concern to prevent the complete disappearance of the physical embodiments of two always related conceptual entities critical in American thought as guarantees of American exceptionalism: wilderness or nature and its human manifestation, the Indian. But both, by the late nineteenth century though clearly endangered, are to remain marginal to American life—Indians in reservations and museums where they can be contained and visited, pitied or marveled at; nature in carefully bounded parks, also to be visited and in as much comfort and convenience as possible. Indians and nature may thus function as images, in packages, but in no fashion are either to become central to American life, sites of struggle and conflict, actualities and persistent actors in history.

4. Throughout the essay I will also be drawing on the experience of teaching *The People Named the Chippewa* for almost a decade. When I refer to readers I usually have in mind specifically about 500 students, mostly at Amherst College but also at the University of California at Berkeley, with whom I have shared the book and who have, as individuals and in community, taught me a great deal about the ways this text works, baffles, delights, frustrates, and teaches. I would like specifically to name my indebtedness most recently to fine essays and comments by Jennifer Burch, Brian Harrigan, Paulus Ingram, Jennifer Mattson, and Peter Vantine at Amherst College, Han Choi at Hampshire College, and Kristin Theis-Alvarez at the University of California at Berkeley.

5. "Virtually," only because I cannot see them as central to much of the poetry, the experiments in haiku, but this may well only indicate the limits of my imagination and understanding.

6. Few important contemporary American writers have created such a substantial and varied body of work. And no other Native American writer has written so well in so many forms. History, poetry, the essay, autobiography, the

novel, journalism, short stories, literary theory are all genres in which Vizenor has worked as well as creating his own marvelous mixtures. The sheer variety recalls Norman Mailer, though in virtually all other regards it is hard to imagine two more different writers. A more apt comparison, to go back yet another generation, might be to Edward Dahlberg. Vizenor and Dahlberg both had largely homeless childhoods, both write about them utterly unsentimentally, and both have a body of work which eludes ready classification.

7. From *The Trickster of Liberty:* "The active reader implies the author, imagines narrative voices, inspires characters, and salutes tribal tricksters in a comic discourse; an erotic motion under the words dissolves the separation between minds and bodies" (xi).

8. In his autobiographical *Interior Landscapes: Autobiographical Myths and Metaphors,* a book I regret not being able to devote attention to in this essay, Vizenor in explaining why he didn't become an actor, draws something like this distinction. One must be playful, but there is more:

. . . because of my insecurities about families and identities. I reasoned that an actor lived in the role, and in my case the role would have become my home. I praised the trickster, our comedies, the turn of egos in a stern world, but there must be more to me than a mere pose. (129)

9. Its use provides one evidence for seeing *The Everlasting Sky, Wordarrows,* and *Earthdivers* as making a family of texts culminating in *The People Named the Chippewa. The Everlasting Sky,* the first of these, and the one most directly anticipatory of *The People,* only uses epigraphs by Native American writers, thinkers, and activists, virtually all of whom are Anishinaabeg.

10. And, more personally, in this passage from *Interior Landscapes:* "My crossblood remembrance, lost tribal souls, uncertain identities, and wounded cranes in the poisoned cities, cause me the most miseries. I learned to remember these stories, and to honor impermanence, tribal tricksters on the run, run, run, run" (130).

11. Vizenor writes more extensively about Marleen American Horse in *Wordarrows* (38-46). The names are fictional.

4

HOLDING WORD MONGERS ON A LUNGE LINE:
THE POSTMODERNIST WRITINGS
OF GERALD VIZENOR AND ISHMAEL REED

Amy J. Elias

"You can go home again," writes Ursula Le Guin in *The Dispossessed*, "so long as you understand that home is a place where you have never been" (157). Gerald Vizenor continually returns to a home where he has never been while warning others of the dangers of nostalgic hearth-longing. Vizenor associates such nostalgia with the reconstruction of Native American history by both colonial anthropology and sentimental "postmodern speciesists," and he combats this nostalgia with postmodern aesthetic strategies that allow him to jettison anthropocentric realism. This Native American writer is particularly severe in his judgments of anthropologists and their work: "I . . . think that their methodology is narrow, bigoted, and colonial, however objective they pretend to be, and that most of what they say, if not all of what they have said about tribal people, is at best, at very best, bullshit" (Coltelli 161).

Instead of mining the fields of historical fiction, Vizenor cultivates a postmodern garden, and consequently his work may be compared to that of another postmodern fabulator, Ishmael Reed. Reed himself, in fact, has noted the overlap between his and Vizenor's notions of comedy as they derive, respectively, from African American and Native American oral traditions (Watkins 610). A comparison between Vizenor's and Reed's works reveals how authors from differing minority discourses may use postmodernist strategies to combat either the hegemonic realist or the modernist narrative tradition. Furthermore, a comparison between the two authors raises key questions concerning the relation of postmodernism to ethnicity and the dangers of defining an author solely on the basis of his/her "ethnic authenticity."

Vizenor and Reed both redefine "tricksters" to some extent, pitting modern-day tricksters against simulacra of minority race and culture. They are both thus complicitous with the processes of postmodern simulation even as they expose its political dangers. This leaves both authors open to charges of inauthenticity, for both writers become entangled in a web of ontological uncertainty characteristic of postmodernist political fabulation.[1]

1. Re-visioning Nativism and the Transcendent Subject

One could discuss at length the various ways both Vizenor and Reed challenge Western genres and forms such as the historical novel, the university novel, the Western, the Hero Monomyth pattern.[2] However, I think it is perhaps even more important to recognize how they both decenter the ideological as well as the aesthetic groundings of literatures that have been in the past defined as both cultural discourses (American Indian Literature, Black Literature) and as literary modes within the Western literary canon (Realism, for example, or Modernism). As postmodernists and minority writers, Vizenor and Reed wage a double political battle. First, they write from the boundary of the cultural mainstream; the most forceful thrust of their satire is directed at the minority Other as created by most Anglo-Western colonial discourse. However, Vizenor and Reed also satirize the "transcendent subject" projected by their own respective cultural literatures: the simulacra paradoxically created through the attempt by realism and modernism to redefine the colonized Other as minority Subject.

There are two kinds of "precursors" with whom Ishmael Reed may be said to take issue and, perhaps like Bloom's ephebe, write against. The first includes African American literary precursors, most importantly Hurston, Wright, Ellison, and Baldwin (Gates 218). (The second includes his contemporaries in the Black Arts Movement of the 1960s and 1970s.) In interviews, Reed has been outspoken about his distance from Wright, Ellison and Baldwin, claiming that they were "created" by the New York intellectuals of the 1950s and as such became tokens of the white critical Establishment. Importantly, Reed distinguishes the Modernism of these writers' works from his own, presumably postmodern, writing: "Saul Bellow and Alfred Kazin were instrumental in Ralph Ellison's getting the National Book Award for *Invisible Man*. They were the judges, and his book epitomizes the modernist values they supported" (Watkins 604). Building from such comments, Henry Louis Gates argues that Reed's postmodernist narrative strategy (which Gates terms pastiche) allows him to challenge "the received idea of blackness as a negative essence, as a natural, transcendent signified" and that

By undertaking the difficult and subtle art of pastiche, Reed criticizes the Afro-American idealism of a transcendent black subject, integral and whole, self-sufficient, and plentiful, the "always already" black signified, available for literary representation in received Western forms as would be the water dippered from a deep and dark well. (218, 237)

Reed's fiction thus argues against the idea that a "black experience" can fit into preconceived "containers" or definitional boundaries by challenging the realist/modernist idea of blackness as a trope of absence (Gates 218). Moreover, not only does Reed imply through parody that his African American literary precursors construct a "transcendent black signified" in this sense; he also "employs a self-referential language, at all points directing attention to itself as rhetoric, to do so," burlesquing through "vulgarity and hyperbole" the notion of "interpretive credentials" to interpret black experience and using self-reflexive language "to expose the nature of conventions and to insist on new and black structures of feeling" (Gates 219).

I would argue that Vizenor does precisely the same thing in a different context. The aesthetic goals of Vizenor and Reed seem to overlap in one very important sense: both writers perceive their own emerging ethnic literatures as compromised by literary tropes established within a received literary tradition. Within realist and modernist Native American literature, Indian-ness too becomes a trope of absence, an " 'always already' [Red] signified," much as Gates perceived blackness within the African American literary tradition. Vizenor plants a depth charge at the base of this tropological construction by identifying a Native American trope of absence in the myth of the "vanishing Indian." Vizenor's primary term for this trope is simulation, which he appropriates from Jean Baudrillard and Umberto Eco.[3]

For Vizenor, as a Native American, there seem to be two kinds of simulation. The first is that of the colonizer, who transforms the Native American subject into a simulation of an Indian-ness that is, in Eco's words, "realer than real." Vizenor alludes to this forced conversion, as it is specific to Native Americans, in nearly all of his writing.[4] According to Eco, in its demand for "the real thing," postmodernism "must fabricate the absolute fake; there the boundaries between game and illusion are blurred, the art museum is contaminated by the freak show, and falsehood is enjoyed in a situation of 'fullness,' of *horror vacui*" (Eco 8). Likewise, Vizenor writes,

Tribal cultures are colonized in a reversal of the striptease. Familiar tribal images are patches on the "pretense of fear," and there is a sense of "delicious terror" in the structural opposition of savagism and civilization found in the cinema and in the literature of romantic captivities. ("Socioacupuncture" 411)

Colonialism turns Native Americans into simulations by putting clothes (e.g., bone choke collars and leather breeches) *on* them, transforming all into simulations of vanished savagism and Wild West comedy. The counter, for Vizenor, is a "reverse striptease": Native Americans must take off the bone collars and refuse their simulated selves, which is precisely what Tune Browne does in "Socioacupuncture": he strips on stage, flinging his Indian costume out into the cheering audience and refusing simulated identity. Those in Vizenor's novels who are seduced by colonial simulacra are doomed to spiritual, or even physical, death. As Eco notes, "for the reproduction to be desired, the original has to be idolized" (19). Vizenor illustrates such idolatry in *Bearheart: The Heirship Chronicles* with Belladonna Darwin-Winter Catcher, who is called on to defend her heritage and can only muster up sentimental simulations of Indian history, and Little Big Mouse, who espouses an evangelical vision of otherness that eventually gets her killed (Keady 61-65).

However, Vizenor does posit a second kind of simulation, one with potentially positive consequences. This is the simulation constructed by Ishi, who appears in many of Vizenor's nonfiction essays. Vizenor reconstructs Ishi's history in *Manifest Manners*. Ishi was a Yana Indian captured at a northern California slaughterhouse in August, 1911; immediately fodder for local newspapers, who called him "the last of his tribe," Ishi was taken by a Sheriff Webber from the slaughterhouse and, because he had no home and spoke no English, was put in jail until he was released to the custody of Alfred Kroeber, an anthropologist who later wrote the book *Ishi in Two Worlds*. According to Vizenor, Ishi lived in rooms furnished by Phoebe Apperson Hearst, who also created the Department and Museum of Anthropology at the University of California. Ishi was housed in rooms at the university's museum, and before he died of tuberculosis in 1916, he was the focus of study by Kroeber, Thomas Waterman (a linguist), Saxton Pope (a surgeon and student of tribal archery) and Edward Sapir.

In retelling Ishi's story, Vizenor indicates that the Yana Indian double-troped colonial simulations, playing the game of simulation while keeping his own name silent. In other words, Ishi simulates simulation. For Vizenor, he becomes a living sign. Ishi is not only absence; he is presence masquerading as absence, playing at absence in a simulation of his own. " 'Ishi is the absence,' *he* [Ishi] might have said."[5] Vizenor calls those who manage this double-simulation "postindian warriors": "Postindian simulations arise from the silence of heard stories, or the imagination of oral literature in translation, not the absence of the real in simulated realities; the critical distinction is that postindian warriors create a new tribal presence in stories" (*Manifest* 12). In other words, Ishi's identity is a performative one. Vizenor's unique distinction between self- and other-directed simulation corresponds to the distinctions he makes between "tragic wisdom" and "Tragic Indians":

The tragic miseries of a chemical civilization are denied in manifest manners, and tragic wisdom is consumed in the esthetic ruins of movies and television; the neocolonial denial of tragic wisdom has become a burden in tribal consciousness and literature. ("Native" 223)

If I am reading his nonfiction essays correctly, "tragic wisdom" for Vizenor is a term denoting experiential and traditional wisdom garnered by native cultures who have had contact with colonizers. "Tragic wisdom" is therefore a positive thing, different from the drama of the "tragic noble savage" constructed by the colonial narratives that Vizenor calls "tragic miseries." "Tragic wisdom" is internal to Native cultures and opposes the colonial simulation of "tragic miseries" ("Native" 223). In Vizenor's nonfiction, "tragic Indians" (the colonial constructions) are associated with the simulated Vanishing Indian and thereby with the trope of absence; Ishi symbolizes one kind of attempt at preserving tragic wisdom.

The metaphor of simulation gives Vizenor a means to challenge the precepts of both anthropocentric literary realism and literary modernism. His neologism for Manifest Destiny—"manifest manners"—aligns him theoretically with postcolonial critics who lambast modernism and structuralist anthropology. As Stephen Slemon's critique of Modernist sculpture (or almost anyone's recent criticism of Conrad's *Heart of Darkness*) reveals, it has become common to view European Modernism as a kind of covert colonial romanticism, incorporating the redactive notions of "other" and "authenticity" as well as a hegemonic binary between "center" and "periphery."[6] Vizenor reveals modernist structuralism to be the red man's burden: these theories "never seem to enter stories as a language game without an institutional advantage; . . . they are academic tropes to power rather than tribal stories in a language game" (*Narrative* xiii). Speaking of Thomas Waterman, Alfred Kroeber, and others who studied Ishi at the museum, Vizenor notes that these men were "not insensitive," but nonetheless

their studies and museums would contribute to the simulations of savagism. At the same time, some of these educated men were liberal nihilists, and their academic strategies dispraised civilization. These men who represented civilization would find in the other what they had not been able to find in themselves or their institutions; the simulations of the other became the antiselves of their melancholy. (*Manifest* 131-32)

Vizenor's critique sounds dramatically similar to that of Ishmael Reed in *Mumbo Jumbo* when he writes that the Atonist Path's creed is "Lord, if I can't dance, No one shall" (65). Reed and Vizenor both satirize an Anglo-Western culture that has grown weary of itself and projects onto the Other both its desire and its fears about its own inadequacy.

Vizenor claims repeatedly in interviews that to corral "Indian Literature" within a set of structural(ist) fences is to kill the living spirit of the writing—in effect, to conventionalize Native American literature. In this sense, Vizenor seems to align himself with theorists who fault modernism for producing not the liberating proletarian or artistic universalism it often theorized, but rather a self-deluded colonial imperialism, one that fetishized nativism in a feverish rush for new artistic energies and non-Western creative mythologies.[7] Like many other theorists of the postmodern, Vizenor constructs postmodernism as the mode which can revitalize a desiccated modernist agenda: "Modernism is a disguise, a pretense of individualism and historicism; postmodern is a pose in a language game that would controvert the institutional power of translation" (*Narrative* x).

Vizenor's central image and character type—the trickster—is central to his interrogation of the trope of absence within realist and modernist narrative, for his poststructuralist trickster opposes an essentialist one (and a "vanished" one) constructed by modernist structuralism.[8] Griever de Hocus in *Griever: An American Monkey King in China* exemplifies how tricksters thwart institutionalization:

Griever holds cold reason and those unctuous word mongers who palm stories and passions on a lunge line when he paints the world. His imagination is a dance to discover interior landscapes; but now and then his trickeries on rough paper are cornered in popular clichés and institutions, abused by those who vest their personal power in labels and tickets to the main events. When this happens, when the world appears overused like a turnstile, he pleats and doubles shrouds and veronicas, creases photographs, folds brochures, dictionaries, and menus, to weaken the plane realities. (201-02)

When tricksters are sought for dissection by the social sciences, then tricksters are in real danger of becoming one of two dead things: either postmodern simulacra or fossilized corpses. Vizenor thus opposes a representational "trickster" with a semiotic one, one that can never be captured because of its location within the play of language itself. "The trickster," he writes, "is a semiotic sign; not cultural material or discovered elements that are recomposed to endorse invented models in social science" (*Narrative* 188).

Whether Vizenor's definition of trickster is *anthropologically* correct may be irrelevant, for his tricksters play at a postmodernist game: how to disrupt when disruption itself (the trickster, the Other's voice) has become co-opted within the System. In interviews, Vizenor approvingly notes the perspective of a medicine healer named Betonie in Leslie Marmon Silko's *Ceremony*. In Silko's novel, Betonie is critical of the tribal medicine healers who cling to the old ceremonies and do not realize that ceremonies, while embedding and preserving the past, must also undergo constant revision and re-creation in order to accommodate the new demands of a changing landscape.[9] Like the fictional Betonie, Vizenor is wary of pasture-ized Indian literature, the equivalent of formula fiction. Vizenor's tricksters may (or may not) violate historical models, but they do "update the ceremonies" and rescue the trickster from a museum death.

It may be important at this juncture to note that Reed also constructs postmodern tricksters, and that the concept of ethnic *humor*—in this case, African humor denied by the Anglo-Western colonial ear—is essential to his notion of trickster potency. While Reed deliberately draws from African and African American myths, oral tales, and cultural traditions,[10] in more recent years his concept of "syncretism" (or multiculturalism) has led him to "update the ceremonies" and draw trickster features from those of various cultural traditions.[11] Raven Quickskill, a main character in Reed's *Flight to Canada,* is such a character construction. Raven, Reed notes,

is based upon the Tlingit Indian myths of the Pacific Northwest. A hereditary chief of the tribe read the book and invited me to his home in Sitka, Alaska. When I arrived they allowed me to view and photograph various totems of their tribe, such as a raven's crest, and these totems were without exception *satirical.* So it is with the classic Afro-American poetry, as well. The Afro-American poet at his best is a humorous poet, not a singer of spirituals. (33)

Like Vizenor, Reed constructs postmodern, even ahistorical, tricksters who deny "tragic misery" and renew "tragic wisdom" through humor.[12] He has been advocating the need to "update the ceremonies" for virtually his entire career. This ethic takes the form of neo-hoodooism, a new Americanized form of Voodoo.[13]

What, then, are the interrogative postmodernist narrative strategies that Reed and Vizenor share? Joe Weixlmann correctly observes that

Reed's novels "shatter the mold of traditional Black American fiction in a manner anticipated by . . . *Invisible Man*: Realism, seriousness, and the *engagé* give way to surrealism and pointed, often hyperbolic comedy and satire" ("Politics" 41). Likewise, Vizenor's response to the threat of sentimentalized or popular realism is a sometimes hallucinatory prose style in a satiric mode. Reed's and Vizenor's postmodernism attempts to unmask colonial simulation and the "transcendent signified" and celebrate play as a political alternative.

Second, both Reed and Vizenor problematize the (a)priority of, as well as the relation between, oral and written stories. Both celebrate written texts over or alongside the "oral traditions" of both African American and Native American cultural literatures. On the one hand, by problematizing the relation between the oral and the written, they launch a postmodernist attack upon binary structuration of concept and language. "For Reed," writes Gates, "this belief in the reality of dualism spells death" (238).

On the other hand, by problematizing the relation between the oral and the written, both Reed and Vizenor simultaneously undermine the anthropological construction of "oral traditions" as simulations of cultural authenticity and difference. Gates writes that *Mumbo Jumbo* argues "against the privileging in black discourse of what Reed elsewhere terms 'the so-called oral tradition' in favor of the primacy and priority of the written text" (223). In agreement, Ashraf Rushdy argues that "Reed is not going to represent writing as inherently dangerous in order to argue that orality is more sacred or sound a means of self-representation"; while writing in the form of racist legal codes denied slaves freedom, slave narratives and other forms of writing actually helped blacks to establish their freedom (120). While Reed's "Neo-HooDoo aesthetic" celebrates African American oral traditions, Reed himself writes literary texts for a somewhat coterie audience.[14] His fictions, such as *Mumbo Jumbo*, in fact depend upon the written page for their spatial effects; typography, pictures, distribution of white space, symbology: all play an integral part in *Mumbo Jumbo* and wed the visual to the aural.[15]

Just as Reed counterpoints written and oral narratives, Vizenor also repeatedly stresses the need for a Native American "crossblood" literature, one that celebrates oral traditions but also transforms colonial written forms. Bo Schöler calls Vizenor's new aesthetic "a new *literary* aesthetic which we might call the transformed visionary oral aesthetic."[16] Likewise, claiming that "the language of tribal novelists and poets could be a literary ghost dance," Vizenor argues that "English, the coercive language at federal boarding schools, has carried some of the best stories of endurance and tribal spiritual restoration, and now that same dominant language bears the creative literature of crossblood writers in the cities" ("Native" 227). For Vizenor, "the postmodern printed word" is "a pose," a kind of secondary simulation in the manner of Ishi's self-directed simulation. Because it is constructed by Native American writers, it inevitably is subversive, *post*colonial, because it will play a tricksterish role within colonial discourse. Coopted, the colonizer's language will turn upon him: *Bearheart* is in fact written as a chronicle complete with prologue; *The Heirs of Columbus* rewrites the historical romance; and *Griever* echoes the form of the epistolary novel. *Griever* also comes replete with a secondary bibliography.

Specific postmodernist narrative strategies shared by both authors include the rejection of narrative closure. Helen Tiffin cogently observes that the "refusal of finality" is "crucial to the process of decolonizing fictions" because

closure, the privileging of one set of cognitive codes over others in the establishment of national or regional traditions, should not occur, for its occurrence replicates the processes of imperial imposition and consolidation. Decolonizing the European fiction does not invoke a simple reversal of centre and periphery, but a dismantling of the constitutive components of such potent characterizations. (29)

In *Bearheart: The Heirship Chronicles,* for example, Proude Cedarfair and Inawa Biwide are reborn and enter the world of the vision bears, transforming a novelistic ending into a spiritual and cultural beginning. Vizenor's *Griever* ends with his protagonist, Kangmei, and the rooster Matteo Ricci sailing into the sunset, plot conflicts (like the political conflicts they re-present) unresolved. Indeed, this defiance of closure is one link between tricksters from different cultures, something that links Griever with the Chinese Monkey King: "He [Mind Monkey] was driven to be immortal because nothing bored him more than the idea of an end; narrative conclusions were unnatural, he would never utter the last word, breathe the last breath, he would never pick flowers, the end was never his end" (128). Significantly, in Griever's epistolary "postscript" to the novel, in a gesture geared to defy and deflate realist plot conventions, the "sacred text" of the sacred bear scrolls turn out to be "nothing more than recipes" (234). Thus, the novel defies closure at a generic level. Viewed from one angle, after all, *Griever* is a detection story, but Vizenor refuses to allow the rationalist logic of detective fiction to control the "mystery" of the scrolls.

Most of Reed's novels end in a similar defiance of realist conventions of narrative closure, and in one instance he uses precisely the same attack on rationalist/realist conventions. At the end of *Mumbo Jumbo*, all the characters gather for the revelation about the "sacred Text" of Jes Grew, only to find that the Text has been destroyed and that the whole intrigue surrounding it has deflated like a spent balloon. Gates specifically aligns *Mumbo Jumbo*'s open-endedness with Reed's postmodern re-visioning of African American literary realism:

Reed's most subtle achievement in *Mumbo Jumbo* is to parody, to Signify upon, the notions of closure implicit in the key texts of the Afro-American canon. *Mumbo Jumbo*, in contrast to that canon, is a novel that figures and glorifies indeterminacy. . . . In its stead, Reed posits the notion of aesthetic play: the play of tradition, the play on the tradition, the sheer play of indeterminacy itself. (Gates 226-27)

As numerous critics have noted, with this postmodern narrative turn Reed manages to deflate the generic logic of the same opponent (the Anglo-Christian European West/The Atonist Path) that he attacks throughout his novel (Paravisini 113-25). Parody is thus often the deflationary strategy shared by Vizenor and Reed; both writers parody "low" aesthetic forms such as the detective novel, the Western, the travel saga, in order to thwart stereotypes and upset hoary narrative conventions.[17]

Of course, these postmodernist tactics won't wash for everyone. Theodore Mason, for instance, argues that both Reed's *Mumbo Jumbo* and Gates's analysis of it are flawed because (1) indeterminacy as an aesthetic ideal presupposes political impotence and insulation from the Real (e.g., history), and (2) if elevated to the status of metanarrative, indeterminacy becomes the very closure and determinacy it opposes (Mason 106). This is precisely the criticism leveled against postmodernism generally by John McGowan, Marxist critics Alex Callinicos or Christopher Norris, and postcolonialists such as Tiffin.[18]

In other words, I think this is the point at which one either buys into postmodernism or one doesn't. For both Reed and Vizenor, either implicitly or explicitly, the "Real" is always already in quotes, always a simulation, a postmodern language game.[19] Both writers attempt to construct a provisional community, a micro-politics, within this postmodern parameter. And this engages both writers in a postmodern paradox, the same that plagues Lyotard's writing and other theories of the postmodern: how to assert value after the death of metanarrative and the Real.

Precisely because their satire constructs a metaphorical or parodic history, both Reed and Vizenor are dangerously close in this instance to advocating the simulation that they politically and artistically oppose. But as Linda Hutcheon notes, postmodern parodic irony "rejects the resolving urge of modernism toward closure or at least distance. Complicity always attends its critique" (*Politics* 99). Like an aesthetics of indeterminacy, the "double process of installing and ironizing" (*Politics* 93) allows both authors to unravel and reweave the fabric of Anglo-Western colonial history, yet at the same time it places both authors' works in the precarious position of unavoidable postmodernist complicity, illustrated most in their satire of the "transcendent minority subject" and particularly in Vizenor's notion of performative simulation.

2. The Problem of Agenda and Authenticity

Both Reed and Vizenor thus share a postmodernist deconstructive agenda with respect to their realist and modernist literary precursors: while respectful of the work of others, both writers criticize the "transcendent signified" constructed by writers within their respective racially defined literatures. Perhaps even more important than this is both writers' choice *also* to challenge their own contemporaries and to refuse merely to construct a political binary opposition to colonial control. As postmodernist writers, they refuse binary structuration in even a political sense, and insist that their works be judged on aesthetic—rather than merely political—grounds. By this I mean that Reed and Vizenor question whether racial identity can be asserted as a "trope of absence" or a "trope of *presence*." Issuing this challenge to many of their contemporaries, both writers have suffered backlash as a result.

While Ishmael Reed takes issue with Hurston, Wright, Ellison, and Baldwin, he also writes against a hegemonic political aesthetics espoused by his contemporaries in the Black Arts movement of the 1960s and 1970s. This was Henry Louis Gates's insight in *The Signifying Monkey:* that while both Ellison and Reed criticized "blackness as a negative essence, as a natural, transcendent signified," they also implicitly repudiated the Black Arts movement's desire to make blackness "a presence, which is merely another transcendent signified" (237). Associated with the Black Power movement specifically by Hoyt W. Fuller, the editor of *Negro Digest* (later renamed *Black World* in 1970), the Black Aesthetic was intended to combat what Fuller considered the colonial subjugation of blacks in the United States. Essentially the same stance was propounded by Larry Neal in his 1968 essay "The Black Arts Movement" (Leitch). LeRoi Jones/Amiri Baraka and the literary critics Stephen Henderson and Addison Gayle, Jr. supported the Black Aesthetic: Black arts, with their roots in Black culture, created for Black readers.

Yet in interviews, Reed repeatedly distances himself from a Black Aesthetic and, while acknowledging the important work done by these writers and critics, takes issue with the idea that his work should fit into a mold formed by political, instead of aesthetic, frames. Opposing what he called "policy poetry," Reed stated that "there was a nonaggression pact signed between the traditional liberal critics and the black aesthetic critics . . . the black aesthetic crowd came in and writers were required to perform to their Marxist blueprints" (Martin, "Interview" 177). Reginald Martin clearly outlines the battles Reed began fighting with reviewers as early as 1969; with Houston Baker (as a result of a scathing 1972 review of *Mumbo Jumbo)* and Addison Gayle—both of whom Reed eventually called "black opportunists in the English departments"; and, finally, Amiri Baraka (Martin, "FreeLance" 41). Ironically, while in these print battles Reed specifically argues for the literariness of his fiction, he is often cited as a "political novelist" in contemporary reviews by certain white critics, and the juvenalian satire in his works often meets with hostility from students defensive about their own racial or cultural positionality.

Reed's print battles with his contemporaries have often been vicious, and they resulted directly from his implied postmodern aesthetic (Gates 237). Reed's challenge to the black trope of presence is a postmodern challenge to metanarrative—even one constructed by a "boundary discourse" of his own constituency. Postmodernism, as Hutcheon has noted, "cannot be considered a new paradigm" in the sense of Lyotard's metanarratives:

Provisionality and heterogeneity contaminate any neat attempts at unifying coherence (formal or thematic). . . . The centre no longer completely holds. And, from the decentered perspective, the "marginal" and . . . "ex-centric" . . . take on new significance. . . . The concept of alienated otherness (based on binary oppositions that conceal hierarchies) gives way . . . to that of differences, that is to the assertion, not of centralized sameness, but of decentralized community—another postmodern paradox. (*Poetics* 6, 12)

Reed specifically correlates the Black Aesthetic to academic institutionalization of African American literature and thus to a neo-colonial academic impulse. He writes in *19 Necromancers from Now:*

in this country art is what White people do. All other people are "propagandists." One can see this in the methodology used by certain White and Black critics in investigating Black literature. Form, Technique, Symbology, Imagery are rarely investigated with the same care as Argument, and even here, the Argument must be one that appeals to the critics' prejudices. (xiv)

Reed's counter to an "authentic" black identity (correlating to his attack of the trope of presence) is now a multicultural approach.[20] The backlash Reed has encountered to his work may be less a response to his racial politics that it is to his subversive challenge to universalization; the provisional and sometimes paradoxical critique in Reed's fictions cannot be coopted by any political platform, even an Afrocentric one.

Gerald Vizenor's postmodern resistance resembles Reed's in two respects. First, like Reed, Vizenor implies a postmodern aesthetic that stands at a precarious position between in-group and out-group politics—though unlike Reed, Vizenor does not seem to have sparked vituperation among critics and political activists. Vizenor's autobiography, *Interior Landscapes* (1990), tells of a life defined by marginality and committed to political action within the Native American community. Yet as a contemporary writer and university professor, Vizenor stands apart from radical Native American separatist literature or politics.

Vizenor's books, including his nonfiction and literary theory, appeal to an academic readership, and his repeated theme is one of subversion from within—from within colonial institutions such as literature, language, academe. Figures such as Dennis Banks become symbolic negatives in Vizenor's nonfiction; repeatedly he satirizes a naiveté bordering on dangerous narcissism of the Pan-Indian Movement. Yet even here, Vizenor's politics hedges, for he implies that Banks was made into "a kitschyman of reservation capitalism"—a simulation of resistance— through media aggrandizement (*Manifest* 42-43).

Second, like Reed, Vizenor consistently castigates those writers who attempt to construct "the romance of racial purities or the antiselves in tribal literature."[21] His notion of "Crossblood identities," like Reed's syncretism, challenges notions of aesthetic as well as racial "purity" and is the postmodernist third alternative to the two poles of representation.

Vizenor also avoids merely opposing a "trope of presence" to a "trope of absence" by resituating Native American literature within the framework of contemporary theory. His image of the trickster is consistently that of a semiotic sign rather than cultural representation: "The trickster is a chance, a comic holotrope in a postmodern language game . . . ; a semiotic sign for 'social antagonism' and 'aesthetic activism' . . . but not 'presence' or ideal cultural completion in narratives" (*Narrative* 192). In *Manifest Manners*, Vizenor draws from the work of theorists such as Linda Hutcheon, Jean-François Lyotard, Terry Eagleton, and Jacques Derrida to formulate a complex theory of Native American subjectivity as it is constructed within literature.

In the chapter of *Manifest Manners* entitled "Shadow Survivance," Vizenor attempts a postmodernist quest to find a third alternative to presence and absence, a Pynchonesque zone between zero and one. This third alternative he finds, as does Reed, in the realm of art, and he calls the alternative "shadows":

> The shadow is that sense of intransitive motion to the referent; the silence in memories. Shadows are neither the absence of entities nor the burden of conceptual references. The shadows are the prenarrative silence that inherits the words; shadows are the motions that mean the silence, but not the presence or absence of entities. (64)

"Shadows" are metaphorical traces of the natural world, which "is a venture of sound and shadows" (72). The oral tradition was able to embed traces of the silences and shadows of the natural world. It makes sense then that the "natural development of the oral tradition is not a written language," a *telos* promoted by Anglo-Western colonialism (72). Because it contains traces of natural silences and shadows, the oral tradition is irresolvably *different* from written narrative. Simply translating oral stories into written narratives does not give one access to shadows, to the natural echoes and imprints of the oral tale. Like Vizenor's breakdown of distinctions between oral and written narrative, the metaphorical concept of "shadows" mixes aural and visual imagery.[22]

Those postmodern Native Americans who wage an aesthetic and/or political war on colonial simulation of Indian-ness become "postindian warriors," and their consciousness perceives and transmits shadows, *hears* shadows—shadows like Derrida's trace within texts.[23] In a postmodern/postcolonial society, one that has both textualized the world and, through simulation, has eviscerated representation, "liberation and survivance" for the colonized can only be found somewhere other than representation. (Vizenor is here rewriting Saussure through Baudrillard.) In a postmodern world, representation *is* simulation, but shadows can avert and subvert this because they are made up of "trickster stones and postindian stories"—traces of the natural world, oral history, the Other (64). In other words, if I am reading this correctly, shadows are a third alternative to representation's two poles of presence and absence: not presence, because the shadows do not construct an "Indian identity" or "Indian history" (which could only be a simulation in this postmodern society); not absence, because shadows recall (but do not construct) tribal humor, memory, and subjectivity in a subversive ironic voice.

Vizenor is reworking Derrida's theory in *Of Grammatology* of "arche-writing" as a means of dealing with the "metaphysics of presence."[24] Ashraf Rushdy identifies precisely this phenomenon in Ishmael Reed's novel *Flight to Canada*. Rushdy notes that for Derrida, arche-writing dismantles the distinction between orality and literacy because it occurs in both graphic and nongraphic expression, both writing and speaking (124). In the concept of arche-writing and the "arche-trace" are addressed the problems of orality and literacy, presence and absence, and self/other—all of which become reformulated in Vizenor's idea of "shadows." "Shadows and silence," writes Vizenor, "have no representations, no presence, no absence, no antishadows" (*Manifest* 73).

In *Manifest Manners,* Vizenor furthermore posits a Native American alternative to Derrida's *différance*:

> We must need new pronouns that would misconstrue gender binaries, that would combine the want of a presence in the absence of the heard, a shadow pronoun to pronounce remembrance in silence, in the absence of postindian names, nouns, and deverbatives. The *pronounance* combines the sense of the words *pronoun* and *pronounce* with the actions and conditions of survivance in tribal memories and stories. The *pronounance* of trickster hermeneutics has a shadow with no person, time, or number. In the absence of the heard the trickster is the shadow of the name, the sound, the noun, the person, the *pronounance*. (97-98)

For a Native American writer, the problem of how the oral/aural intersects with the visual/written (especially in narrative) is intimately connected to the problem of semiotic and racial difference and deferral of meaning. Vizenor thus supplements Derrida's "arche-writing" and "différance" with the concepts of "shadows" and "pronounance" to produce a neo-Native deconstructive vocabulary. The concepts of "shadows" and "pronounance" thus comprise Vizenor's challenge to the trope of presence in Native American contemporary literature.

Vizenor has not suffered the backlash resulting from this radical revisioning as has Ishmael Reed from a number of his contemporaries. But Vizenor does challenge a contemporary realism (exemplified, for instance, in the more commercially popular novels of James Welch, Louise Erdrich, and Linda Hogan, and in movies such as *Thunderheart*), a realism that is, by now, in danger of becoming formulaic in its presentation of Native American life. At the least, this mode of writing can focus on a Pan-Indian universalism rather than on unique experiences of specific Native American peoples. Popular realism (for lack of a better term) can entomb Native characters in the "homing pattern" identified by William Bevis or a Native rite-of-passage pattern, where a young person moves from innocence or stability (the tribal life), through experience or psychological turmoil (the city life, war, etc.), back to a Blakean organized innocence (new perspective on self as tribal participant).[25]

In his afterword to Vizenor's *Bearheart: The Heirship Chronicles*, Louis Owens relates how three mixedblood college students in his own class reported him to a dean for teaching Vizenor's novel: the students "had known how to respond to the familiar tragedies of Indians . . . played out in novels by other Native American writers. But *Bearheart,* with its wild humor, upset them" (247-48). Ironically, Ishmael Reed has identified this same problem in relation to teaching African American contemporary literature: "Students who would never think of turning a seminar on Melville into a political rally would not hesitate to dictate to a Black instructor what emphasis should be made, or what works should be covered, in his course" (xiii-xiv).

3. A Perspective

Ironically, both Ishmael Reed and Gerald Vizenor are open to charges of inauthenticity because of the liberating strategies of their work. Both authors problematize postmodern authenticity through political fiction that paradoxically refuses closure. In this particular respect, Reed's and Vizenor's political voices are more like one another's than the voices within their respective literary/cultural constituencies. Any comparison of the two authors thus raises uncomfortable questions concerning the relation of postmodernism to ethnicity and the dangers of defining an author solely on the basis of his or her "ethnic authenticity." Inherent in Reed's and Vizenor's work are warring quests: to recognize and draw strength from one's ancestral past, and, simultaneously, to avoid a Dorothy-in-Oz-like sentimentality of "home." In fact, both authors ironically literalize the message of Baum's story: for them, there is "no place like home." For both authors, returning to a sentimental past implies acceptance of the artificial closure constructed by postmodern simulation. For both, resisting this closure constitutes a political act in the word wars. To the consternation of those who would assert difference, indeterminacy and play meld the dancer and the dance in the fiction of these writers; the journey, not the destination, is "home."

Notes

1. Defined by Robert Scholes as literature which (1) has an extraordinary delight in design; (2) asserts the authority of the shaper through the structure of the tale, by way of its very shapelessness; (3) has a didactic quality, tending toward ethically controlled fantasy; and (4) has a spirit of playfulness. See Scholes, *Fabulation and Metafiction* (U of Illinois P, 1979).

2. For discussions of Vizenor and generic revisionism, see Hochbruck 274-75, 277, A. LaVonne Brown Ruoff, "Woodland Word Warrior: An Introduction to the Works of Gerald Vizenor," *MELUS* 13.1-2 (1986): 24-25; and Bo Schöler, "Trickster and Storyteller: The Sacred Memories and True Tales of Gerald Vizenor," *Coyote Was Here: Essays on Contemporary Native American Literary and Political Mobilization, The Dolphin* 9 (1984): 134-46.

Critical discussions of Reed's generic revisionism are too numerous to cite here. See, for instance, on slave narrative: Ashraf H. A. Rushdy, "Ishmael Reed's Neo-HooDoo Slave Narrative," *Narrative* 2.2 (1994): 112-39; Hortense J. Spillers, "Changing the Letter: The Yokes, the Jokes of Discourse, or, Mrs. Stowe, Mr. Reed," *Slavery and the Literary Imagination,* ed. Deborah E. McDowell and Arnold Rampersad (Baltimore and London: Johns Hopkins UP, 1989), 25-61. On Reed and Westerns, see Peter Nazareth, "Heading Them Off at the Pass: The Fiction of Ishmael Reed," *Review of Contemporary Fiction* 4.2 (1984): 208-26; Norman Harris, *Connecting Times: The Sixties in Afro-American Fiction* (Jackson and London: UP of Mississippi, 1988). On Reed and detective fiction, see Joe Weixlmann, "Culture Clash, Survival, and Trans-Formation: A Study of Some Innovative Afro-American Novels of Detection," *Mississippi Quarterly* 38.1 (1984-85): 21-32. On Reed and genre, see Keith E. Byerman, *Fingering the Jagged Grain: Tradition and Form in Recent Black Fiction* (Athens and London: U of Georgia P, 1986).

3. One might compare Vizenor's "four postmodern conditions in the critical responses to Native American Indian and postindian literatures" to Jean Baudrillard's four "successive phases of the image." See Gerald Vizenor, *Manifest Manners: Postindian Warriors of Survivance* (Hanover and London: Wesleyan UP, 1994), 66; Jean Baudrillard, "The Precession of Simulacra," *Art After Modernism: Rethinking Representation,* ed. Brian Wallis (New York: New Museum of Contemporary Art; Boston, MA: Godine, 1984), 256; Umberto Eco, *Travels in Hyperreality,* trans. William Weaver (New York: Harcourt Brace Jovanovich, 1986).

4. Vizenor's attacks on colonial transformations of Indian subjectivity is frequently noted by commentators. See, as examples, Ruoff 23; Patricia Haseltine, "The Voices of Gerald Vizenor: Survival through Transformation," *American Indian Quarterly* 9.1 (1985): 31-47.

5. Vizenor, *Manifest Manners* 128, italics mine. There is a marked similarity between what Vizenor says Ishi is doing and what a character, the grandfather, is doing in the anthologized first chapter of Ralph Ellison's novel *Invisible Man.* The grandfather's dying words haunt and confuse Invisible Man:

"I never told you, but our life is a war and I have been a traitor all my born days, a spy in the enemy's country ever since I give up my gun back in the Reconstruction. Live with your head in the lion's mouth. I want you to overcome 'em with yeses, undermine 'em with grins, agree 'em to death and destruction, let 'em swoller you till they vomit or bust wide open. . . . Learn it to the younguns," he whispered fiercely; then he died. (Ellison 16)

Significantly, the protagonist of Ellison's novel learns the truth of his grandfather's words, but his only recourse at that point is to become "invisible." As Gates notes, this is the modernist validation of blackness as absence. In contrast, Ishmael Reed constructs characters such as Uncle Robin in *Flight to Canada* who play at this game of willful Tomism, but Reed also creates characters— such as Raven Quickskill or, more explicitly, PaPa LaBas in *Mumbo Jumbo*— whose performative alternative to colonial simulation is *presence.* Like the grandfather in Ellison's *Invisible Man,* Ishi (implies Vizenor) simulates absence in a modernist revisionary gesture. As does Reed, Vizenor honors Ishi as a "first step" away from modernist colonial domination yet demands a more radical postmodern response.

6. See Stephen Slemon, "Monuments of Empire: Allegory/Counter-Discourse/Post-Colonial Writing," *kunapipi* 9.3 (1987): 1-16; and Stephen Slemon, "Modernism's Last Post," *Past the Last Post: Theorizing Post-Colonialism and Post-Modernism,* ed. Ian Adam and Helen Tiffin (Calgary: U of Calgary P, 1990), 1-11. I do not have the space here to discuss Vizenor's fascinating situation between the postmodern and the postcolonial. (For a general discussion, see Arnold Krupat, "Postcoloniality and Native American Literature," *Yale Journal of Criticism* 7.1 [1994]: 163-80.) I do think Vizenor politely rejects the modernist revisioning of nativist realism exemplified in, for instance, N. Scott Momaday's *House Made of Dawn* (New York: Harper & Row, 1966). In *Bearheart,* Vizenor gently critiques himself among other Native American writers and significantly assigns Momaday the nomer "romancioso" (Gerald Vizenor, *Bearheart: The Heirship Chronicles* [Minneapolis: U of Minnesota P, 1990: 113-14]).

7. This idea is common to many writings about postcolonialism, too numerous to cite here. For an introductory discussion and sources, see Bill Ashcroft, Gareth Griffiths, and Helen Tiffin, *The Empire Writes Back: Theory and Practice in Post-Colonial Literatures* (London & New York: Routledge, 1989).

8. On Vizenor's use of the trickster figure, see also Franchot Ballinger, "Sacred Reversals: Trickster in Gerald Vizenor's *Earthdivers: Tribal Narratives on Mixed Descent,*" *American Indian Quarterly* 9.1 (1985): 55-59.

9. See Vizenor's comments in "Dead Voices," *World Literature Today* 66.2 (1992): 225. See also Vizenor's epigraphs to *Narrative Chance;* Haseltine; Leslie Marmon Silko, *Ceremony* (New York: Viking P, 1977).

10. See Gates; Norman Harris, "Politics as an Innovate Aspect of Literary Folklore: A Study of Ishmael Reed," *Obsidian: Black Literature in Review* 1.2 (1979): 41-50; Robert Gover, "An Interview with Ishael Reed," *Black American*

Literature Forum 12 (1978): 12-19; Robert Elliot Fox, "Blacking the Zero: Toward a Semiotics of Neo-Hoodoo," *Black American Literature Forum* 18.2 (1984): 95-99.

11. See Jerome Klinkowitz, *Literary Subversions: New American Fiction and the Practice of Criticism* (Carbondale and Edwardsville: Southern Ilinois UP, 1985); Reginald Martin, "Ishmael Reed's Syncretic Use of Language: Bathos as Popular Discourse," *Modern Language Studies* 20.2 (1990): 3-9.

12. In the same interview, Reed stated, "I'm into American folklore now, and totemism, which I learned from the Native Americans. The coyote stories, that sort of thing" (Domini 34). See also Joe Weixlmann, "Ishmael Reed's Raven," *Review of Contemporary Fiction* 4.2 (1984): 205-08.

13. Virtually all critics writing about Reed's work must deal in some way with his neo-hoodoo. For an introduction to Reed's aesthetic, see Reed's "Neo-HooDoo Manifesto," *Conjure: Selected Poems 1963-1970* (Amherst, MA: U of Massachusetts P, 1972), 20-25; the comprehensive discussion in Robert Elliot Fox's *Conscientious Sorcerers: The Black Postmodernist Fiction of LeRoi Jones/Amiri Baraka, Ishmael Reed, and Samuel R. Delany* (New York: Greenwood P, 1987); Neil Schmitz, "Neo-HooDoo: The Experimental Fiction of Ishmael Reed," *Twentieth-Century Literature* 20 (1974): 126-40; Chester J. Fontenot, "Ishmael Reed and the Politics of Aesthetics, or Shake Hands and Come Out Conjuring," *Black American Literature Forum* 12.1 (1978): 20-23; Fred Beauford, "A Conversation with Ishmael Reed," *Black Creation* 4 (1973): 12-15; Frank McConnell, "Ishmael Reed's Fiction: Da Hoodoo Is Put on America," *Black Fiction: New Studies in the Afro-American Novel Since 1945*, ed. A. Robert Lee (New York: Barnes & Noble, 1980), 136-48; Fox, "Blacking the Zero"; Carter.

14. See Gates; Erik D. Curren, "Ishmael Reed's Postmodern Revolt," *Literature and Film in the Historical Dimension,* ed. John D. Simons (Gainesville: UP of Florida, 1994), 139-48.

15. See Fox, "Blacking the Zero"; Brian McHale, *Postmodernist Fiction* (New York: Methuen, 1987), 179-97.

16. Schöler 143. See also Hochbruck 274; Velie 135.

17. See, for instance, Ruoff 25; Velie 145. McConnell notes that VooDoo can be thought of as "as a form of creative parody and purification-through-possession" that is reformulated into a faster, Americanized version as Reed's neo-Hoodoo (McConnell 143-44). See also Byerman 217-37. Rushdy notes what Reed calls "Reed's Law": "When the parody is better than the original a mutation occurs which renders the original obsolete." Reed's comments in interviews about the need to "update the ceremonies" is a form of parody that to some extent also renders the original obsolete.

18. See John McGowan, *Postmodernism and Its Critics* (Ithaca and London: Cornell UP, 1991); Alex Callinicos, *Against Postmodernism: A Marxist*

Critique (New York: St. Martin's, 1990); Christopher Norris, *What's Wrong with Postmodernism: Critical Theory and the Ends of Philosophy* (Baltimore: Johns Hopkins UP, 1990) and *The Truth about Postmodernism* (Oxford UK and Cambridge, MA: Blackwell, 1993); and Tiffin.

19. See Reed's comments in Beauford; Curren 145.

20. Reed has been an outspoken proponent of multiculturalism for some time. In his early interviews, the term he uses is "syncretism" to describe this melding of European, African, Native-American, African American influences. See Reed's introduction to *The Before Columbus Foundation Fiction Anthology,* ed. Ishmael Reed, Kathryn Trueblood, and Shawn Wong (New York and London: Norton, 1992); Martin, "The FreeLance PallBearer Confronts the Terrible Threes" 181-82; Martin, "An Interview" 185-86; Klinkowitz.

21. See Vizenor's evaluation of Charles Larson's *American Indian Fiction* in *Manifest Manners* 81.

22. In *Earthdivers,* Vizenor introduces the notion of a "word cinema," another mixing of the oral with the visual. See Haseltine 41.

23. For a discussion of Saussure and Derrida in relation to Native American literature, see also Arnold Krupat, "Post-structuralism and Oral Literature," *Recovering the Word: Essays on Native American Literature,* ed. Arnold Krupat and Brian Swann (Berkeley: U of California P, 1987), 113-28.

24. Elaine Jahner has also identified this influence of Derrida on Vizenor's aesthetics. See Jahner, "Cultural Shrines Revisited," *American Indian Quarterly* 9.1 (1985): 25. Also Krupat, "Post-structuralism and Oral Literature"; Jacques Derrida, *Of Grammatology,* trans. Gayatri Chakravorty Spivak (Baltimore: Johns Hopkins UP, 1976).

25. See William Bevis, "Native American Novels: Homing In," *Recovering the Word: Essays on Native American Literature,* ed. Arnold Krupat and Brian Swann (Berkeley: U of California P, 1987), 580-620. See Hochbruck 275-76 for a clear discussion of the emerging "formula" for contemporary Indian novels.

Works Cited

Ashcroft, Bill, Gareth Griffiths, and Helen Tiffin. *The Empire Writes Back: Theory and Practice in Post-Colonial Literatures.* London and New York: Routledge, 1989.

Ballinger, Franchot. "Sacred Reversals: Trickster in Gerald Vizenor's *Earthdivers: Tribal Narratives on Mixed Descent.*" *American Indian Quarterly* 9.1 (1985): 55-59.

Baudrillard, Jean. "The Precession of Simulacra." *Art After Modernism: Rethinking Representation.* Ed. Brian Wallis. New York: New Museum of Contemporary Art; Boston, MA: Godine, 1984. 253-81.

Beauford, Fred. "A Conversation with Ishmael Reed." *Black Creation* 4 (1973): 12-15.

Bevis, William. "Native American Novels: Homing In." *Recovering the Word: Essays on Native American Literature*. Ed. Arnold Krupat and Brian Swann. Berkeley: U of California P, 1987. 580-620.

Blaeser, Kim M. *Gerald Vizenor: Writing in the Oral Tradition*. Norman and London: U of Oklahoma P, 1996.

Byerman, Keith E. *Fingering the Jagged Grain: Tradition and Form in Recent Black Fiction*. Athens and London: U of Georgia P, 1986.

Callinicos, Alex. *Against Postmodernism: A Marxist Critique*. New York: St. Martin's, 1990.

Carter, Steven R. "Ishmael Reed's Neo-Hoodoo Detection." *Dimensions of Detective Fiction*. Ed. Larry N. Landrum, Pat Browne, and Ray B. Browne. Bowling Green: Popular Press, 1976. 265-74.

Coltelli, Laura. "Gerald Vizenor." *Winged Words: American Indian Writers Speak*. Ed. Laura Coltelli. Lincoln and London: U of Nebraska P, 1990. 154-82.

Curren, Erik D. "Ishmael Reed's Postmodern Revolt." *Literature and Film in the Historical Dimension*. Ed. John D. Simons. Gainesville: UP of Florida, 1994. 139-48.

Derrida, Jacques. *Of Grammatology*. Trans. Gayatri Chakravorty Spivak. Baltimore: Johns Hopkins UP, 1976.

Domini, John. "Ishmael Reed: A Conversation with John Domini." *American Poetry Review* 7 (1978): 32-36.

Eco, Umberto. *Travels in Hyperreality*. Trans. William Weaver. New York: Harcourt Brace Jovanovich, 1986.

Ellison, Ralph. *Invisible Man*. New York: Vintage, 1952.

Fontenot, Chester J. "Ishmael Reed and the Politics of Aesthetics, or Shake Hands and Come out Conjuring." *Black American Literature Forum* 12.1 (1978): 20-23.

Fox, Robert Elliot. "Blacking the Zero: Toward a Semiotics of Neo-Hoodoo." *Black American Literature Forum* 18.2 (1984): 95-99.

——. *Conscientious Sorcerers: The Black Postmodernist Fiction of LeRoi Jones/ Amiri Baraka, Ishmael Reed, and Samuel R. Delany*. New York: Greenwood P, 1987.

Gates, Henry Louis. *The Signifying Monkey: A Theory of African-American Literary Criticism*. New York: Oxford UP, 1988.

Gover, Robert. "An Interview with Ishmael Reed." *Black American Literature Forum* 12 (1978): 12-19.

Harris, Norman. *Connecting Times: The Sixties in Afro-American Fiction*. Jackson and London: UP of Mississippi, 1988.

——. "Politics as an Innovate Aspect of Literary Folklore: A Study of Ishmael Reed." *Obsidian: Black Literature in Review* 1.2 (1979): 41-50.

Haseltine, Patricia. "The Voices of Gerald Vizenor: Survival through Transformation." *American Indian Quarterly* 9.1 (1985): 31-47.

Hochbruck, Wolfgang. "Breaking Away: The Novels of Gerald Vizenor." *World Literature Today* 66.2 (1992): 274-78.

Hutcheon, Linda. *A Poetics of Postmodernism: History, Theory, Fiction.* New York and London: Routledge, 1988.

——. *The Politics of Postmodernism.* London and New York: Routledge, 1989.

Jahner, Elaine. "Cultural Shrines Revisited." *American Indian Quarterly* 9.1 (1985): 23-30.

Keady, Maureen. "Walking Backwards into the Fourth World: Survival of the Fittest in *Bearheart*." *American Indian Quarterly* 9.1 (1985): 61-65.

Klinkowitz, Jerome. *Literary Subversions: New American Fiction and the Practice of Criticism.* Carbondale and Edwardsville: Southern Illinois UP, 1985.

Krupat, Arnold. "Postcoloniality and Native American Literature." *Yale Journal of Criticism* 7.1 (1994): 163-80.

——. "Post-structuralism and Oral Literature." *Recovering the Word: Essays on Native American Literature.* Ed. Arnold Krupat and Brian Swann. Berkeley: U of California P, 1987. 113-28.

Le Guin, Ursula. *The Dispossessed.* New York: Avon, 1974.

Leitch, Vincent B., ed. *American Literary Criticism from the Thirties to the Eighties.* New York: Columbia UP, 1988.

Martin, Reginald. "The FreeLance PallBearer Confronts the Terrible Threes: Ishmael Reed and the New Black Aesthetic Critics." *MELUS* 14.2 (1987): 35-49.

——. "An Interview with Ishmael Reed." *Review of Contemporary Fiction* 4.2 (1984): 176-87.

——. "Ishmael Reed's Syncretic Use of Language: Bathos as Popular Discourse." *Modern Language Studies* 20.2 (1990): 3-9.

Mason, Theodore O., Jr. "Performance, History, and Myth: The Problem of Ishmael Reed's *Mumbo Jumbo*." *Modern Fiction Studies* 34.1 (1988): 97-109.

McConnell, Frank. "Ishmael Reed's Fiction: Da Hoodoo Is Put on America." *Black Fiction: New Studies in the Afro-American Novel Since 1945.* Ed. A. Robert Lee. New York: Barnes & Noble, 1990. 136-48.

McGowan, John. *Postmodernism and Its Critics.* Ithaca and London: Cornell UP, 1991.

McHale, Brian. *Postmodernist Fiction.* New York: Methuen, 1987.

Momaday, N. Scott. *House Made of Dawn.* New York: Harper & Row, 1966.

Nazareth, Peter. "Heading Them Off at the Pass: The Fiction of Ishmael Reed." *Review of Contemporary Fiction* 4.2 (1984): 208-26.

Norris, Christopher. *The Truth about Postmodernism*. Oxford: Blackwell, 1993.

——. *What's Wrong with Postmodernism: Critical Theory and the Ends of Philosophy*. Baltimore: Johns Hopkins UP, 1990.

Owens, Louis. "Afterword." *Bearheart: The Heirship Chronicles* by Gerald Vizenor. Minneapolis: U of Minnesota P, 1990. 247-54.

Paravisini, Lizabeth. "*Mumbo Jumbo* and the Uses of Parody." *Obsidian II: Black Literature in Review* 1.1-2 (1986): 113-25.

Reed, Ishmael. *Conjure: Selected Poems 1963-1970*. Amherst, MA: U of Massachusetts P, 1972.

——. *Flight to Canada*. New York: Atheneum, 1989.

——. *Mumbo Jumbo*. New York: Macmillan, 1972.

——. *19 Necromancers from Now*. New York: Doubleday, 1970.

Reed, Ishmael, Kathryn Trueblood, and Shawn Wong, eds. *The Before Columbus Foundation Fiction Anthology*. New York and London: Norton, 1992.

Ruoff, A. LaVonne Brown. "Woodland Word Warrior: An Introduction to the Works of Gerald Vizenor." *MELUS* 13.1-2 (1986): 13-43.

Rushdy, Ashraf H. A. "Ishmael Reed's Neo-HooDoo Slave Narrative." *Narrative* 2.2 (1994): 112-39.

Schmitz, Neil. "Neo-HooDoo: The Experimental Fiction of Ishmael Reed." *Twentieth-Century Literature* 20 (1974): 126-40.

Schöler, Bo. "Trickster and Storyteller: The Sacred Memories and True Tales of Gerald Vizenor." *Coyote Was Here: Essays on Contemporary Native American Literary and Political Mobilization. The Dolphin* 9 (1984): 134-46.

Scholes, Robert. *Fabulation and Metafiction*. Champaign: U of Illinois P, 1979.

Silko, Leslie Marmon. *Ceremony*. New York: Viking, 1977.

Slemon, Stephen. "Modernism's Last Post." *Past the Last Post: Theorizing Post-Colonialism and Post-Modernism*. Ed. Ian Adam and Helen Tiffin. Calgary: U of Calgary P, 1990. 1-11.

——. "Monuments of Empire: Allegory/Counter-Discourse/Post-Colonial Writing." *kunapipi* 9.3 (1987): 1-16.

Spillers, Hortense J. "Changing the Letter: The Yokes, the Jokes of Discourse, or, Mrs. Stowe, Mr. Reed." *Slavery and the Literary Imagination*. Ed. Deborah E. McDowell and Arnold Rampersad. Baltimore and London: Johns Hopkins UP, 1989. 25-61.

Tiffin, Helen. "Recuperative Strategies in the Post-Colonial Novel." *Span* 24 (1987): 27-45.

Velie, Alan R. *Four American Indian Literary Masters: N. Scott Momaday, James Welch, Leslie Marmon Silko, and Gerald Vizenor*. Norman: U of Oklahoma P, 1982.

Vizenor, Gerald. *Bearheart: The Heirship Chronicles*. Minneapolis: U of Minnesota P, 1990.

——. "Dead Voices." *World Literature Today* 66.2 (1992): 241-42.

——. *Griever: An American Monkey King in China.* Minneapolis: U of Minnesota P, 1987.

——. *The Heirs of Columbus.* Middletown, CT: Wesleyan UP, 1991.

——. *Interior Landscapes: Autobiographical Myths and Metaphors.* Minneapolis: U of Minnesota P, 1990.

——. *Manifest Manners: Postindian Warriors of Survivance.* Hanover and London: Wesleyan UP, 1994.

——. "Native American Indian Literature: Critical Metaphors of the Ghost Dance." *World Literature Today* 66.2 (1992): 223-27.

——. "A Postmodern Introduction." *Narrative Chance: Postmodern Discourse on Native American Indian Literatures.* Albuquerque: U of New Mexico P, 1989. 3-16.

——. "Socioacupuncture: Mythic Reversals and the Striptease in Four Scenes." *Out There: Marginalization and Contemporary Cultures.* Ed. Russell Ferguson et al. London and Cambridge, MA: MIT P, 1990. 411-19.

——. "Trickster Discourse: Comic Holotropes and Language Games." *Narrative Chance: Postmodern Discourse on Native American Indian Literatures.* Albuquerque: U of New Mexico P, 1989. 187-211.

Vizenor, Gerald, ed. *Narrative Chance: Postmodern Discourse on Native American Indian Literatures.* Albuquerque: U of New Mexico P, 1989.

Watkins, Mel. "An Interview with Ishmael Reed." *Southern Review* 21.3 (1985): 603-14.

Weixlmann, Joe. "Culture Clash, Survival, and Trans-Formation: A Study of Some Innovative Afro-American Novels of Detection." *Mississippi Quarterly* 38.1 (1984-85): 21-32.

——. "Ishmael Reed's Raven." *Review of Contemporary Fiction* 4.2 (1984): 205-08.

——. "Politics, Piracy, and Other Games: Slavery and Liberation in *Flight to Canada.*" *MELUS* 6.3 (1979): 41-50.

5

"A CROSSBLOOD AT THE SCRATCH LINE":
INTERIOR LANDSCAPES

Richard Hutson

"I would be a writer a decade later, a crossblood at the scratch line."[1]

The title of Gerald Vizenor's autobiography, with its hint of the oxymoronic, may disorient a reader right at the outset. Landscapes, after all, usually belong to the exterior, are exteriority itself. The title could thus be translated as "Interior Exteriors." The subtitle, "Autobiographical Myths and Metaphors," in turn, enhances the disorientation. An autobiography, we say, is a "continuous narrative" of an actual life, one that can be verified by historical detective work, and a "systematic history of the personality" (Beaujour 2). The protagonist of an autobiography refers to a real world, and he or she is presumed to be a unity. Even if we admit that the representation of a verifiable life must consist in some fictionality, we do not care to be reminded that a person's life is made up of "myths and metaphors" *even before* we undertake our voyeuristic adventure of reading the narrative of the experience at hand.

Vizenor's slight swervings away from the scratch-line of readerly expectations not only disorient the reader, then; they also usurp the work of the literary critic and analyst. Readers of autobiography like to be left the task of pointing out that there is a self-behind-the-self, that the autobiographer is, in fact, using metaphors and fictions and myths unintentionally, and it is the happy task of the reader to bring these matters to everyone's attention. Vizenor has anticipated the reader's critical task in advance. In the last chapter of *Interior Landscapes,* he actually cites passages from a number of the leading analysts of the autobiographical genre. Writer and reader, creative author and critic are thereby mingled in the narrative from the beginning to the end. Where will one draw the line? What is left for the reader?

And whereas Vizenor presents his life in a chronological order, each chapter with a date, the narrative is by no means continuous. The life is presented as a series of remembered stories, with large gaps between them. Moreover, the narrator leaps, without much warning, from a temporally dated early event to the much later time of the writing, tempting us to construct a teleology, which always turns out to be improvisatory, a direction that gives no direction. And his constant invocation of myth, whose writerly usefulness might be to fill in, or cover up, gaps in the continuity of a life, instead contributes to the sense of readerly dislocation. Even when the narrator asserts the marks of a controlled interpretation, there is an identity confusion among spheres that we tend to think should rightfully be held separate and distinct. The effect is a crossing of the lines, as if whatever scratch-lines might be sketched or presumed are difficult, but richly productive, to hold.

Again, a reader might reasonably expect a thematic unity from the collection of narratives, but Vizenor does not seem anxious to posit a general or easily recognizable theme by which the individual stories could be subordinated. Vizenor's tales "give the appearance of discontinuity, of anachronistic juxtaposition, or montage," an organization by narrative chance and laconic chronology which might tempt us to suggest that *Interior Landscapes* belongs to the tradition that Michel Beaujour calls the "self-portrait" rather than autobiography (3). The coherence or permanence or totality of the life is not present, is, thus, not controlled by the anticipated death of the protagonist, a basic premise behind the genre of autobiography. The life we are offered is controlled by a kind of systematic uncontrol—"the contingency of writing" (Barthes 136), semantic slippage or "wild words," the possible presence of tricksters as "metaphors on the borders" (73), "coincidences and chance encounters" (127)—by language and the practices of writing as both a "game" (75) and a "dump for our culture's refuse" (Vizenor, "Trickster" 196), "comic shit" (Beaujour 6), the multiple forms of survivance. Vizenor does not seek "permanence from the past" (75), but, "making do with whatever means he believes to be at his disposal, attempts to say what he is, right then, while writing" (Beaujour 6).

In many instances, however, traces, echoes (maybe ghosts?), of the traditions of autobiographical writings can be seen. Something like themes, more or less coherent, are recoverable, re-iterated. In the last chapter of *Interior Landscapes,* Vizenor quotes from his previous autobiographical writings as well as from theorists and critical readers of the autobiographical genre, suggesting that he wishes readers to understand that he is, assuredly, writing autobiography, autobiographical stories. But he is conducting his own style of autobiography in a highly self-reflective manner, so that, to use Paul Jay's analysis of modernist autobiography, basic aporias of the genre become "foregrounded." What might have been once left to the critical reader now becomes inscribed within the text of autobiography. "What once merely disturbed now becomes a structural principle" (180).

Writing in 1989, Vizenor does not have the luxury to write unself-consciously within the terms of a genre that was, in an important sense, founded upon the bad faith of an innocence which long masked the problems and contradictions of the genre, the possible incongruities or gaps, for instance, between the author, the narrator and the subject of autobiography. He could well say, with Roland Barthes: "I . . . *rewrite* myself —at a distance, a great distance—here and now . . . I am not contradictory, I am dispersed" (Barthes 142-43). Vizenor, accordingly, is not trying to subvert or transgress the "rules" of the genre, nor is he trying to compete with previous practitioners of the genre. But by invoking the genre, he joins an extended tribal order of fellow autobiographers, making only a claim of difference. "'A good hunter is never competitive,' I wrote in an [earlier] autobiographical story" (263), says Vizenor. He understands autobiography as the ongoing acts of survivance, as a rewriting of the self.

Interior Landscapes is, then, one more book in Vizenor's project of writing, not the last book. Autobiographical writing, for Vizenor, is not a tomb for its subject, "such as into himself eternity changed him" (Mallarmé). The "seal of completeness" is missing (Lang 13). Instead of a closure of the narrative of a life, the last chapter presents eight different stories of events, as if the ending of the book is arbitrary, anticipating a proliferation of future narratives. Death has been encountered from time to time, as in any game of life, but the terminating force of death has been subsumed by, for instance, the substitute death of the squirrel that urban hunter Vizenor shoots. "I owe so much to that red squirrel who dared me to hunt him in the oaks, who died in me" (170). After shooting the squirrel a number of times, Vizenor says, "I begged him to forgive me before he died" (169). He cannot be sure that the gift of forgiveness is forthcoming. Death may have been made secondary now, but Vizenor's life will remain unforgiven and impure despite his need for purity and his improvisatory conversions: "I sold my rifle and never hunted to kill animals or birds again" (170). The one death has been sufficient for his imagination, so that the anticipated death of the author does not determine the sense of the narrative of a life. The life, like the book, remains open.

But what is especially disorienting for the practised reader of autobiography is the simultaneous presence and absence of the Anishinaabe trickster figure, Naanabozho. As Vizenor argues in his essay on "Trickster Discourse," the trickster does not belong to presence. Naanabozho seems to be everywhere without ever appearing in person, as a character. Whatever it/they is/are, it withdraws before anyone can see them. Its or their presence may be felt, but it/they is/are constantly disappearing as it/they goes/go along. What may be detectable is the "trickster signature," a sign of absence. A trickster has no stable character, no autonomy, no identity, no substance. A trickster is a reserve, a reservation, an excess. All kinds of oppositions may be generated within the non-essential essence of the trickster as a foundation myth. The result is a synthesis without unity, always holding the account offered as open to accident, chance, suffering, humor. Trickster writing uncovers an alterity that lies within the same, within comprehension and communication; it generates self-effacement and withdrawal, in the manner of the photographed father whose death is not subject to closure. In the "synthesis," contradictions are generated and sustained without ever resolving or sublimating or destroying them.

Such a trickster signature sounds like the very muse of autobiography, if we look at the genre as "inherently contradictory," even impossible (Lang 13). The synthesis or unity (highly ambivalent in its warlike polarities: good/evil [gambler], menace/protector, authentic/inauthentic, individual/tribe) that trickster provides is "a unity of combat" (Gasché 152). It is this mythic figure that Vizenor invokes and within whose aura he finds the profound relevance for contemporary life of the Native American perspective, of the Objibwa/Chippewa or Anishinaabe heritage. This trickster, as "infrastructure," to use Rodolphe Gasché's term, is an archaic mode of synthesis, more simple than Western civilization's various discursive and murderously totalitarian synthesizings. What we find in this figure is a foundational synthesis, alien and archaic, a simulacrum of unity at the beginning of any possible conflict and contradiction within which the multiple and contingent parties to conflict may live in "a minimal organizational unit" without the "benefit of homogeneous unity" (Gasché 152).

Almost any chapter of *Interior Landscapes* will take the reader into the heart of this complicated vision, with stories that may be read as simply good stories, autonomous and self-enclosed, or as tales with extensive ramifications and resonances. Take, for instance, the story about Mean Nettles, the "titan," a merciless figure in Gerald Vizenor's young world, "so mean that even the demon mosquitoes on the river circled his head out of reach," like an evil halo (66). This person resembles a trickster figure from the Anishinaabe traditions. "He was silent," a sign of the trickster's refusal to enter into the realm of ordinary discourse. The twelve-year-old Vizenor and his friend Frog are "pleased to torment the titan who lived on the river," and they sabotage the construction of the titan's sailboat, for no other reason than "to torment the titan" (67). (And, from the later perspective of the proven writer, for no other reason than to capture the poetic assonances of the line.) When Vizenor ("or Petesch as I was known to some people then" [67]) and Frog are caught by Mean Nettles and his cohorts, the six Pitcher brothers, after Gerald and Frog sabotaged the titan's sailboat construction, the brothers chant: "'Badtize 'em, badtize 'em'" (67). They remember that Mean Nettles had once "threatened to baptize his enemies with water from Green Lake" (66). Green Lake is not a pristine pastoral body of water, as its name suggests, but "a huge gravel pit near the river; it filled with sulfurous waste from the concrete block factory up the hill. The lake was chartreuse, clear, and smooth; the water turned flaxen at dusk, as thick as cough medicine, and clotted at the bottom" (66). Gerald and Frog naturally try to avoid their "badtism," considering it worse than a beating, since they had already experimented with the water from the lake and already know that water from the lake will dry their skin "into thin white wrinkles." The Pitcher brothers' pun suggests a baptism that is an inversion of the more conventional purification rites. As it turns out, they are not "badtized" in the polluted lake, but they are, nevertheless, given another version of the titan's parodic baptism when he catches them in a hole and "urinated on our heads" (69).

Even so, Vizenor and Frog carry on their cunning battles with Mean Nettles, trickster battles of spontaneous strategies and counter-strategies. They decide to steal his boat and sail around Green Lake, knowing that Mean Nettles will be too tired to catch them (69). But once they run ashore, the titan "and his legion of cross-eyed squatters," the Pitcher brothers, begin a search. Gerald and his friend try to hide in the trees, "crows perched at the top of the trees" (70). (Such is Vizenor's young imagination that he actually takes on the identity of a crow. The crow is not a metaphor but a new identity.) But Mean Nettles is a "wise tracker" (70) and locates the crows.

This whole experience might be folklore, or perhaps an updating of a Tom Sawyer and Huckleberry Finn story, or of young William Wordsworth's remembrance of stealing a boat. The story reads as a combination of exaggeration and reality suggesting that all of the participants are figures from a tribal myth, an established story in which the participants do not know that they are caught within the framework of a tribal tale. Life and death activities seem at once playful and authentic, simulations and the real thing. The captive Gerald and Frog are "transported to the island on a raft and left there naked with our hands and feet tied to trees" (71). They are "banished" by Mean Nettles to this island in the river "for the rest of our lives" (71) and remain tied to the trees until nightfall. "The demon river mosquitoes, bloated with too much blood, rolled over on our shoulders, arms, back and dropped from our bodies into the moist thick grass" (71). In the writing of these experiences, Gerald and his friend seem to live outside of an ordinary world; their activities are truly adventurous, even liberatory. And, most importantly, such activities depend upon the trickster ability of the protagonists to take on different identities at will—pirate, crow, titan, demon—and to become lost in the dialectic of the *agon*. Trickster, Vizenor suggests elsewhere, "does not distinguish between friend and foe in carrying out his pranks" ("Trickster" 207). Trickster is the reciprocity of strategies and cunning intelligence of the different parties, a battle which asserts a communication between what we might be tempted to call evil and good, although these obvious polarities are never mentioned.

We might expect, furthermore, to find in the Mean Nettles story the trace or shadow of a conversion narrative, a conventional element in the genre of Anglo/American autobiography. But Vizenor's initiation does not wash away an old self in order to give birth to a more pure identity. The young crossblood's impurity and illegitimacy are left intact. An epic, mythic, battle has taken place, imaginary and actual, with a positive outcome for Gerald: "we needed to be punished and tortured by the titan." He doesn't say why. Perhaps he feels that he has confronted and survived the evil trickster and need no longer live in fear for the rest of his life. Gerald and Frog enter the battle for the sake of the battle itself, knowing that Mean Nettles will reciprocate with unwavering resolution. The recognition they will gain in the end is to be "praised for our courage as little people" (72). Recognition as dimunition will preserve them, at least partially, from being entrapped within epic and/or theological purity.

The whole episode is a game, and, cruel as it might be, Vizenor affirms its value. He has undergone a conversion to a self-aware nontheological position of tricksterism, a "badtism" into impurity, not so much an inversion of the traditional conversion narrative which obliterates the impure past of a life, purifies the self for "entry into a new life" (Starobinski 78), as a confirmation of what he has always been, an impure and illegitimate identity (as established by his crossblood genealogy), a verification that will subsequently allow him to acknowledge the "trickster signature" in later events. And although the characters— Vizenor, Frog, Mean Nettles, the Pitcher brothers—are the visible figures in the narrative action, in effect, they are at once persons and masks of the trickster who remains behind the scene, the self-effaced and self-effacing generator of "story."

Through the trickster figure, the subject of this autobiography confronts himself (the self) as illegitimate, as impure, as marginal. Like Henry Adams who finds that he cannot get an "education," Vizenor moves in and out of sites for legitimation but can never achieve "legitimacy." And, as Adams finds that he will have to make do without an education, Vizenor has a counter move available to him from his cross-blood heritage, to embrace illegitimacy.

Consequently, he will be plagued throughout the course of his life, for instance, with various problems about his high school and college records. Some basic mark of legitimacy and accreditation always seems to be missing, and Vizenor himself is a party to this lack; "graduation is death," he tells a social worker as he is about to graduate from high school and join the army (114). As a new recruit in the army, he is told that his "masturbation papers" are missing. Something about his records is always amiss, so that it will often be difficult for Vizenor to get, for instance, post-high school education. He and a bureaucracy seem to conspire to maintain his illegitimacy. Upon his return from Japan, he will be accepted by New York University "on the condition that my high school records would be provided at a later date; naturally, my records would never be revealed" (155). Through perseverance, resolution, exams and bureaucratic amnesia, he will be able to enroll in a number of schools, universities and law school. "My liberation was the military in Japan; my education, chance and coincidence" (156).

Vizenor will always wear the marks of impurity and illegitimacy. Instead of conducting his life as a quest for legitimacy, he will work for the recognition of substitutes, alter egos, like Thomas White Hawk, whom he saves from the electric chair, or Ishi, whose name Vizenor tries to get the University of California to honor. He will take on, in a vocation he appears to have inherited from a long genealogical line, a role as a journalist, an "advocate" for Native American peoples, and a spokesman for all kinds of designated underclass Americans. Here again, it is Vizenor's tricksterism—i.e., his willingness strategically and imaginatively (and illegitimately?) to inhabit the official position of his adversary—that gives him efficacy. Vizenor can be effective in his advocacy by identifying with the official discourse of the dominant culture, with what the culture officially advocates but does not practice. The dominant culture operates like Roger, a kleptomaniac orderly at a mental hospital, who, fellow orderly Vizenor says, "understood the manners of the game, but not the rules of the game" (177). Vizenor becomes a militant remembrancer of the "rules of the game" and always fights against the "manners of the game." He thereby honors the official claims that justice must include all humanity, especially the "little people," the marginalized, the illegitimate, even as he opposes official practice.

If we consider Private Vizenor's encounter with the Army officer in Japan, we can see another and different instance of the trickster's accompaniment in the narrative of Vizenor's life. Major Brown was "pleased to hear the call to attention when he entered a communal toilet area" (119).

It seems that the Major wished to test the loyalty of the men, or to test the authority of his rank under these unusual circumstances. As "a compeer shouted attention," Vizenor relates, "I refused to move from the stool, but others leapt to their feet, trousers down, and saluted the major in search of a war" (119). There is no hesitation here for the crossblood protagonist, no split in his loyalty. Vizenor, inheritor of the trickster identity, will remain loyal to trickster materiality, to shit. As the Major walks through the latrines in the morning to garner the embarrassed salutes from the men, Vizenor concentrates, instead, upon his shitting and ignores the Major. When the Major asks him why he is not at attention, the private replies, "I'm taking a shit, sir." And he follows with an elaboration which invokes what he takes to be a basic scratch-line: "This is our crapper, sir, not an orderly room" (120). The Major is trying to divide loyalty between a voluntary and an involuntary act. If he can catch the men in their involuntary acts of bowel movements, he will have proven their loyalty to the bureaucracy of the military, to a military code which has also been usurped by the Major for his personal enhancement. Major Brown has confused personal and anonymous obeisance, crossing the lines of the proper and the improper. But he encounters the limit to his ventures in authority when he tries to interrupt a primary trickster activity.

In order to counter the Major's future vengeance, Vizenor understands that he will have to make himself into a completely anonymous military figure and follow the strict letter of the military code as an act of strategy. Taking a shit and refusing to salute the Major are the trickster's way of setting up a situation, a challenge. The Major responds by personalizing his strategies of control, working out the delayed manipulations of "a trained avenger" (120). Vizenor's counter-strategy is to remain intently aware of the military code without necessarily thinking about the Major specifically.

On a particularly nasty winter night when Vizenor and his outfit are on combat maneuvers in the mountains, "the duty guards [including Vizenor] gathered in a large tent to avoid a blizzard" and to play poker. "No one would venture into the mountains in a winter storm, we agreed, and passed the duty clock around the poker table. Our tour of duty was the game. At midnight the clock was mine for two hours" (120-21). The Korean/U.S. truce has just been signed, so that there is no particular anxiety about keeping the guard. Nevertheless, Vizenor arises from the game in time to assume his midnight guard. He puts on his coat and takes up his duties in the freezing night. His decision to honor his guard duty, even on an unlikely occasion, appears to be simply a case of obeying military orders, of acting by the book. But the Major goes out into the night thinking he will be able to catch someone off guard.

٭ The story suggests that the level of communication here between the Private and the Major is extremely complex, composed as it is of anticipation, projection, expectation, hunches, strategies and counter-strategies. Why would the Major venture out into this weather to check up on the guard? Has he somehow intuited that Vizenor is the designated guard on duty? Is he just trying to be the good army man, making sure that everything is in order, especially when there are many excuses to relax the rigor of surveillance? Does Vizenor have a hunch that the Major will be checking up? He refers to his "apprehension" about a "paranoid officer" (121), without, however, referring to the Major. Is this hunch a rational anticipation or just a matter of chance?

The result is that Private Vizenor, by carrying out his designated duties as the midnight guard, transgresses the best expectations of the Major's evil gambling, a better game than the one he had left at the card table. He has outplayed the Major, who has gambled that Vizenor, or any soldier, will be derelict on such a night. Instead, Private Vizenor carries out his duties with the rigor of the military regimen. As a consequence, he humiliates the Major, forcing him, by the letter of military regulations, to stand and identify himself in the proper military manner, as if the Major were the object of suspicion, a possible enemy rather than the commander in charge. He forces the Major to humiliate himself before the Army Private, by making him obey the strict letter of military procedure. In the story, trickster appears on the side of the figure most rigorously and impersonally identified with the anonymous procedures of an anonymous bureaucracy.

Despite the cruelty in the different scenes in Vizenor's life, the unseen omnipresence of trickster maintains a certain restraint over the violence, holding it within the boundaries of a game. No matter how cruel, "the tribal trickster is a liberator and healer in a narrative" (Vizenor, *Narrative* 187). For instance, the trickster myth is a source of comfort in Gerald's experience with his mother, especially after the accidental death of his stepfather, Elmer Petesch, since it can account for the wide swings of loyalties and moods, of lies and truths. When his mother calls the police to have Gerald arrested for stealing and threatening her, the narrator relates that "My mother was obsessed with fear, death, and loathing. She was wicked that winter; she sputtered her hatred, seethed, and scorned my independence and responsibilities to the man who trusted me more in five months than she had ever dared to care in seventeen years" (97). She is so outrageously exaggerated in her denunciation of her son ["He's a criminal, no good, he'll never be any good, he should be in jail, teach him a lesson" (97)] that even the police see through her accusations and rescue Gerald from the scene. The trickster is never mentioned here, but these wild turns of mood, in his mother and in other figures, including Elmer, may be understood as allusions to the aleatory activities of a trickster. The mark of the trickster is rapid and unaccountable change, the unanticipatable event.

Understanding the events in life as the activity of the trickster allows Vizenor to accept his own changes of mood and reinforces his refusal to be submerged, to be a victim, in the desolation of betrayal, and gives him the capacity to forgive. "Tricksters," he says, "eased the pain in stories," become inscribed in stories so that "wounds would be healed in stories" (74). There is here a counter mythology to the traditions of Christianity, a paganism that maintains a distance between Gerald and the actions of others, the trickster as an emotional buffer against the most severe kinds of depression, desolation, betrayal and violence. We may note that Gerald's experience with his mother, in her return from Los Angeles to try to get Elmer's worldly goods, is presented as comic, and that this comic sense derives from the temporal distance between the actual scene in 1951, when Gerald is seventeen, and the writing or telling of this scene some 35 years later. But it is also the case that a remembered emotion is absorbed and softened by the aura of the trickster figure who always hovers behind the narrative sketches of a crossblood life.

One of the trickster's specialties is to turn the antagonist's weapons back upon himself. This means that the trickster must always be able to enter into the subjectivity or thinking of the other person. The other person, the antagonist, uses premeditation, deceit, the surprise attack and the sudden assault. But the trickster projects his intelligence onto the other's line of thinking and can always, thus, outwit the other because he has secret intelligence of the other's designs. The trickster subject of an autobiography must always be multiple, must always be able to stand outside of himself in an identity that can adapt immediately to the multiple antagonists around him. If we ask, what is the nature of the trickster, we must say that there are at least two dimensions to his/hers/its abilities: to premeditate designs of action, which entails being able to project subjectivity onto the other subject, and to improvise spontaneously.

What this character allows Vizenor to do is to present "the Indian" as utterly non-primitive, as the character who has an advantage by being able to see the relationship between the past and the future, self and other. The trickster's power may well lie in not getting completely seduced into the present. He is not a simple or pure presence, but a presence deeply enriched, or crossed, by history and cunning. He is a saturated temporality, a figure whose temporality cannot be divided into past, present and future. He can be cunning because a sense of the past as non-linear, extending back into the pre-history of myth, can be brought to bear upon an event. The trickster gives Vizenor both weight and lightness, both reflective and practical abilities. The temporal range and comprehensiveness allow the crossblood to cope excellently in the contemporary world precisely because he is not lost in nostalgia for past glories and for past forms of life and imaginary integrities. The trickster develops his abilities to cope from a life of hunting and war, but the ability to anticipate and identify with an antagonist's action is a general framework of flexibility or instant adaptability. By invoking the trickster (in other writings as well as his autobiography), Vizenor is developing a myth of the Native American's mode of living in the world that makes him the hero of modern or postmodern life, not the hero of romantic bygone eras of a nomadic hunter-warrior tribe. In his loyalty to trickster, he is loyal to everything and to nothing. He is loyal to the play of life. He tends to jettison all hints of what Louis Owens calls "ethnostalgia" (43).

His guard against nostalgia does not necessarily eliminate the possibility of experiences of return, the return to the *nostos,* the home. "The White Earth Reservation returned to my past in a most unusual manner" (57). A thirteen-year-old Gerald becomes a member of the "Viking Council of the Boy Scouts of America" and goes with the group to a summer camp which turns out to be on the White Earth Reservation. This chapter becomes a narrative of complexities between mothers and Native Americans, a crossblood inheritance. Young Gerald is urged "with love and cookies to be part of her den" by Mary Norman Haase, who becomes his substitute mother, "a wise mother who cared for more than a dozen boys, most of them on familial margins" (58). This Scout den mother performs elementary acts of recognition for Gerald which his biological mother fails to do. In an important sense, Mary Norman Haase serves as an origin for Vizenor the writer ("she presented me with my first desk"), and he, in turn, dedicated "my first book of haiku" to her (58). Vizenor has multiple origins, as he has multiple parents, even multiple names.

As a Boy Scout, he is supposed to earn honors and merits by performing "dubious ceremonies" "borrowed from tribal cultures" (58). In a "pretend" letter he writes to his real mother, he tells her that the camp is on tribal lands that belong to his own family past ("My father grew up here you know"). Sometime "later," he comes to understand that the Order of the Arrow ceremonies performed by the Scout masters were pretend ceremonies, "an adventitious comic opera with racialism, wild dancers, shamanic simulations, and a bearded man who ate fire" (60). "I wondered who these white men thought they were, playing Indian on stolen tribal land" (61). As a Boy Scout, he is doubled in mothers and in Indians—a pretend mother who is his real mother to whom he writes pretend letters; pretend Indians led by his symbolic mother, the den mother who gives him cookies and encouragement, to whom he later writes haiku poetry. We are offered here a rich drama of the implications of crossblood existence and his many experiences of simulacra. There must be a line, a "scratch line," between the literal and the symbolic, between the pretend and the real, but even so, Gerald does not belong clearly to one or the other. Opting for the Scouts because of a den mother, Gerald is invited to participate in the pretend, racist culture of the Scouts.

One event in his Boy Scout experience seems to be Vizenor's complicated way of mapping his "home" while still acknowledging his traveler status. The Boy Scouts are given a compass reading exercise, but Gerald's group, under his leadership, take off on a spontaneous, unplanned outing instead. They spend the day walking around a lake. Gerald's activity is interpreted by the white leaders as "giving the Scouts a bad name." The senior Scouts insist on believing that Gerald and his group were lost—i.e., were not able to follow the compass. (This accusation is particularly insulting since the compass has been specious. If the tenderfoot scouts could not read the compass, they had simply to follow the dirt road back to the camp.) Indeed, Vizenor does give the Scouts a bad name, but in the literal sense. He "bad-names" the senior Scouts by dismissing them as "pretenders to the land, abusers of gasoline, and artless readers of the compass" (61).

Gerald's relationship to the scouting trip on White Earth land is typically complicated. His crossblood consciousness cannot obliterate the reality of the white man's theft. The white Scouts do not live with this double consciousness, do not have to be aware that they are camping on land stolen from the Anishinaabe. The white man has stolen and distorted the Native American culture in his ceremonies just as he has stolen the land. Even true motherhood has been stolen, in a sense. And young Vizenor is at once complicit in and resistant to the multiple theft. The regions that have been crossed here are at once clear and blurred. His discovery of a home that is not a home ("I had no home" [149]) is achieved by chance, improvisation, simulation.

Vizenor does have a strong sense of what he calls "tribal consciousness" (130), however. Despite all of his playfulness with identity, despite the model of the trickster, there is for Vizenor some aura of the belief in authenticity. We see the emergence of such underground rumblings in his decision to leave Japan when his enlistment in the Army is ended. "I might have pretended to be the modern crossblood Lafcadio Hearn at Sophia University," he speculates. "He became Japanese, and he could have become Anishinaabe; we were brothers with the trees and stones" (129). His decisions are, at this moment, unstable: "I changed my mind at the last minute." But the temptation to stay in Japan is great, and, in retrospect, he would regret his decision to leave. "Japan was my liberation, and the literature, the haiku poems, are closer to me now in imagination, closer to a tribal consciousness, than were the promises of missionaries and academic careers" (130). As his mind changes, he struggles to find an explanation for leaving Japan. "I was worried that my past would be unforgiven, that my temper and experience would be abandoned." He considers going into acting for a career, "but I changed my mind about that too, because of my insecurities about families and identities. I reasoned that an actor lived in the role, and in my case the role would have become my home. I praised the trickster, our comedies, the turn of egos in a stern word, but there must be more to me than a mere pose" (129).

In his reasoning about the insecurity of identities, he has an inkling that there is an identity that may be his, or a role that can truly be his "home." He ends up accepting Hearn's words about loving that for which one sacrifices as his ultimate explanation for leaving Japan. He decides to leave Japan, "his lover in the mountains," and return to America as the land which has caused him the most pain. "My crossblood remembrance, lost tribal souls, uncertain identities, and wounded cranes in the poisoned cities, cause me the most miseries. I learned to remember these stories, and to honor impermanence, tribal tricksters on the run, run, run, run" (130). For Vizenor, a more genuine identity is constructed by the pain and sorrow that the U.S. bequeaths him in "the burdens of racialism and the hard rind of ideologies, and terminal creeds." At the core of his identity lie his "passions, curiosities, rage and resistance" (130). We might be tempted to refer to this core as a center, a home, from which radiates the adventures and insecurities and ironies. The contemplated tentative identities of the actor which might tempt him in Japan cannot win out, in the end, over the master of tentative and contradictory identities, the trickster figure native to his Anishinaabe heritage. His identity as an American crossblood turns out to be stronger than his imaginary propensities to identify with the Irish and Greek crossblood, Lafcadio Hearn. Imagination, the creative possibilities of new identities, falter here against chance and contingency, which in turn become a version of destiny.

There is a tendency to believe that every new autobiography, especially those by ethnic writers, challenges or subverts the genre. Vizenor's work is no exception. But can there be a challenge to the genre of autobiography? It would seem not. Autobiography as a genre has a name but no laws. Or, rather, the law of the genre has, since the Romantic era, demanded a sense of the originality of an individual subject within the terms of cultural discourse. Our fascination with this genre lies, beyond the pleasures of voyeurism, in the demand for the representation of the singularity of individual experience, an impossibility, since to represent commits one to the terms of a cultural discourse in general. A singular life, as presented in writing, always ends up having to mean something, to take on some universal cultural significance, since one has, for the contractual exchange, only the common coin of the realm, language, discourse. "At its most naive, autobiography really does claim to represent a self and its experience," but in our post-Romantic era, not to mention our postmodernist era, hardly any practitioner of the genre can escape the sense that s/he can "represent anything but the impossibility of self-representation" (Burt 18).

Is there a design, a pattern, in this depiction of a life? Vizenor tends to offer the reader episodes, so that the experience of any one design gets lost in the reading. But this does not mean that the reader is forced to construe his autobiography as postmodern, for one aspect of the textual tradition of autobiography has always been the picaresque, a postmodernism, as it were, way before its time. Why does not Vizenor feel any anxiety about the episodic nature of his autobiography? There is a sense in which a postmodern text forces us to play with our inability to decide whether a text really has a plausible or discoverable coherence, a hidden or analogical unity, or whether it is fragmentary and chaotic. As readers, especially of autobiography, we desire a unity or we expect an underlying narrative thread. The more disjunctive the appearance of the text, the more obsessive is our desire to find the hidden unity of a self. A genealogical record of family life may look like the beginning of a grand narrative, a personal narrative that can also serve as the trellis for the weaving of history and culture. But Vizenor seems not to be tempted by such possibilities. His account of his family does not anticipate a grand narrative, even though it does suggest a fragmentary, or non-linear continuity with a long past, one that begins with the mythic division of the original five totems of the Anishinaabe. His genealogical account suggests the mongrel composition of the narrative subject. If genealogy is a search for origin and the continuity of a life from that origin, what Vizenor presents is the autobiography of a multiple, divided origin—a disseminated father, mother, identity, even a proper name. (The name "Vizenor" is "despotic transcription" by an early Indian Agent of the name "Vezina" [17].) If there is an evaded or a hidden foundation for American culture in the pre-existent Native American occupation of the continent, this foundation is really the trickster, who has no center or stability or identity. The trickster as the founding of a culture is not a center or a ground, but instability and contingency.

Vizenor's life zig-zags rather than moves toward a clear revelation of a fixed identity. The incidents of the life do not move toward some kind of frame or unity of analogy. That is because the trickster enters into the picture as if by chance. We cannot claim that the protagonist here is trickster. But the identity of the narrator/protagonist may always swerve in its narrative path, in its building and unbuilding, in its numerous fosterages, in its chance encounters with trickster. We could say that the author refuses to give the reader the clues that could be used to form a framework of unification. But a theorist of autobiography like Philippe Lejeune might also say that it is we the readers who refuse to fill in the gaps that the author has left. Postmodernist literary practice is still a contract in which the author and the reader consent to remain within the fragments of experience and thinking without any irritable straining toward unity (Lejeune 3-30). The contract states that the writer has not presented the enigmatic fragments of a life in order for the reader to discover the invisible meaning. As post-modernist readers, we live in the era of suspicion about unified imaginations.

For, in theory, the notion of representation and the idea of a person's individual life seem incompatible, even impossible. For some ethnically identified Americans, the very idea of autobiography is a contamination, a pure sign of the loss of an ethnic identity. Although we do not know the rules of the genre, we know that autobiography belongs to the dominant culture. "Commencing before the Revolution and continuing into our own time, America and autobiography have been peculiarly linked" (Sayre 147). From Vizenor's Native American perspective, however, the native American is the effaced writing of American identity, the forgotten original, or foundational, figure of the continent.

A crossblood becomes the model of metaphor, not exactly the metaphor of metaphors, but the saturation of metaphor, human life as derived from catechresis, the improper. Origins are purely mythical, but the mythic origin may also be an after-effect of the crossing that is metaphor. The trickster does not have a face, but what does it have? It is a holotrope, says Vizenor ("Trickster" 187), the framework of tropology, perhaps something like the metaphor of metaphors. Metaphor is always the unruly, the improper within language itself. Metaphor presents itself with many faces, all of which are not the proper face. What Vizenor shows us is that the proper face cannot appear, and any sense that we might have of a proper face is a ghostly effect of the improper; the proper name got lost along the way. Vizenor is the proper name, the signature of the author. But it is an improper name, the only name which has survived. In metaphor, the force of the origin has been worn away, but the result is a linguistic surplus value. The zig-zag of loss and gain, presence and absence, is the trickster figure who moves in and out of the autobiography, receding and appearing arbitrarily. At times, the trickster looks like a guardian angel; at times, it looks like a cruel demon, the "titan."

Once, at least, it appears as Vizenor taking a shit and thwarting a zealous army major's petty games of authority. At another time, it is the mongrel in northern Japan who awakens Vizenor and saves him from certain death by an uprooted tree in a devastating typoon. Vizenor, and the reader, cannot always identify lucidly the presence or absence of this figure who is perhaps a "signature," a trace of a figure. If the author and the reader could, the trickster would already have become, per impossible, a terminal creed. As holotrope, trickster is the metaphor who remains outside the field, what Derrida calls the "extra metaphor" (Derrida 220), the metaphor that has been denied. Native Americans have to strive to avoid all of the traps that the dominant culture has laid for the representation of Indians. In Vizenor's mythology, the vanishing of the American generates the trickster as holotrope, a newly enriched field. Metaphor preserves the crossblood; the crossblood preserves the metaphor. The metaphor is the crossblood; the crossblood is the holotrope. Metaphor and crossblood lock into each other. And like metaphor, and also like trickster, a crossblood can never be pure.

And so the crossblood dislocates the subject of American autobiography, or, at the very least, maintains a dislocation that may have always been a feature of its absence/presence. Vizenor seems to play with the possibility that there is a dislocation before the experience of language. What he offers us in the "autobiographical myths and metaphors" is the undecidable of metaphor versus some cultural otherness at the heart of the subject. Or perhaps we should say that the dislocation in Vizenor's book is double; there is a supplementary dislocation to the dislocation of language. The symbolic order that makes up American culture is schizophrenic. What this crossing points to is that no culture, and certainly not the mythic melting pot of the United States, has an apparatus for adjudicating the priority of one "blood" over another. Native Americans, like Vizenor, remain loyal to two states, as it were. Both "bloods" are sovereign. There can be treaty negotiations between them, but they cannot be merged into one nation, one identity, a unified subject. One might ask why these two bloods are not at war with each other, since violence would be the supplement to this lack of a judgment. They can, at times, as Vizenor narrates, be at war. But they can also be held in peace by the trickster who was always already divided and never anxious about unity.

The writer of the autobiography is the ghost of the subject of the text. Who is, or can be, the writer of an autobiography? What is the status of this kind of survivance? The narrator as survivor or surplus of the text cannot be merely an idea. But the trickster is a kind of idealization of things in the world, that surplus which thus makes the things of the world graspable, as well as ungraspable, by the subject. In this sense, the genre of autobiography belongs to the Native American, the figure of survivance, as well as to the trickster, who must always survive because uncontainable, an origin divided from its origin. Only trickster can write autobiography.

Note

1. Gerald Vizenor, *Interior Landscapes: Autobiographical Myths and Metaphors* (Minneapolis: U of Minnesota P, 1990), 58. All future page references will be to this edition and will be included in the text.

Works Cited

Barthes, Roland. *Roland Barthes by Roland Barthes.* Trans. Richard Howard. New York: Hill and Wang, 1977.

Beaujour, Michel. *The Poetics of the Literary Self-Portrait.* Translated from the French by Yara Milos. New York and London: New York UP, 1991.

Burt, E. S. "Poetic Conceit: The Self-Portrait and Mirrors of Ink." *Diacritics* Winter 1982: 18.

Derrida, Jacques. "White Mythology." *Margins of Philosophy.* Trans. Alan Bass Chicago: U of Chicago P, 1982.

Gasché, Rodolphe. *The Tain of the Mirror: Derrida and the Philosophy of Reflection.* Cambridge, MA, and London: Harvard UP, 1986.

Jay, Paul. *Being in the Text: Self-Representation from Wordsworth to Roland Barthes.* Ithaca and London: Cornell UP, 1984.

Lang, Candace. "Autobiography in the Aftermath of Romanticism." *Diacritics* Winter 1982: 13.

Lejeune, Philippe. *On Autobiography.* Trans. Katherine Leary. Minneapolis: U of Minnesota P, 1989.

Owens, Louis. *Bone Game.* Norman: U of Oklahoma P, 1994.

Ricoeur, Paul. *Oneself As Another.* Trans. Kathleen Blamey. Chicago and London: U of Chicago P, 1992.

Sayre, Robert F. "Autobiography and America." *Autobiography: Essays Theoretical and Critical.* Ed. James Olney. Princeton: Princeton UP, 1980.

Starobinski, Jean. "The Style of Autobiography." *Autobiography: Essays Theoretical and Critical.* Ed. James Olney. Princeton: Princton UP, 1980.

Vizenor, Gerald. *Interior Landscapes: Autobiographical Myths and Metaphors.* Minneapolis: U of Minnesota P, 1990.

——. *Narrative Chance.* Albuquerque: U of New Mexico P, 1989.

——. "Trickster Discourse: Comic Holotropes and Language Games." *Narrative Chance.*

6

KID VIZENOR:
CONTRARY JOURNALIST

Joe Rigert

He was an unlikely candidate for print journalist. Emerging from the military and the university, he became a social worker, and then an advocate. Counseling prison inmates at first, later he would work on an employment program for Native Americans, and still later would be one of the founders of the confrontationist American Indian Movement.

This was hardly the proper beginning for a journalist, who is supposed to be detached, committed to no cause, able to apply critical thinking to any group or any situation, regardless of how this may conflict with his personal beliefs.

But Gerald Vizenor did have one of the primary attributes of any successful journalist. He learned quickly. He learned the ways of journalists and journalism, and used his knowledge to the benefit of his causes. He learned, for example, that journalists are prone to hype their stories in their never-ending thirst for ego and page one. He also learned that journalists like to feel that they are close to sources, especially among the deprived and dispossessed. It fits their liberal instincts, and makes them feel special.

So Vizenor got to know a few key journalists personally, and could count on them to carry his message, or to show up for the confrontations with the racist white establishment. Vizenor also played to their need to make the most of their stories; he fed them high numbers on the urban count of Native Americans, illusionary numbers, the numbers of a trickster. Repeated a few times in the popular press, however, they become authoritative. High numbers gave good stories to the journalists, and gave the politicians good reason to respond to the needs of a long-neglected group of Americans.

But Vizenor himself as journalist? Well, maybe it was possible. He did know the ways of journalism. And he had the skeptical view of the journalist; nobody could work in the prisons without learning to recognize the art of the con, and without being able to see through it. Prison inmates are always getting religion and reforming themselves, while they remain in prison.

Business and political leaders are often sacrificing the truth to further their goals: To look good, stay in office and maintain power. Prison counselors and journalists—the good ones—have no illusions about much of anything. And Vizenor was good at what he did, whatever it was in a variegated life as errant youth, military man, poet, counselor, confrontationist, con man for a cause. And then, of course, as journalist.

And that's what this chapter is all about: Vizenor as journalist. It was a relatively brief period in his life as teacher and author. But it was noteworthy as a commentary on those times and on this person.

Those times in the late 1960s and early 1970s were times of social turmoil, times of war at home and abroad, times of action and reaction. And this person, Vizenor as journalist, became a caustic critic as well as crusading causist.

But this was not a critic of the running dogs of white racism, or a critic of the reactionary opponents of equal rights for all Americans, or a critic of the politicians who promised much and delivered not much. In a startling editorial series in the *Minneapolis Tribune,* March 1973, this was Vizenor the journalist critic of the American Indian Movement he had helped to create, of confrontation heroes who made headlines and accomplished little, of romantic white liberals who financed them out of a patronizing guilt, of Native American ripoff artists who fed on the desire of politicians to get rid of them.

In "confrontation heroes," a scathing critique of his onetime comrades of the American Indian Movement, he described the "extravagant parody" of members of a cop-watch program trailing police cars in expensive convertibles. He chided the confrontationists for punching out racist adversaries at the front door, but walking out the back door without bothering to take part in the negotiation of change. Change was occurring, he wrote, but they were not part of it or even happy with it. When elected tribal leaders won hunting and fishing rights through a federal court decision, he pointed out, the AIM activists appeared with firearms to raise a protest and express a willingness to die for the cause. "The issue was won through the courts, and suicide was not necessary," Vizenor declared in a delicious dismissal of their tactics.

Was Vizenor getting old, losing his radical mind? Had he sold out to the demands of journalism, to the need to make a good story? Or had he merely sought out and reported the truth, as much of it as he could find, in the best tradition of journalism? As he would put it, his words were the arrows that hit their mark.

It was the sad, alarming and jarring truth he was after. "During the occupation of the offices of the Bureau of Indian Affairs in Washington, radical leaders demanded another investigation and reorganization of the paternalistic bureaucracy that has controlled the lives of tribal people on reservations for more than a century," he reported. "The militants had a powerful position from which to negotiate their demands: It was an election year and scores of congressional liberals were sympathetic. But rather than negotiate the demands, the leaders of AIM accepted more than $60,000 to leave the building and the city. They left with hush money."

Vizenor was not finished with that story. He was like a mythical God, hovering over his creation, watching, holding his people to account. He performed in this new role not because he was opposed to revolution and change. Rather, he knew from history that revolutions can be ruined when the revolutionaries become corrupted. He also knew that confrontations are often necessary, and he had taken part in his share of them. Then, as if the Gods had deigned it, Vizenor was journalist observer at Wounded Knee 1973, the ultimate AIM confrontation. "Members of the American Indian Movement held 11 people hostage at this Pine Ridge Reservation town where more than 200 Indians were massacred by cavalry troops in 1890," he wrote for the *Minneapolis Tribune*.

Later he would write of the irony and hypocrisy, of AIM leaders voicing the very same demands that they sold out in Washington when they took the hush money and left town. He praised the leaders and their followers for raising important issues—in government, law enforcement and education. But he chided them for deflating the merits of the cause when they left in the wake of reports of widespread shoplifting, unpaid motel bills and damaged property.

For all the corruption of some leaders, however, the movement helped bring about some change, and helped inspire other tribal people to join their newly publicized cause. In his chronicles of the people and events, Vizenor quoted a Roman Catholic priest giving credit to AIM for accomplishing in two weeks what others could not have done in two years. He described the transformation of tribal attorney Ramon Roubideaux, who was finally feeling good about himself as he filed a court complaint against old white friends in high places. He wrote of challenges to the corruption and nepotism of tribal leaders. And he saw the spiritual revivalism of some AIM radicals as a recognition that tribal people could not defeat the white man by force or political rhetoric, but could transform themselves in regenerating past traditions of spiritualism.

Some of the AIM leaders and their followers, however, were not impressed by the truth-telling of the co-founder of their movement. Either he was for them, all the way, through all their twists and turns, or he was against them. While they consorted with white liberals, in and out of the churches, seeking their money and support, they turned on their chronicler, threatening his life, treating him as traitor.

Vizenor laughed.

The kid—he was actually in his early thirties—got his start in newspaper journalism under the best and the worst of city editors. Frank Premack was right out of the "front page" tradition of old-time journalism. This was long before the time of empowerment, sensitivity training and political correctness. Premack shouted at his reporters from the desktops. He had no time to worry about their personal problems or to tolerate their incompetence. Either they produced often and well or they went on his shit list. The reporters respected his news instincts, but many—maybe most—hated him as a human being. It was rumored that his wife loved him, but that was never confirmed, and seemed implausible. He died of a heart attack in his forties, because he ignored chest pains for too long and then insisted on driving himself to the hospital.

Vizenor was not one of the man's favorites; he had none. But there was a certain bond between the two of them, born of a similarity in their natures. Both were direct, outspoken, moody, individualistic, defiant, out of the mainstream, unwilling to be labeled or boxed in. As a political reporter in an earlier life, Premack the liberal had been just as tough on the liberals as the conservatives, just as Vizenor later would expose the hypocrisies of his former Native American compatriots in the fight against racism and paternalism.

In fact, Vizenor had already demonstrated his defiance—that was how he got the job. At a conference of editors and writers for the Minneapolis Star and Tribune Company, he had demanded that editors "be tried for crimes against humanity" for their treatment of tribal cultures. His powerful indictment was well received for one reason: Newspaper journalists love to be excoriated, mainly because they love attention, good or bad. The worst that can happen to an editor or reporter is to be ignored. Their response to this upstart critic at that conference has been lost in the mist of history, but undoubtedly they admitted their failures, professed to be trying, and promised to do better. Editors and reporters have been doing that at conferences for a long time, and they have taken just as long to make any profound changes.

Vizenor gave the top print bosses a chance, however, to do more than beat their breasts in guilt. He gave them an opportunity to show their concern and their liberalism on a newspaper known for its own defiance of powerful interests. They offered him a job, and he took it in June 1968. He came to the newspaper not as an unproved reporter, but as poet and social activist who had already demonstrated his ability to dig up and write the truth of a story. The kid reporter had gone behind the headlines of a brutal murder of an old woman, and found the circumstances that turned a talented and upward striving Thomas White Hawk into her killer. This was the classic story of how the people of a violent culture, thriving on inequity and iniquity, could beget a son who would commit the ultimate act of violence, with a vengeance. Vizenor told that story not as an excuse for the killer, but as an explanation of the act.

Americans spend much of their time discussing how to stop conflict and violence, and how to promote cooperation and peace. They never succeed, and well they should not. Cooperation and peace tend to support the status quo; out of conflict and violence come change—sometimes for the better, although not always.

Vizenor, the emerging print journalist, under the tutelage of the orally violent editor Premack, would soon be back on the frontlines of confrontationist politics. One of his early assignments was to observe and report on challenges to the Roman Catholic Church, sometimes revolutionary itself, but more often a force to maintain the established theology and secular ideology. Catholic lay people were crashing the ceremonies of the Holy Mass to raise seminal questions.

A veteran of confrontation politics himself, Vizenor quickly caught the ironies of the encounters. His first paragraph in his first story quoted the intruder asking, could man act against civil authority on the basis of his conscience (women were busy raising children in those days)? His second paragraph noted that the question came at a time in the sermon when the priest told the congregation to look forward to the time that the human spirit would be liberated.

The time had not yet come. According to Vizenor's strictly factual account, the ushers quelled the disturbance and the priest quickly ended his sermon, reminding the faithful of his policy to get them home early for lunch.

The confrontationists obviously knew that they could have significant impact only if they were able to spread their message through the news media. They let it be known when and where they would strike next, just as police invite reporters along to watch them break down the doors of suspected drug dealers. Vizenor had used the press to further his own goals in his earlier career as advocate, and now he was being used, and enjoying it. Why not? The holy intruders were raising good issues, and producing good stories for the hungry reporter on the make.

In his second story, he described how angry Christians threatened violence against the outsiders who were raising questions and seeking a dialogue. And, then, his third account told a tale of violence unleashed: three of the outsiders were removed from the church when they criticized the omission of the sermon. A father slapped his challenging daughter and called them all Communists. The reporter was threatened with a lawsuit.

But change comes slowly, if at all. The protestors disbanded, the church continued as before, and Vizenor went on to other stories. The attempt to create a dialogue, he wrote in a summary piece, changed little more than the conversation in the parish parking lots.

The life of the print journalist is not all conflict and confrontation and prominently played stories. Vizenor covered his share of events that wound up being reported on page 16 or 24 or 10B. A boutique offers items for the poor. A young adult center opens on south side. South American birth-control myths are cited. Those were some of the headlines. Even on the lesser stories, however, Vizenor caught the pathos of the people who were in the news, unwittingly or not. When the Indian director of an Indian identity program was fired for failing to "think Indian," he said he would stay with the program. "I want to learn how to be an Indian," is the quote Vizenor put in his last paragraph. A good editor would have moved it way up the story, near the top.

Vizenor was not type-cast as "the Indian" reporter in the years he toiled full-time for the *Minneapolis Tribune*. As a general-assignment reporter, he was expected to be a generalist, able to write about home education, a prison riot and school desegregation, all of which he did. But his editor would have been a fool not to take advantage of the newly hired reporter's knowledge of the Native American population, and editor Premack, no fool by any measure, saw the opportunity through Vizenor to give an inside perspective to this large body of Minnesota residents too often viewed in stereotypes and categories. It was also a great opportunity for Vizenor, whose father's violent death had been treated stereotypically in another Minneapolis newspaper, and he made much of that chance.

The stories he wrote were not only of the problems of people who had long been ignored by the late-arriving white settlers. He described the funeral of John Ka Ka Geesick, who had practiced herbal medicine until his death at age 124. The white doctors with all their high-tech medicine might have learned something from him. He also wrote of the computer plant that offered hope in dealing with the persistent unemployment problem on reservations. Hope was needed, as well as jobs.

But Vizenor also took the opportunity to portray in human terms the "problems" of the original inhabitants of the state. When Minneapolis city agencies released surveys on deplorable housing conditions, the print journalist did more than just report the results. He went out to see for himself. "A cockroach zipped across the back of a porcelain sink in a fourplex . . . and disappeared behind a dripping faucet," he wrote in his first paragraph. The newspaper followed with an editorial titled, "The urban Indian housing scandal."

There was more to come. The father of Dane White, age thirteen, had asked the sheriff to pick up his son and put him in jail—just to give him a scare. Dane was a runaway. He and other boys had stolen a car. He was frequently truant from school. So the sheriff stuck him in a cell made for drunks, thieves and wife-beaters. He languished there for six weeks, and then hanged himself.

After covering the funeral for the *Minneapolis Tribune,* Vizenor tried to make sense of the tragedy. He didn't dress it up in the language of the romantic white journalists of the East Coast and Europe, putting it all to alienation from his culture or loss of identity or inability to deal with white oppression. As Vizenor would piece together the story, Dane White was a victim first of a broken family; much of the time he was running to, as well as running from. He was running from his father and stepmother, who were trying to cope with eleven children, and running to his grandmother or his mother. Dane White also was a victim of a juvenile justice system that meant no harm, but couldn't seem to arrange for foster care in less than six weeks, a system that considered lockup an acceptable alternative. And Dane White was a victim of his parents.

Just as he would be brutally honest in his reporting of the Native American confrontationists, Vizenor portrayed no romantic version of this boy's father and stepmother. Cyrus White, wrote Vizenor, had bothered to visit his son only once in the forty-two days he spent behind bars; his stepmother the same. He had asked the sheriff to take him away from his grandmother.

As he wrote of Dane White, Vizenor must have thought of his own childhood: the murder of his father; a mother who had too many problems of her own to contend with a contentious son, and the foster parents who tried. He heard White's grandmother describe young Dane as a happy-go-lucky kid, and Vizenor imagined the grandson and grandmother together, with Vizenor on the run.

Senator Walter F. Mondale would decry the suicide a few days later, blaming it on an educational system that destroys "the Indian's respect for himself and his culture." As Vizenor had already reported, it wasn't all that complicated.

Vizenor conformed to the norms of print journalism for a full four months; for him, it was an amazing performance. Then, on September 26, 1968, he could contain himself no longer. He rose up against the big print boss, Bower Hawthorne, executive editor, the man who had hired him. After complaining many times and getting no response, he filed a complaint with the city accusing his newspaper company of carrying derogatory and racist images and messages of Native Americans.

The print boss was outraged, and hardass subeditor Premack figured that Vizenor was finished as his reporter. But like Premack, Hawthorne was no fool. He knew that the Cowles family, owners of the *Minneapolis Star* and *Minneapolis Tribune,* were liberals on racial and social issues, as well as concerned about their image as enlightened members of their progressive community. Hawthorne capitulated in three hours, promising to establish policies to correct the problem. Vizenor withdrew his complaint and took a leave of absence to teach at a college for one year, and returned to write columns as a contributing editorial writer.

It was in this latter phase as print journalist that Vizenor produced some of his most critical work. It was not only his truthtelling about the American Indian Movement, but also his journalistic recognition of other problems within the Native American communities themselves. But he was not engaged in heavy-handed attacks on the leaders of people who had been victimized by the Caucasian invaders who won the wars. Rather, he was often writing a gentle criticism, pointing to the problems within that were helping to keep a people from moving ahead, in whatever cultural mode they preferred.

So he joined with another reporter to examine the failures of Indian education. Or he wrote about the promise and failure of economic development on Indian reservations. Or about the implications of casino gambling.

In his critical reporting on Native American affairs, Vizenor was way ahead of the hound dogs of the press. Never one to go with the pack, he rejected the prevailing liberal mode: Expose the abuses in business, government and the powerful institutions, but do not delve into the internal affairs of the weak and oppressed. It was a paternalistic approach that allowed leaders in the communities of the poor to exploit their compatriots, or damage their causes, with impunity.

Vizenor had seen enough and knew enough from experience to have no illusions. Indians had a special way with their children? Had a profound reverence for the earth? Were protectors of the environment? Like the Caucasian invaders, some of the original inhabitants measured up to the romantic ideals, although some of their "ideals" were merely creations of the latecoming settlers. Others ignored or defied the ideals, out of circumstance or inclination. In early years, many denuded the land where they lived, and moved on. In later years, others suffered from the dysfunctional family life of poverty. How could anyone expect them to be different?

In the "Politics of Paraeconomics," written for the Federal Reserve Bank, Vizenor told of highly educated Indian people returning romantically to reservations to live out their visions of tribal life in years past. But he went on to say, "Reservation tribal people are too preoccupied with survival to afford the luxuries of linguistic retreats from the present." And he said those abandoning the realities of urban life might soon be outnumbered on the roads back to the reservation by tribal people with the technical skills and college educations needed to manage programs and enterprises.

As Vizenor the critic described it, tribal politics, poor management and paternalistic government controls had hurt the economies of the reservation people, prompting him to call them paraeconomics, lacking in any real benefit. But he saw the potential for change. It would take tribal control of natural resources, educated and experienced management of new, aggressive enterprises and enlightened political leadership. This was journalist Vizenor in yet another role: visionary.

Beware of journalists who have visions. They are often wrong; and Vizenor was no exception. By the 1990s, economic development had been achieved on many reservations, but not from control of natural resources or other idealistic projections. Employment and unprecedented riches came from casino gambling: bingo, slot machines and all the other methods of extracting money from the weak and foolish.

Vizenor took time off from teaching and writing books to make some journalistic observations. "Who could have imagined that casinos would rescue communities and reduce chronic unemployment rates on reservations?" he wrote. As white people once threw money at Indian children, now they were throwing it to whole tribes, by the tens of millions. In just two states, Minnesota and Michigan, casinos provided 8,000 jobs and a payroll of $90 million for twenty tribes.

Never one to accept anything uncritically, however, Vizenor pointed to the dangers of this kind of "economic development." There was conflict, even violence, between the advocates of gambling and the proponents of traditional ways of life. There was the question of whether the tribes, required by federal law to negotiate with the states for casino gambling, were placing their sovereignty in jeopardy. And there was the prospect that the sudden riches would incite the enemies of the tribes to seek restrictions on their new enterprises.

Vizenor proposed a strategy to neutralize the opposition: To demonstrate their sovereigny, the tribes should name ambassadors to various nations and negotiate the liberation of stateless families, relocating them to reservation communities. The liberation of Kurdish, Tibeta, Haitian and other families would sustain the moral traditions of tribal cultures. It was another Vizenor vision, unlikely to be realized, but then Vizenor had no illusions about the perfectibility of the human species. He had seen and written too much for that.

Nor did Vizenor have any unrealistic expectations for print journalism. He well knew its limitations and its prejudices, from past to present. One day he had gone back to read the story in the *Minneapolis Journal* of June 30, 1936, reporting the death of his father in the clichés and stereotypes of those times. As the newspaper told it, "police sought a giant Negro today to compare his fingerprints with those of the rifled purse of Clement Vizenor, twenty-six years old, found slain yesterday with his head nearly cut off by an eight-inch throat slash." Later the newspaper reported that police had given up on the Negro and were considering such suspects as half-breed Indians and the jealous husband of a showgirl. They never solved the case.

Journalists don't solve many problems either, but they give a rough account, from day to day, of the happenings of their times. They try to make sense out of the senseless; get to the truth of the matter. Vizenor, in his short time as print reporter, did more than many to follow the truth, wherever it might lead, and however painful it might be.

7

GRIEVER: AN AMERICAN MONKEY KING IN CHINA:
A CROSS-CULTURAL RE-MEMBERING

Linda Lizut Helstern

Critics who have found William Bevis's "homing in" an apt paradigm for the contemporary American Indian novel have generally viewed Gerald Vizenor's work as the exception that proves the rule. This has certainly been the case with *Griever: An American Monkey King in China,* but it should not be forgotten that Gerald Vizenor is a contrary. The logic of the trickster reversal, contrary to prevailing critical opinion, suggests that *Griever* is the premier example of the Native homecoming novel. The best-known story about Indians, after all, is the story of their migration to the Americas from their original Asian homelands. Just how much at home he was in China dawned on Vizenor the night he attended his first Chinese opera, a performance of *The Havoc of Heaven.* It was 1983, and Vizenor was a Fulbright fellow teaching in Tianjin. While he had long been familiar with the story of the Chinese Monkey King through Arthur Waley's translation, watching the audience response to the universally beloved Monkey in action brought home the reality that the Chinese trickster had for centuries played exactly the same role as his tribal counterpart—a reminder that the irrepressible power of life is always stronger than any force established to control it (Vizenor, personal communication).

With biting satire and an array of trickster reversals, Gerald Vizenor's Chippewa-Chinese-American tour de force captures the particular historical moment in the early 1980s following the restoration of diplomatic and trade relations between China and the United States after a hiatus of some 30 years: East meets West again. Incorporating his personal observations of contemporary China, Vizenor underscores the irony of a number of Native American Indian/Chinese cross-cultural parallels, particularly the brutal suppression of an artistic and religious heritage. He attempts to convey the essence of the Chippewa, or *anishinaabe,* and the Chinese cultural legacies to a reading public equally unfamiliar with both—to tell traditional stories in ways that would demonstrate their cultural meaning and import. For this purpose Vizenor creates in Griever de Hocus—a mixedblood university teacher from the White Earth Reservation—a protagonist who can be simultaneously identified with the most popular heroes of the most popular literary forms of the *anishinaabeg* and the Chinese: *naanabozho,* the tribal trickster, and Sun Wu-k'ung, the trickster monkey of Chinese opera, the Chinese analog of Native American storytelling. Within the framework of the Chinese lunar calendar and festival cycle, Vizenor weaves together traditional *anishinaabe* and Chinese stories using the conventions of Chinese opera.

It is through his effort to give new life to the old stories, perhaps more than anything he could have observed about Chinese culture in the early 1980s, that Vizenor captures the historic moment. With the condemnation of the Gang of Four and the cessation of the activities of the Red Guards who had sought to purge China of all ties to its "reactionary" cultural history in the decade between 1966 and 1976, the nation had just begun the process of recovering its heritage. As Colin Mackerras noted,

The overwhelming impression which emerges from a consideration of the Chinese performing arts since 1976 is an attempt to revive a lost culture. During visits to China, one of the commonest terms I came across among performing arts circles was *huifu,* to restore, recover. Failure to restore was always regarded as a pity, success was the highest good. (Mackerras, *Performing* 204)

It is the ultimate cross-cultural irony that Native American Indian writers, including novelists N. Scott Momaday, Leslie Marmon Silko, James Welch, and Vizenor himself, had so recently begun the process of imaginatively re-membering their own heritage.

An appreciation of the subtlety of Vizenor's art begins with an understanding of the Native American trickster, and particularly the trickster of the *anishinaabe* oral tradition. Vizenor refers to him as "*naanabozho,* the compassionate woodland trickster" (*People* 3). Whatever name or form he takes as he moves from tribal legend to tribal legend across North America, "the Native American Trickster is the quintessential wanderer" (Ballinger, "*Ambigere*" 32). Trickster lives at the margins of society, again and again manipulating and violating conventional moral notions. With his super-sized penis and virtually endless intestine, he is frequently "lascivious, gluttonous, arrogant, disobedient, greedy, cruel, restless, lazy," but he is just as frequently a "clever, tricky, creative, transforming, funny fellow" (Radin 165; Ballinger, "*Ambigere*" 24). Despite everything, Trickster remains sympathetic, if not loveable, and ultimately, elusive as a subatomic particle, he defies "final definition of time, place and character" (Ballinger, *"Ambigere"* 31).

While the emphasis on Trickster's various personality traits differs from tribe to tribe, Paul Radin notes in his classic study that five Trickster exploits came to be told in virtually all Native American tribal cycles in practically identical form. Vizenor utilizes all five of these plots in singular adaptations in *Griever:* Trickster's plot to kill the ducks by giving a dance where they must keep their eyes closed; Trickster's plot to marry the chief's son by changing sexes; Trickster's plot to send his penis across the lake to have intercourse with the chief's daughter; Trickster's test of the talking laxative bulb; and Trickster's flight on the turkey buzzard's back, which ends when the turkey buzzard drops him into a hollow tree (Radin 132-40). In each case, Vizenor reverses some significant aspect of the story. Franchot Ballinger views such reversals in light of the Native American tradition of Heyoka, whose practitioners honor the creative spirit of the universe by doing the opposite of what is expected in every instance: every "no" becomes a "yes," and every "yes" a "no" (*"Ambigere"* 35; "Sacred" 38).

Vizenor's version of the dancing ducks takes place in the Chinese market during Griever's first walk through the city. Not a duck story at all but a chicken story, it grows out of a scene Griever has painted on a scroll he carries around with him in a holster: "a proud white cock leading all the caged hens to freedom" (Vizenor, *Griever* 34).[1] The two-dimensional scene takes on a life of its own, but the would-be liberator has to do some serious persuading to get help with his Chinese. "This is real, this is freedom, not some precious recipe," he barks at the lesbian management consultants Jack and Sugar Dee in his final persuasive plea (44). After an hilarious bargaining session, the trickster-teacher succeeds in buying the chickens, forcing the butcher to close up shop for the day. In this reversal of the original trickster story, no one dies, everyone lives.

The rooster which first caught Griever's attention becomes not only his pet but the emblem of his outrageous trickster sexuality. With the cock free, Sugar Dee immediately becomes the object of Griever's erotic attention. She escapes and vanishes, but for Griever, the reality of the mind is at least equivalent to physical reality. Exercising his significant mental powers, Griever transforms himself into Sugar Dee's lover:

He spread his fingers beneath the poppies, moved to the rise of her stomach. Sugar Dee tossed her hair back, wide over his neck as he leaned on her shoulder close to her breasts. He became a woman there beneath her hair, and with thunder in her ears, she peeled the blossoms. (54-55)

In a homoerotic reversal of the old story, Trickster's victim is no chief's son with a male wife but a woman's woman. Hester Hua Dan is the next object of Griever's lust. Hers is also a story of gender reversal, a variation on the story of Trickster's penis crossing the water. Sensing an impending seduction, Hester wades into the ocean both to escape Griever and to urinate. Vizenor's description is laced with eroticism:

> She raised her dress higher and waded deeper until the wild moons lapped between her thighs and a cold undercurrent soused her groin. She trembled, rose higher on her toes, and then eased back to the current, deeper in the water, and urinated. Warm waves circled her thighs. (104)

Here it is the trickster who is caught waiting as the waves lap the shore. Griever's Venus steps out of the foam—and a pool of her own garlic-scented urine—to become, unlike the chief's daughter, the trickster-teacher's willing sexual partner. There is no awl through the penis to separate these lovers, and Griever's erotic style remains pure trickster throughout their encounter. When he engages Hester in cunnilingus, for example, Griever's "nose brushed her clitoris, he burrowed and inhaled the wild humors" (105).

Griever finds himself in deep shit in the public bathroom in Victoria Park, but at least it isn't his own. In a variation of the story of Trickster's laxative, Griever is given a bundle of "garlic peace" by Hua Lian to facilitate his trip to the open toilet. This, apparently, is the traditional way to survive the stench (120). In one last trickster reversal, Vizenor updates the story of Trickster's flight. Here an ultralight aircraft, not a turkey buzzard, carries Griever across China to his finish. His apparent failure to arrive in Macao, where he told China Browne he was headed, suggests Griever's end may be as ill-fated as Trickster's, but the novel leaves both Griever and the reader up in the air.

Vizenor incorporates the stories into a framework that underscores their ultimate meaning within Native American cultures: Trickster is a liberator. In cultures which sought to balance cosmic dualisms through ritual action, Trickster stands as a reminder of the times when the desta-bilizing power of life is stronger than the controlling rituals. Franchot Ballinger suggests that the laughter he elicits is laughter at the patness of our human beliefs ("*Ambigere*" 31). Like Navajo and Pueblo sacred clowns who honor the sacred by defying cultural taboos as a part of a ritual itself, "Trickster frees man from the imaginative and moral impov-erishment attending enslavement to codified and solidified thinking" (Ballinger, "*Ambigere*" 31). He shows us that reality is all too often conditioned by human expectations and perceptions. Trickster's ultimate gift is creativity, the ability to effect change.

The compassionate *anishinaabe* trickster *naanabozho* is both teacher and healer, whose gifts to the people include medicinal plants, wild rice, maple sugar, basswood, and birch bark. Still, this does not fully explain Vizenor's use of the adjective *compassionate.* In the context of the Chippewa origin myth is a group of stories detailing *naanabozho*'s search for his own origins which suggests a rationale for Vizenor's choice of words. As it happens, these trickster stories in written form came down to Vizenor as a family legacy. They were published in an eleven-part series by his great uncle Theodore Beaulieu in *The Progress,* the newspaper he founded on the White Earth Reservation (Velie 126). Originally published in 1887-88, the stories were re-edited by Vizenor for a collection published in 1970. They were recently incorporated into a new edition of *Summer in the Spring.*

The cycle begins with the conception of *naanabozho,* whose father, the north spirit, was attracted to a beautiful young woman gathering food. In the wind's way he made love to her without her knowledge or consent, and she became pregnant. Just after giving birth, the young woman is carried off by her *manidoo* lover, leaving behind a newborn to be raised by his grandmother. The orphan *naanabozho* is haunted by his mother's absence and determines to find her killer and avenge her death. *Naanabozho* ultimately confronts his father. Seeking at all costs to avoid a show of power, the *manidoo* placates *naanabozho* by giving him full control over the earth. This is a realm of great darkness and terrible evil, but with the eyes of the owl and the light of the firefly, *naanabozho* begins to explore. He encounters the terrible suffering of the victims of the great gambler and vows "that if he ever destroyed the *gichi nita ataaged,* he would liberate the victims who were being tortured" (Vizenor, *Summer* 127). Laughing in the face of death, *naanabozho* takes on the gambler and keeps him from winning the first round of the game with a well-timed whistle. In other versions, *naanabozho* goes on to defeat the gambler, but the Beaulieu version ends here.

In *Griever,* a novel built on a similar lack of closure, liberation becomes both a motive and a motif. The transformation of Griever the trickster-teacher into the American Monkey King turns on the crux of liberation, which in China is an old, old theme. If the Communists divided Chinese history into two parts, "before liberation" and "since liberation," the concept of liberation came to China with the first Buddhist scriptures, some 1700 years ago. Liberation from the round of birth, suffering, and death—the achievement of nirvana by all beings—is the ultimate goal of Buddhism. Its saints are the compassionate teachers, the boddhisattvas, who have chosen to forego the buddhahood they have earned until every being in all six realms of existence has also attained enlightenment.

The Chinese Monkey King attained buddhahood and literary immortality in a novel first published in China in 1592. Frequently but not definitively attributed to Wu Ch'Eng-en, *The Journey to the West* is an account of the travels of the monk Hsuan-tsang (596-664 A.D.) to bring Buddhist scriptures from India to China. It was not the first fictionalized account of Hsuan-tsang's quest nor the first to include a monkey companion, but *The Journey to the West* became an immediate popular hit and never lost its appeal to Chinese of all ages and classes (Yu 1-21). The Monkey King Sun Wu-k'ung, both audacious and irrepressible, is the novel's comic hero. Monkey, his two novice monk companions Hog and Sha Monk, and their immortal dragon-horse, are charged with protecting the scripture pilgrim through the exigencies of the quest, which ultimately takes seventeen years to complete.

The quest begins from the same motivation which brought *naanabozho* face to face with the evil gambler—a compassionate desire to release the souls of the dead from their suffering. The Tang Emperor promises to celebrate the Grand Mass of Land and Water "for the salvation of those orphaned spirits" who gave their help in returning his spirit to life after his visit to the underworld (*Journey* 253).[2] When advised by the Boddhisattva Kuan-yin herself that the mass cannot be effective without the Great Vehicle Laws of Buddha, the Tang Emperor authorizes the worthy monk Tripitaka to make the necessary journey to obtain them. Kuan-yin has paved the way for his success by promising three fallen immortals (Monkey, Hog, and Sha Monk) that their own punishments will end if they lend their assistance to the scripture pilgrim. The monkey, the traditional Buddhist symbol for the active and irrepressible mind, is perhaps the most recognizable element of Buddhist allegory in the novel. *The Journey to the West* serves as an extended reminder that finding a way out of the eternal round of birth and death and achieving enlightenment requires taming both "the monkey of the mind and the horse of the will" (Yu 59). The novel, however, simultaneously develops a Taoist allegory of personal cultivation through its incorporation of alchemical, yin-yang, and *I Ching* lore (Yu 34).

Monkey's close kinship with the Native American trickster is established in the opening thirteen chapters of the one-hundred-chapter work. Monkey's beginning is no less miraculous than *naanabozho*'s: he hatches from a stone *"exposed to the wind"* (my emphasis) and soon earns the title *Handsome Monkey King* through his daring. It is neither food nor sex which motivates this Monkey King but a voracious appetite for immortality. Some "three or four hundred years" into his reign, Monkey recognizes that ultimately he will die and begins a quest which leads him to his first teacher, Master Subodhi. It is Master Subodhi who gives Monkey the religious name Sun Wu-k'ung, "Wake-to-Vacuity" (82). The auspicious name with its Buddhist resonance, pointing "to the emptiness, the vacuity, and the unreality of all things and all physical phenomena," plants the seed of Monkey's ultimate enlightenment (Yu 38). A superb pupil, within a few years Wu-k'ung masters the Art of the Earthly Multitude, seventy-two physical transformations which will protect him from all calamity. His magical weapon, a 13,500-pound iron rod which can be reduced to the size of an embroidery needle, makes him all but invincible. When the Monkey King dares to eradicate his name from the Register of Death, the Jade Emperor determines to bring him to heaven to keep an eye on him. After creating havoc in a number of ways, Monkey here finds the opportunity to devour the peaches of immortality and after a five-hundred-year imprisonment, begins his quest with the scripture pilgrim.

Monkey's theft of the magic peaches is one of the best-known episodes of *The Journey to the West,* in large measure because it lends itself so readily to the stage. It was as traditional Chinese opera that famous literature became widely known to mass audiences of illiterate peasants. From spring to mid-fall, outdoor theatrical performances were a staple at major religious festivals held for centuries at temples throughout China. The performances competed in a carnival atmosphere against such favorite entertainments as stilt walkers and acrobats (Bredon and Mitrophanow 392-94). While most operas were primarily love stories or war stories, they retained a vestige of their original religious nature in their opening scenes, which often dealt with some Buddhist or mythological theme (Mackerras, *Chinese* 96). As entertainment with a moral enjoyed by the entire population, the Chinese opera may be considered the analog of traditional Native American Indian storytelling.

The potential for education through popular entertainment did not escape the Chinese bureaucrats. From time immemorial, they "viewed the drama as a means of propagating correct ethical values" (Mackerras, *Chinese* 92). The plots and characters admitted to the imperial Chinese repertory had to uphold Confucian moral standards, and any violation by any character demanded appropriate punishment. In the theatre, death came to every unfilial child. Yet the actors, knowing their real audience, frequently improvised upon the approved scripts, peppering their performances "with references to current events which were usually hostile to the Confucian *status quo*" (Mackerras, *Chinese* 17). Even as he borrows traditional characters and plot-lines, taking the unfilial Hester Hua Dan to her death, Gerald Vizenor honors with his satire the Chinese tradition of the politically subversive performance.

It is not a tradition the Communist government has honored, but government rewrites have not dampened the popular enthusiasm for traditional operas. During a 1982 visit to his boyhood home of Tianjin, John Hersey observed "a Chinese teenager walking along with a stereo tape deck held on his shoulder, music blasting full volume into his ear. He was playing classical Peking operas" (Hersey 66). Many operas survived the Communist revolution because they adapted themselves readily to post-liberation politics. These included stories about rebellions against feudal authorities, wars of resistance against foreign aggressors, the righting of injustices, and love stories which could promote women's equality (Mackerras, *Performing* 79). During the Cultural Revolution of the late 1960s and early 1970s, only four operas, none traditional, were permitted performance. One of the first operas revived afterward, however, was *The Havoc of Heaven*—Monkey's theft of the magic peaches. While political virtues of the revival were extolled in the *People's Daily* on July 13, 1978, Colin Mackerras takes a skeptical view of the justification:

The real reason why Monkey dramas have been revived is the simplest one: Chinese people love them, no matter what age, sex or political colouring. This has been so for centuries and will quite likely remain so for more. (Mackerras, *Performing* 98)

The Monkey King that Gerald Vizenor creates in his own revival might have leaped right off the Chinese stage. Vizenor even provides an appropriate Buddhist prologue. Griever's first acts in China are acts which liberate sentient beings from bondage—first a caged nightingale and then the chickens. Enjoined not to take the life of any sentient being, a faithful Buddhist gains special merit by saving a sentient being from unnatural death. In a story that directly parallels Griever's rescue of the chickens, Heinrich Harrer describes dining with a Tibetan friend in a Lhasa restaurant. One of the day's offerings, a goose, wandered through the dining room while they were eating. Harrer's friend promptly bought the goose, took it home and loosed it in his garden where it lived happily for years (Harrer 74). From the fifth grade, the White Earth trickster-teacher has understood his Boddhisattva role—not that all beings, or even most, are liberated willingly. Fear of liberation is an obstacle that some characters in the novel cannot overcome, even with Griever's help. China Browne, the news reporter from the White Earth Reservation who tracks the missing Griever in China, is trapped in the Wheel of Becoming. She "worries about bad blood, small insects near her ears, and those wild moments when she loses connections with time. She is worried that she could be suspended without a season, severed from the moment; these fears have delivered her to the whims of clowns and the vicarious adventures of tricksters" (21). While Griever flies, China is hobbled, fixated on bound feet. Even the prisoners Griever frees from the execution caravan are, by and large, too afraid to make a break for freedom.

Hester Hua Dan is no less afraid. While Griever is prepared to celebrate the impending birth of their illegitimate child and take Hester flying with him, she is worried about the judgement of society, and her father's judgement in particular. She doesn't want to be seen with Griever, a foreigner, and she doesn't want any part of his escape plan: "'Never fly in airplane,' she told the trickster but held back the real reason: her fear, resignation to paternal power, and her dedication to the nation" (200). Hester is wiping away tears the last time Griever sees her alive. She is ultimately found drowned, along with the tiny bones of five unwanted babies, in the pond behind the teachers' residence. She has been killed by her own dogmatic father—her worst fears realized. The moment Griever discovers his loss, the trickster assumes another dimension of his identity. With a tenderness he has never previously shown, Griever bids Hester a final farewell: "He loosened the blue stone rabbit, washed her hair back, raised her face to the moon, touched the scar, and kissed her bloated cheeks" (225). Griever finally earns the name his mother has given him, a name that recalls his father, a Gypsy in the Universal Hocus Caravan who taught his lover about "griever time" and "griever meditation," which she practiced faithfully three times a week. Until Hester's death her eldest son had owed "his name to this compulsive practice, but not much more" (50).

True to its opera conventions, from the beginning the novel seems to leave no doubt about Griever's character. The retired opera warrior clown Wu Chou identifies him early on as both "a mind monkey" and "a natural clown" (21, 25). This is a bit of carefully contrived multicultural trickery: Vizenor builds his novel not only by playing on the Western conception of the clown, the closest American analog to the tribal trickster, but also on a thorough understanding of the stock character types in traditional Chinese opera—the leading man, or *sheng;* the woman (*tan* or *dan*); the painted face character (*ch'in* or *ching*), a rough, strong man; the comedian, or *chou;* and the limited number of permutations of each (Mackerras, *Chinese* 15; Zung 37-38). All four character types include a warrior permutation, which requires actors with a high degree of acrobatic as well as vocal skill.[3]

From Vizenor's clues we might expect the Monkey King with his painted face and acrobatic antics to be a *chou.* Another guess, given the actual list of types, would be a "painted face." In fact, the traditional Chinese opera Monkey is neither. He is a *wu-sheng,* the military type of the leading man (Mackerras, *Chinese* pl. 28). Griever, however, a thoroughgoing trickster, is not about to be typecast. Vizenor gives him all three male roles. Like his Western counterpart, the *chou* is often stupid or ribald and frequently improvises. According to Mackerras, "spontaneous or local jokes are very much a part of his technique" (Mackerras, *Chinese* 25). This role is a natural for Griever. When one of the American teachers demands, "Do you have toilet paper in this country?" Griever mocks the pat Chinese answer to all unanswerable questions: "Well, our leaders will report on that soon" (95). The exchange is all the more biting because it comes in the middle of Griever's first love scene with translator Hester Hua Dan, and this would ordinarily have been her line. When Griever and Hester later begin a conversation about pets as they watch Griever's rooster on the beach, Hester comments that the Chinese have no pets. Griever responds, "Chinese eat their pets." Asked if there are many pets in America, Griever assures her, in an equally biting tone, "Even pet cemeteries . . . headstones and cameos, mongrels with precious middle names, burial services, and real flowers, believe me" (103). Even the satire crosses cultures.

Behind the scenes, the *chou* traditionally had another and very different role. According to Yang Mou-chien, he was charged with offering the sacrificial incense to Lao-lang shen, the patron god of actors (Mackerras, *Chinese* 76). Religious life was an extremely important aspect of ensemble performance. The sacrifice to Lao-lang shen might with some justification be compared with traditional Chinese clan sacrifices. By virtue of their profession, Chinese actors were virtually cut off from normal family life. Much like Western actors of previous centuries, they lived on the margins of society, associated with drugs, prostitution, and homosexuality. The acting troop was, effectively, the only family they knew (Mackerras, *Chinese* 78-79).

Wu Chou, who is repeatedly described in terms of the warrior clown's traditional emblematic butterfly, apparently took his roles very seriously (Zung 38). "When he was too old to tumble as an acrobat," we learn, "he studied the stories of tricksters and shamans in several countries around the world" (23). Wu Chou formally initiates Griever into the mysteries of the Monkey King, thereby providing Griever with a Chinese identity for his Chinese identity card. The old clown bears a suspicious resemblance to the elders responsible for the conduct of Native American tribal rituals and the religious training of younger men. Wu Chou ritualistically paints Griever's face, garbs him in one version of the traditional Monkey costume (a yellow opera coat and biretta with two blue tassels), and cautions Griever on the language and behavior appropriate to the Immortal Monkey. Griever now shows the world his true character. The lines which define the simian face form a heart, which, ironically, carries both of its Western symbolic meanings, eros and agape.

Face paint, or more typically "war paint," has been so closely associated with American Indians as to be a cliché. It is just one more irony functioning in the novel that ties traditional Chinese opera and traditional Native American culture together. In both cases, make-up color and design convey meaning: a man's character can be read in his face. The Monkey King's face paint is predominantly red with black and white accents. In China, red is traditionally the color of loyalty and uprightness. Black conveys simplicity and straightforwardness. White here functions as an accent, but a predominance of white in the face of a male character signifies a wicked and vicious man (Zung 41). When Scaticook storyteller Truman Coggswell appeared wearing traditional Native American red and white face paint, he was asked about its importance to his culture. The Scaticook tribe is linguistically related to the Chippewa and shares a common origin history. Coggswell responded that face paint carries a twofold meaning. First, it ties a man to his clan, in his case the Turtle Clan. Second, it speaks "the truth of the heart" of the person who wears it (Coggswell).

Scroll in holster, Griever, the scholar-lover, also takes the role of the *sheng,* Western-style. Having heard the dawn broadcast of "The East Is Red" one too many mornings, Griever determines to change the tune. He singlehandedly liberates China by substituting the traditional American military favorites "The Stars and Stripes Forever" and "Semper Fidelis." In the end, Griever wins the blond, the woman of his dreams with her own scroll. They fly off into the sunrise together, but not before Griever finally assumes the traditional "painted face" role of the "black face" (Zung 38). It is his disguise for the Marxmass Carnival. Blackface, of course, has a significant place in American theatrical traditions, and its comic and racist associations function importantly in the carnival scene, which foregrounds racism Chinese-style. Griever has invited both the African students and the Algerian watchmakers, who are always excluded from social events where Chinese women are present. Griever's blackface disguise simultaneously honors "the truth of the heart" of the Chinese mixedblood artist-turned-coal-hauler Lindbergh Wang, who has openly challenged the authorities on both their politics and their aesthetics. Chinese blackface is the ultimate disguise for the trickster suddenly turned honest and straightforward.

So insistent is Griever on delivering moon cakes and liberation to Wang in his prison cell that Wu Chou is forced to tell the authorities a trickster version of *The Havoc of Heaven* to save the White Earth trickster-teacher from himself. While Kangmei laughs up her sleeve, Wu Chou returns Monkey's punishment for stealing the magic peaches to its origin in Chinese story. Griever, according to Wu Chou, has been playing the part of the scholar-lover Wu Gang, sentenced for some misdemeanor to labor until he can earn his freedom by chopping down the sacred, self-healing cassia tree—effectively for eternity. In *The Journey to the West,* the ostensible source of the opera plot, Monkey is actually imprisoned under Five Phases Mountain for his theft of the magic peaches, but such a punishment could not practically be staged. During the rehearsal, Wu Chou reports, there was an accident: the eminent foreign actor-teacher hit a brick pile instead of the tree and was buried by fallen bricks until Lindbergh Wang freed him. This trickster story-before-the-story suggests what could happen if Griever isn't careful: Wang's cell, we will learn, is a carefully constructed pile of loose bricks with his "obscene" drawings on the unseen side. Himself a master of trickster liberation, Wang needs no help from an overzealous Griever, who could so easily destroy the freedom Wang has built. Yet another story-before-the-story can be read in Griever's blackened face. Among the traditional *anishinaabeg,* blackface would, among other things, signify mourning (Vecsey 66). Griever will soon enough learn of the death of his lover and their unborn child.

Throughout the novel, Griever acts his roles in the best operatic tradition. The Chinese acting style is based on highly symbolic gestures and movements calculated for their aesthetic effect. No gesture, no movement lacks significance. In *Secrets of the Chinese Drama,* Cecelia S. L. Zung includes chapters on sleeve movements, hand movements, arm movements, foot movements, leg movements, waist movements, pheasant feather movements, and symbolic actions. Griever can be recognized by three characteristic gestures: pinching his ear, pulling out one of the hairs on his temple, and folding his ear. Pinching the ear lobe is a well-known French gesture meaning "crazy," totally appropriate to a trickster monkey. No indicator of frustration here, "pulling out his hair" ties Griever directly to his predecessor in *The Journey to the West.* In one of the seventy-two shamanic transformations he learned from Master Subhodi, the Great Sage could create multiple clones by pulling out one of his hairs and ordering, "Change!" Monkey uses this trick, known as *The Body Beyond the Body,* on several occasions. The Great Sage also attaches special significance to his ear. This is where he keeps his weapon of choice, reduced to the size of an embroidery needle, but he is ready to do battle with the single word *change.* As with many of the esoteric facts in this novel, Vizenor provides a key to their origin. In

Griever, as in the original, these gestures clearly signal body/mind transformation (129).

While it is possible to identify most of the novel's Chinese characters by their stock opera roles, Shitou, the stone shaman, is essentially an *anishinaabe* character. Griever himself acknowledges the connection. As Shitou breaks stones with his bare hands, Griever watches, "proud to be a mixedblood trickster and related to the stone in his own tribal origin stories" (72-73). The stone, missing from the Beaulieu version of the origin stories, is, in fact, *naanabozho*'s brother, one of the three sons born of the meeting between *naanabozho*'s mother and her *manidoo* lover. *Naanabozho* ultimately kills the other two. Stone assists him in the process by teaching him that stones will crack with alternate applications of cold and heat (Barnouw 15-17). Shitou not only offers Griever instruction in stonebreaking, it is he who finds Hester's body and tells Griever of her death.

Egas Zhang, Hester Hua Dan, Hua Lian, and Kangmei are all readily identifiable as stock types from the Chinese opera. Zhang, the director of the foreign affairs bureau and Hester's father, is a *ching,* the type of the crafty and evil minister (Mackerras, *Chinese* 25). Vizenor warns us to expect Zhang's calculated, mind-numbing villainy: he has been named for the father of the lobotomy. Zhang's unfilial daughter Hester is a loose woman in both English and Chinese, a *hua dan* indeed. Hua Lian, whose names means "painted face," would under normal circumstances be classified as a *ching.* To Chinese audiences she would immediately be recognized as a supernatural being by her make-up and duster, "a highly-esteemed object," carried only by gods, goddesses, spirits, nuns, or monks (Zung 23 note). The gold and silver make-up Hua Lian uses to highlight her eyes is used primarily by gods and fairies (Zung 41). Like Buddha's, her brows are "luminous" (115). Because she is a woman rather than a man, however, Hua Lian falls into a special category, perhaps "Vizenor-Trickster *ching.*"

Kangmei, the daughter of Egas Zhang's wife and the Oklahoma-born Sinophile Battle Wilson, is a *ch'ing-i,* the most typical *tan.* Unlike Hester, she is a dutiful daughter to her father. She modestly hides not only her eyes but her entire face as she travels through the novel in her emblematic prairie schooner. She successfully, if accidentally, resists Griever's sexual advances (176-77). Kangmei is a character ultimately true to her name: *strong/beautiful* (Chong). But as with many mixedbloods, Kangmei's story is not a simple one. In the Buddhist version, she will play the horse of the will to Griever's monkey of the mind. Kangmei's Chinese origins can be traced directly to the Taoist pantheon, where the Patroness of Silkworms is also known as the Horse-Head Lady. Kangmei, known as "the moth walker," raises silk worms on Obo

Island. She protectively carries the "moth seeds" with her "in small bundles under her arms" (165).

In a popular Chinese legend, a daughter is promised to anyone who can rescue her kidnapped father. When the family's horse wins her hand, however, his claim is vigorously denied. When he insists on the marriage, the horse is killed and his hide hung out to dry. The young woman walks past it one day, and the hide envelops her and carries her off to heaven. After ten-days' search the hide is found under a mulberry tree; the girl has been turned into a silkworm. Her parents grieve until the day they see a vision of their daughter, who tells them that she is now a Princess in Heaven (Bredon and Mitrophanow 66 note). In traditional iconography the Horse-Head Lady is represented with a horse's hide thrown over her head and shoulders. Instead of a horse's hide, Kangmei wears a silk burnoose over her blond hair. With Griever, the horse opera hero, she will indeed ascend into the heavens.

The Horse-Head Lady's story is not the only traditional Chinese story Vizenor weaves into the fabric of the novel. The motif of the scar, which not only identifies the elusive Hester for Griever but connects her with his earliest memories of adult (and illicit) sexuality, is well known from a Tang dynasty legend. In this story a young traveler meets a sage along the road and inquires about the book he is reading. It happens to be the record of marriage fates for everyone on earth. When the young man asks about his own, he is told that he will marry the daughter of a vegetable seller standing nearby. Unsatisfied with her lower-class status, the young man hires a killer, but the killer succeeds only in scratching her over the eyebrow. Fourteen years later, when the young traveler marries a girl from another province, the bridal veil is raised to reveal the scar. Inquiries prove the bride to be, in fact, the vegetable seller's daughter (Bredon and Mitrophanow 414-15). Ironically, the scar motif is also the key to identifying Trickster in an *anishinaabe* story of *naanabozho*'s incest with his daughters. *Naanabozho* fabricates his own death, having warned his daughters in such an event to marry the first man who comes along rather than risk starvation. They do just what he has told them, marrying none other than *naanabozho* himself, who is recognized ultimately by the scar on his forehead (Barnouw 86-87).

Such motifs function effectively in the novel, whether or not we understand their multicultural associations. When Vizenor tells us that he is retelling an old story, however, it is useful to look for a trickster transformation. To honor Hester Hua Dan and the five dead children, at the end of the Marxmass Carnival, Hua Lian tells the story of a hungry shaman bear who accepts offerings of food from otter and raven. Rabbit has no offerings to give the bear and so offers himself, leaping into the fire and earning the bear's praise. In commemoration of the sacrifice, the rabbit is transformed into the moon, henceforth known as Jade Rabbit. This story, rewritten to incorporate the most powerful Native American Indian healing spirit, originated as a Buddhist parable with Buddha in the role of the shaman bear. Throughout the Buddhist world the moon is known as the "Hare-Marked."

The Taoists made the popular story their own with the creation of Jade Rabbit, who lives in the moon pounding the Pill of Immortality, otherwise known as the Elixir of Jade (Bredon and Mitrophanow 406-09). Jade Rabbit, as Hua Lian notes, has a companion similar to Griever. In the traditional story, her companion is the scholar condemned for some misdemeanor to spend eternity trying to chop down the sacred, self-healing cassia tree to gain his freedom (Bredon and Mitrophanow 410). This is the very role Wu Chou cast Griever in during their meeting with Lindbergh Wang's prison guards. Hester can be identified as Jade Rabbit by the lapis lazuli (read "blue jade") rabbit she wears as a pendant, an emblem that connects her with both death and the moon. The blue color highlights the rabbit's sacred character, for according to Chinese tradition blue is the color of heaven (Bredon and Mitrophanow 55). In *anishinaabe* tradition, blue is the color of the land of death, the south (Coleman, Frogner, and Eich 61).

Hester can also be identified with another inhabitant of the moon, the Moon Lady, protagonist of the most popular of all traditional Chinese stories (Hu). In a version of the story retold by Amy Tan in *The Moon Lady,* she, like the Monkey King of the Chinese opera, succumbs to the temptation of immortal peaches. The Moon Lady steals a bite of the peach of immortality bestowed on her husband by the Queen Mother of the Western Skies. As punishment, she and her husband must live separately, he on the sun and she on the moon, but they are permitted to meet one night each year. It is no accident that Griever seductively invites Hester to the beach pavilion, telling her, "The peach emperor created this place for the night" (104). Vizenor is simply translating Hester's temptation into plain English as he links trickster lust with spiritual quest: *peach* is one of many Taoist names for the female sexual organ. The Taoist quest for immortality, "from the humblest effort right up to the peaks of spiritual achievement, is based upon manipulating sexual energy." The prototype of the successful Taoist male practitioner is the star god of longevity Shou-lao, always depicted with a peach in his hand. The crane, the traditional Chinese symbol of longevity, is often shown inside the peach (Rawson and Legeza 24-25).

The night Hester dies, the night of Griever's Marxmass Carnival and the autumn moon festival, is the very night when the traditional Chinese opera season closed. This is Griever's cue to exit, but in typical trickster fashion, the novel seems to resist closure, leaving Kangmei and Griever in-flight. The four-part novel is not as open-ended as it seems, however. Louis Owens notes that the number four is "especially power-ful in Indian tradition. For Native Americans a four-part structure, paral-leling the seasonal cycles, suggests completeness and wholeness as well as closure" (Owens 243). *Griever* begins with the summer solstice and ends with the harvest moon festival. Each section of the novel bears the name of one of the two-week "joints" of the traditional Chinese lunar calendar, and Vizenor carefully develops a theme appropriate to the time. *Xiazhi*/Summer Solstice spans late June/early July. It is known in China as the time of the garlic harvest. According to Bredon and Mitrophanow, "There is even a popular proverb which says: 'At *Hsia Chih,* dig up the garlic'" (Bredon and Mitrophanow 21). The proverb takes on new life at the street market where, after Griever frees the chickens, one of the peas-ants shouts that he should next "free the garlic" (53).

Dashu/Great Heat falls in late July/early August, vacation time, when the American teachers find themselves unexpectedly at the beach. Here Griever, in great heat indeed, consummates his affair with Hester. *Bailu*/White Dew falls during the middle two weeks of September, time to get back to work with renewed energy. The trickster-teacher, now thoroughly recognizable as the Monkey King, undertakes his most daring feat, the liberation of the prisoners in the execution caravan. *Quifen*/Autumn Equinox spans the end of September and early October, ending with the harvest moon festival, one of the most joyous of tradi-tional Chinese celebrations (Bredon and Mitrophanow 19-22). Vizenor, characteristically, celebrates it with a trickster reversal, making the cele-bration a time of deep sorrow.

It should be noted that the novel's time frame is an exact reversal of the winter period when traditional stories are allowed to be told in Native American Indian communities, and Vizenor astutely uses the time frame to underscore his trickster liberation theme. The summer solstice festival and the autumn moon festival both celebrate historical Chinese political protests and are the only traditional holidays to do so. The former commemorates an upright government minister of the fourth cen-tury B.C. whose prince would not implement the reforms he so earnestly urged. Ch'u Yuan chose a culturally accepted suicide by drowning as his form of moral protest. A grateful populace made offerings to his spirit, and the summer solstice festival grew up around their efforts to thwart the greedy water monster who tried to steal them (Bredon and Mitro-phanow 301-03). The moon cakes traditional to the autumn moon festi-val had their origin in the fourteenth century when they became the means for conveying secret messages to the Chinese patriots fighting Mongol oppression. The Mongols had gone so far as to billet one of their men in every household. The moon cake messages led to the successful overthrow of the Mongol dynasty (Bredon and Mitrophanow 399-400). Moon cakes are still sent from neighbor to neighbor and from friend to friend, just as Griever takes them to share with the imprisoned artist/ coal hauler Lindbergh Wang.

In Vizenor's re-membering of Chinese culture, these cyclical holidays underscore the importance of another meeting of East and West after a long hiatus. Griever gives his pet cock, emblem, and alarm clock, the name Matteo Ricci. Ricci, a Jesuit missionary who landed in Macao in 1582 and remained in China until his death in 1610, established the first successful mission to China since the time of Kubla Khan. Thoroughly versed in Chinese language and civilization, Ricci used Western technical achievements to gain the respect of the Chinese bureaucrats for his own culture and religion. It was he who brought the first clock, the Western Wheel of Becoming, and the first map of the world to China. (Ironically, missionaries were almost always the point of first contact between European culture with its linear conception of time and Native American Indian tribes, who like the Chinese, conceived of time cyclically.) In Buddhist iconography, the cock of desire is one of the "Three Poisons" at the hub of the Wheel of Becoming. Associated with sexuality in both Eastern and Western cultures, Griever's emblem thus provides a clear link with life and death, time and history.

Griever has come to China with exactly the opposite mission from Ricci's. Like his mythic trickster predecessors—and the Buddha— Griever seeks to liberate culture from what Louis Owens calls "spatial and temporal repressions" (Owens 241). As Wu Chou tells China Browne, Griever hated clocks and "carried a holster to shoot time" (26). His singular weapon is the imagination—his scroll of "pictures from wild histories," the histories Griever envisions and projects. As he himself says, "imagination is the real world, all the rest is bad television" (28). When the butcher kills chickens, Griever resurrects them on paper and, more than that, sets them free: "he holds cold reason on a lunge line while he imagines the world. With colored pens he thinks backward, stops time like a shaman, and reverses intersections, interior landscapes" (34). Griever, like Vizenor, re-members. Griever's mistake, and it may be a fatal one, supplies the ultimate trickster ending. He stops to ask for directions, bringing orthodox reality to bear on imaginative flight.

Notes

1. Subsequent references to *Griever: An American Monkey King in China* will be indicated by page number only.
2. Subsequent references to *Journey to the West* will be indicated by page number only.
3. In *The Chinese Theatre in Modern Times,* Colin Mackerras elaborates on these four basic character types, noting first of all, that there are civilian (*wen*) and military (*wu*) types of each character, including the *tan.* In addition to the *wu-sheng,* the principal male characters include the *lao-sheng,* a bearded old man always played by a baritone, who might be a court official or a general, and the *hsiao-sheng,* a younger scholar and lover with a tenor falsetto vocal range. The main civilian *tan* is the *ch'ing-i,* a faithful wife or lover or a virtuous daughter. The "faster" woman is the *hua-tan.* There are a wide range of *ching,* or painted face characters, known for the volume of their singing. These include warriors, judges, and statesmen who are brave, upright, and loyal, as well as bandits, crafty and evil government ministers, and gods. The *ch'ou,* or clown, is often stupid or ribald but can also be an evil character (24-25).

Works Cited

Ballinger, Franchot. "*Ambigere:* The Euro-American Picaro and the Native AmericanTrickster." *MELUS* 17.1 (1991-92): 21-38.

——. "Sacred Reversals: Trickster in Gerald Vizenor's *Earthdivers: Tribal Narratives on Mixed Descent.*" *American Indian Quarterly* 9.1 (Winter 1985): 55-59.

Barnouw, Victor. *Wisconsin Chippewa Myths and Tales.* Madison: U of Wisconsin P, 1977.

Bredon, Juliet, and Igor Mitrophanow. *The Moon Year.* 1927. New York: Paragon, 1966.

Chong, She-Kong. Telephone communication with the author. 22 April 1994.

Coggswell, Truman. African American and Native American Storytelling. Duff's Reading Series. St. Louis. 21 March 1994.

Coleman, Sr. Bernard, Ellen Frogner, and Estelle Eich. *Ojibwa Myths and Legends.* Minneapolis: Ross and Haines, 1961.

Harrer, Heinrich. *Return to Tibet.* Trans. Ewald Ossers. London: Weidenfield and Nicholson, 1984.

Hersey, John. "A Reporter at Large (China—Part I)." *New Yorker* 10 May 1982: 49-79.

Hu, Hua-ling. Telephone communication with the author. 18 October 1994.

The Journey to the West. Vol. 1. Trans. and intro. Anthony C. Yu. 4 vols. Chicago: U of Chicago P, 1977.

Mackerras, Colin. *The Chinese Theatre in Modern Times.* London: Thames and Hudson, 1975.

——. *The Performing Arts in Contemporary China.* London: Routledge and Kegan Paul, 1981.

Owens, Louis. *Other Destinies: Understanding the American Indian Novel.* Norman: U of Oklahoma P, 1992.

Radin, Paul. *The Trickster: A Study in American Indian Mythology.* London: Routledge and Kegan Paul, 1956.

Rawson, Philip, and Laszlo Legeza. *Tao: The Chinese Philosophy of Time and Change.* London: Thames and Hudson, 1973.

Tan, Amy. *The Moon Lady.* New York: Simon and Schuster, 1992.

Vecsey, Christopher. *Traditional Ojibwa Religion and Its Historical Changes.* Philadelphia: American Philosophical Society, 1983.

Velie, Alan R. "The Trickster Novel." *Narrative Chance: Postmodern Discourse on Native American Indian Literatures.* Ed. Gerald Vizenor. 1989. Norman: U of Oklahoma P, 1993. 121-39.

Vizenor, Gerald. *Griever: An American Monkey King in China.* Minneapolis: U of Minnesota P, 1990.

——. *The People Named the Chippewa: Narrative Histories.* Minneapolis: U of Minnesota P, 1984.

——. Personal communication with the author. 29 April 1994.

——. *Summer in the Spring.* Norman: U of Oklahoma P, 1993.

Yu, Anthony C. Introduction. *The Journey to the West.* 4 vols. Chicago: U of Chicago P, 1977. 1-62.

Zung, Cecelia S. L. *Secrets of the Chinese Drama.* 1937. New York: Benjamin Blom, 1964.

8

WHODUNWHAT?
THE CRIME'S THE MYSTERY IN GERALD VIZENOR'S
THE HEIRS OF COLUMBUS

Elizabeth Blair

"Yes, but we never believe anything the government has ever said about the tribes, least of all the information about the heirs and our nation," said Stone.

—The Heirs of Columbus

Vizenor's 1991 novel, *The Heirs of Columbus,* continues his long-standing tradition of refusing to conform to genre conventions.[1] In a recent review, the Columbus scholar Kirkpatrick Sale comments that *Heirs* "is hardly a novel, at least in the standard narrative sense."[2] Other critics would appear to agree, labeling the book variously as satire, science fiction, fantasy, and even a "mythopoeic space-age chronicle."[3] In addition to all of these labels, one little-noted possibility arises: the book mimics and mocks the conventions of the murder mystery. The act of appropriating and overturning the conventions of the crime story allows Vizenor to reinterpret five centuries of "New World" history to startling comic and satiric effect. The crime story proves to be an apt trope for the history of contact between European colonizers and aboriginal Americans.

Published in 1991, *The Heirs of Columbus* is Vizenor's response to the anticipated 1992 quincentenary celebrations of Christopher Columbus's "discovery" of America. Not content with a mere critique of the concept of discovery, Vizenor expropriates the practice itself. Through his crossblood protagonist, Stone Columbus, Vizenor (or Vizenor's text) becomes the "discoverer" *par excellence,* and *what* he discovers is nothing short of revolutionary: Christopher Columbus is an Italian-Sephardic-Jew-Mayan mixedblood! The controlling metaphor of Columbus as mixedblood not only serves to reinforce the hybrid nature of the text but also comments on the dubiousness of what the white world calls "history." This revisionist version of American history is fully as plausible as the standard history-book version that claims Columbus "discovered" a "New World." *Heirs* refuses to validate the invented Indian "discovered" by Christopher Columbus. Instead it offers a contradictory, tongue-in-cheek interpretation of the man who named the tribes "Indian."

The Heirs of Columbus blends elements of the Native American trickster tale with the tenets of the postmodern detective story. In past books, Vizenor's oppositional stance with respect to the mimetic tradition has placed him squarely in the postmodern camp. In *Heirs*, Vizenor continues to blend oral myth with post-structural narrative, while utilizing the conventions of the postmodern detective story. According to David Lehman, these conventions consist of sham appearances, fallible sleuths, comic upsets, shifting identities, multiple outcomes and disruptions and subversions of the plot.[4] Says Lehman, "When the world refuses to behave in compliance with the expectations of a rationalist, you get the postmodern detective tale."[5]

When a trickster is set loose in a detective story, the result is the carefully calculated and arranged "chaos" that is typical of both trickster texts and postmodern crime stories. While the Native American trickster shares some qualities of the conventional detective hero (typically, both are outsiders and both are easily led astray by a consuming interest in sex), their differences are manifest. The prototypical detective represents rationality and order, while the trickster and the postmodern sleuth represent irrationality and disorder. The signature of the detective is "reason," while the signature of Vizenor's trickster-sleuth is chaos and chance.[6]

In *Heirs of Columbus*, chaos is the order of the day. Plots proliferate. Vizenor evokes the Santa Maria bingo barge only to sink it almost as soon as it appears, then picks up a second narrative thread in a posh club in New York City, where events precipitate a court hearing in which tribal imagination triumphs over judicial ratiocination. Next, the scene shifts to a new "crime" across the sea and, finally, the narrative returns to a utopian re-enactment of "discovery" in which the tribal heirs discover/invade Point Assinika exactly 500 years after the arrival of Columbus. Along the way, "crimes" accumulate on both sides of the cultural divide, and, to further complicate matters, the classic murder mystery triangle is thrown out the window. Instead, *Heirs* posits multiple possibilities for the roles of sleuth, criminal, and victim.

While the typical "whodunit" offers a solitary detective who possesses highly developed powers of reasoning, *Heirs* offers multiple candidates for the role, none of whom measures up to the classic sleuth. The first candidate, Felipa Flowers, is a fashion model turned criminal lawyer, who wakes up one day and realizes she would rather "poach" than represent the law in San Francisco, California. Now she liberates cultural artifacts and shamanic stories from museums and "colonial dioramas." True to the dictates of the postmodern detective story, Felipa's investigative style more closely resembles that of Inspector Clouseau than that of Hercule Poirot. Like Clouseau (and like Trickster) she has refined self-sabotage to a high art. To her peril, she fails to note the myriad clues such as dreams and augury that point to her demise. As a consequence, she dies halfway through the book. She is replaced by additional detective figures, including police inspector Captain Treves Brink, tribal detective Chaine Riel Doumet, and Lappet Tulip Browne, an imaginative detective resurrected from Vizenor's 1988 novel, *The Trickster of Liberty.* The three tribal detectives, Felipa Flowers, Chaine Riel Doumet and Lappet Tulip Browne, all favor intuition and narration over detection and ratiocination.

In *Trickster,* Tulip explains her unusual investigative practices to a prospective client:

First, my report will be in the oral tradition and told to you, no one else, in less than a week . . . I will describe several scenes and imagined events as stories, but the interpretation and resolution of the information will be yours, not mine . . . You must agree to these conditions. (72)

Tulip offers stories rather than clues, words rather than material evidence. Her mission as detective is to bring about harmony and balance rather than to support institutions and return lost goods. In fact, *Heirs* is out to demonstrate that institutions often justify or legitimize crimes and return goods to those who never owned them in the first place.

Because *Heirs* poses multiple possibilities for the roles of criminal, victim, and sleuth, it should be no surprise that Flowers plays all three— detective, suspect, and murder victim. But Felipa's murder proves to be a red herring, a diversionary tactic. Solved offstage and presented to the reader as a *fait accompli,* it signals that the real crime, the real mystery, lies elsewhere. The task of the armchair detective thus becomes not to discover *who* done it, but to sort out who done *what,* then to decide which act is the *real* crime. Locating the crime of crimes in this chronicle of crimes proves to be no simple task. Possible crimes include: the tax violations of Stone Columbus's high stakes bingo caravel; the theft of stones from the tavern on the mount; the conquistadors' burning of the tribal bear codex; the theft of New World gold; Spain's banishment of the Sephardic Jews; Columbus's enslavement of the Indians; his theft of New World names; Henry Rowe Schoolcraft's theft of the medicine pouches; their repatriation or theft back by the mixedblood shaman, Transom; Felipa Flowers's repatriation of tribal medicine pouches, ceremonial feathers, and bones; the theft of the remains of Columbus and Pocahontas. And the "crimes" go on, *ad infinitum,* in this trickster-thriller where the good guys are the healers and the bad guys are the stealers—except that things are never that simple in either the trickster or the postmodern text. Vizenor himself steals-and-heals the perpetrator of the crime of crimes; he co-opts the man who stole America by reimagining him as a Mayan mixedblood, who carries the strains of both healers and stealers.

According to Barbara T. Rader and Howard G. Zettler, the function of the typical detective story is to examine "how society defines, deals with and internalizes what is conventionally viewed as crime."[7] But Vizenor has little interest in the conventional crimes that his narrative decenters, destabilizes and deconstructs. After much bigger game, his goal is nothing less than to redefine "crime" itself in tribal terms.

In previous works, Vizenor has expressed intense interest in the numerous legal battles that face contemporary tribal people, including treaty rights, water rights, and thefts by museums. *Crossbloods: Bone Courts, Bingo, and Other Reports* (1990) and *Wordarrows: Indians and Whites in the New Fur Trade* (1978) concentrate on many of the concerns that animate *The Heirs of Columbus.* In these and other books, Vizenor writes eloquently about victims of the criminal justice system, such as Dane Michael White, a young Sioux boy who hung himself while awaiting a custody decision, and Thomas White Hawk, whose "Indianness" was socialized out of him, to tragic effect.[8]

In the satiric sketch "Bone Courts: The Natural Rights of Tribal Bones," Vizenor argues that stones, trees, birds, water, bears, and bones are the repositories of tribal narrative and thus should be granted the right to confront their oppressors in court.[9] In *Heirs,* Flowers presents a similar proposition. When she meets with Doric Michéd to discuss the recovery of Ojibway ceremonial items, she tells him:

The medicine pouches are tribal stories, not capital assets . . . What would the old shamans say if they knew their stories were offered for sale by an explorer in New York? (46-47)

A descendant of Schoolcraft and the sole mixedblood member of the Brotherhood of American Explorers, Doric Michéd resists Flowers's stories. Instead, he puts his faith in the Brotherhood's motto: "Explore new worlds, discover with impunities, represent with manners, but never retreat from the ownership of land and language" (50). Flowers and Michéd bump heads as they quibble over terms:

"Schoolcraft stole the medicine pouches," shouted Felipa.
"The shamans pitched their pouches into the lake," said Doric . . .
"*Stolen* is the right word," whispered Felipa.
"*Discover* is more accurate," said Doric. (50)

After her tribal operative, Transom, succeeds in stealing back the medicine pouches, Flowers does a similar semantic dance with police investigator Captain Treves Brink. Questioned about the pouches, Felipa responds, "Nothing was stolen." Brink quips, "You even stole the crime," and she retorts: "True, but the liberation of our stories is no crime" (60).

Since the crime has been "stolen," there is no material evidence, no charges can be filed, and no trial can be held. Instead, Federal Judge Beatrice Lord orders a hearing "to discover what a crime means in this particular case" (66). A bit of a trickster herself, Judge Lord charges spectators for a seat in her courtroom and upsets usual courtroom practice by stacking the judicial deck in favor of tribal consciousness; she announces that imagination will take precedence over material evidence. The hilarious proceedings that result include videotapes of the stolen crime, magic socks, electronic moccasins, laser shrouds, testimony by a shapeshifting panther, crows flying out of boxes, and laser holograms into which the judge enters to initiate sex with a bear.

Brink, the first witness in this cock-eyed, chaotic court, states: "Your honor, the real crime here is that the reported crime was stolen, and we would have indicted with even minimal evidence, but the bones seem to have walked out on their own" (67). But the judge insists that further testimony is necessary to determine "how to treat the repatriation of tribal stores . . . as a crime" (69). Open-minded and imaginative, Judge Lord adopts the terminology of the heirs and is willing to consider ideas like repatriation and the right of bones in court because this approach would favor "tribal consciousness" (65).

The next witness is Chaine Riel Doumet, a military intelligence agent turned tribal investigator. Asked to explain the cultural distinction between imagination and possession or stories and material ownership, Doumet testifies: "Your honor, some tribal people would say that the real world exists and is remembered nowhere else but in stories" (75). When asked how ownership is determined, Doumet explains that the tribal sense of possession is spiritual and that nothing can be owned or sold. Straining to understand, the judge remarks: "Stories, then, are at the core of tribal realities, not original sin, for instance, or service missions" (80).

"Stories and imagination, your honor, but of a certain condition that prescinds discoveries and translations," responds the next witness,

Lappet Tulip Browne (80). Now Judge Lord begins to take issue with this view: "Tribal stories and their traces, it seems to me, are not much more than hearsay . . . the legal contentions would be vagarious . . . capricious, erratic, unreasonable" (81). Lappet counters by contending that one achieves spiritual balance through imagination, myth, ritual, and story, not through the appropriation of land and language. Defending the right of tribal stories to their day in court, she testifies: "Tracks are traces, words are traces, and stories hold the wild traces of the told and heard, the sounds of imagination and creation" (81). In other words, stories are evidence.

In *The Trickster of Liberty,* Ginseng Browne takes essentially the same stand. On trial for theft, Ginseng tells the federal judge: "The problem's pure white . . . whites stole the hardwoods, our ginseng, and they even stole our stories" (151). When this judge also retorts that stories are hearsay evidence, Ginseng responds: "If you don't believe what tribal people say in my stories, then I don't believe what whites have said in those stories printed in your law books" (145-46). To steal one's stories, one's traditions, is to deny a people its history, Vizenor suggests.

While *Heirs of Columbus* is Vizenor's first novel to fully exploit the crime story trope, detective figures play cameo roles in previous works. The protagonist of "The Sociodowser," is described as everything but a detective.[10] "Father Bearald One became better known on urban reservations as a map dowser, a tribal sensitive, a shaman dowser, a water and spirit witch, and a healer and medicine man," Vizenor writes (150). Nonetheless he "finds people, solves crimes, calls animals, and he even does strange things in court, man, he can cause people to think they are really innocent" (143). Hired to locate impounded tribal vans, Father Bearald One uses "visions and intuitive memories" to track them down rather than the powers of ratiocination. When ne'er-do-well members of the Prospect Park American Indian Center cook up a scheme to "enter the fur trade by force" using the repatriated vans, Father Bearald One exercises his transformative powers to stop the theft. By mentally concentrating on the crime, he is able to alter the outcome "from potential violence to satire" (156). The real mission of this trickster detective is to "outwit evil and balance the universe," not to support institutions and return lost goods (159). In an example of this balancing act, Father Bearald One influences the outcome of tribal bingo games through mental telepathy, concentrating on people "whose needs he could feel" and who were "responsible for the care of others" (155).

While Lappet Tulip Browne, Felipa Flowers, and Father Bearald One practice an imaginative detection designed to serve their tribal communities, other Vizenor protagonists mock such activities altogether. In the sketch "Four Skin Documents," intelligence gathering serves as a screen for sacred and mythic connections that will never be revealed to the white establishment.[11] As graduate student, novelist, and informer for an intelligence firm, Vizenor protagonist Cedarbird uses three computer programs to write his stories. One converts the material into information for the "metaphrase editor at the intelligence firm," one creates commercial stories, and one is a secret code that cannot be understood by either the commercial editor or the intelligence firm editor (*Landfill Meditation* 163).

Vizenor's "metaphrase editor" is a strange kind of intelligence officer. Like many white readers of Indian literature, she demands myth rather than fact from her Indian informant and is most pleased when Cedarbird celebrates Mother Earth and tells stories about "mythic racial divisions" (167). Given this, it is not surprising that her favorite character is Touch Tone, an "urban skin" who shoots other Indians with a red plastic water pistol (167). Author Cedarbird is more than willing to give the intelligence firm the invented Indian they seek, so long as he can maintain his secret and sacred third code. This code he keeps locked in his computer, where, presumably, it is safe from the social scientists who seek to steal the sacred history of the tribes by appropriating their oral stories. Cedarbird's guise as intelligence-author is one more "secular reversal from the sacred" designed to prevent translation by the white establishment.[12]

The character of Chaine Riel Doumet in *Heirs,* like Cedarbird of *Landfill Meditation,* serves three masters. He produces "simulations of political evidence," "consumer notices," and "observations in a personal third narrative" (161). These he delivers to the central intelligence agency, the tribal president, and the heirs of Columbus, whom he favors for "reasons of cultural identity" (166). His clear bias toward the heirs shows in the description of Stone that he presents to his opponent, the tribal president:

His point is to make the world tribal, a universal identity, and return to other values as measures of human worth, such as the dedication to heal rather than steal tribal cultures. (162)

In fact, institutional intelligence is responsible for much of what happens in this novel. We learn that the murder of Felipa Flowers was effected through the joint cooperation of the Brotherhood of American Explorers and the intelligence agents, who supplied the lethal venom used by Doric Miché d to poison Felipa. Shamed by what he has learned about "the savages of intelligence" (167), who steal tribal culture, murder tribal operatives, and spread disinformation, Doumet ends his career as an operative.

Elsewhere, Vizenor makes a more explicit point about the adversarial relationship between Native Americans and the law, a preoccupation that has taken many forms in his work. In his sketch "Retake on Colonialism," he presents verbatim testimony on Ojibway treaty rights (*Earthdivers* 47-62). The white legal representatives say nothing at great length and answer each direct question with obfuscation and equivocation. In the *Earthdivers* sketch "The Sociodowser," District Court Judge Silas Bandied snaps his teeth and, like Judge Lord, denies the reality of animal spirits and avian visions; when Bandied asks why he is beginning to itch, the prosecutor reports the presence of "bear tics trained to disrupt our system of justice" (145). The judge drops the charges because these tribal ticks turn out to be more convincing (and more irritating) opponents than the wielders of law court logic. Despite their differences, Vizenor's witnesses, tricksters, and tribal detectives all attempt to subvert or undermine the dominant culture, to get under its metaphorical skin and make it itch, just as Vizenor himself does.

For Vizenor, narrative is a better forum in which to revise white history than law courts, which insist on white logic rather than tribal realities. In *Heirs*, Vizenor seeks to counter white history with tribal story, white logic with word play. Stories regenerate the imagination and recover tribal identity; they are both historical and generative because they tell what has been and create what will be. Vizenor's stated task in the trickster text is to remain historical while eluding historicism. In order to do this, he must recreate the New World in stories rather than in law courts.

To reclaim history, to convert *his*tory to *our*story, is a challenge Vizenor takes very seriously in *Heirs of Columbus*. When Admiral Lucky White of Carp Radio asks the British book-collector Pellegrine Treves how Columbus could know he had discovered America, Treves answers: "I should think language is our trick of discovery, what we name is certain to become that name" (169). In *Heirs*, Vizenor demonstrates that two can play the "name" game. He "names" a new world and suggests that tribal people need not take on the white myth of "Indianness" along with the invented name. As Vizenor writes in *Earthdivers*:

We are aliens in our own traditions: the white man has settled with his estranged words right in the middle of our sacred past . . . our vision is to imagine like earthdivers a new world. (107)

It is the aim of *Heirs of Columbus* to resurrect and reinstate that "new" world. In stark contrast to the old "culture of death," the heirs would create "the first nation in the histories of the modern world dedicated to protean humor and the genes that would heal." (119)

For Vizenor, humor and healing are nearly synonymous terms. Paper presenters at a Modern Language Association convention in New York City argued that Vizenor's imaginative version of the Columbus story may serve to deflate myth balloons about the validity of the Euro-American version of history but does little to establish an alternative version of that history—that Vizenor critiques the invented Indian but offers only satire and humor in place of identity—that the playful is not the political. I would assert that the opposite is true. That we laugh because something is true and often painfully so. That humor may establish a less rational but potentially deeper acknowledgment of that truth. That to establish what one is *not* may be a necessary prelude to asserting who and what one *is*. That to joke about the "serious" is to deconstruct the conventional "truths" that deny and distort historical and contemporary tribal realities.

Vizenor's version of the Columbus story is neither static nor definitive, but rather mythic, imaginative, and above all, funny. Humor in Vizenor is both antidote and entertainment. While the Heirs are heartened by the resistance of Metis rebellion leader Louis Riel, who was "seditious to the end for the rights and claims of tribal members" (159), they choose a different route. Avoiding both open rebellion and legal recourse, they establish a New World based on the trickster humor that heals. As Tune Browne puts it in *Trickster of Liberty*, "This is comic, and we are serious" (58).

Vizenor's Columbus text proclaims the generative and regenerative possibility of the word. *Heirs* suggests that language can be an agent of redemption, at once powerful and transformative. To redefine crime and the crime story is to redefine history, an act Vizenor views as necessary in order to re-envision tribal identities.

Notes

1. This paper is an expansion of a review of *The Heirs of Columbus* that was published in the spring 1992 edition of *Wacazo-Sa Review* and a paper delivered at the 1992 Modern Language Association Convention in New York City.

2. Kirkpatrick Sale, review of *The Heirs of Columbus, The Nation*. Sale also comments that Vizenor "understands the wilder, irrational, half-mad parts of the Discoverer's soul as few people ever have" (465).

3. Elizabeth Cook-Lynn, "The Trickster and Mr. Columbus," *Los Angeles Times Book Review* 8 Sept. (1991): 10.

4. David Lehman, *The Perfect Murder* 204.

5. Lehman 203.

6. Gerald Vizenor, *Narrative Chance: Postmodern Discourse on Native American Indian Literatures.* See Vizenor's introduction to this volume, "A Postmodern Introduction," and his essay "Trickster Discourse: Comic Holotropes and Language Games" for his prose articulation of the Native American trickster figure. In his view, the social sciences attempt to control chaos by means of monologues. The trickster, on the other hand, celebrates chaos. Thus the proper signifier for the trickster is "chance."

7. Barbara T. Rader and Howard G. Zettler, eds., *The Sleuth and the Scholar: Origins, Evolution, and Current Trends in Detective Fiction* xi.

8. For an account of Dane Michael White, see "Sand Creek Survivors" (33-46) in *Earthdivers: Tribal Narratives on Mixed Descent.* For accounts of Thomas White Hawk, see "Prosecutors and the Prairie Fun Dancers" (149-64) in *Wordarrows* and "Capital Punishment" (100-55) in *Crossbloods.*

9. *Crossbloods* 62-82.

10. Gerald Vizenor, *Earthdivers: Tribal Narratives on Mixed Descent* 141-60.

11. Gerald Vizenor, *Landfill Meditation: Crossblood Stories* 162-79.

12. See "Rubie Blue Welcome" in *Earthdivers* 107. Cedarbird also narrates this sketch.

Works Cited

Blair, Elizabeth. Review of *Heirs of Columbus. Wicazo-Sa Review.* Spring 1992.

Cook-Lynn, Elizabeth. "The Trickster and Mr. Columbus." *Los Angeles Times Book Review* 8 Sept. (1991): 10.

Lehman, David. *The Perfect Murder.* New York: Free P, 1989.

Rader, Barbara T., and Howard G. Zettler, eds. *The Sleuth and the Scholar: Origins, Evolution, and Current Trends in Detective Fiction.* New York: Greenwood P, 1988.

Sale, Kirkpatrick. Review of *The Heirs of Columbus. The Nation* 21 Oct. 1991: 465.

Vizenor, Gerald. *Crossbloods: Bone Courts, Bingo, and Other Reports.* Minneapolis: U of Minnesota P, 1990.

——. *Earthdivers: Tribal Narratives on Mixed Descent.* Minneapolis: U of Minnesota P, 1981.

——. *The Heirs of Columbus.* Hanover: Wesleyan UP, 1991.

——. *Landfill Meditation: Crossblood Stories.* Hanover: Wesleyan UP, 1991.

——. *The Trickster of Liberty.* Minneapolis: U of Minnesota P, 1988.

——. *Wordarrows: Indians and Whites in the New Fur Trade.* Minneapolis: U of Minnesota P, 1978.

Vizenor, Gerald, ed. *Narrative Chance: Postmodern Discourse on Native American Indian Literatures.* Albuquerque: U of New Mexico P, 1989.

9

"STORIES IN THE BLOOD":
RATIO- AND *NATIO-* IN GERALD VIZENOR'S
THE HEIRS OF COLUMBUS

Arnold Krupat

Its publication in 1991 positioning it as a sort of pre-emptive strike against the anticipated excesses of the Columbian quincentenary, Gerald Vizenor's *The Heirs of Columbus* seemed most immediately to present itself as a Native American re-appropriation of the Admiral of the Ocean Sea, a post-modern or post-colonial re-colonization of the Columbian legacy. The novel's comic re-invention of Columbus for our time is, to be sure, important; yet *The Heirs of Columbus,* as its title should have— although, in '91 it probably could not have—made clear, is as much about the *heirs* of Columbus as it is about the old sailor for Spain.

The nature of heritage has been an important concern of Vizenor's for some time. The novel preceding *The Heirs of Columbus, The Trickster of Liberty,* published in 1988, is subtitled *Tribal Heirs to a Wild Baronage,* and in 1990, Vizenor's first novel, *Darkness in Saint Louis Bearheart* (1978), was reissued under the new title, *Bearheart: The Heirship Chronicles.* In 1991, *The Heirs of Columbus* moves heirship to titular and thematically controlling status, and I will read the novel as an intervention in the ages-old battle between *natio*—the Latin verb means to be born, and carries with it all the filiative, and racial claims of birth, descent, and blood inheritance—and *ratio*—the verb means to reason, and it carries the affiliative, cultural, and consensual claims of chosen values. In his Columbus book, Vizenor, as I hope to show, takes what might seem a very surprising position on the importance of *natio-* in the establishment and cohesion of what I'll call post-tribal utopian communities.[1]

Even a short history of the relations between *natio-* and *ratio-* in the West would take us far afield and take me well beyond my competencies, but a few things do need to be said. By the time of Columbus, as Marc Shell writes, the

Statutes of the Purity of the Blood (*limpieza de sangre*) adopted in Toledo in 1449—and elsewhere a little earlier or later . . . made the distinction between Christian and *converso* [Jewish convert][2] solely on the basis of blood *lineage*. (309-10, my emphasis)

The Spain that expelled its Jews in 1492 (and its Moors ten years later) rejected the notion of a distant consanguineous kinship with all those of Jewish heritage. It rejected, that is, the logic of those who argued that we are all brothers in Adam, or, for that matter, the logic of those who made the point that, after all, Jesus was a Jew. And it rejected as well the logic of a spiritual kinship with Jews, denying—irrationally, it would seem— that a Jewish convert was a brother in Christ. By 1492, as Shell continues, "The myth of Pure Blood (*sangre pura*) unmixed with Muslim or Jewish blood" (311) had taken hold, and so the Jews were expelled. In his log for the day he set sail, Columbus remarks the heavy traffic in the harbor caused by the many ships bearing Spain's Jews away.

The various types of traditional "blood" reasoning—only my directly traceable blood kin are my brothers; those who are my brothers must be my directly traceable blood kin—was to be left behind by a modern or "enlightened" world view for which, in time, brothers and sisters become, for example, *citoyens* and *citoyennes,* eventually comrades, or, indeed, "my fellow Americans." In the modern world of the *aufklarung,* not *natio-* but *ratio-* was to be the basis of kinship: my brothers and sisters are those who choose to share my values and principles. From this perspective, all *natio*-nalisms—appeals to birth and blood as the basis of kinship and heirship—would be seen, in the phrase of Tony Judt, as "pathological condition[s] of incomplete 'modernity'" (44). Nonetheless, we know it to be the case that, as Theodor Adorno observed, "Nationalism today is at once obsolete and current." With only this brief background let us return to Vizenor's *Heirs of Columbus.*

Who was Columbus and who are his heirs? On the first page of the novel, Columbus is said to be "an obscure crossblood who bore the tribal signature of survivance" (3). Columbus is a "crossblood" in that—this is one of the novel's central conceits—"Columbus was Mayan" (8), and also Jewish on his mother's side. According to Stone Columbus, one of the heirs of Columbus, and the protagonist-*figure* in the novel,[3] it was "The Maya [who] brought civilization to the savages of the Old World" (9).[4] Columbus's achievement was to bring "tribal genes back to the New World"; his was no voyage of discovery, but, rather, a return "to his homeland" (9). The Maya are important to Vizenor's ethnomythology in that "The Maya were the first to imagine the universe and to write about their stories in the blood," a phrase—stories in the blood—that occurs some 53 times in a novel of 189 pages, and a phrase to which I will return.

Not only was Columbus Mayan, but so, too, we are informed, was Jesus Christ—who, like Columbus, also had a Jewish mother, and was, thus, himself a crossblood. Jews, in Vizenor's account, in particular Sephardic Jews, like the Mayans, "bear their stories in the blood" (101). Not only Mayans and Jews, but Moors are also (although in somewhat lesser degree) important to the novel. For the Moors' "ancient leaders were crossbloods" as well, and Moorish people also "bear the signature of survivance and remember stories" (34).

This "signature," alluded to many times in the novel, is a specifically genetic signature, and Stone Columbus can legitimately claim to be an heir of Columbus because he has "naturally" inherited "the same signature" as Columbus, as "confirmed in several reliable studies of his bones and dried blood on a lead ball found at the bottom of his casket" (135).[5]

It is Stone Columbus who leads the heirs, along with a motley crew of—to take a phrase from Vizenor's *Bearheart*—"weirds and sensitives" (37), in the founding of a post-tribal utopian community at Point Assinika (Point Roberts in the Strait of Georgia between Washington state and Vancouver Island, Canada).[6] On October 12, 1992, exactly five hundred years after Columbus's first day in the New World, a "sovereign nation" dedicated to healing is founded. In a parody of a well-known passage of Columbus's journal, the narrator says that "At dawn," the heirs "saw pale naked people, and . . . went ashore in the ship's boat," to take "possession of this point in the name of [their] genes and the wild tricksters of liberties" (119).[7] Thus is established "the first nation in the histories of the modern world dedicated to protean humor and the genes that would heal" (189). The healing that is to take place in this "natural nation" (126) is to be achieved both by the humor in stories, and also by means of advanced genetic therapies—*ratio-* and *natio-* in tandem, it would seem, as these are conjoined in the key phrase to which I have already alluded, "stories in the blood."

I admit to having found this a troubling locution. I don't, that is, believe there is any gene for narrative orientation or preference, nor that stories can be inherited "naturally," remembered, listened to, heard "in the blood." Certain genetic inheritances are most certainly advantages for survival under specific ecological conditions, but that is not the issue here.[8] What is centrally at issue, as we shall see further, is the commitment "to heal rather than steal tribal cultures" (162). But when, very early in the novel, Stone Columbus announces that "The truth is in our genes" (10), what is one to think?[9]

As if to forestall worries of this sort, it is said that the phrase "stories in the blood" is a *"metaphor* for racial memories, or the idea that we inherit the structures of language and genetic memories" (136, my emphasis). But these phrases are simply variants of one another; "stories in the blood" is in synonymous rather than metaphorical or figurative relation to the notion of "racial memories," and so on. What to make of this apparent embrace of the logic of *natio-,* of race and blood, in a writer all of whose work has been militantly anti-racist?

For Vizenor surely agrees with Stone Columbus, of whom it is said that he

resists the notion of blood quantums, racial identification, and tribal enrollment. The heir is a crossblood, to be sure, but there is more to his position than mere envy of unbroken tribal blood. Indians, he said, are "forever divided by the racist arithmetic measures of tribal blood." He would accept anyone who wanted to be tribal, "no blood attached or scratched." (162)

Stone's intention in founding the nation at Point Assinika is

to make the world tribal, a universal identity, and return to other values as measures of human worth, such as the dedication to heal rather than steal tribal cultures. (162)

Yet Stone himself, as we have noted, is an heir of Columbus not only because of his values and his dedication to healing, but because of his genes, or "blood."

The narrator asserts that "scientists have established the genetic signatures of most of the tribes in the country" (162), so that now,

anyone could, with an injection of suitable genetic material, prove beyond a doubt a genetic tribal identity. Germans, at last, could be genetic Sioux, and thousands of coastal blondes bored with being white could become shadow tribes of Hopi, or Chippewa. (162)

This commitment to the *genetic* possibility of "a universal tribe would cause no harm, 'because there was nothing to lose but racial distance'" (162). So it is clear, as I have said, that any racialist argument in *The Heirs of Columbus* is set squarely against racism. But, then, why the embrace of *natio-* as equally or even more important than *ratio-* in the conceptualization of heirship and community?

I think the answer has to do with Vizenor's quite conscious adoption of a postmodern strategy that sees the best form of opposition in an apparent acquiescence to—in Marcuse's old phrase—"the real as rational"—which today would seem to mean the real as national. For surely it is the case that not secular reason but blood ties are in ascendance everywhere. The keynames are all too familiar: Bosnia, Rwanda, the France of Le Pen, Berlusconi's Italy, and so on and on. In the face of all this (and, unfortunately, a very great deal more), one might very well believe that the best way to fight those who appeal to birth, blood, and race as the basis of heirship might be not to fight but apparently to join them.[10]

Thus, in *The Heirs of Columbus,* Vizenor seems to accept the fact that, in Marc Shell's phrase, "Blood *counts*" (310n). Let us dare to state, for example, that the "truth is in our genes" (10), and let us agree to accept as members of our community only those who share our blood lineage, a certain genetic inheritance or "signature." But then let us democratize that signature, as it were, by means of technologies that now (so it is claimed) allow us to assure that anyone can share our blood—Germans can be Sioux, blondes can be dark, and so on. Of course, those with whom we will share our blood must be people who also share our values, the commitment of Columbus and his heirs to healing by means of the humor in stories—but if they do share those values, they can now literally be our brothers and sisters "in the blood." If blood does indeed count—as for all the rationalists' efforts to the contrary it seems to—then, let it count: and let all those who want a transfusion or implant come to the Dorado Genome Pavilion at Point Assinika where they can have whatever genes they want.

Does the Ku Klux Klan worry about the "mongrelization" of the race? Well, says Vizenor, they should only be so lucky: for, as Caliban, "the great white reservation mongrel" (16) puts it, it was mongrels who

dreamed humans into being and then out to sea in search of their own stories in the blood, but humans lost their humor over land, gold, slaves and time.

Mongrels created the best humans, we had that crossblood wild bounce in our blood. (16)

It is the "crossblood wild bounce" that the novel celebrates, insisting that "the best humans" are mongrels—crossbloods like Columbus and Jesus, Mayans, Jews, and Moors.

In the United States, of course, Moorish or Jewish or Mayan Indian blood tends to make one a second-class citizen or outcast, the victim of anti-Semitism or racism. But in Vizenor's novel, Moorish or Jewish or Indian blood is just the kind of blood to have. This "good" blood, in *The Heirs of Columbus,* is not, of course, the mythical *sangre pura* privileged by racists of every stripe, but always-already mixed blood. As

Sergeant Alex/Alexina Hobraiser had put it in *The Trickster of Liberty,* "Mixedbloods are the best tricksters, the choice ticks on the tribal bloodline" (xii). Tricksters, as Vizenor has asserted repeatedly, are mythic comedians, and the "protean humor of tricksters," indeed, humor in general, as Chaine Louis Riel, heir of a great *métis* rebel, states explicitly, "has political significance" (166). Vizenor has always taken his humor as having "political significance," and, for *The Heirs of Columbus,* he signals that fact from the outset by prefacing his book with a lengthy epigraph from Jean-Paul Sartre's *What Is Literature?* In Bernard Frechtman's translation, the quotation Vizenor has chosen from Sartre begins with a variation on Marx's famous shift in philosophical purpose: Sartre writes, "We are no longer with those who want to possess the world, but with those who want to change it." For all his recognition that "The most beautiful book in the world will not save a child from pain," nonetheless Sartre insists, "we want the work to be . . . an act; we want it to be explicitly conceived as a weapon in the struggle that men wage against evil."

As we have remarked, the post-tribal community established at Point Assinika is centrally concerned with healing children, saving them from pain; Stone's "ambitious course" in founding the nation looks forward to the rescue of "millions of lonesome and wounded children" (122). It is at the Dorado Genome Pavilion under the direction of Pir Cantrip, accused by nefarious figures of being a former Nazi, but, in fact, a "wounded Jew," and one of the good guys, that genetic research in the interest of healing is carried out; and children arrive from all over to be saved from pain.[11]

But how can a self-identified postmodernist embrace Sartre's "left modernism," in Anthony Appiah's phrase, his belief in the book as weapon? Sartre's commitment to cultural politics, to say what is obvious, bases itself upon distinctions between "authenticity" and "inauthenticity," "good faith" and "bad faith," indeed on the determinable difference between social "good" and "evil." But these distinctions and differences are only an illusion from the perspective of the Baudrillardian, DeLeuze- and Guattari-an postmodernism with which Vizenor has again and again allied his practice.

Postmodern fiction, as Linda Hutcheon notes, is marked by "a deliberate refusal to resolve contradictions" (*Poetics* x). Certainly Vizenor has consistently and militantly refused to resolve contradictions. But this stance entails the conclusion that postmodernism cannot be or imply a politics. Postmodernism "is certainly political," as Linda Hutcheon affirms, "but it is politically ambivalent, doubly encoded as both complicity and critique" (*Politics* 168). Now it is obvious that there is no avoiding complicity of some sort and degree whenever one writes—that is the nature of cultural practice which cannot not be embedded in an *a priori* world which provides its conditions of possibility.

Indeed, on one hand, as Fredric Jameson has argued, "postmodern fantastic historiography," "Fabulation," "mythomania," or "outright tall tales" (368) (all of these, of course, apt as descriptions of *The Heirs*) may be symptoms "of social and historical impotence, of the blocking of possibilities that leaves little option but the imaginary" (369), the complicitous side of things. But Jameson points out another possibility, that postmodernist fiction may, by "its very invention and inventiveness endorse . . . a creative freedom with respect to events it cannot control," thereby stepping "out of the historical record itself into the process of devising it." Postmodern fantastic historiography, thus, may proliferate "new multiple or alternate strings of events," which can

rattle the bars of the national tradition and the history manuals whose very constraints and necessities their parodic force indicts. Narrative invention here thus becomes the figure of a larger possibility of praxis. (369)

The "figure of a larger possibility of praxis": it would almost seem as though Jameson had Vizenor's trickster actually in mind in writing these words. And Jameson's words more generally accord well with Vizenor's claims for the postmodern imaginary fabulations in which he has for so long engaged, claims which emphasize the intensely critical dimension of his project.[12]

But if *The Heirs of Columbus* rattles "the bars of the national tradition," parodies, and indicts—and it most certainly does all of those things—yet it does one thing more: it imagines, as I have said, a post-tribal community dedicated to healing—which, indeed, it insists can achieve its utopian goals of, again in Sartre's words, saving children from pain. The last sentence of the novel reads (there is, however, an Epilogue), "The children danced on the marina, and their wounds were healed once more in a moccasin game with demons" (183).[13] Such a conclusion cannot come from postmodernist proliferations of relativism, or ironic celebrations of irresolution. So where does it come from? For a theoretical answer to this question we must step outside First World postmodernism.

I turn here for some help to Anthony Appiah's account of what he calls the second stage of the postcolonial African novel as exemplified most particularly in Yambo Ouologuem's *Le Devoir de Violence* (1968), in English, *Bound to Violence* (1971). For all the differences between the postcolonial African novel of the past twenty-five or thirty years, and the

Native American novel of the same period, I think Appiah's remarks may be useful for our purposes.[14] Opposed to the Western imperium, such a novel, according to Appiah, is also opposed "to the nationalist project of the postcolonial national bourgeoisie," celebrated by the first stage of the postcolonial African novel, and works to delegitimate such a project.[15] But the basis of such "delegitimation cannot be the postmodernist one," writes Appiah; rather, "it is grounded in an appeal to an ethical universal, . . . an appeal to a certain simple respect for human suffering" (353). As for Ouologuem's novel, "If we are to identify with anyone," says Appiah, "it is with the [*sic*] 'la négraille,' the 'nigger-trash,' who have no nationality" (353).

I am not competent to judge the accuracy of Appiah's account in general or his particular reading of Ouologuem, but I find his remarks highly suggestive for understanding the political stance of Vizenor's *Heirs of Columbus*. For it seems to me that for all of Vizenor's repeated insistence on a postmodernist orientation, he no more than Ouologuem can make the book a weapon by postmodern means, and, indeed, he, too, must finally appeal to the "ethical universal" of a "certain simple respect for human suffering" (353). We have several times noted that *The Heirs of Columbus* is committed to the healing of children at Point Assinika. Are these healers with whom we may perhaps identify, people joined in what I have called a post-tribal utopian community, like Ouologuem's "la négraille"? As mixedbloods and "mongrels," a term I take as related to—in Appiah's translation—"niggertrash," they, too, have no nationality. There is, to recall, Pir Cantrip, the wounded Jew, survivor of the holocaust; Sir Pellegrine Treves, also a Jew, and an expatriate from London; the manicurists Teets Melanos and Harmonia Dewikwe, from where, exactly, we are not told; a child named Blue Ishi; the no name first lady transvestite; Memphis the panther; Caliban the great white mongrel, and so on and on.

"Africa's postcolonial novelists, novelists anxious to excape neo-colonialism," Appiah writes, "are no longer committed to the nation; in this they will seem . . . misleadingly postmodern" (353). So, too, in this regard, do I see Vizenor as "misleadingly postmodern" in that his explicit commitment to the "sovereign nation" at Point Assinika clearly is a commitment to what I've called a post-tribal utopian community. In Africa, Appiah believes, "Postcoloniality has become . . . a condition of pessimism" (353). I can't compare and contrast the material prospects in the various African nations with those of Native American nations here, but Vizenor's political humor seems to me decidedly optimistic. Intended as "a weapon in the struggle that men wage against evil," his book is directed against those attached to foregone conclusions, "terminal creeds," and the "tragic" closures of birth and blood. Anyone dedicated to healing and comic liberation can become a genetic heir of Columbus at the Genome Pavilion at Point Assinika, but only those so dedicated need apply. "Stories in the blood" is a troubling phrase, and yet *The Heirs of Columbus* is a text unqualifiedly opposed to racism in the Americas, defending, in what only appears to be the manner of postmodernism, *ratio-* by means of a comically reinvented *natio-*.

Notes

1. A post-tribal utopian community, I should say, specifically devoted to healing. I'll take this up further in regard to *The Heirs* below. *Bearheart* and *The Trickster of Liberty* also conclude with the estabishment of post-tribal utopian communities of healing. The survivors of the western pilgrimage in *Bearheart* come to rest at Pueblo Bonito, in Chaco Canyon, New Mexico, where they encounter three tribal holy men who "laughed and laughed knowing the power of their voices had restored good humor to the suffering tribes" (243). *The Trickster of Liberty* does not end with the laughter of the sages but with the barking of mongrels ("the mongrels barked on the meadow" [154]), a very positive presence and a very salutary sound in Vizenor's work, as we shall see further. My use of post-tribal is an analogue of Vizenor's delineation of what he calls the "postindian," most particularly in his *Manifest Manners: Postindian Warriors of Survivance*. I note that of five epigraphs to this volume, two deal directly with matters of "race," my subject in this essay.

2. A *converso* is a Jew who has more or less voluntarily chosen to become a Christian, as opposed to a *marrano,* a Jew who has accepted forced conversion, e.g., under torture or threat of death. *Marrano* means pig. *The Heirs* speaks of both *conversos* and *marranos* and does not explain the difference, such as it is.

3. I'm thinking of Donald Barthelme's novel of 1967, *Snow White,* in which various characters are, with witty, postmodern irony, the prince-*figure,* the wicked witch-*figure,* and so on. Vizenor would no more create a traditional *protagonist* than Barthelme would offer a straight analogue of the characters in the fairy tale.

4. Carter Revard's brilliant satire, "Report to the Nation: Reclaiming Europe," may well have provided a partial source for this notion.

5. Barry Laga's recent study of *The Heirs* expends a good deal of ingenious energy relating Derrida on the "signature" to Vizenor's use of that term. I think, unfortunately, that this is wasted ingenuity, inasmuch as signature, in Vizenor's text, whatever it *might* mean, is pretty clearly *used to mean* genetic signature.

6. The citizens of this new nation are a rather strange lot. They eventualy include, among others, Admiral Luckie White, revealed to be a Sephardic Jew,

and the host of a talk show on Carp Radio; Harmonia Dewikwe, a "government manicurist" (118); the "no name man, . . . a pale weaver with a doctorate in consciousness studies from the University of California" (118), a transvestite who crossdresses as the wives of the presidents, in particular, Lady Bird Johnson; Dr. Pir Cantrip, a scientist and a "wounded Jew" (on him, somewhat more below); and, to mention no others, eventually Sir Pellegrine Treves, a Sephardic antiquarian bookseller in London, actively involved in the storyline-plot-action of arranging for the remains of Pocahontas to be buried alongside the remains of Christopher Columbus at the base of the Trickster of Liberty, the statue which parodically (it is taller than you know what) watches over or represents (take your pick) the "sovereign nation" at Point Assinika.

7. An odor of sanctity for these proceedings is provided by the fact that the heirs make "all the necessary declarations and [have] these testimonies recorded by a blond anthropologist" (119). The mockery of anthropology is an ongoing trope in Vizenor's work. I say something more about this in note 15, below.

8. Quite to the contrary: for Columbus is said to have possessed "an enormous clubbed penis curved to the right, a disease of fibrous contracture during an erection" (31), the source not of pleasure but of great trouble and pain. If this genetic legacy has been passed on to Stone or other heirs "in the blood," it is not mentioned.

9. The only rejoinder to Stone's remark is Luckie White's rapid and rather bemused, "Right, we are what our genes must pretend" (10). To my mind—a mind anachronistically committed to making *sense*—this works only in translation, i.e., Right, whatever we are, we pretend comes from our genes. But that is not what Vizenor has written.

10. I want to make it absolutely clear that I am *not* claiming to retrieve Vizenor's *intentions* here. My position in relation to Vizenor's use of "stories in the blood" is a little like that of the talk radio host and Sephardic Jew Luckie White in relation to the heirs. For, like her, I am, as a reader, "impatient for conclusions," possessed of "a worldview that was frustrated by the heirs who imagine the starts but never the ends" (173). Vizenor imagined the starts, and, as I make the point below, probably would rather bracket the "ends," leaving things famously "open." Thus I am reading against the grain in trying to sort out the ends, that is, the implications of his procedure. When I say such things (see just below) as Vizenor apparently joins the racists in order to fight them, or, that he seems to accept, etc., I do not mean that that is what he *intends,* but that that is the effect of his procedure.

11. Along with the Dorado Genome Pavilion in which genetic research in the interest of healing takes place, the second major institutional edifice of the new nation is the Felipa Flowers Casino. This is often crowded, "as usual with wounded gamblers" (138). In the Casino, behind the bingo tables, "at the back near the restaurant and concessions" (138) is located the "Parthenos Manicure

Salon" (138). Here, those like Teets Melanos, along with Harmonia Dewikwe, "hear the secrets of women and the concessions [*sic*] of men, more than a shaman or a priest would hear on the reservation" (141), and, by their loving attention to the hands of their clients, perform important acts of healing. But they also save "thousands of secret bits of skin and fingernail from the hands" (141) of those they manicure—in the interest, of course, of the positive genetic research being carried on at the Genome Pavilion. It needs to be said, however, that traditionally, the saving of bits of skin and nails is an activity engaged in not by those with benevolent intentions, but, rather, by witches who mean harm. This traditional aspect of the novel, unlike others (e.g., reference to the windigoo, to mythical gambling, to medicine pouches, miigis shells, and so on) seems one the reader is called upon more nearly to ignore than to integrate.

12. I am grateful for my understanding of Hutcheon and Jameson on the postmodern novel to Brian McHale's "Postmodernism, or The Anxiety of Master Narratives." Complicitous critique is, as McHale underlines, a fairly unstable oxymoronic construction, and, as McHale further notes, in Jameson's analysis of specific texts (the phrase itself, however, is Hutcheon's) it is unclear on what basis he determines that there is more complicity than critique and vice versa. My reading of *The Heirs of Columbus* takes the complicity of the text (e.g., the acceptance of a logic of *natio-*) as a means to the end of a progressive political critique, as if it were possible somehow to arrive at Sartre by way of Baudrillard. But once again this reading can in no way be authorized by an appeal to Vizenor's intentions. His procedure has regularly been to have Baudrillard when he wants Baudrillard, Sartre when he wants Sartre, and so on, and not to worry, with the likes of Luckie White and me, about irresolution or contradiction.

13. Gaming, gambling, and "narrative chance" have been important throughout Vizenor's work. Louis Owens (in *Other Destinies*) offers the most useful comments, commenting as well on the ethical dimensions of a commitment to "chance."

14. I've argued elsewhere (in "Postcoloniality and Native American Literature") that while some of its hybrid features—the linking of elements of the indigenous oral tradition, for example, to the various conventions of Euro-American fiction—may permit the Native American novel to be considered in the context of postcolonial literature, it is, nonetheless, not best seen in that context for the simple reason that there is not yet a post- to the colonial status of Native American peoples.

15. Part of that delegitimation is a violent attack on the claim of Western anthropology to "know" or speak for African or Native American people. Ouologuem's novel offers a withering satiric portrait of an anthropologist called Shrobénius—obviously, as Appiah notes, with reference to "the German Africanist Leo Frobenius" (352)—and of what he calls "*Shrobéniusologie*" (354). Vizenor, too, has never missed an opportunity to inveigh against anthro-

pology, often—and in *The Heirs* as well—in the form of "blond anthropologists," as noted above. His Shrobénius is Eastman Shicer, "aerobics instructor and cultural anthropologist" in *The Trickster of Liberty*, a character based upon the eminent southwestern anthropologist Edward Spicer.

Works Cited

Appiah, Kwame Anthony. "Is the Post- in Postmodernism the Post- in Postcolonialism?" *Critical Inquiry* 17 (1991): 336-57.

Barthelme, Donald. *Snow White*. New York: Atheneum, 1967.

Hutcheon, Linda. *A Poetics of Postmodernism: History, Theory, Fiction*. New York: Routledge, 1988.

——. *The Politics of Postmodernism*. New York: Routledge, 1989.

Jameson, Fredric. *Postmodernism, or, the Cultural Logic of Late Capitalism*. Durham: Duke UP, 1992.

Judt, Tony. "The New Old Nationalism." *New York Review of Books* XLI (May 26, 1994): 44-50.

Krupat, Arnold. "Postcoloniality and Native American Literature." *Yale Journal of Criticism* 7.1 (1994): 163-80.

Laga, Barry. "Gerald Vizenor and His *Heirs of Columbus:* A Postmodern Quest for Discourse." *American Indian Quarterly* 18 (1994): 71-86.

McHale, Brian. "Postmodernism, or the Anxiety of Master Narratives." *Diacritics* 22 (1992): 17-33.

Ouologuem, Yambo. *Bound to Violence*. Trans. Ralph Manheim. New York: Harcourt, 1971.

——. *Le Devoir de Violence*. Paris: Plon, 1968.

Owens, Louis. *Other Destinies: Understanding the American Indian Novel*. Norman: U of Oklahoma P, 1992.

Revard, Carter. "Report to the Nation: Reclaiming Europe." *Earth Power Coming*. Ed. Simon J. Ortiz. Tsaile, AZ: Navajo Community College P, 1983. 166-81.

Shell, Marc. "Marranos (Pigs); or, From Coexistence to Toleration." *Critical Inquiry* 17 (1991): 306-35.

Vizenor, Gerald. *Bearheart: The Heirship Chronicles*. Minneapolis: U of Minnesota P, 1990.

——. *Darkness in St. Louis Bearheart*. Saint Paul: Truck P, 1978.

——. *The Heirs of Columbus*. Hanover: Wesleyan/UP of New England, 1991.

——. *Manifest Manners: Postindian Warriors of Survivance*. Hanover: Wesleyan/UP of New England, 1994.

——. *The Trickster of Liberty: Tribal Heirs to a Wild Baronage*. Minneapolis: U of Minnesota P, 1988.

10

TEXTUAL INTERSTICES:
MIRRORED SHADOWS IN GERALD VIZENOR'S *DEAD VOICES*

Douglas Dix, Wolfgang Hochbruck, Kirstie McAlpine,
Dallas Miller, and Mary Tyne

Even before the publication of his fifth novel, *Dead Voices,* Gerald
Vizenor had been recognized as one of the most inventive and versatile
of contemporary Native American authors.[1] So much said, *Dead Voices*
represents a surprising turn after the dense and metaphorical *Heirs of
Columbus,* which took its own ironical aim at the Columbus anniversary
in 1992. The narrative of *Dead Voices* is comparatively accessible, the
stories self-contained and—as in *The Trickster of Liberty*—there is a per-
vading gentleness and good humor. Perhaps, too, Vizenor's taste for
Zen-Buddhist teaching plays a more important part than previously.[2]

For the first time in a Vizenor novel there is an "I"-narrator—with
some "autobiomythical" references to the author, but they should not be
overestimated (Krupat).[3] The stance of the academic first-person narrator
in *Dead Voices* is for the most part one of autocritical self-consciousness.
He remains nameless except for the epithet "Laundry" given to him by
the urban trickster figure of Bagese, an old woman whose stories are
parts of a wanaki card game in which each card turned on seven successive days (re-)presents a mythical animal (including stones, some of
which are apparently animated in Ojibwa/Anishinaabe tribal thought
and grammar). The cards, however, are not turned on successive days in
Laundry's game, but over a period of nine months, Laundry's initiation
and gestation period.

This non-linear chronology and the thirteen-year time span suggest
periods of silence within which we are invited to imagine Laundry
coming to grips with all he has seen and heard. Bagese is a strain on the
nose and, initially, on the imagination of her visitor, whom she in return
outfits with yet another one of those typical Vizenor urban tribal nicknames, Laundry, referring to *his* smell: "You smell like television soap,"
Bagese says to Laundry, "the sweet smell of laundry is a dead voice"
(16). As a teacher, Bagese not only has the right to name but also to pre-

178

sent riddles and tasks to her disciple, and when they are not answered satisfactorily, she resorts to the kind of violence a Zen-master purportedly exacts against his or her disciples: she pounds him on the head.[4]

Our main concern in this collective paper takes up, precisely, the question of textualization. For "textualization" in the stories of *Dead Voices* is at once problematic and of the essence. It foregrounds a defense of the aural, which Bagese states, and restates, throughout the reported telling of her stories. As Laundry says right from the beginning, ". . . she said that tribal stories must be told not recorded, told to listeners but not readers, and she insisted that stories be heard through the ear not the eye" (6). However, the existence of the text as artifact and its construction through the voice of the narrative "I" points to and criticizes the accepted fabrication of tribal life in books. Laundry exemplifies the "as-told-to" position in metatribal discourse, but he does so consciously, raising the question of appropriation and representation in comical turns.[5]

First, the apparent elision of the aural and the printed actively plays with the notion of audience. Laundry is, after all, a university lecturer on tribal philosophies and his projection of Bagese's stories upon the page not only effects a transgressive play of boundaries but situates him in a mediating position simultaneously as both the teller and the audience. The trick to the narrative lies in the elision of both tellers—beneath the containing texts of Laundry's translations are Bagese's own representations of fragments of an aural matrix of stories: the "shadow" Vizenor sees uncovered in "the ruins of representation" ("Ruins"). Vizenor's own use of the Earthdiver myth serves as a model for this process: the aural appears as recoverable through the construction of the printed text as fragments of the old world form the seeds of the new.

What appears problematic about such a model is the rigidity of its own terms. Developing the notion of a world view drowned out by the constructions of the colonial, this model also cites a paradoxical notion of discovery and repossession. An erasure of the uppermost layer of colonial turds (to stay within the metaphorical frame of the Earthdiver myth) would reveal the old world in its entirety; the aural as an artifact may be recovered. This, however, is not what Vizenor seems to be saying.

Second, tribal life did not and does not exist in definable layers like geographical strata. Overwhelmed and intertwined within one another, many different forms become finally irrecoverable in the drowning out of the old world. The postcolonialist endeavor is then situated in the model of a palimpsest: the debris floating to the top is unreadable in itself, but within the watery matrix of the flood, shadows and traces of the designs of other stories can be found. Recoveries are—and can only be—ironic. The palimpsest represents a melding of constructions that no longer have any referent in the real. There is no original to recover but traces remain within the fixed indeterminacy of an infinitely overlaid artifact.

The palimpsest model again is limited in that everything is rendered in terms of textual positions. By adding the Earthdiver model we arrive at an including narrative, centering around the transgressive figure of the trickster as the site from which the constructions of the new emerge. Much as Leslie Marmon Silko's use of "witchery" destabilizes a polarized attack on colonialism by including it within a creation story, so Vizenor's use of the trickster incorporates the controlling narratives within his own world view. The turds may float upon the water or the uppermost layer of constructions, but originally they come from the trickster himself.[6] As a language gamester, the trickster permeates all levels of the infinitely fluid discourse and renders closed narratives obsolete. The turds are the tangible artifacts of a limiting construction, but it is from within the fluid medium of unfixed narrative that a new form of discourse can be formed. Thus Vizenor writes of the fleas in *Dead Voices*:

We turn the leaves and bright water runs down our hands, under our sleeves, over our hard bodies to the road, and on to the storm drains and the underground rivers to the ocean. We are fleas and water, we are stories in the ocean. (55)

Similarly, there is a reference to the emergence of new discourses in this "fluid" medium of postmodernity in the following chapter, "We are squirrels, and our stories run with the water beads out to the stories in the sea" (61).[7]

The discussion so far has centered upon an abstract evaluation of Vizenor's structures of textual histories without acknowledging *Dead Voices* itself as embedded in the very traditions Vizenor seeks to challenge. This paradox is played out in *Dead Voices* through the figure of the trickster. Her apparently central role is complicated in Vizenor's stories; the three tricksters in the "Stones" chapter are bound to one another, and Naanabozho is constricted by the water of the flood. The trickster's creative role is curbed and complemented in that she cannot act and create out of her own accord. She needs outside help, other spirits or animals perform the necessary dives for material—a decentralized image running counter to the possibilities of master narratives. The trickster's immersion within the flood of narrative situates him on a fine borderline.

Vizenor's text acknowledges this principle by including signposts within the text that point to its existence as a construction. The trickster becomes a language game within a text she both constructs and yet which confines her. The free play of this language game is only as free as the bounds of the construction, unless it takes a form that the construction does not recognize. Vizenor's line "I would rather be lost at war in the cities than at peace in a tame wilderness" (136) reflects this. The city as a confining discourse can only enclose that which it recognizes. Being lost in the cities is analogous to a virtual submersion in the flood; the text of the city is a self-reflexive loop. Within its lumen, that which remains unsignified in the larger text is free to play. Pointing to the looped constructions of his own text, Vizenor highlights its transgressive center. In order to elaborate on this point, we shall trace the roles and images of two signifying signposts in the text, namely mirrors and maps.

As "narrator," Laundry casts himself in the role of a voyeur looking through a glass darkly at Bagese. Significantly, his vision is smudged: "The rain came in bursts, cold and hard, and blurred the window" (15). While he negotiates with the larger narrative constructions of the "Indian" woman, Bagese in turn engages a bear vision in her mirror in mythical discourse. Gradually, Laundry moves from his initial analytical assessment of an exotic "other," from the safe distance of his position as an academic critic, to an engagement directly with the mirror. The movement is ambivalent. Spatially, Laundry moves from the boundary to the center; at the same time, he acknowledges the existence of an as yet unsignified beyond. The translation of these stories on the fringes of the imagination into the larger discourse through the appropriative gaze of the outsider is the problem dominating the whole sequence. Yet Vizenor includes the appropriative gaze within a matrix of subversions. In contrast to the narrations of traditional anthropologists, Laundry's self-reflexive accounts are more representative of what he (and he only) sees in the mirrors than of what he wants to see through the window. The text incorporates Bagese's sanctions and warnings against the publication of her stories in a paradoxical loop of argument that, if taken literally, would efface its own validity.

I listened, I held my breath, and promised not to publish what she told me. I was in her scent and could do nothing less, of course, and she told me stories about the liberation of animals, birds, and insects in the cities. She even encouraged me to tell my own stories, but my stories were lectures, or dead voices, so she told me to imagine in my own way the stories she had told me. (7)

Within this optional interface, Laundry's text is legitimized as a voice of his own, but by calling the novel *Dead Voices* the *positive* implications within the above quotation are again turned in on themselves. Laundry's texts remain fragmented, but it is within the interstices of his accounts that the shifting shadows of the bear appearing in the mirror in Bagese's apartment can—so to speak—be "heard." The medium contains another medium, and the message can only be imagined, never real.

Bears and shadows of bears are familiar to Vizenor readers as mythical referents, possible visions in special characters since Proude Cedarfair and Inawa Biwide became vision bears walking through the solstice window at Pueblo Bonito in *Bearheart.* In *Dead Voices,* Bagese turns into a bear simultaneously on the first and the last pages of the novel, and throughout the text "bear" is a possible vision in a mirror, visible to children and animals. Adults, and academics above all, may learn to see, even if their reports and reproductions are likely to not move beyond the realm of the dead voices.[8]

In a discussion of the bear as an "archshadow in the silence of tribal stories," Vizenor uses passages from Luther Standing Bear's *My Indian Boyhood* to emphasize the notion of the shadow as "the unsaid sense in names, the memories in silence and the imagination of tribal experiences" ("Ruins" 11). Luther Standing Bear uses the image of the bear to mirror the human by eliding their common vanity: bears look at their own image in the water. Luther Standing Bear frames this with an account of his community doing the same "Before we had looking-glasses" ("Ruins" 11). The position of the observer has changed. The bear is watched looking into the water; in doing so he is shadowing past behavior. The approach to the reflective surface is multiple, and the question that must be asked is, what is seen in the water? Luther Standing Bear offers a reflection of the bear from his own position as a watcher of the process; yet his account of the bear's satisfaction is implied from his own appreciation of the animal as an analogue to himself.

In the linkage of the bear and the mirror, the dangers of this subjective reading disappear when it is considered along with the presence of mirrors in *Dead Voices.* In his use of mirrors and mirroring, Vizenor seems to be investigating the possibility of infinite shadows within the reflection. The position of the observer changes again: the voyeur, standing back from the lake's edge watching others or an "other" as they look into the mirroring water, moves forward to engage with the mirror. The one face presented to the mirror becomes part of, in Vizenor's phrase, the "shadow memories" of the others. The mirror no longer attaches to what it is reflecting through a single knowing gaze, but disperses it amongst a new range of interpretations.

Although this is not strictly relevant to Vizenor's scheme, this process is analogous to the paradigm asserted by Freud in his analysis of the child's mirror game.[9] Assuming control over the disappearing and reappearing mirror image reassures the child that the mother will come back. It would be easy to see the relation between Laundry, Bagese, and the bear in the mirror contained in this motif. Vizenor's mirror, however, is not part of a self-contained negotiation with the self (nor, it must be stressed, is it part of a romantic revision of the "lost mother earth" motif) but the notion of self-effacement as a means to hear obliterated shadows is an important and complex one.[10] This concept is contained in the Earth-diver story in the assumption of powers to create and recreate. It is also developed in the story of the three tricksters in the "Stones" chapter of *Dead Voices*. Naanabozho, wanting to free himself from his obligation to his brother Stone, attempts to kill him. In the process of ridding himself of the one object which (and to which he) was bound to return, he frag-ments Stone into "thousands and thousands of pieces" (27). These being cast "in the four directions of the earth" (27) means that Naanabozho can never efface or move away from Stone and of course this also means that he is now free to travel. The implication is that there is a unity in frag-mentation and that survival lies in the intangible. The stories connect the fragments that survive as shadows in the mirror. Recovery of the stories depends upon an awareness of seemingly disparate connections.[11]

This brings us back to the situation of Laundry in relation to the window, the mirror and the stories, and to the second signifying sign-post: the making of maps. Initially, Laundry negotiates with Bagese from behind a window through which he can only see distorted images. The images he wants to discover (and to map) lie beyond his "eye" into this world. It is not, therefore, possible for him to dive into her world and recover the particles out of which a new construction of the world is made. His "mirror" does not contain the flood. The window is constantly washing clean and paradoxically the constant washing only serves to occlude his ability to see. He resembles the "I" of the explorer, in the process of discovering with the anthropological "eye," and with intent to map out territories in order to appropriate them. It is the appropriative gaze of the voyeuristic subject as he views the "other," the object he desires. One of the results of Laundry's translation or transfer of the sto-ries onto the two-dimensional chart, which the page resembles, is to draw the reader into an inclusive chain of voyeurisms; the text becomes a window.

Laundry's unified map of the room is shattered into an infinity of fragmented visions as the room itself and everything in it is reflected in the countless mirrors that line the apartment. The wanaki game Bagese plays and Laundry learns about charts the world in a miniature reenact-ment of Lake Merritt. Even though the notion of map-making denotes a colonizing process, the objects from which these maps are made—"... a collection of stones, many stones, birds, leaves, flowers, insects and other mysterious things ..." (15)—produce documents of a different kind. The maps, as a result, are illegible in a conventional sense. Their configuration works against an appropriative delineation of difference within cartographic discourse.[12] What these maps seek to catalyze are the shadows and traces of stories within each component part.

Within the notion of the map as text lies the irony that all of Bagese's maps are virtually identical, yet the configurations of the stories contained within each of them are vastly different. The trails cover the same ground with stones as symbols representative of the animals Bagese meets on each trail and all of them are representatives of fragmented Stone. According to the rules of the game,

[W]hen animals, birds, insects and living things are seen on the trail a stone is placed to remember the place. In this way Stone is always present where life would be in the wanaki game. (29)

This works against the notion of cartographic discourse as a central part of the colonial endeavor, as a means to demarcate the boundaries of discovered land, but it is more than that. Vizenor is also using the stone and mirror trails to chart a mode of writing in another way. The stones are not the stories; they are not even mnemotechnic devices in the conventional sense. The maps re-emphasize the point that they are in themselves and as themselves redundant in the storytelling. It is within the intangible space of the aural interpretations of the maps that the creative text lies, as Bagese says, "I hear to see, and stories come to me over the dead voices. I see in the mirror what others fear to hear" (138). The maps are therefore, as much as published texts, dead voices. And in a way Bagese's differently encoded trails of stones and mirrors are another ossification of the aural into the tangible. The difference lies in the quality of the viewer or listener who is aware of the shadows and traces behind the signs.

Even after Laundry enters Bagese's apartment and negotiates with her and the mirror, his fear of the reflection (not *his* reflection, though) reflects his uneasy position within the map of the story, as he expresses in the form of a koan: "I avoided the mirrors for fear that my face would vanish ..." (20).[13] It betrays his absolute faith in himself as an individual at this point whilst underlining the fragility of his position. Individual identity is both tenuous and pervasive. For Laundry, the mirror is initially the site of an antagonistic exchange; the reflection simultaneously being what he most desires to ingest and that which he cannot face or see. This also connects to the image of the trickster as a being with a mirror instead of a face, a transitive figure that is both faceless and many faced.[14] Laundry's fear is less that his face will adorn the image of the trickster than the inverse—that he will become trapped within the frame of the mirror. The central image is no longer that of a faceless trickster but of a disembodied face within the mirror. Laundry fears that his position of absolute selfhood as an agent of discovery behind the appropriating gaze of the window will be translated into a fragmented identity in which he himself becomes the artifact. The irony is, of course, that within the construction of the narrative, he is already there.

In this respect, also, the text is both a window and a mirror. Bagese's stories contain shadows and infinite resonances behind the words of the text. The wanaki game pursues these multiple reflections and connections. Laundry's accounts of trails and stories offer a frame to the work that—superficially read—accords to the "as-told-to" tradition of dual authorship mostly found in anthropologically inspired (auto-) biographies. The inclusion of Bagese's sanctions against producing the very text the reader is reading endows it with a salacious taint of arcane knowledge. The look through the window remains: whether Laundry enters the apartment or sees the bear in the mirror, the stories are still contained within the written text. Even ten years after her disappearance, Bagese's teaching appears to have left Laundry with a strong inhibition with regard to using her materials. Nevertheless, after the receipt of both copper dish and mirror, the texts are published. Maybe she didn't pound him on the head hard enough.

The irony lies in Vizenor's situating of criticism of the written within the published speech of Bagese's stories. The apparently polarized view of the aural and the written that would exculpate this attempt at transcription is compared and weighted strongly against the bleached texts of "wordies," "anthropologists," and "blondes." But *Dead Voices* is not one of the many self-styled brimming-with-self-righteousness initiation stories of the type: "sacred tribal knowledge transferred to worthy white man as Indian medicine man prepares to sing his death dirge." Laundry is initially counted, or counts himself, among the "wordies," and the critique of the written contained in *Dead Voices* is facing inward on itself from the title onwards. Being situated within a printed text, the argument draws attention to its frame, the text itself. This is not an easy appropriation from a voyeuristic stance. Vizenor is pointing to the water-logged glass and containing frame of the gaze in a postmodern endeavor to problematize the reader as a reader. The arguments within the text against the text constitute a "final vocabulary"[15] which cannot be accepted from the text itself without question.

Vizenor seems to be arguing against the absorption of a polarized world view of liberal guilt and spiritual recovery (the window) to present more complex and shifting mediations with the text (the mirror). At the same time, the final paragraph of the novel makes clear that a perception focusing on Laundry's position as a "dead voice" representative would also be inaccurate. His final interaction with the mirror is not one of essentialist closure, but an acknowledgment that the shadows it contains are merely that, shadows. "Once or twice a year," we read, "some visitor might see the shadow of a bear in the mirror" (142). There are no essential experiences to appropriate but only stories to hear. At the same time, their visual (re-)presentation on the page is not a foreclosure against aural perception, as Laundry says, "I never doubted that she had the power and the stories to bring back the dead, even dead voices at a great distance" (19).

This statement expresses a dual possibility: if it is possible to bring back the dead voices in an oral discourse, then it is possible for the stories to "winter out" in *Dead Voices*. Publishing the stories sets up the window through which the inquisitive may peer, and those who see the mirrors beyond can hear the shadows of other stories. When Laundry recovers the tabernacle mirror he comments that, "those who hear the bear are there to hear the stories of the old woman" (142). Laundry's final argument, however, seems to be that the published stories themselves are shadows, traces of the aural in the ruins of representation. Much as the wildness of the treelines is translated into acts of survivance in the city, the printed text becomes the site of a new conflict. The closed discourses of "dead voices" are unaware of the aural shadows within their bounds. The text is a window, signposts to the stories of a tribal woman, but of course these constructions are also dead voices themselves. The paradox is unsolvable, no final solution, but the shadows dance behind the dead voices and survivance lies in the translation of the window into the endless play of mirrors. The reader is left with a koan: what is the sound of one story printed? Likewise, Laundry's final statement of connection in separation, "We must go on" (144), harkens back to the Zen level of Dead Voices, to a "just so" in which Bagese, Laundry, and the stories disappear—but not forever.

Post-Text

The bear in the mirror is me, more than manners and poses. The bear is there, the bear is me, the bear is never at peace. We are the stories of the war, the chance in the mirror. We hear each other and we must go on. (139)

We have been writing about textualization, about the layerings and fragmentations of a postindian narrative in, to deploy Vizenor's own terms, the ruins of representation of a dominant civilization. The text we have been writing about shatters the window of objective representation into a thousand slivers, and our own text has and must continue this shattering, must turn against even our own attempts to make sense of what we find, must open up new stories, because, to quote Gerald Vizenor, himself quoting Samuel Beckett, "we must go on."

It has become fashionable to say, post Jacques Derrida and Paul de Man, that "there is nothing outside the text." What many critics forget when they subsequently reduce the world to textuality is that this very same statement also implies its opposite meaning as well: *everything remains outside of the text.* Everything that is beyond language, everything that is beyond intelligibility, everything that is beyond the dead voices. These seemingly irreconcilable statements must be held in the mind simultaneously, for to reduce the world to text alone is, in fact, to reduce the world to dead voices.

So what is "outside" the text entitled *Dead Voices: Natural Agonies in the New World?* We might begin by looking outside the text proper (and yet inside, still), where we find three epigraphs by Samuel Beckett, John Neihardt, and Maurice Blanchot. Three more stories are being told: Beckett's "Unnamable" exhorts that we "must go on," Neihardt's Black Elk warns of the shadows that can cloud our visions, and Maurice Blanchot urges that we "write in the thrall of the impossible real" and to continue writing in the face of our own mortalities. These three statements, chosen to stand outside the text by the author, must give us some sense of what lies within and beyond this text, although each of these statements opens out further to infinitely complex texts and contexts.

The theorist Jean-Luc Nancy has created the term "exscription" to describe certain works where the words of the author exist with such an intensity that they shatter the text, the voice emerging and plunging straight out of the text and into our lives. One might just as well describe this process of exscription as "live voices"—voices so full of life that they drive straight through the printed page and into our hearts, "exscribing" the life of the author through and beyond the printed words. A feature of such texts is that they bring us to speak in turn, for we cannot remain unmoved having read them. Gerald Vizenor's stories, printed and aural, have precisely this quality, and have motivated us all to continue with our own voices, our own stories. This quality of perpetuating ever more stories is the crucial feature of exscripted texts, for it is what prevents texts, what hopefully will prevent our text, from becoming simply more dead voices. Such texts enliven others to look into the mirrors at themselves and begin telling their own stories, to join in the war against the dead voices of the "wordies" (who, alas, inhabit us all at times). For we must go on.

Our own stories are necessary for our own survivance, and that survivance exists within a world that is forever at war, whatever our race, creed or color. We don't need the forever unchanging stories of a stable canon, we don't need the rational or empirical analyses that drive home a point the way a hammer drives a nail, but rather open, fluid, plural stories and interpretations that we tell from where we ourselves stand, and tell again in another way, and tell still again, for,

There is no peace, and our best stories must be heard in a trickster war, in the shadows, in a world of chance. Peace is a tragic end, we are lost in peace. Once our stories are written there is no war to hear, to remember our voices and the way we carried on in stones and stories. We must go on and be heard over the dead voices. (135)

We are all bears in the mirror, brought to the world by chance, brought to a world of chance, a world continuously at war. We have all been "brought down from the wild treelines to our natural agonies in the cities" (30), and the war we must fight is one of survivance, for we must go on. Gerald Vizenor's stories are there to help us in that struggle.

Notes

1. The authors of this collective essay all met at the third annual Stuttgart Seminar in Cultural Studies, which was organized by Professor Heide Ziegler of the University of Stuttgart, at the Monrepos Castle Hotel from August 1-15, 1993. Gerald Vizenor was a member of the faculty. Every afternoon and sometimes long into the night, Gerald and the five of us talked about the morning's plenary session, we discussed Native American literature, we told each other stories, and we laughed a lot together. *Dead Voices* was one of the texts discussed; our discussion of this book has continued long after the intensive days of Monrepos and long after we bade each other our fond farewells. Our cooperation in compiling this essay is indicative of the fact that together we have indeed fared well, collectively inspired by the initial guidance of Gerald Vizenor.

2. A potential reading of *Dead Voices* as a Zen-type initiation of Laundry by Bagese has support within the text as well as outside it. First, Laundry seeks Bagese out as a disciple seeks a master. Laundry has traveled some distance on this path already, allowing him to recognize Bagese as the "master" he is in

search of, in keeping with the Zen saying "when the disciple is ready, the master will come." And so we find, for example, Laundry saying, "She should have been my discovery at the cages, but as you can see, she must have waited there to catch my ear" (9). As is common among some forms of Zen, Bagese becomes Laundry's personal "master," and she confuses him with stories which stretch his conception of the possible. In Bagese's stories there are many examples of haiku, a form of poetry written by Japanese Zen monks.

3. Also unusual for Vizenor are the instances of "direct address" in Laundry's narration, a stereotypically "Indian" form. These are found less often in the sections in which Laundry is apparently relating Bagese's stories. Laundry begins with a direct address to the reader (5) and ends with a direct address to Bagese (144). Only the "Stones" chapter, early in Laundry's initiation and prefatory to the wanaki game itself, uses direct address in what should be Bagese's voice. This suggests that a part of Laundry's initiation involves learning to communicate the stories.

4. If Laundry is to be read as a Zen-type initiate and Bagese as a "master," two points must be recognized at the outset: first is the question of Laundry's race and second is the fact of Bagese's sex. Vizenor never specifies Laundry's race, and within his body of work, the position of a white university lecturer on tribal philosophy would be expected to be very different from that of a "crossblood" tribal philosopher. Vizenor is here leaving an open space, a silence in the text which plays with racial stereotypes by leaving race completely out of the picture.

By creating a female "master," Vizenor is creating a tribal initiation story that overturns the traditional Zen-type process. The exclusively male world of the Zen monk is opened up by placing it squarely in the city—no ordinary place for an ashram—and subverted by placing a male initiate in a world of female "masters," the desert "bear women." To western readers this may go almost unnoticed, but to a reader familiar with Zen traditions, this is revolutionary. Laundry is already engaged in the "word wars," but intellectually, as an academic. His experience, apprenticeship, with Bagese results in a spiritual enrichment of his place in the word wars. This is also a critique of academia, in which the word wars, without this spiritual grounding, are fought entirely within the realm of the colonizers. That is, by educating himself within the institutions imported by the colonizers, by qualifying himself as a university lecturer, Laundry has agreed to limit the scope of the discourse. From Bagese's position the entire discourse, the word wars, has taken place within the realm of the dead.

5. As an initiate-narrator, Laundry can also be placed among the disciples recording the stories of Jesus, Plato recording the dialogues of Socrates or the recorders of the Tao Te Ching. Laundry's story has parallels to Gary Snyder's and to Janwillem van de Wetering's initiation into Zen. This sort of narrator presents a unique set of problems, as the humility befitting an initiate tends to

underplay the accomplishments of the narrator in contrast to the achievements of the "master." The written-oral question shows up here as well. Jesus, Socrates, Lao Tzu and Zen masters function entirely orally, while for most of us, our knowledge of the life and wisdom of the masters is based on the written accounts of their followers.

6. In talking about the androgynous figure of the trickster, we are presented with the problem of which pronoun to use. In order to avoid the rather clumsy use of, for example, him/herself or s/he, we have as it were taken a leaf out of *Dead Voices* ("What seems to be a game is not a game, the opposites are never the other, the plurals, even the pronouns we write, are not in the natural world . . ." [111], and "The luminous trickster might have taken over our game if she had not tired and returned to his perch as a crow" [115]) and we will sometimes refer to the trickster as being male, sometimes female.

7. An alternative to this reading is suggested in the myth itself. The new form of discourse can be seen as a chance survivance of older constructions, brought up through the discourse at great risk by the trickster's mythological animal helpers. Through this imposing layer they dive one after another until eventually a pawful of earth is retrieved, from which the trickster recreates the world in its new forms.

8. "*Listen, ha ha ha haaaa*" (Vizenor, *Bearheart* vii).

9. "He had discovered his reflection in a full length mirror which did not quite reach to the ground so that by crouching down he could make his mirror image 'gone'" (Freud 284 n1). We of course see the relevance of Lacan here, but due to restrictions of space we choose not to hear him now.

10. Laundry's "graduation" from the initiation process, his self-effaced hearing of shadows in the mirror, is effected after Bagese's disappearance. His ability to see the bear in the mirror and his calm, affectionate manner toward the vision are proof of his acceptance of the world into which Bagese has brought him. See note 13 below.

11. The second trickster brother is a clear example of silence in Vizenor's work. His participation is marginal within the story of the three tricksters, like Laundry he is nameless and he is described as "a manidoo child with some human features" (25). He joins Naanabozho in his nightly adventures, but he is silent and "never answered the question" when asked to kill Stone (26). More is not disclosed about this silent manidoo child who may be seen to be a sort of counterpart to Laundry.

12. See Harley for example.

13. A koan is "a riddle used in Zen Buddhism to demonstrate the inadequacy of logical reasoning" (*OED*). Bagese deliberately brings Laundry to face and accept his fear; she brings him slowly to initiation. Bagese recognizes the fact that Laundry is between two worlds and she ironically explains that the bear-knowledge she gives is "too much to endure at rush hour, in line at the

bank, or in a lecture at the university" (20). Laundry must incorporate this new spiritual understanding into his compromised world, even its fearful sexual element: "her lust almost did me in when at last . . . she appeared to me as a bear in the tabernacle mirror" (20).

14. An interesting comparison would be the German trickster figure Ulenspegel, "owlglass," and the fact that a contrasting mythological figure, that of the vampire-destructor, does not show in mirrors.

15. Vizenor used Richard Rorty's term to delineate constructions (not only) of the Native American experience that reduce or abolish the possibility of irony, when he lectured on "The Aesthetics of Translation" on August 3, 1993, as part of the Stuttgart Seminar in Cultural Studies.

Works Cited

Freud, Sigmund. "Beyond the Pleasure Principle." *On Metapsychology: The Theory of Psychoanalysis.* Penguin Freud Library vol. 11. Ed. Angela Richards. London: Penguin, 1991.

Harley, J. B. "Maps, Knowledge and Power." *The Iconography of Landscape: Essays on the Symbolic Representation, Design and Use of Past Environments.* Ed. Dennis Cosgrove and Stephen Daniels. Cambridge: Cambridge UP, 1988.

Krupat, Arnold. "Trickster's Lives: The Autobiographies of Gerald Vizenor." Toronto: MLA Convention, December 29, 1993.

Nancy, Jean-Luc. "Exscription." *The Birth to Presence.* Stanford: Meridian P, 1993. 319-40.

Silko, Leslie Marmon. *Ceremony.* New York: Penguin, 1977.

Vizenor, Gerald. *Bearheart.* 1978. Minneapolis: U of Minnesota P, 1990.

——. *Dead Voices: Natural Agonies in the New World.* Norman & London: U of Oklahoma P, 1992.

——. "The Ruins of Representation: Shadow Survivance and the Literature of Dominance." *American Indian Quarterly* 17.1 (Winter 1993): 7-30.

11

TRIBAL IMAGES OF THE "NEW WORLD":
APOCALYPTIC TRANSFORMATION IN *ALMANAC OF THE DEAD*
AND GERALD VIZENOR'S FICTION

David Mogen

Like Leslie Silko's *Almanac of the Dead,* Gerald Vizenor's *Bearheart, Dead Voices,* and *The Heirs of Columbus* utilize apocalyptic and futuristic themes to comment on cultural conflict and world view dislocations. Yet these fictions also dramatize conceptions of time, space, and causality that question the very models of linear history structuring traditional Western treatments of apocalypse and the future.[1] Most fundamentally, by dramatizing the emergence of "new worlds" shaped in visions and prophecies, all of these novels adapt aspects of American and Native American tradition to reinterpret the meanings of cultural apocalypse from a primarily tribal point of view.

Many of Vizenor's transformational themes are grimly paralleled in *Almanac of the Dead,* in which Silko evokes underlying patterns of Indian prophecy to project apocalyptic images of cultural and spiritual crisis. Similarly, in *Bearheart* Vizenor extends trickster tradition into a postapocalyptic future landscape to examine the destructive effects of "terminal creeds." In *Dead Voices* he creates a subtle apocalypse of the spirit in a contemporary setting. And in *The Heirs of Columbus,* Vizenor constructs a kind of parallel history narrative that cannot be located precisely in conventional Western time and space, but seems to be located in a mythic, trickster universe that interpenetrates with conventional history and "reality."

Though in Western tradition apocalypse is deeply identified with disaster, it can also evoke images of transformational regeneration, and it is this aspect of the theme that Silko and Vizenor ultimately project in their apocalyptic fictions. In all four of these major Native American novels the apocalyptic theme recapitulates grim aspects of tribal experience under colonization, yet it also projects possibilities for the survival of tribal values into an emerging "new world"—the imminent revolution in *Almanac of the Dead,* the "fourth world" to which Indian pilgrims escape in *Bearheart,* the bizarre world of the "wanaki game" in *Dead Voices,* and a kind of tribal utopia in the new nation established by Stone Columbus in *The Heirs of Columbus.*

To discuss such connections between major works of Native American literature and a theme usually associated with science fiction is, of course, to plot lines of convergence between two frequently marginalized traditions, perhaps even to run the risk of further marginalizing both as margins in the margins. But the connection to "science" provides at least the potential for illuminating how Native American tradition, imaginatively understood, impinges upon the most powerful validation system of our time. Though science fiction still is marketed and perceived primarily as "genre" entertainment for a limited audience, it has gained some limited recognition as an art form that at its best interprets the impact of science on culture: almost all universities have integrated science fiction into their curricula in some form, and increasingly specific books and authors break through to a mainstream audience. Though much science fiction is indeed formulaic adventure fiction, the genre has created a mythic environment and a vocabulary of themes and symbols that, at its best, explores the possibilities and dangers created by Western ideals of "progress."

The most general theme common to both Native American writing and science fiction is, of course, the theme of being "caught between two worlds,"[2] a phrase that by its tendency to evoke cliché invites deconstruction. In Native American texts this theme often becomes a trickster survival story, in which the implied tragedy is reconstituted to portray creative transformation and cultural adaptation. For the character or the people "caught" between worlds also have the positive potential for integration, for creatively transforming the terms of conflict to emerge into a "new world" (whether a literally conceived world of the future, a transformation of consciousness, or a next world of Indian prophecy).

Like Native American protagonists who move between their traditional cultures (or remnants thereof) and modern mainstream culture, many science fiction protagonists move from the "known" world to encounters with the alien—whether set in the earth's future, on another planet, or in a parallel universe. And many science fiction writers have quite consciously adapted this convergence of themes, as can be seen not only in such juvenile creations as Andre Norton's "Sioux Spaceman," but also in some of the most well-known classics of the field: thus, Aldous Huxley's *Brave New World* depicts "John Savage" leaving the reservation to enter "Utopia"; Ray Bradbury's *The Martian Chronicles* (like countless other space-colonization novels) portrays frontiersmen from earth encountering alien civilizations clearly modeled on those encountered by Europeans in the "New World"; and an experimental novel like Roger Zelazny's *The Eye of Cat* portrays a Navajo bounty hunter of the future using elements of his traditional culture to track a dangerous alien adversary.[3]

The most interesting writing in all of these traditions explores such thematic convergences between genres through a kind of postmodernist play with contradictory dramatic and philosophical implications. Just as some science fiction writers have integrated Native American themes into extrapolation about the future and outer space, so Native American writers such as Silko and Vizenor, consciously or unconsciously, adapt traditional science fiction themes to their own purposes. And in all of these traditions apocalyptic conflicts between worlds portray both imminent disaster and possibilities for transformative cultural integration.

In this very general sense the themes of many Native American writers converge with those of an extensive ironic tradition of science fiction, expressed in endless elaborations of the Frankenstein Myth, in which the scientific world view creates horrors ranging from Doomsday weaponry to bio-engineered monsters to ecological disaster. But Silko's and Vizenor's adaptations of specific conventions traditional to science fiction, such as the apocalyptic collapse of technological culture and utopianism, illustrate that, consciously or not (in Vizenor's case especially this enterprise appears to be overt) some of the best Native American writers explore boundaries that both separate and connect speculative science and Indian tradition.

The post-holocaust future provides one of science fiction's extensive ironic traditions, warning about the dangers of unexamined "progress" by dramatizing the aftermath of physical and cultural apocalypse, and both *Almanac of the Dead* and *Bearheart* adapt variations of this environment to their authors' purposes. (Though *Almanac of the Dead* presents essentially a pre-apocalyptic setting, it clearly leaves us poised on the brink of radical upheaval—politically, culturally, and environmentally—as revolutionary forces converge in Tucson; and *Bearheart* presents an essentially Indian pilgrimage through a future West returned to a state of frontier anarchy created by depletion of energy resources.) Though nothing in these texts suggests that either Silko or Vizenor conceived of them in terms of science fiction categories, their theme of post-technological apocalypse suggests fundamental affinities with this ironic, mythic tradition. The future here is both a warning, an ominous prediction of possible disaster, and, more fundamentally, a mirror that refracts in mythic images contemporary dislocations in values and philosophy: thus, in conventional political terms *Almanac* portrays racial and class conflict escalating into revolution, and *Bear-*

heart depicts the aftermath of technological dependency and unrestrained ecological exploitation. But in the context of tribal experience this mirror refracts repressed history as well, since nightmare images of the future evoke hidden horrors of the past. Like the desolate futures of Wells's *The Time Machine* or Walter Miller's *A Canticle for Leibowitz* or J. G. Ballard's *Terminal Beach* or Philip K. Dick's entropic post-war landscapes (translated into film imagery in such works as *Bladerunner* and the Mad Max and Terminator series), the futures presented in *Almanac of the Dead* and *Bearheart* function both as predictive forewarnings and as mythic extensions of the present and past.

Yet if *Almanac of the Dead* and *Bearheart* are informed by forms of irony that are deeply associated with science fiction, they also dramatize assumptions that are alien to most science fiction tradition (writers such as Ursula K. Le Guin and Octavia Butler are to some extent exceptions). These visions of the future arise more fundamentally from tribal patterns of prophecy than from scientific extrapolation, and the fictions themselves incorporate non-Western conceptions of "story" derived from oral tribal traditions: traditional stories, trickster tales, dreams, and visions provide primary bases for extrapolation, along with predictive, science-based speculations. Most fundamentally, perhaps, these contemporary Native American fictions are shaped within a metaphysics that challenges fundamental Western assumptions about time, space, and causality. If these novels are in some sense tribal (to use Vizenor's generalized sense of the term "tribal") "science fictions," they are science fictions whose design radically alters traditional Western images both of "science" and "fiction."

In an eloquent essay about the origins of *Almanac of the Dead,* Silko discusses the Indian conceptions of time and metaphysics that partially inspired her fiction:

My interest in time comes from my childhood with the old-time people who had radically different views of the universe and reality. For the old-time people, time was not a series of ticks of a clock, one following the other. For the old-time people time was round—like a tortilla; time had specified moments and specific locations so that the beloved ancestors who had passed on were not annihilated by death, but only relocated to the place called Cliff House. At Cliff House, people continued as they had always been, although only spirits and not living humans can travel freely over this tortilla of time. All times go on existing side by side for all eternity. No moment is lost or destroyed. There are no future times or past times; there are *always all* the times, which differ slightly, as the locations on the tortilla differ slightly. The past and future are the same because they exist only in the "present" of our imaginations. We can only think and speak in the present, but as we do it is becoming the past which is always present and which always contains the future encoded in it. Without clocks or calendars we see only the succession of days . . . but the succession is cyclic. . . . Nothing is lost, left behind, or destroyed. It is only changed. (Silko, "Notes" 136-37)

Silko here essentially deconstructs from a tribal point of view some of the fundamental categories within which science fiction traditionally has been conceived: time is cyclic rather than linear, causality derives from spirit rather than mechanism, and even in apocalypse nothing is destroyed, only changed. Past and future, the Other World of spirits and this world we experience—all are connected in "imagination" of the present. But as the novel's title suggests, once we learn that the almanac survives from the ancient Mayas, time here is conceived within a specifically Mayan context as well, in which calendars and clocks record the cyclical nature of time, in which purpose and intent animate time itself: "What interested me about the Mayas was their notion of time; they believed that time was a living being that had a personality, a sort of identity. Time was alive and might pass but time did not die; moreover, the days and weeks eventually would return" (Silko, "Notes" 135).

Though the novel's action appears to take place in a setting familiar to science fiction readers—an imminent, unspecified future in which the world we know is transformed radically through disaster—within Silko's larger conception this future is not comprehensible to any conventionally "scientific" inquiry. Though the novel is rich in detail, chronicling dislocations on an epic scale, weaving together historical facts and fictions from diverse points of view on two continents throughout five hundred years of history, this future is not merely an apocalypse happening in time, but an apocalypse of time itself. Time is not merely the theater, but the active agent of the drama as well.

Silko's portrayal of impending apocalypse expresses political protest on many fronts—about historical and ongoing colonial carnage, eco-destruction, insular Marxist ideology, political and bureaucratic corruption—but the revolutionaries here recognize that they are merely agents of larger forces, the furious spirits of the coming days. The motley collection of holistic healers at the novel's conclusion, like the gathering crowds following the twins and the sacred macaws on their mysterious pilgrimage to the Mexican/American border where the forces of apocalypse converge, are literally attuned to energies of the time, for the climactic convergence in Tucson has been anticipated in centuries of tribal prophecy: "the world that the whites brought with them would not last. It would be swept away in a giant gust of wind. All they had to do was wait. It would only be a matter of time" (Silko,

Almanac 235). Ultimately, this revolution cannot be entirely explained through conventional political or economic theory (hence the elaborate commentary on the limitations of Marxism). Its forces come from Mayan metaphysics, from the angry energies of the returning days.

In Vizenor's *Bearheart* the apocalypse has already occurred, and the disintegration of civilization as we know it has created a new frontier in which an Indian pilgrimage retraces the historical course of American westward expansion through the ruins of technological civilization. An ironically inverted "Western" as well as an Indian science fiction, *Bearheart*'s postapocalyptic landscapes satirize sterile, destructive ideals of progress, as Vizenor's comments on the novel suggest: "I conceived of it as an episodic journey obliquely opposed to manifest destiny, a kind of parallel contradiction, of Indians moving south and southwest rather than West. What they're travelling through is the ruins of Western civilization, which has exhausted its petroleum, its soul" (Vizenor, *Bearheart* 249).[4]

But though this ravaged landscape does warn of the dangers of overdevelopment and ecological exploitation, Vizenor's primary satirical target is not technological but conceptual, the "terminal creeds" that trap Indians and non-Indians alike into constricted, lifeless roles. These "ruins of Western civilization" are simply products of an inadequate world view, and the novel's opening page establishes a context which integrates the gothic science fiction landscape into the structures of Indian prophecy:

> The earth turtles emerge from the great flood of the first world. In the second world the earth is alive in the magical voices and ceremonial words of birds and the healing energies of plants. . . . The third world turns evil with contempt for living and fear of death. . . . In the fourth world evil spirits are outwitted in the secret languages of animals and birds. . . . The crows crow in their blackness. Ha ha ha haaaaa the bears call from sunrise. (*Bearheart* 5)

This description of the prophesied cycle of "worlds" defines the character of our third world in its final stages (become a "third world" indeed after the exhaustion of energy resources), and it also foreshadows the central action of the novel, whose pilgrims ultimately pass through a "vision window" to enter as bears into the fourth world. Whether taken literally or figuratively, this metaphysical context fundamentally shapes Vizenor's presentation of the postapocalyptic journey, whose episodic structure derives at least as much from trickster tradition as from ironic recapitulation of Western epic.[5] In this science-fictional landscape of technological ruin, trickster energies replace vanished petroleum, and reconstructed oral traditions shape the Indian pilgrims' quest.

The story of Sir Cecil, the "evil gambler, the monarch of unleaded gasoline" (102), illustrates this fusion of science fiction imagery and trickster tradition: created by technology's disintegration, sadistically manipulating travelers desperate for gasoline into his web of pain, he is both Frankenstein monster and an evil witch of Indian tradition. When Proude Cedarfair defeats him at his perversion of a tribal gambling game, itself an evil parody of ritual ceremony, Cedarfair defeats both the culture of death in its final agonies and a radically reconceived Indian symbol of evil. And just as Vizenor's symbols of evil integrate tribal stories with apocalyptic gothicism, so too his myth of survival and transformation fuses Euro-American "New World" imagery with tribal prophecy. The pilgrims' quest for a "new world paradise in New Mexico" (97) ultimately leads to the fourth world, where trickster/animal warriors transform evil, just as Cedarfair defeated the malignant gambler.[6]

This transformation of the Indian protagonist into a bear in another world also provides the closing image to Vizenor's later novel, *Dead Voices,* when the old storyteller and master of the "wanaki game," Bagese, seems to disappear into the mirrors as a bear. Here Vizenor subtly adapts the apocalypse theme into an intimate interpersonal drama in a contemporary setting. Through Bagese the primary narrator, himself a Native American scholar versed in the Western arts of speaking in "dead voices," encounters in the urban setting in which he lives the reality of animal spirits and living, though transformed, Indian tradition. In this complex postmodernist play on the connections between forms of discourse and "reality," Vizenor dramatizes recovery of an apparently lost relationship to nature through personal transformation.

Like Vizenor's earlier work both in essays and in fiction, *Dead Voices* dramatizes the complex "word wars" waged between tribal peoples and mainstream culture. Indeed, as the title suggests, this strange "novel" creates a living trickster voice—at once profane, lyrical and wondrously bizarre—through which to dramatize a radical perspective on the Western tradition of written culture, embodying "dead voices" that suppress the "natural agonies" of tribal peoples and the natural world. By giving written "voice" to the internal narrator Bagese, a recluse tribal woman who is at once a bear and the vehicle through which we hear the agonies of animal beings surviving in the urban landscape, Vizenor paradoxically translates unspeakable realities into a written medium that historically has obliterated them in wars of words. Because the very voice of the novel embodies a paradox of articulation, this is a difficult book to read, one in which meaning and narrative alike seem to hover just beyond the reach of written language. Like the mirrors in Bagese's home that provide glimpses of her bear identity, the language here presents tantalizing refractions from realms of experience that never entirely come into focus. But this effect of suspension between worlds of discourse creates a curious poetry as well, in which conventional images of tribal cultures, nature, and reality itself are radically transposed.

The novel's messages are implicit in its paradoxical point of view, which integrates "voices" that are inherently untranslatable, so that decoding the perspectives of the various voices telling the narrative becomes part of the process of "reading." The three major categories of "voice" are suggested in the opening chapter, "Shadows," which serves as a fictional author's preface to the tales that follow. Here the tribal storyteller Bageese warns the scholarly narrator of the dangers of translating her stories into the "dead voices" of lectures and printed words: "She was a bear . . . [who] said that tribal stories must be told not recorded, told to listeners but not readers, and she insisted that stories be heard through the ear not the eye" (Vizenor, *Dead Voices* 10-11).

This introductory warning about the difficulty of translating oral into written "hearing" is later compounded by the nature of the stories themselves, which originate in the tribal "wanaki game," and which must be experienced and told from a first person plural point of view, in which the human narrator's voice is fused with those of the beings whose stories are being told. Bagese's education of the narrator also prepares the reader for the uniquely conceived voice of the stories that follow: "The secret, she told me, was not to pretend, but to see and hear the real stories behind the words, the voices of the animals in me, not the definitions of the words alone" (7). Thus we are introduced to the wanaki game, in which the "we" of the stories become, in turn, the beings designated in the story titles: "Stones," "Bears," "Fleas," "Squirrels," "Mantis," "Crows," "Beavers," "Tricksters," and finally, the plurality of plurals, "Voices," before the transformed narrator returns to conclude the novel by chronicling Bagese's final disappearance.

In his quincentennial novel, *The Heirs of Columbus,* Vizenor translates this theme of personal transformation of consciousness into a more general theme of cultural transformation, creating an epic reconstruction of the last five hundred years of history in the "New World." To turn from *Almanac of the Dead* and *Bearheart* to *The Heirs of Columbus* is (like the tribal pilgrims entering the fourth world) to leave the gothic environment of the postapocalypse future for utopia, science fiction's mythic counterpoint to the Frankenstein story. Here Vizenor re-envisions "progress" in tribal terms, developing the theme of quincentennial apocalypse as a trickster romance of cultural transformation. In keeping with their quincentennial theme both *Almanac of the Dead* and *The Heirs of Columbus* chronicle the conclusion of a story that began with Columbus's arrival in the New World, but whereas Silko dramatizes the return of angry days and vengeful spirits, Vizenor portrays an essentially peaceful transition in which tribal heroes "created one more New World in their stories and overturned tribal prophecies that their avian time would end with the arrival of the white man" (Vizenor, *Heirs* 5). Both *Almanac of the Dead* and *Bearheart* identify tribal prophecies with violent apocalypse, disintegration of the Euro-American order. But in the utopian vision of *The Heirs of Columbus* the "New World" is ushered in quietly by enchanting trickster conversation on late night radio talk shows, by a creative tribal community that integrates perceptions of animal spirits with computer technology to create public visions in laser light shows. In tribal utopia science and vision work in harmony, as the new nation employs genetic researchers and engineers both to tap into "the ultimate tribal power . . . the healer genes" (161) and to scramble forever all racial definitions of identity (162).

In tribal utopia Columbus himself is a primal crossblood—both the Old World's first agent of the culture of death and ancestor to the crossblood survivors who begin constructing the tribal "New World" as the quincentennial ends. Apocalypse comes not from destruction but from delight and wonder, not from tragic resistance but from comic liberation. Reflecting on the tragic death of tribal hero Louis Riel, Stone Columbus, crossblood descendant of Christopher himself, states the novel's utopian theme: "Stone was heartened by the wild heat of his [Riel's] resistance and spiritual visions, but not by the cold weather of his tragic creeds. The heirs pursued the same mission of resistance and tribal independence, but theirs liberated the mind with the pleasures of trickster humor, and held no prisoners in the heart" (160).

To ask where this utopia exists in time and space is, of course, to revisit the ironic pun in Sir Thomas More's title, describing a "perfect place" that is "no place." Or perhaps this irony itself is a product of Old World metaphysics, of linear time, bounded space, and mechanistic causality. Perhaps in the next New World utopia can finally escape the mechanistic definition of perfection that has doomed all Western utopias to become anti-utopias. And more fundamentally, perhaps in this mythic space/time utopia can truly exist both as symbol and reality, in that Other World of spirit that is no less real because it is accessible only through a "vision window." The novel tells us only that utopia actually began on October 12, 1992, when Stone Columbus established a sovereign tribal nation at Point Assinika, where he originally harbored the *Santa Maria Casino,* his "tribal flagship" (6), as well as the floating restaurant on the *Nina* and the tax-free market on the *Pinta*. And we know that this perfect no-place shares most of our vexed history of five hundred years of word wars and physical and spiritual carnage.

But in *The Heirs of Columbus* fundamental alterations of history reconstruct the present to make tribal utopia possible. Here, as Stone Columbus explains, "The Maya brought civilization to the savages of the Old World" in ancient times, and "Columbus escaped from the culture of death and carried our genes back to the New World, back to the great river," for "he was an adventurer in our blood and he returned to his homeland" (9). If the present truly consists of past and future constructed in the imagination, perhaps utopia could become our present, now that the myth creates it. Perhaps novels can be "vision windows" into new worlds, where trickster humor integrates re-visioned "science" with tribal "fictions" to transform both science and fiction in a new "New World" paradigm.

Perhaps these two quincentennial novels best illustrate the range of possibilities explored in contemporary Native American fiction, the ways that cultural conflict can generate both despair and creative cultural transformations. In these quincentennial fictions we can visualize alternatives—apocalypse through tragedy, or apocalypse through laughter. We can choose convergences of tribal fictions and science fictions that create a crossblood metaphysics for a new era, in which the Old World and the New World merge in new constructions of time, space, and causality. Or we can choose the constructions of our tragic creeds, in which we can only hope a phoenix will arise from ashes. As Silko's and Vizenor's imagined Mayas might put it, only time will tell.

Notes

1. For an extensive analysis of this apocalyptic theme in American science fiction see David Ketterer's *New Worlds for Old*.

2. This parallel is fundamentally important to fantasy as well (whether science fiction is simply a specialized category of this often loosely defined "genre" is a subject of never-resolved dispute about definitions). But I am most interested here in the convergences between images of the future at least obstensibly founded in scientific speculation ("extrapolation," in science fiction terminology) and those founded in Native American oral tradition and prophecy, since they most dramatically illustrate postmodernist exploration of divergent cultural contructs of "reality."

3. For a more general discussion of convergences between science fiction and traditional themes of frontier fiction see my *Wilderness Visions*.

4. Quoted in Louis Owens's afterword to Gerald Vizenor's *Bearheart*.

5. This basic plot—centering on a hero and/or a group traveling west in pursuit of often contradictory goals and dreams—is, of course, an archetype of American frontier fiction, from Young Goodman Brown's journey into the forest to the epic scale of action in novels such as Willa Cather's *My Antonia* and A. B. Guthrie, Jr.'s *The Big Sky*. For an extended discussion of Vizenor's fusion of trickster tradition and American Frontier Gothic in this novel see Louis Owens's "'Grinning Aboriginal Demons': Gerald Vizenor's *Bearheart* and the Indian's Escape from Gothic" in *Frontier Gothic* (Mogen et al.).

For further discussion of Vizenor's use of trickster figures to engage in "word wars" with mainstream culture see Louis Owens's chapter, "Ecstatic Strategies: Gerald Vizenor's Trickster Narratives," in *Other Destinies: Understanding the American Indian Novel* (Owens). See also Alan Velie's "The Trickster Novel" and Gerald Vizenor's essay, "Trickster Discourse: Comic Holotropes and Language Games," in *Narrative Chance: Postmodern Discourse on Native American Indian Literatures* (Vizenor).

Works Cited

Ketterer, David. *New Worlds for Old*. Garden City, NY: Doubleday, 1974.

Mogen, David. *Wilderness Visions: The Western Theme in Science Fiction Literature*. 2nd ed. San Bernardino, CA: Borgo P, 1993.

Mogen, David, Mark Busby, and Joanne Karpinski, eds. *Frontier Gothic: Terror and Wonder at the Frontier in American Literature*. London and Toronto: Associated UPs, 1993.

Owens, Louis. "Ecstatic Strategies: Gerald Vizenor's Trickster Narratives." *Other Destinies: Understanding the American Indian Novel*. Norman and London: U of Oklahoma P, 1992. 225-54.

——. "'Grinning Aboriginal Demons': Gerald Vizenor's *Bearheart* and the Indian's Escape from Gothic." *Frontier Gothic*. 71-83.

Silko, Leslie Marmon. *Almanac of the Dead*. New York: Simon and Schuster, 1991.

——. "Notes on *Almanac of the Dead*." *Yellow Woman and a Beauty of the Spirit: Essays on Native American Life*. New York: Simon and Schuster, 1996. 135-45.

Velie, Alan. "The Trickster Novel." *Narrative Chance* (Vizenor). 121-39.

Vizenor, Gerald. *Bearheart*. 1978. Minneapolis: U of Minnesota P, 1990.

——. *Dead Voices*. Norman and London: U of Oklahoma P, 1992.

——. *The Heirs of Columbus*. Hanover, NH: UP of New England, 1991.

Vizenor, Gerald, ed. *Narrative Chance: Postmodern Discourse on Native American Indian Literatures*. Norman and London: U of Oklahoma P, 1992.

12

TO HONOR IMPERMANENCE:
THE HAIKU AND OTHER POEMS OF GERALD VIZENOR

Tom Lynch

the arrogance of academic discoveries[1]
Poems on a page bear a decidedly, yet deceptively, fixed being. The Western literary tradition (if I may invoke such a creature) has historically preferred fixed texts. Even when confronting slippery oral traditions, an enormous effort has been expended to canonize an originary Ur-form of each tale. Such a tendency, akin to mounting a bird species rather than pondering the flight of feathers, is the antagonist of Vizenor's poetic art. In what follows I seek to explore some of the ways Vizenor's haiku and longer poetry melt fixation and celebrate the transformative possibilities of impermanence.

—HAIKU
I think my first important experience as a writer, my most ecstatic experiences, were with poetry.[2]

> *November trees*
> *Fine lines of delicate twigs:*
> *The twilight sky.*

When readers discover that Gerald Vizenor writes haiku poetry, they may be reminded of Richard Wright. Both are writers concerned with, if not consumed by, ethnic and racial identity politics and resistance to the multiple manifestations of racist ideologies. In 1959, late in his life, Wright discovered haiku through R. H. Blyth's books and from his death bed composed more than 4,000 of his own. His title for his selected haiku, *This Other World,* suggests the distinction he saw between haiku and the political literature he spent most of his life writing. Though at first glance one might suspect that for Vizenor as well, haiku is an adjunct to, perhaps an escape from, his more serious project of assailing the terminal creeds of manifest destinarian ideologies, such an assessment would be mistaken. Unlike Wright, Vizenor came to haiku at the start of his literary career. Indeed his experiences in Japan and with haiku were formative in the development of his literary aesthetic and impelled his political consciousness.

Vizenor's academic career is also obliged to haiku, which were responsible for his first academic position: "Professor George Mills hired me to teach at Lake Forest College in Illinois and inaugurated my career as a college teacher in the most unusual manner: haiku poems, not a doctorate, earned the highest honors" (*Interior* 218).

Because Vizenor's current reputation rests so strongly on his status as a theorist and novelist, haiku, a genre that eschews theoretical content, seems peripheral. Given the obscurity of the genre in academic discourse, who would notice his haiku—however excellent—if they constituted his sole output? Yet haiku may be postulated as enacting, rather than discussing, his theoretical positions. Through them one encounters, not the essence, but the presence of Vizenor's imagination. Haiku, slight though they may be, embrace the wide expanse of his concerns:

Haiku thought is intuitive, a manner of meditation at a dreamscape, a clear distance from dense grammatical philosophies and dominant political ideologies. Haiku turns are moments of wonder in the natural world, surprises at the treelines near the trail, at the woodland rim; internal transformations through mythic word cinemas, visions and dreams, memories, unusual symmetries, and imaginative relationships between words, birds, fur, water, insect sounds, twists in the snow. Haiku is blue, tactile, musk, tribal, and a dance. (*Matsushima* n.p.)

Haiku imbue Vizenor's theoretical prose and his fiction, no doubt exasperating some critics when a prose essay on a theoretical aspect of tribal identity suddenly cascades imagery across the page.

—JAPAN
The Japanese and their literature were my liberation. ("Envoy" 27)

> *calm in the storm*
> *master basho soaks his feet*
> *water striders*

Sent to Japan as a GI in 1953, Gerald Vizenor escaped transfer to Korea and so had opportunity to encounter Japanese literature. Illustrating the transformative power of that trickster—chance—Vizenor, an urban crossblood Anishinabe, discovered the power of literature, gained access to his own poetic heritage, and found a literary voice in occupied Japan. "How ironic," he says "that my service as a soldier would lead me to haiku, and haiku an overture to dream songs. Haiku would be my introduction to the pleasures of literature, a national literature that did not exclude the common reader by dominance, decadence, or intellectual elitism" ("Envoy" 26). Encountering haiku in the season of his 18th summer, Vizenor was "liberated from the treacherous manners of missionaries, classic warrants, the themes of savagism and civilization, and the arrogance of academic discoveries" ("Envoy" 26).

In part at least, his haiku are an effort to glean a remembrance bordering nostalgia: "I would regret my decision to leave, and over the years told stories and wrote poems to remember the sound and scent of Japan" (*Interior* 130). His remembrance of those times in Japan exude desire: "Japan was my lover in the mountains" (130). With Aiko Okada, his Japanese lover to whom he later dedicated several of his haiku collections, Vizenor pilgrimaged on the route of the Master Bashô.

Matsuo Bashô visited Matsushima and wrote in his haibun travel diaries about the moon over the pine islands. We were there three hundred years later and remembered the master haiku poet. Aiko told stories and poems and touched the sand creases near shore; we held the water, raised the moon in our hands, wished in silence to hold that night under the pines. Leashed boats turned on their moorage in the bay. We waited in the fresh shadows and then crossed the wooden bridge back to the mainland and the hotel. (*Interior* 145)

His haiku serve in part to "hold that night under the pines." The wish is fulfilled in the imagistic line that follows that phrase: "Leashed boats turned on their moorage in the bay." Calling that image to mind returns him to that delicate evening vigil.

Vizenor was accepted as a student to Sophia University in Tokyo, where he imagined himself studying "Japanese language and literature, tea ceremonies, haiku poetry, the soul of the crane" (his Anishinabe clan totem and an honored being in Japan). At the last moment, however, he rejected the position and returned to the United States, a decision he recalls somewhat wistfully in his autobiography (*Interior* 127).

Vizenor seems to have felt more at home in Japan than Minnesota. On his departure, he "cried and walked for hours to the train depot. I wanted to change my mind," he says, "to stay at home in Japan. I had no home; how ironic that there was no home at the end of my last road home" (*Interior* 149). To honor impermanence in haiku seems an oddly apt trickster gesture for one who found surcease from homelesness in a land not his home.

His desire to recall Japan seems to have grown stronger with time. His earliest collections of haiku have titles that do not explicitly invoke

Japan: *Two Wings the Butterfly* (1962), *Raising the Moon Vines* and *Seventeen Chirps* (1964), *Slight Abrasions: A Dialogue in Haiku,* with Jerome Downes (1966), and *Empty Swings* (1967). But his substantially revised collected haiku from 1984, *Matsushima: Pine Islands,* has a title that explicitly returns us to the Japanese experience that propelled his haiku performances. As his visit to Matsushima, and all that it configures, grows more remote in time, it looms more strongly in imagination: "shamans and other tribal healers and visionaries speak the various languages of plants and animals and feel the special dream power to travel backward from familiar times and places" (*Earthdivers* xvii).

Pondering Vizenor's haiku in the context of his expressed literary themes, several intertwined topics surface: impermanence and tradition, seasons, *oshki anishinabe,* Zen tricksters, nature, dissolving words, shadows, and attributes of development.

—IMPERMANENCE AND TRADITION
I learned to remember these stories, and to honor impermanence. (*Interior* 130)

> *sweet bouquet*
> *abandoned on a park bench*
> *set upon by bees*

When Vizenor returned to the United States from Japan he entered college and in 1960 again encountered haiku, this time in the University of Minnesota classroom of Professor Edward Copeland, who, Vizenor says, "opened his course on Japanese literature that summer with haiku in translation. The sense of impermanence, he said, is in the weather, the seasons, and in haiku; at the same time, we are aware of culture and tradition" (*Interior* 171). These remembered course notes, with their emphasis on impermanence, encapsulate Vizenor's haiku aesthetic:

Copeland recited and translated one of the greatest haiku poems by Basho: *furuike ya,* the ancient pond; *kawazu tobikomu,* frog leaps, or jumps; *mizu no oto,* the sound of water, or splash. The poem shows the season, and suggests tradition and impermanence in the most subtle images and motions. (*Interior* 172)

Summarizing the views of Kyorai, one of Bashô's disciples, Donald Keene explicates this notion of impermanence in more detail: "Bashô insisted that a worthwhile hokku must contain . . . eternal validity and not be a mere flash of wit, but it must also be in tune with the moment and not a fossilized generalization. . . . a hokku had to be at once about the observed moment . . . but also about the eternal element that was momentarily disturbed" (136).

This juxtaposition of permanence and change might also suggest a parallel to the condition of the postindian tribes confronting the dilemma of how to maintain tribal being yet remain alive to the flux of the contemporary world, not "a fossilized generalization" in a colonialist matrix. "The impermanence of natural reason and tribal remembrance," Vizenor says, "was close to the mood of impermanence in haiku" ("Envoy" 28).

The vicissitudes of Vizenor's own life (his father's murder, his mother's abandonment, his step-father's death, his passage from home to home) also emphasize—perhaps exaggerate—the wistful tragedies and occasional delights of impermanence. His recollection of Professor Copeland's description of Issa as one who "celebrated common creatures, the earth as it turns, runs, and blooms, impermanence and human ironies; he was poor, an orphan, and he loved nature" (*Interior* 172) could as well describe himself, and suggests a deeply personal basis for his interest in haiku.

—SEASONS
The greatest source of experience and inspiration comes from the seasons of Spring and Autumn and the transition and motion of life during these seasons. (Two Wings 6)

In the darkness
Only the scent of Autumn:
Smouldering leaves.

Impermanence most manifests itself in the great cycle of the seasons. Traditionally, for some people definitively, though less so in modern times, a haiku poem refers to the seasons, either overtly or through a conventional season word. In the *Spring* volume of R. H. Blyth's *Haiku* Vizenor would have read that for Bashô the season was the essential component of haiku, not, Blyth contends, simply "as a principle, but as a mode of intuition, a vaster way of seeing particular things. As we look more carefully at the object," Blyth continues, "we see in it the whole world working out its perfect will. And this comes from the historical, the accumulated experiences of the Japanese race during more than a thousand years" (v). Vizenor identifies a close affinity between this culturally inherited Japanese appreciation for the seasonal cycle and his tribal heirs' seasonally patterned life.

The *anishinaabe* learned to hear the seasons by natural reason. . . . The first tribal families trailed the shores of *gichigami* to the hardwoods and marshes where they touched the maple trees for *ziizibaakwadaaboo* in the spring, speared fish on the rivers, and then gathered *manoomin,* wild rice, in the late autumn. Before winter and the cold snow the tribes returned to their communities at *mooningwanekaning* on Madeline Island in Lake Superior. (*Summer* 5-6)

All his haiku books are seasonally organized. In several books each page of haiku also contains the Japanese character for the season. So one reads a poem, then the calligraphic name of the season, then a second haiku. The calligraphy serves more than a decorative function, it endorses the broadest context for the poems, it serves as the cosmic cycle of impermanence of which the image in the poem is a specific case. The season is at both the literal and imaginative center of each page.

An example from *Matsushima:*

sudden rain
scarecrows share an umbrella
bingo night

calico kittens
crowd around a bowl of milk
garden stones

Perhaps because the seasons, unfixed, energize the flux of life and embody in the largest cosmic sense the power of transformation, "the motion of the seasons," he says, are among those aspects that constitute "the hermeneutics of trickster stories" (*Summer* 10).

—ZEN TRICKSTER

Naanabozho . . . is related to the wind, and his brother is a stone. (*Interior* 129)

The cool breeze
Bends the whiskers of the cat
Napping in the window.

Kimberly Blaeser suggests that "many of Vizenor's haiku . . . readily exhibit a connection to the trickster tradition in Native American literature" (345). One might postulate various reasons for this link. For one, haiku, at least those in the Zen tradition, like the trickster, seek to delace the shrouds of what Vizenor calls "terminal creeds," or fixed categories of thought. The outlooks of both Zen and the trickster avoid dualities. Vizenor notes that "the images in a haiku are not reduced to structural polarities, the opposites are dissolved in words" (*Matsushima* n.p.).

Toward this end, both outlooks cherish intuition. Haiku poet and theorist Eric Amann says "a haiku is said to resemble the 'koan' in Zen teaching, inasmuch as it makes use of paradox, 'unresolved tension' and the juxtaposition of apparently unrelated images, forcing the reader into an intuitive rather than an intellectual perception of reality" (33). Such could as well be said of the trickster's service. Indeed Vizenor refers to Paul Reps's book *Zen Flesh, Zen Bones* as "a collection of trickster and meditation stories" (*Matsushima* n.p.).

—OSHKI ANISHINABE
The oshki anishinabe writer is a visual thinker. (Everlasting 69)

> *With the moon*
> *My young father comes to mind*
> *Walking the clouds.*

This poem, a bit mystical by haiku conventions, is more kin to Anishinabe dream songs and links Vizenor's immediate vision of the moon with his memory of his long-deceased father, his connection to his Anishinabe heritage. Vizenor's sense of the poetics of what he terms the *oshki anishinabe* (new Chippewa) writer could also serve as a definition of the haiku writer. When discussing Ted Mahto he states that "the *oshki anishinabe* writer is a visual thinker soaring on the rhythms of the woodland past through the gestures of the present" (*Everlasting* 69). This poetics is possible because "the *anishinabe* language of the past was a language of verbal forms and word images. The spoken feeling of the language—and thought processes—is a moving image of tribal woodland life. The visual images are not static or inferred from logic" (*Everlasting* 75).

Vizenor believes that a "mythic parallel" exists "between haiku and dream songs. . . . fundamental to both forms" is an "intensity of imagery and the idea of comparisons—the kind of mythic transformations, comparisons between human behavior, and comparisons in life without a superior relationship to it" ("An Interview" 42). According to Kimberly

Blaeser, Vizenor's haiku "seeks to combine the traditions of the Ojibway dream song and the Japanese haiku" (344). It may be useful to recall here that haiku poetry stem from and seek to reinvoke a moment of intense insight, what the Haiku Society of America calls "the essence of a moment keenly perceived, in which Nature is linked to human nature" (82). As Blaeser says, "the Ojibway dream songs also stem from a moment of intense personal awareness which, as the name indicates, may have come during a dream or visionary experience" (346). For Vizenor, she says, haiku and dream songs "intend to surpass or forgo the goals of any philosophy of literary esthetics for the sake of actual experience, for a moment of enlightenment" (349). Extending the parallel further, Blaeser suggests that "both haiku and dream songs also seek not merely to give voice to this visionary experience, but also, acting as stimuli, to assist the reader or listener in the attainment of a similar moment of spiritual awareness or illumination" (350). As Blyth says, haiku "are for you to use in your own poetic experience. You are not to be a mere observer of literature, but to play your part in its dynamic re-creation" (v). Several places in *Earthdivers,* a work concerned with the idea of creation and re-creation, Vizenor echoes Blyth by claiming that "creation takes place . . . between tellers and listeners" (*Earthdivers* 26). "Creation myths are not time bound, the creation takes place in the telling" (*Earthdivers* xii). In this sense, creation myths are like haiku, in which the events in the poem recur in the act of their telling. Each haiku is, in a very real sense then, a microcosmic creation myth calling into new being the events reinscribed through the telling. The creation of both the poem, and the events enacted in the poem, take place in the telling.

—NATURE
moments of wonder in the natural world. (Matsushima n.p.)

> *thunder clouds*
> *leech lake applauds at the dock*
> *crows mark the poplars*

Haiku are first, foremost, and fundamentally a poetry of nature. Even those poets who choose to write haiku about exclusively human topics generally justify this decision by arguing that moments of human existence are also subsets of nature (Willmot 211-25). This riveted concentration on the natural world, this acknowledgment of the validity, the ontological equivalence, of even the tiniest and seemingly most innocuous of creatures as the focus of important poetic art, draws another affinity between haiku and Anishinabe poetry.

While haiku is usually seen in the context of Buddhism, R. H. Blyth discusses the influence of Shinto in a way that suggests some parallels with Anishinabe culture. Blyth declares that the essence of "non-political Shinto" is "animism, the belief in indwelling spirits, together with animatism, or simple nature worship" (158). Though A. Irving Hallowell suggests that the Anishinabe are not entirely animistic, the possibility for animism exists. Indeed in Ojibwa grammar, he concludes "stones are grammatically animate" (24). Vizenor retells in *Earthdivers* how Hallowell "once asked an old *anishinaabe* man about the animation of stones: 'Are *all* the stones we see about us alive?' He reflected for a long while and then replied, 'No! But *some* are'" (xvii). One needn't propose any great similarity between Shinto and Anishinabe belief to see a basic compatibility on this issue. Vizenor quotes the neglected genius Lafcadio Hearn, to indicate the connective possibilities. Hearn, he says, though "born Irish and Greek"

became Japanese, and he could have become Anishinaabe; we were brothers with the trees and stones. "Until you can feel, and keenly feel, that stones have character, that stones have tones and values, the whole artistic meaning of a Japanese garden cannot be revealed to you." Naanabozho, the Anishinaabe earthdiver and tribal trickster, is related to the wind, and his brother is a stone. (*Interior* 129)

Both haiku and tribal literatures take the tiniest of creatures seriously for their own sake, not for what, like Shakespeare's lark arising or Burns's "Wee, sleekit, cow'rin, tim'rous beastie," they might be made to symbolize of the human condition. Like Issa's haiku, Vizenor's abound in the doings of the tiniest creatures:

Issa	Vizenor
Fleas of my hut,— I'm sorry for them; They become emaciated soon enough (Trans. Blyth)	Harried mosquito I am not the last of my kind Ticking my neck.
Do not kill the fly! See how it wrings its hands Its feet! (Trans. Blyth)	breakfast flies first at the table rural habits

—DISSOLVING WORDS

Not ersatz existence, but the sentiments of natural experiences when words dissolve. (Matsushima n.p.)

april ice storm
new leaves freeze overnight
words fall apart

In the preface to *Earthdivers* Vizenor quotes Karsten Harries that "there are moments when the inadequacy of our language seizes us, when language seems to fall apart and falling apart opens us to what transcends it. . . . As language falls apart, contact with being is reestablished . . ." (xvi). Haiku has been called "the wordless poem," and according to haiku poet and theorist Rod Willmot, "haiku's special characteristic as a form of literature is to seem not to be literature. In different terms: a haiku has 'presentational immediacy,' setting objects and events right before us without words getting in the way. At least, that is the illusion—an illusion created by words and our expectations about them" (Willmot 211).

This illusion is a paradox. In most literature the word signifies an external object, and that object in turn signifies symbolically some transcendent meaning. The words "old pond" on a page evoke the image of a pond, and that pond must, if we are to value the poem, we think, stand for something else, some significant meaning. In haiku, this is a mistake. If a Japanese haiku seems a meaningless image to a Western reader, it is not because that reader lacks familiarity with Japanese culture and so misses the symbolic significance, it is because the haiku is indeed, perversely, meaningless. Haiku seek to slide back down the chain of signifiers, eliminating the final stage and, by eschewing most literary tropes, creating an illusion that it has evaded the first stage of signification. As Eric Amann puts it,

The problem for the Western reader . . . is not to find the hidden meaning, the "symbolic signficance" of a haiku, for there is none, but to re-convert the images of a haiku into his own intuitions. And the answer to that lies in the art of reading haiku. A haiku is not meant to be read like a longer poem. It is more of an object for contemplation. First we must empty our minds of all pre-conceived ideas and re-experience what the poet saw or heard or felt. (Amann 3)

Vizenor concurs: "The reader creates a dreamscape from haiku; nothing remains in print, words become dream voices, traces on the wind, twists in the snow, a perch high in the bare poplar" (*Matsushima* n.p.). In the dreamscape of the imagination, the words "become" these things. Conversely, he continues, "Deconstruct the printed words in a haiku and there is nothing; nothing is in a haiku, not even a poem. The *nothing* in a haiku is not an aesthetic void; rather, it is a moment of enlightenment, a dreamscape where the words dissolve." For haiku provoke "not ersatz existence, but the sentiments of natural experiences when words dissolve" (*Matsushima* n.p.).

As an introduction to his book *Eating a Melon,* haiku poet Bob Boldman retells a Zen parable that further elaborates on this idea:

> Ken-O and his disciple Menzan were eating a melon together. Suddenly the master asked, "Tell me, where does all this sweetness come from?"
>
> "Why," Menzan quickly swallowed and answered, "it's a product of cause and effect."
>
> "Bah!, That's cold logic!"
>
> "Well," Menzan said, "from where then?"
>
> "From the very 'where' itself, that's where." (n.p.)

The Zen trickster Ken-O's "very 'where' itself" dissipates language and is an ally of Vizenor's shadow, the Anishinaabe "*agawatese.*"

—SHADOWS
The shadows are the prenarrative silence that inherits the words. (Manifest 14)

> *Even my shadow*
> *Moves as I do in the moon*
> *Listless October.*

One of the most common words in Vizenor's critical vocabulary is "shadow." When the words dissolve, only their shadows remain. In the essay "Shadow Survivance" he argues that

> the shadows are the silence in heard stories, the silence that bears a referent of tribal memories and experience. The shadow words are active memories, and the memories of heard stories. . . . The word *agawaatese* is heard in the oral stories of the *anishinaabe,* the tribal people of the northern woodland lakes. The word hears silence and shadows, and could mean a shadow, or casts a shadow. The sense of *agawaatese* is that the shadows are animate entities. (*Manifest* 72-73)

He relates the concept of shadow explicitly to haiku in which the dissolved word is replaced with a shadow in the evoked sensation. "The haiku poem, for instance, ascribes the seasons with shadow words." Vizenor goes on to quote Blyth: "'Haiku is the result of the wish, the effort, not to speak, not to write poetry, not to obscure further the truth and suchness of a thing with words, with thoughts and feelings,' wrote R. H. Blyth in *Haiku*" (65). Though quiet, haiku is sensational in that its design is to evoke a sensory experience. The shadow inheres in the sensation that precedes and postcedes language.

—ATTRIBUTES OF DEVELOPMENT
The notion, in the literature of dominance, that the oral advances to the written, is a colonial reduction of natural sound, heard stories, and the tease of shadows in tribal remembrance. (Manifest 72)

> *november storm*
> *hearts painted on the bridge*
> *crossed out*

Vizenor constantly revises his haiku. The flux of the poems seeks to avoid what we might call the "terminal poem" syndrome. Since each republication involves a reenactment, there are no scriptural versions of his haiku. Vizenor himself identifies three levels of variation or what he calls "attributes of development" ("Envoy" 30). The haiku in his first books, he says, "were common comparative experiences in the past tense." In *Matsushima*, however, the haiku "were more metaphorical, concise and with a sense of presence" ("Envoy" 30). A comparison of a poem originally published in *Empty Swings* and recomposed for *Matsushima* indicates some of the changes:

> Like silver buttons
> The moon comes through his shirt
> Threadbare scarecrow.

> october moonrise
> scarecrow in a threadbare shirt
> silver buttons

Haiku juxtapose image components, but the logic of a simile constrains response. In this revision Vizenor has taken the silver buttons out of the realm of the imagined simile and stitched them onto the scarecrow's shirt, allowing for a more suggestive and intuitive reading.

In his recent revisions he has also exchanged the past tense for the present, an alteration foregrounding his notion that "creation takes place in the telling, in present-tense metaphors" (*Earthdivers* xii). The change also gives the poems a greater sense of immediacy, as the following pairs indicate. The first in each pair is from *Seventeen Chirps* and the revised versions are from *Matsushima:*

The charcoal
Stored all summer in the shed
Smelled of urine.

birch wood
stacked all summer in the shed
scent of urine

The red bucket
Frozen under the rain spout
Began to leak.

wooden buckets
frozen under the rain spouts
springs a fast leak

To suggest, however, that the changes have always been improvement may be to commit the folly of canonizing a scriptural version in direct contradiction to Vizenor's desire to avoid such fixing. Perhaps it is better to see the various manifestations of the poems as akin to the seasonal flux. This spring is not an improvement on the last one, and a more recent version of a poem is not necessarily an improvement on a previous one—though the momentum to interpret it as such is strong.

His most recent revisions add what he terms an "envoy"

a prose concentration and discourse on the images and sensations. This practice combines my experience in haiku with natural reason in tribal literature, a new haiku hermeneutics. Tribal dream songs and haiku are concentrated in nature. For instance, the haiku poems that follow have an envoy, or a discourse on the reach of haiku sensations and tribal survivance. The envoy is interpretative; the three lines of the haiku are heard in shadow words and printed without punctuation. The envoy is in prose. ("Envoy" 30-31)

In the following he takes a poem from *Matsushima* and adds a discussion:

those stubborn flies
square dance across the grapefruit
honor your partner

Fat green flies dance on the backs of spoons, turn twice, and reach for the grapefruit. The flies allemande left and right in a great breakfast dance, but the owners of the spoons in the restaurant would terminate the insects to save the grapefruit. We are the lonesome dancers over the remains of so many natural partners in the world. ("Envoy" 31)

This practice of mixing prose and haiku has an honored history in Japan as a genre loosely referred to in English as haibun. Usually, however, haibun mingles haiku with either a descriptive travel journal, such as Bashô's *Oku no Hosomichi* (*The Narrow Road to the North*) or with a diary, such as Issa's *Oraga Haru* (*The Year of My Life*). In both cases, the prose provides a context for the haiku, but not, as in Vizenor's "envoys," an explicit analysis. Given the frustrations a haiku poet in America may experience with the limited ability of his audience to appreciate his art, Vizenor's desire to explicate is certainly understandable. But it also engenders a possible authorial interpretive hegemony, alien to the haiku spirit, which grants far more sovereignty to the reader. Even if, as Vizenor contends, "the interpretations of the heard and written must consider the shadow words and sensations of haiku," and even if "the envoys to haiku are the silent interpretations of a 'haiku spirit'" ("Envoy" 32), these envoys are nevertheless authorial interventions into the reader's experience of the image. Blaeser praises "the open text of Vizenor's haiku," which, she says, "generally works through images of the natural world. . . . In his poetry, he employs natural images but refrains from dictating connections or meaning. Instead, he holds faith with the visual imagination of the reader" (354). One seems compelled to ask, though, whether the addition of an envoy implies a retreat from this faith.

This question has arisen elsewhere in considerations of Vizenor's work. Discussing the film *Harold of Orange,* Robert Silberman has pondered this tendency in Vizenor's work:

In the movie, as, at times, in the introduction to his books . . . we can see Vizenor struggling to explain what he is doing and, because he is taking an essentially romantic view of the imagination as sacred and beyond rationalism, attacking the notion of explanation. There is a tension underlying Vizenor's double role as the self-conscious and self-critical individual who writes introductions [and envoys] "explaining" to the audience, a gesture of guidance and aid, and as the artist who then turns around and attacks explanations. (11)

The envoys to haiku may suggest an attempt on Vizenor's part to write a more elaborated form of haiku as an alternative to the longer poetry he composed earlier in his career.

—LONGER POEMS

I have never overcome my wearisome want to raise the word from the page, to sound out the passion and the sacrifices of literature in the voice of the crane. (Interior 144)

> grandchildren following
> clumsy and clover stained
> tasting the rain
> singing
> the world will change

Though longer poetry was important earlier in his career, in recent years Vizenor seems to consider it less so. In a 1981 interview Vizenor asserts that "I think my first important experience as a writer, my most ecstatic experiences, were with poetry." He then admits, however, to the declining importance of the longer poems: "I'm not sure now; except for haiku I'm much more moved by longer prose pieces" ("Interview" 43). He has never published a collection of his longer poetry, but many can be found in anthologies, most extensively in *Voices of the Rainbow: Contemporary Poetry by Native Americans* and *The Harper's Anthology of 20th Century Native American Poetry*.

His first serious poems were written in Japan. "The Balcony," which he calls "one of my earliest poems" was written for Aiko Okada (*Interior* 140). The poem is mainly a sequence of three-line imagistic stanzas, such as "Where the summer sun/Bakes and bleaches the stone,/Where the birds land, rest and sing." The dependence on imagery and the mood of pleasant melancholy show the influence of haiku and Japanese poetics. The poem is organized through a process of incremental parallelism, a design he will use frequently in his later poetry.

His later poems are similarly imagistic, but much more emotionally intense, a sort of extended haiku often transforming under the pressure of the post-colonial condition into a surrealistic expression of agony. The innocent image, brayed in the mortar of manifest destiny, excretes a tragicomic unction. For example, the poem "White Earth," subtitled "Images and Agonies," (a subtitle that could apply to many of his poems) opens with a seasonally explicit haiku-like image: "late october sun/breaks over the cottonwoods." One could almost expect a third line to complete this poem as a haiku, but instead the poem transforms with the slinking arrival of the trickster:

> tricksters
> roam the rearview mirrors
> government sloughs

The view in the rearview mirror, a compressed historical angle of vision, provides the perspective for the remainder of the poem. Grim, the poem is not entirely bleak. Though "beaded crucifixion/double over in the reeds," nevertheless somehow "shamans at the centerfolds/pave the roads/publish their poems." And although "fiscal storms/close the last survival school," we discover that "animals at the treelines/send back the hats and rusted traps" and might be reminded of the fur trade and imagine the beavers returning the beaver hats and rusted traps of their agony.

A similar but more personal, perhaps less overtly politicized poem, is "March in North Dakota":

>   the whole moon
>   burns behind jamestown
>
>   seven wings of geese
>   light the thin ice
>
>   asian sun
>   bleeds on the interstate
>
>   pressed flowers
>   tremble in the prairie stubble
>
>   paced on the mirror
>   my fingerprints blot the past

In this poem we are again traveling the highways of the northern plains, this time explicitly near Jamestown, North Dakota (though the name Jamestown might also prick a recollection of the early colonial village). The poem moves through a sequence of imagistic moments until the poet's fingers step across the rearview mirror to obscure the past. Bathed in prairie light, with the full moon rising on one side and the sun's glow burning on the other, the flowers tremble, and in flight across North Dakota the poet seeks to evade personal and/or cultural history.

A poem that explicitly shows the connection between his haiku and his longer poems, as well as the way his images exude a complicated political stance, is "Shaman Breaks"

>   1
>   colonists
>   unearth their wealth

and tease
the old stone man
over the breaks

moths batter
the cold windows
their light
is not our day

leaves abide the seasons
the last crows
smarten the poplars

2
tourists
discover their ruins
and mimic
the old stone woman
over the breaks

nasturtiums
dress the barbed wire
fences down
to the wild sea

magnolias
bloom under a whole moon
words fall apart

3
soldiers
bleach the landscapes
hound the shamans

wild stories
break from the stones

This poem echoes numerous lines and other poems of Vizenor's in one of the more overt gestures of self-referential intertextuality to be found in his work. For example, the lines "their light/is not our day" in the middle stanza of section 1 recall the lines from "Tyranny of Moths" "tonight the moths/go stitching with their kind/up and down the net/they may never know/my light is not my day." The second stanza of section 2 repeats almost verbatim a haiku from *Matsushima:* "bold nasturtiums/dress the barbed wire fences/down to the wild sea," as well as a phrase from *Interior Landscapes:* "Remembrance is a natural current that beats and breaks with the spring tides; the curious imagine a sensual undine on the wash, as the nasturtiums dress the barbed wire fences down to the wild sea" (*Interior* 263). And the third stanza, essentially a haiku, repeats a line from another haiku in *Matsushima,* "april ice storm/new leaves freeze over-night/words fall apart."

Each section begins with a different representative of the colonial enterprise: colonists, tourists, soldiers. The first two sections are structurally identical. While in the first section the "colonists/unearth their wealth," in the second section the "tourists/discover their ruins." And while the colonists of the first section then "tease/the old stone man/over the breaks," the tourists in section 2 "mimic/the old stone woman/over their breaks."

Though each stanza begins with a colonial master, each also expresses a transcendence of that condition. The colonists' stanza opens out into moths (perhaps images of transformation?) and concludes with leaves and crows in the poplars. The tourists' stanza is transformed as the nasturtiums dress the colonial barbed wire fence and the magnolias beneath the moon supersede language. And finally in the soldiers' stanza, though the soldiers bleach the landscape and hound the shamans, wild stories still manage to break from the stones—the brothers of Nanabozho. In their various transformations, the elements of nature in the turn of the seasons escape the strictures of colonial dominance.

A less hopeful poem, perhaps tragic-romantic, but among his best, is "Indians at the Guthrie." Presenting a tapestry of cultural and personal loss, the poem ties performances of terminal representations with both historic and contemporary genocide. The opening stanza presents damaged urban Indians outside a theater:

> limping past the guthrie theater
> wounded indian
> saluting with the wrong hand

This external scene contrasts with the next stanza, which portrays those inside the theater as a sort of white royalty erecting the stage props for a performance of manifest destiny:

> blond children in purple tapestries
> building castles
> barricades on stage with reservation plans

The poem then leaps into history, recalling the massacre of Cheyenne in 1864 and, so many years earlier, of the Pequots, "the first of the New England tribes to sense the genocidal intentions of the English" (Drinnon 43-44):

> rehearsing overscream from sand creek
> five hundred dead on the mystic river stage

The theatrical tropes of "rehearsing" and "stage" link these literal massacres with the colonialist performance in the theater. In his essay "Sand Creek Survivors" Vizenor connects the Sand Creek massacre with the suicide by hanging of thirteen-year-old Dane Michael White. Dane had been imprisoned for forty-one days, mostly in isolation, for truancy. Vizenor's essay is a prose meditation and gloss on the poem, made more obvious in a stanza that recounts contemporary versions of massacre:

> once more at wounded knee
> sniffing glue in gallop
> sterno in bemidji
> cultural suicides downtown on the reservation

The urban reservation provides no escape from the relentless pursuit of the cavalry. The concluding stanza explicitly links "acts" inside the theater with actions in the outside world:

> when the theater acts are over
> the players mount up for new parties in the hills

The pun on "acts" reveals the bond between colonialist portrayal and genocidal behavior.

Like his haiku, Vizenor's longer poems change with each published incarnation. A notable example of this is the poem about his father published as "Family Photograph" in *Voices of the Rainbow* and as "The Last Photograph" in *Interior Landscapes,* where it appears in the context of a discussion of his father's murder. The two poems contain few exact lines in common, yet they match up almost precisely stanza for stanza. The motifs in each stanza are the same, but the language varies, just as a story in the oral tradition varies with each telling yet maintains a comparable sequence of events: "It's pretty obvious in my work," he says, "that stories are not static; there are no scriptural versions of oral traditional stories. There are great variations" (Coltelli 164). The first few stanzas illustrate the effect:

FAMILY PHOTOGRAPH	THE LAST PHOTOGRAPH
among trees my father was a spruce	clement vizenor would be a spruce on his wise return to the trees
corded for tribal pulp he left the white earth reservation colonial genealogies taking up the city at twenty-three	corded on the reservation side he overturned the line colonial genealogies white earth remembrance removed to the cities at twenty three
telling stories sharing dreams from a mason jar running low through the stumps at night was his line	my father lived on stories over the rough rims on mason jars danced with the wounded shaman low over the stumps on the fourth of july

This matching pattern continues with little variation throughout the two poems. "Family Photograph" is more condensed than "The Last Photograph," but we would be hard pressed to say if one version were superior to the other.

Like much of his work, these poems echo images from other works; most notably in this case the image of tree stumps recalls his poem "Tribal Stumps," which concludes with the lines "my father returns/with all the mixed bloods/tribal stumps/from the blood-soaked beams of the city." On initial reading, this stump imagery suggests the vestiges of living beings, the wounds to once vital forces. On the other hand, however, the stump may be just another trickster disguise. For example, we read in Christopher Vecsey's structural consideration of Ojibwa creation myths that "Nanabozho's power as a shaman was particularly illustrated by his ability to transform himself and appear in various disguises, most particularly by his transformation into a stump" (83).

Such transformations provide a fluid key to Vizenor's art. Fixity is the impress of the tragic-colonial enterprise. Flux is the comic-compassionate trickster's habitation. Whether altering his longer poems with each publication, revising his haiku through the moods of the years, or celebrating the turn of the seasons, Vizenor maintains his desire to dismember terminal creeds, to remember the chances of change, and, as he says, to "honor impermanence."

Notes

1. Gerald Vizenor, "Envoy to Haiku," *Shadow Distance: A Gerald Vizenor Reader,* ed. A. Robert Lee (Hanover, NH: Wesleyan UP, 1994), 27.
2. Gerald Vizenor, "An Interview with Gerald Vizenor," interview by Neal Bowers and Charles L. P. Silet in *MELUS* 8.1 (1981): 43.

Works Cited

Amann, Eric. *The Wordless Poem: A Study of Zen in Haiku.* Toronto: Haiku Society of Canada, 1969.

Blaeser, Kimberly. "The Multiple Traditions of Gerald Vizenor's Haiku Poetry." *New Voices in Native American Literary Criticism.* Ed. Arnold Krupat. Washington: Smithsonian Institution P, 1993. 344-69.

Blyth, R. H. *Haiku.* 4 vols. Tokyo: Hokuseido, 1949-52.

Boldman, Bob. *Eating a Melon: 88 Zen Haiku.* Glen Burnie, MD: Wind Chimes, 1981.

Coltelli, Laura. *Winged Words: American Indian Writers Speak.* Lincoln: U of Nebraska P, 1990.

Drinnon, Richard. *Facing West: The Metaphysics of Indian-Hating and Empire-Building.* Minneapolis: U of Minnesota P, 1980. New York: Schocken, 1990.

Haiku Society of America. *A Haiku Path: The Haiku Society of America, 1968-1988.* New York: Haiku Society of America, 1994.

Hallowell, A. Irving. "Ojibowa Ontology, Behavior, and World View." *Culture in History: Essays in Honor of Paul Radin.* Ed. Stanley Diamond. New York: Columbia UP, 1960. 19-52.

Jahner, Elaine. "Cultural Shrines Revisited." *American Indian Quarterly* 9.1 (1983): 23-30.

Keene, Donald. *World within Walls: Japanese Literature of the Pre-modern Era, 1600-1867.* Rutland, VT: Tuttle, 1978.

Niatum, Duane, ed. *Harper's Anthology of 20th Century Native American Poetry.* New York: HarperCollins, 1988.

Rosen, Kenneth, ed. *Voices of the Rainbow: Contemporary Poetry by Native Americans.* 1975. New York: Arcade, 1993.

Silberman, Robert. "Gerald Vizenor and *Harold of Orange:* From Word Cinemas to Real Cinema." *American Indian Quarterly* 9.1 (1983): 5-21.

Vecsey, Christopher. *Imagine Ourselves Richly: Mythic Narratives of North American Indians.* New York: Crossroad, 1988.

Vizenor, Gerald. *Earthdivers: Tribal Narratives on Mixed Descent.* Minneapolis: U of Minnesota P, 1981.

——. *Empty Swings*. Minneapolis: Nodin, 1967.

——. "Envoy to Haiku." *Shadow Distance: A Gerald Vizenor Reader*. Ed. A. Robert Lee. Hanover, NH: Wesleyan UP, 1994. 25-32.

——. *The Everlasting Sky: New Voices from the People Named the Chippewa*. New York: Crowell-Collier, 1972.

——. *Interior Landscapes: Autobiographical Myths and Metaphors*. Minneapolis: U of Minnesota P, 1990.

——. "An Interview with Gerald Vizenor." By Neal Bowers and Charles L. P. Silet. *MELUS* 8.1 (1981): 41-49.

——. *Manifest Manners: Postindian Warriors of Survivance*. Hanover: Wesleyan UP, 1994.

——. *Matsushima: Pine Islands*. Minneapolis: Nodin, 1984.

——. "Sand Creek Survivors." *Shadow Distance: A Gerald Vizenor Reader*. Ed. A. Robert Lee. Hanover, NH: Wesleyan UP, 1994. 247-59.

——. *Seventeen Chirps*. Minneapolis: Nodin, 1964.

——. *Summer in the Spring: Ojibwe Lyric Poems and Tribal Stories*. Minneapolis: Nodin, 1981.

Vizenor, Gerald, and Jerome Downes. *Slight Abrasions: A Dialogue in Haiku*. Minneapolis: Nodin, 1966.

Willmot, Rod. "Mapping Haiku's Path in North America." *A Haiku Path: The Haiku Society of America, 1968-1988*. New York: Haiku Society of America, 1994. 211-25.

13

"IMAGINATION IS THE ONLY REALITY. ALL THE REST IS BAD TELEVISION": *HAROLD OF ORANGE* AND INDEXICAL REPRESENTATION

James Ruppert

To date *Harold of Orange* is Gerald Vizenor's only excursion into the world of cinema and visual representation. We can be certain that Vizenor did not intend for *Harold* to come off as bad television, but rather that it carries forward his artistic thrust toward imaginative liberation, comic play, and the rethinking of timeworn representational formulas. Yet the very nature of cinema presents Vizenor with a problem. As many film theorists have mentioned, the immediacy of the act of watching a film creates an "impression of reality." The immediate correlation of object to image may not be as powerful as it was with the first viewers of motion pictures, who jumped right out of their chairs when an image of an approaching, steaming locomotive was shown to them, but our acceptance of the realistic representation of cinema has been carefully nurtured by the Hollywood Standard and our film culture.

Vizenor's writings have always attempted to overthrow realistic expectations. Robert Silberman so observes of the characters in *Harold of Orange*, "Vizenor's Indians remain unlike any real Indians; they are Indians of his imagination" (15). Vizenor's dedication to *mythic* verism undermines any one-note, representational realism and constantly reminds the social sciences and history of the crisis of "representation" that has shaken the theoretical basis of all the social sciences and humanities for thirty some years. What, then, is a radical thinker to do with a medium like this?

Well, the standard artistic answer is to allow a symbolic level of discourse to ride the back of the mimetic image. By careful editing, the symbolic can become dominant in the viewer's perception, or as Keith Cohen writes, "mimesis is subsumed in the automation of the medium itself" (70). This dilemma would be unsuitable for Vizenor. As he has written, "The trickster is comic nature in a language game, not a real person or 'being' in the ontological sense. Tribal tricksters are embodied in imagination and liberate the mind; an androgyny, she would repudiate translations and imposed representations, as he would bare the contradictions of the striptease" (*Trickster* x). As language game, perhaps tricksters don't belong in the cinema. The trickster, so hard to pin down in his writings, would now be perceived as a real, male person. However, in a trickster discourse such as *Harold* a symbolic relationship could not present the trickster as a "comic holotrope," the whole figuration as Vizenor insists trickster discourse does. Symbolic representation merely reestablishes a fixed connection between the signifier and a more abstract signified. At this point let me turn to some discussions of cinematic theory and semiology to explain how I believe Vizenor is able to avoid this dilemma.

In his influential *Signs and Meaning in the Cinema,* Peter Wollen calls on the work of C. S. Peirce to ground his theoretical methodology, and to extend the analyses of visual images in the cinema done by Roland Barthes and Christian Metz. Quoting Peirce, Wollen contends that "a sign is either an icon, an index or a symbol." The icon, "according to Peirce, is a sign that represents its object mainly by its similarity to it; the relationship is not arbitrary but is one of resemblance or likeness. Thus, for instance, the portrait of a man resembles him . . . An index is a sign by virtue of an existential bond between itself and its object" (122; compare Peirce 101-15). Examples of this might be footprints in the sand, weathercocks, or medical symptoms. Lastly, a symbol is an arbitrary sign that requires no resemblance nor existential bond; it is a matter of convention like the meaning assigned the American flag or specific words.

As an iconic sign, viewers would believe Charlie Hill was like Harold Sinseer, the compassionate trickster. The trickster and trickster discourse would be perceived as having a solid reality. Audiences would know how tricksters walk, talk, and act. The inherent iconic emphasis of cinematic representation insists on the reality of the trickster. Indeed it does appear that Vizenor's film and original filmscript conform to many viewer expectations established by the Hollywood Standard (certainly more so than in his novels). Robert Silberman comments that despite Harold's address to the audience, "Harold remains a conventional narrative" (16). However, I think Vizenor wanted to use this mimesis, but then to subvert it.

If he had chosen the typical symbolic approach such as a film like *The Seventh Seal* does, he could have had the trickster appear in far less human form. He could have changed sexes, sizes, voices, etc. Perhaps Charlie Hill could have become a symbolic sign, symbolizing liberation, amorality, creativity, humor, or any of a dozen other tricksteresque abstracts as determined by Vizenor. He would have had to rely on convention, on an accepted array of symbolic signifieds to connect to the image of Charlie Hill (the signifier). Wollen, using Peirce's semiotics, supplies an alternative in the concept of the indexical sign, and this is the path Vizenor takes.

As an indexical sign, Harold Sinseer, the image of Charlie Hill can be perceived in a variety of ways. The weathercock bears an existential relationship to the east wind; then it bears a similar relationship to the west wind. Hill/Harold is not an icon nor a symbol, but Vizenor can make use of either when the wind blows that way. At any one moment the existence of Harold doing or saying something creates its essence, its meaning. This is the closest Vizenor cares to come to the free play of the language game and still work inside the iconic nature of cinema and with the conventional expectations of his viewers.

The film has a symmetrical structure. Scenes at the reservation coffeehouse begin and end the film. Scenes at the boardroom come second and second to last. These recurrences help focus the viewers on the three nonsymmetrical scenes that comprise Harold's presentation. Like the concentric circles of a target, they center the film on the scene in the Anthropology Department where the indexical sign becomes dominant, and receives its most complete cinematic expression. In each major scene, Harold is involved in the creation of an action or image which functions as an index to express trickster nature and its effect on the viewer. Each of these indexical signs bears an existential relation to its signified since its essence and its meaning are created immediately as the sign comes into existence. None is ever used consistently enough in the film to develop symbolic significance nor do any of them carry over specific trickster-related symbolism from a particular cultural code. Moreover, none of these major actions or images carry the icon significance of represented realism.

In the first scene, neckties are distributed to the warriors of Orange, and Harold informs them that they are the uniform necessary for the foundation presentation. He observes, "No one can resist a skin in a necktie" (58). Viewers are led to consider a situation where Indians appear to have adopted a mainstream American lifestyle. They may even be invited to reflect on how proponents of an assimilationist philosophy might be tempted to pat themselves on the back and to believe in the inevitable appropriateness of contemporary values. Yet the appearance masks a different reality. The practical con-man type evaluation is undercut by the expectation of an almost mythic response to the indexical sign. Harold says that when they show up in ties the directors won't "remember nothin' we tell them but the truth." Any mere talk or simplistic understanding of truth will have no effect; rather, the ties will act as signs behind which the trickster's truth will emerge even as it is being created. The ties will lead the foundation directors in the intended direction as well as it does the warriors and the viewer.

The scenes in the boardroom serve to introduce the directors to the viewer while establishing the context for the all important three central episodes. Harold's indexical sign in this episode is not something he wears, but someone he meets, Fannie. She swings us toward the lustful aspect of trickster, but also she sets up the final action when Harold gives her the director's check. The question of the thousand dollar debt and the implication that trickster's past actions may eventually catch up with him, run as a motif through the film. These questions shift the viewer's concern for lustfulness to resourcefulness, from the foundation question to an individual question. They will eventually indicate a different code of signification being used in the film, a trickster code perhaps.

The first of the three central episodes in the film is the urban naming ceremony. In this scene, the naming event functions as the indexical sign of the trickster forming a point of mythic verism for Harold, the comic holotrope. Certainly, it is not an iconic representation for it is not a real ceremony nor is it symbolic. No clear consistent symbolism accrues to linking Fannie with the signifier "chance" nor Kingsley with "Baltic" or Marion with "Connecticut." The fact that the new names come from a game may lead the viewer to consider the arbitrary nature of the language game.

Though Harold claims he is directed by a dream, the truth of dream reality is not championed. Indeed Harold says, "Who can be serious about anything in a parking lot . . . use your imagination" (69). With this, Harold informs the viewer that the two primary modes of cinematic representation will not be adequate for this cinematic experience. As the first of the three scenes which make up the presentation, it establishes the thematic focus of the film. Indexical signification in the entire film will require imagination to establish an existential relationship. Harold points us toward the creativity of the trickster, toward the possibilities of ceremonial rebirth through imagination, toward the arbitrary nature of language, toward dream reality and mythic representation. As we experience any of those aspects of the sign, we create its essence, momentarily, through imagination, not through realistic or symbolic representation.

The scene in the Anthropology Department gives the viewer a visual representation of the indexical relationship. Harold the contemporary trickster stands on the artifact case while slides are projected on him the way meaning is projected on the indexical signifier. As the slides change, the relationship between Harold, the visual image, and the viewer changes. When images of the ghost dance are projected on Harold, he explains the power of vision to create a new world, a trickster world we presume. But as the slides change from pictures of the dead at Wounded Knee to pictures of wild west shows and Buffalo Bill Cody, viewers are encouraged to appreciate the relationships between reality and projection. The trickster essence shifts from visionary to showman and yet Harold remains the same. As the weathercock moves so does its meaning. The viewer is allowed to overhear the foundation directors Kingsley and Andrew discussing Harold. Kingsley describes him as serious and innocent, someone who wants to stop time and change the world through imagination. This conversation introduces the viewer to the importance of imagination, which will be reemphasized in the next scene, but the visual image of shifting projection and shifting meaning is intended to structure the way the viewer sees the rest of the film, especially the rest of the presentation. Much of Vizenor's approach to the writing of trickster narratives can be observed in the film. The importance of imagination and multiple representations in the creation of a comic and liberating consciousness can be observed when he writes:

"The trickster is real in those who imagine the narrative, in the narrative voices."

Tropes are figures of speech; here the trickster is a sign that becomes a comic holotrope, a consonance of sentences in various voices, ironies, variations in cultural myths and social metaphors. Comic holotropes comprise signifiers, the signified, and signs, which in new critical theories provide a discourse on the trickster in oral narratives, translations, and modern imaginative literature. This *sui generis* discourse is named "mythic verism" in this discourse, which assumes that the theoretical arbitrariness of signs has been resolved in comic holotropes. ("Trickster Discourse" 190)

Perhaps Vizenor intends that we look at Harold/Hill as something similar to a comic holotrope, combining cultural myths and social metaphors. However, iconic and symbolic representation would not resolve the arbitrariness of signs, rather they would reinforce it. Indexical representation alone can establish mythic verism.

The softball game is the last scene of the presentation. In it, the Indians and the Anglos change places, and Vizenor satirizes stereotypical attitudes about Indians held by the Anglos and even the Indians themselves. However, the major visual image is that of Harold changing his shirt, moving from one cultural identity to another, from one social metaphor to another. Certainly Vizenor intends for the viewer to appreciate the quality of transformation central to the essence of the trickster.

But again the action is not realistic nor is it symbolic. The T-shirts don't really stand for cultural identity and no real transformations take place. The changing of the shirts is such an obvious opportunity for Harold to satirize, that to see the act as a consistent, developed symbol is taking things far too seriously and not using our imagination. The action is merely an indicator, an index. Indeed, the softball game is just a game within another larger language and cultural game designed to move us in a variety of directions. Vizenor, seeing the trickster as a "semiotic sign," concludes, "in translation the isolated voice or representation of the trickster is neither real nor mythic" ("Trickster Discourse" 190).

Returning to the boardroom and to the coffeehouse rounds out the structure of the film. The final boardroom scene culminates with two tricks from the wit and wiles of the trickster. As Harold convinces the directors that the coffee is a booze-blocker and pays Fannie with a check she cannot cash, he draws the viewer into a perception of the reversals in which the trickster engages. Harold neatly resolves the personal and public questions that have run as a thread through the film. The imaginative trickster survives again.

While *Harold of Orange* is rich in visual images and satire, it is surprisingly thin in action. Robert Silberman refers to it as "a movie with a great deal of talk—far more talk than action" (7). This is, of course, Vizenor's approach to narrative as it is expressed in cinema. For him, discourse defines the nature of things and reforms the reader or in this case, the viewer. In *The Trickster of Liberty,* he writes, "The trickster narrative arises in agonistic imaginations; a wild venture in communal discourse, an uncertain humor that denies aestheticism, translation, and imposed representations. The most active readers become obverse tricksters, the waver of a coin in a tribal striptease" (x). To become obverse tricksters, readers and viewers must enter a world of imagination and discourse; something action-oriented experience hinders. To use Roland Barthes's terminology from his book *S/Z* concerning codes of narrative, we could see Vizenor's trickster narratives dominated by the hermeneutic code rather than the proaieretic code, the code of truth rather than the code of actions. Peter Wollen, in *Readings and Writings,* combines this concept of the hermeneutic code with a Lacanian appreciation of the psychoanalytic structures of the secret and the quest to discuss Hitchcock's *North by Northwest.* It seems appropriate to borrow some of his methodology here because Vizenor's narrative strategy involves a hermeneutic code in which secrets are revealed to be non-secrets, where the code of truth is revealed as holding an indexical relationship to truth, especially the truth of the trickster. Silberman insists that in *Harold,* Vizenor "has therefore surrendered his narrative voice, the privileged position he holds as the writer of texts" (8). However, it seems to me Vizenor has retained much of that commanding position.

The normal assumption is that for a trick to be successful it must be a secret. The trickster's wily nature, his efforts to change things, indeed his very essence require a certain secretiveness on his part. If we assume that the audience is not the object of the trick, then we can understand the film's perspective. The audience is let in on the trick, the scam of the foundations. In the first scene one of the warriors asks Harold who would believe in pinch beans. The answer is, of course, the same people who fell for the miniature orange scheme. Harold later talks to Fannie and acknowledges that this is the old foundation game, implying that Fannie knows all about it. But what should be a secret from the directors seems already known by them. When the two board directors discuss Harold, they share a knowing smile about Harold, his proposal, and the efficacy of foundations to change the world. For them there is no secret; it is the old foundation game. Harold gets the money; the foundation gets a good name; the truth or the actual efficacy of the proposal is irrelevant. The essence of the trickster is transformed. In place of secrecy, Vizenor erects the game, a language game. On the public, social level, truth becomes secrets that are agreed upon. Such agreements facilitate discourses built on common assumptions of truth because under such conditions a hermeneutic code can become established, and function as a narrative strategy.

On the personal level, the suspense maintained by Harold's attempt to get one thousand dollars from Kingsley is released when Harold gives Fannie the check she cannot cash. He has paid her and yet not paid her. Her secret of a previous relationship with Harold is kept from the directors. Harold's secret of the lie he has told Kingsley remains a secret. The essence of the trickster is retained on the personal level, in private acts. Discourse is hindered, but the narrative strategy based on the proaieretic code is encouraged.

The mixing of these two codes of narrative, which underlie the visual representation of the film, tends to create a dialogic relationship between them. Neither becomes dominant, each contributes to the complete narrative. An illusion of realistic representation is defeated as well as symbolic representation. Moreover these codes stand in an indexical relationship to the truth of the trickster, a relationship that requires the development of the imagination of the viewer. As Buffy St. Marie sings, "trickster change what everything mean, trickster hi hi ho."

Works Cited

Barthes, Roland. *S/Z*. Trans. Richard Miller. New York: Hill and Wang, 1974.

Cohen, Keith. *Film and Fiction: Dynamics of Exchange*. New Haven: Yale UP, 1979.

Peirce, Charles S. *The Philosophy of Peirce: Selected Writings*. Ed. Justus Buchler. London: Kegan Paul, Tilench, Trubner, 1978.

Silberman, Robert. "Gerald Vizenor and *Harold of Orange*: From Word Cinemas to Real Cinemas." *American Indian Quarterly* 9.1 (Winter 1985): 4-21.

Vizenor, Gerald. "Harold of Orange: A Screenplay." *SAIL: Studies in American Indian Literatures* 5.3 (Fall 1993): 53-88.

——. "Trickster Discourse: Comic Holotropes and Lanugage Games." *Narrative Chance: Postmodern Discourse on Native American Indian Literatures*. Ed. Gerald Vizenor. Albuquerque: U of New Mexico P, 1989. 187-212.

——. *The Trickster of Liberty: Tribal Heirs to a Wild Baronage*. Minneapolis: U of Minnesota P, 1988.

Wollen, Peter. *Readings and Writings: Semiotic Counter-Strategies*. London: Verso Editions and NLB, 1982.

——. *Signs and Meaning in the Cinema*. Bloomington: Indiana UP, 1968.

14

THE LAST MAN OF THE STONE AGE:
GERALD VIZENOR'S *ISHI AND THE WOOD DUCKS*

Louis Owens

"Ishi was never his real name." So begins Gerald Vizenor's "Ishi Obscura," in the Chippewa author's *Manifest Manners: Postindian Warriors of Survivance*. An essay on the last "wild man" of America captured in a museum and photographs, "Ishi Obscura" interrogates both the construction of Ishi as museum artifact and the invention and simulation of Indianness, while it illuminates the humanity of the man who was not Ishi, the lonesome survivor who evaded the photographs. Vizenor has had a long and intense fascination with Ishi, the latest fruit of which is a four-act play, *Ishi and the Wood Ducks*,[1] a work that deploys compassion, humor and the ironies of trickster to dissect Euramerica's invention of Indians at the same time that it pays homage to the man called Ishi. At the heart of the play's deconstruction of Ishi as the invented "other" is what Vizenor defines as "trickster hermeneutics": "the interpretation of simulations in the literature of survivance, the ironies of descent and racialism, transmutation, third gender, and themes of transformation in oral tribal stories and written narratives."[2] As a "postindian" survivor, Vizenor's Ishi steps outside the frame of the nostalgic colonial camera, defies the melancholy and terminal definition called "Indian," and appears on stage in the play as a good-humored signifier of indeterminate human consciousness. In the end, despite Euramerica's desperate attempts to fix Ishi as a phenomenon called a "primitive Indian," Vizenor makes it clear that Ishi exists forever in the moment of his stories, reinventing himself within the oral tradition with each utterance. While the first line in Vizenor's opening "Historical Introduction" to *Ishi and the Wood Ducks* quotes a description of the newly discovered Ishi as "a pathetic figure crouched upon the floor," Ishi's first words in the play are "Have you ever heard the wood duck stories," a telling contradiction.

Together, "Ishi Obscura" and *Ishi and the Wood Ducks* provide Vizenor with a way of boring deeply into the almost pathological impulse that has driven Euramerica for five centuries to discover an aboriginal something commensurate to its own needs, and to call that something "Indian." Imagining the Indian as a kind of natural resource free of its own volition—a resource to be mined for some kind of catalyst that will make the "American" alloy so much the stronger—the Euramerican metanarrative peels away the man or woman to find the Indian. Vizenor's art peels away the artifactual veneer of Indianness to find the humanity at the center, to liberate the original American from the entropic servitude of Indianness.

In the writings of Gerald Vizenor, as his serious readers know well, "real" life permeates fiction and fiction warps real events and recognizable contemporary and historical figures into trickster's endless and endlessly self-reflexive tropes. Those who know Vizenor's work will also be familiar with the powerfully utopian impulse that drives his often harsh satires, the same utopian desires that lie at the paradoxical heart of trickster stories. The goal is to illuminate hypocrisies and false positions, to challenge all accepted mores or fixed values, to shock and disturb us and cause us to re-examine and readjust moment-by-moment our conceptions of and relationships with both self and environment. The purpose of "holotropic" trickster,[3] with his/her indeterminable shape-shifting, contradictions, and assaults upon our rules and values, is to make the world better. *Ishi and the Wood Ducks* has its inception in Vizenor's "real life" challenge to the University of California, a challenge arising out of his desire to readjust history, force the university and the rest of society to recognize its false positions and culpability, and do honor to an exceptional man we erroneously call Ishi.

In the fall of 1985, as a visiting professor in Ethnic Studies at the University of California, Berkeley, Gerald Vizenor formally proposed that the north part of the campus's Dwinelle Hall (which housed and still houses the offices of Native American Studies) be renamed Ishi Hall. The student senate at Berkeley voted unanimously to support Vizenor's proposal, praising in their bill Ishi's "intellectual contributions to the University of California in the fields of anthropology, linguistics, and Native American studies."[4] When an administrator in the university's splendidly titled Space Assignment and Capital Improvements Group demurred and offered instead to consider naming a proposed addition to Kroeber Hall after Ishi, Vizenor said no: "We're not about to yield to anthropology and a new intellectual colonialism," he declared.[5] For seven years—that powerful tribal number—the matter rested there.

Who doesn't know the name of Ishi? "He was the last of his tribe," Mary Ashe Miller, a reporter for the *San Francisco Call,* wrote on September 6, 1911, before going on to declare that "[t]he man is as aboriginal in his mode of life as though he inhabited the heart of an African jungle; all of his methods are those of primitive peoples" (MM 128). Discovered weak and starving in a slaughterhouse in northern California in August of 1911, Ishi the prototypical "primitive" was immediately placed in jail by the county sheriff because "no one around town could understand his speech or he theirs" (MM 131). Not the first or last Native to be imprisoned for possessing liminal linguistic identity, Ishi was quickly transferred to the proprietorship of the U.C. Berkeley Museum of Anthropology and the care of noted anthropologist Alfred Kroeber, as Theodora Kroeber explained with undoubtedly unconscious irony: "Within a few days the Department of Indian Affairs authorized the sheriff to release the wild man to the custody of Kroeber and the museum staff" (MM 131). A statement replete with wonderfully authoritative language, Kroeber's words make it clear that at once Ishi was recognized as property of a federal agency (the BIA) which could "authorize" his transfer, as property, to the "custody" of another institution. Nowhere in this statement is there room for the possibility of the indigenous person's own individual agency.

The last known survivor of the Yahi, a division of the Yana tribe of California, Ishi—as he was understood by the white world—was the perfect Indian for colonial Euramerica, the end result of five hundred years of attempts to create something called "Indian." With his family and entire tribe slaughtered and starved to death like countless thousands of the original inhabitants of California by white miners and ranchers, he became the quintessential last Vanishing American, a romantic, artifactual "Indian" who represented neither threat nor obstacle but instead a benign natural resource to be mined for what white America could learn about itself. And when, after living for five years in the anthropology museum at Berkeley, he did perish as scripted, on March 25, 1916, of tuberculosis contracted from his white captors, the *Chico Record,* a little newspaper in a minuscule northern California town, saw through the staged drama with cynical insight:

Ishi, the man primeval, is dead. . . . He furnished amusement and study to the savants at the University of California for a number of years . . . but we do not believe he was the marvel that the professors would have the public believe. He was just a starved-out Indian from the wilds of Deer Creek who, by hiding in its fastnesses, was able to long escape the white man's pursuit. And the white man with his food and clothing and shelter finally killed the Indian just as effectually as he would have killed him with a rifle.[6]

236 · *Loosening the Seams*

Perhaps most exceptional in this newspaper account is the writer's recognition that the "white man's pursuit" of the Indian is inexorable. Central to the extensive body of Gerald Vizenor's writing is his recognition that the white man's pursuit of the Indian is indeed unending, that it represents an unrelenting desire to capture and inhabit the heart of the Native just as surely as Euramerica has appropriated and occupied the Native landscape. Key to this pursuit is language, the struggle for definition and dominance through authoritative discourse.

The University of California must have thought, with considerable relief, that the irritating matter of Ishi Hall had ended when Visiting Professor Gerald Vizenor left the campus to teach elsewhere. However, in January of 1992, having given up an endowed chair at the University of Oklahoma to return to Berkeley as a tenured full professor, Vizenor raised the banner of Ishi's cause once more, writing to Chancellor Chang-Lin Tien to say: "This is a proposal to change the name of the north part of Dwinelle Hall to Ishi Hall in honor of the first Native American Indian who served with distinction the University of California." This time, a full seven years after his first proposal had vanished into the bowels of a university committee, Vizenor cleverly made sure that his proposal coincided with the hullaballoo surrounding the quincentenary of Columbus's "discovery" of America. "This is the right moment," he explained to the chancellor, "the quincentenary is time to honor this tribal man who served with honor and good humor the academic interests of the University of California."[7]

Vizenor's proposal was forwarded to a committee once again. Two months later, in March, after hearing nothing, he wrote politely to the chancellor: "I understand the administrative burdens at this time, even so, my proposal is urgent because it is tied to an unmistakable historical moment." Three months later, in June of 1992, he wrote to the chancellor yet again, this time a bit more heatedly:

Consider the sense of resentment and anger that you might feel if your reasonable initiatives to honor a tribal name and emend institutional racism were consigned to the mundane commerce of a campus space subcommittee. Sixty-eight years ago today, on June 2, 1924, Native American Indians became citizens for the first time of the United States. Indeed, these historical ironies, and the national sufferance of the quincentenary, could be much too acrimonious to resume; the very institutions and the foundational wealth of this state are based on stolen land and the murder of tribal people.

On August 31, 1992, the Director of the Space Management and Capital Programs Committee on campus circulated a memo informing everyone that "The Naming of Buildings Subcommittee did not approve naming a wing of Dwinelle after Ishi. It suggested instead that the central court-yard of Dwinelle Hall be named *Ishi Court*."

On May 7, 1993—almost eight years after Vizenor's initial pro-posal—*Ishi Court* was officially dedicated on the Berkeley campus. In his dedication address, Vizenor said, "There is a wretched silence in the histories of this state and nation: the silence of tribal names. The land-scapes are overburdened with untrue discoveries. There are no honorable shadows in the names of dominance. The shadows of tribal names and stories persist, and the shadows are our natural survivance." He con-cluded his speech by declaring, "Ishi Court, you must remember, is the everlasting center of Almost Ishi Hall."

"Ishi was never his real name," Vizenor writes in "Ishi Obscura." "Ishi is a simulation, the absence of his tribal names. . . . Ishi the obscura is discovered with a bare chest in photographs; the tribal man named in that simulation stared over the camera, into the distance" (MM 126).

A Yahi word meaning "one of the people," the name Ishi masked the Native survivor's sacred name, which he never told to anyone. Ishi became the man. "The notion of the aboriginal and the primitive com-bined both racialism and postmodern speciesism," Vizenor writes in "Ishi Obscura," "a linear consideration that was based on the absence of monotheism, material evidence of civilization, institutional violence, and written words more than on the presence of imagination, oral stories, the humor in trickster stories, and the observation of actual behavior and experience" (MM 128).

For Euramerica, the Indian is defined by absence, not presence. Attention is directed not to what is there but to what is absent. The pre-determined goal is to know the "other" as not-European and to thus delineate the European, while paradoxically to find and extract some aboriginal distillation that, like the single drop of black in the white paint of Ralph Ellison's *Invisible Man,* will somehow make white America greater. The goal is, as Vizenor stresses, never to *know* the "other." The Indian, like Ishi, must be defined by absence so that he/she can be cap-tured as the ethnostalgic other, the lost original fixed in what Vizenor calls "a linear consideration." "The word Indian," Vizenor writes, "is a colonial enactment, not a loan word, and the dominance is sustained by the simulation that has superseded the real tribal names. The Indian was an occidental invention that became a bankable simulation; the word has no referent in tribal languages or cultures. The postindian is the absence of the invention, and the end of representation in literature; the closure of that evasive melancholy of dominance. Manifest manners are the sim-ulations of bourgeois decadence and melancholy" (MM 11). Finally, once the Native is fully defined as the "absent other" the aboriginal space has been figuratively (and, of course, quite literally through concerted programs of genocide) emptied so that it may be reoccupied by the colonizer, realizing the invader's wistful dream of achieving an "original" relationship with the invaded space.

For indigenous Americans, the paradox that arises from the ironies of invention is that it seems the Native person must pose as the absent other—the "Indian"—in order to be seen or heard, must actually become the simulation at the border. Simply put, the central paradox of Indian identity is that Indians must pose as simulations in order to be seen as "real." Vizenor quotes Umberto Eco on this point: "This is the reason for this journey into hyperreality, in search of instances where the American imagination demands the real thing and, to attain it, must fabricate the absolute fake." Vizenor adds that "Indians, in this sense, must be the simulations of the 'absolute fakes' in the ruins of representation, or the victims in literary annihilation" (MM 9). "Ishi," he writes, "has become one of the most discoverable tribal names in the world; even so, he has seldom been heard as a real person" (MM 137). In *Ishi and the Wood Ducks,* the gentle and patient Yahi survivor becomes the "postindian," one of the original people of America freed from the humorless "melancholy of dominance" that requires the invented Indian.

Vizenor's play opens with an introduction that sketches the history of Ishi's discovery in northern California and his transfer from jail to museum. The introduction quotes a number of statements by those who surrounded Ishi in the museum, including Kroeber's declaration that Ishi "has perceptive powers far keener than those of highly educated white men. He reasons well, grasps an idea quickly, has a keen sense of humor, is gentle, thoughtful, and courteous and *has a higher type of mentality than most Indians*" (my italics) and Thomas Waterman the museum linguist's observation that "this wild man has a better head on him than a good many college men." Following the introduction, a Prologue opens with the characters of Ishi and an "old woman" named Boots Story both waiting on a bench outside a federal courthouse, Ishi dressed in "an oversized suit and tie" and carrying a leather briefcase. Boots, a Gypsy, informs Ishi that she must appear in federal court in order to get a "real name." Otherwise she will be deported, or sent "home."

The cast is drawn from the same ten characters in each of the play's four acts, but, with the exception of Ishi himself and his choral accomplice, Boots, the roles and identities of the characters change in each act, a strategy the author explains: "The actors are the same but the names of characters are repeated in the prologue and four acts of the play. The sense of time, manifest manners, and historical contradictions are redoubled and enhanced by the mutations of identities in the same characters."

As noted above, Ishi's first words in the Prologue, addressed to Boots, are "Have you ever heard the wood duck stories?" A few lines later he says, "Ishi is my museum name, not my real name." Turning to the audience, he explains with nice irony, "Kroeber was an anthropologist and got me out of jail to live in a museum (*pause*), he was one of my very first friends." He adds: "Kroeber named me (*pause*), in my own language, he named me the last man of the stone age."

This Prologue foregrounds the contradictions and values of names, museums and stories: "How about a museum of stories?" Ishi asks Boots. When Boots says, "Who can remember stories anymore?" Ishi replies, "That's why you need your own museum." "Names without stories are the end," Ishi says with finality. *Ishi and the Wood Ducks* discovers the dead end of the name "Indian," which arises out of a static, monologic story of cultural dominance (and ethnocide) central to the Euramerican metanarrative, but which has no story at all within the hundreds of cultures it supposedly comprehends, or as Vizenor explains above, "has no referent in tribal languages or cultures."

The first act of the play takes place in the Museum of Anthropology at Berkeley, where Ishi is first seen flaking arrowheads (including one out of a piece of broken glass) in front of a "wickiup." Boots Story has "mutated" into a custodial worker who pushes her duster around the room and offers silent facial responses to the words and events of the act. The act centers on a visit to Ishi by characters associated with the museum and attempts by Ashe Miller, a newspaper reporter, to interview Ishi while Prince Chamber, a photographer accompanying her, tries unsuccessfully to take Ishi's picture. In the opening lines of the act, Saxton Pope, "the medical doctor," praises Ishi as a natural healer and asks Ishi to "show us your home in the mountains" and to teach Pope's son "how to hunt and fish with a bow and arrow, and how to make arrowheads out of broken bottles." Ishi turns to the audience to say, "The mountains are dangerous." When pressed by Pope, he explains that the danger comes from the "savages": the gold miners who "have no stories" and "no culture." When informed of the photographer's visit, Ishi says, "Pictures are never me," and "My stories are lost in pictures." Ishi's words here echo Vizenor's insistence in "Ishi Obscura" that "[t]he miners were the real savages; they had no written language, no books, no manners . . . no stories in the blood. They were the agents of civilization," and "[t]he gaze of those behind the camera haunts the unseen margins of time and scene in the photograph; the obscure presence of witnesses at the simulation of savagism could become the last epiphanies of a chemical civilization" (MM 127). "Savages land in your pictures," Ishi tells the anthropologist Kroeber.

When Ashe Miller says, "Big Chiep [Ishi's nickname for Kroeber] said you come from a 'puny civilization' and that you are 'unspeakably ignorant' (*pause*). Do you know anything?" Ishi's response is "Too much pina." "Pina," we are quickly told, means "pain," an explanation that embarrasses Kroeber. Act one ends with the photographer's request that Ishi engage in what Vizenor has called "cultural striptease": "Ishi, bare your chest, the light is good." Ishi, content to remain unseen and unheard as a "primitive," and refusing to simulate Euramerica's fake Indian, whispers to Kroeber, who explains (in an instance drawn from Ishi's "real life" in the museum): "Ishi say he not see any other people go without them, without clothes (*pause*), and he say he never take them off no more."

Act Two is set in the Mount Olivet Cemetery columbarium, where Zero Larkin, a "native sculptor with a vision," has come seventy years after Ishi's death in order to receive inspiration from Ishi's ashes. He is accompanied by Ashe Miller, the reporter from Act One, and Prince Chamber, the photographer who asked Ishi to bare his chest in that act. Trope Browne, undoubtedly one of the enormous mixedblood Browne dynasty that populates Vizenor's 1988 work *The Trickster of Liberty* (in which Ishi graduates with Tune Browne from the University of California), serves as attendant at the columbarium. When Zero asks Trope "are you a brother?" Trope responds that his answer depends on "How much money you want." Observing and commenting upon the scene, unseen by the others, are Ishi and Boots Story.

Act Two targets both invented Indians and those who would pose as experts on such inventions. When Ishi denies to Boots that he was ever a shaman or that he made the pot in which his ashes are held—both of which "facts" are maintained by the manager of the cemetery, Angel Day—Boots says, "Angel lied then." Ishi replies, "Not really, she's an expert on Indians. . . . Indians are inventions, so what's there to lie about?"

Zero Larkin, the posturing, scathingly satirized native sculptor, intones, "Ishi is with me, our spirit is one in his sacred name," before adding, "I'm going to blast his sacred signature . . . at the bottom of my stone sculpture, my tribute to his power as an Indian." When asked if he's finished the sculpture, Zero says, "Not yet, but with the inspiration of his name it won't take long." Ashe Miller, the penetrating journalist from Act One, asks, "Zero does it make a difference to anyone that you are not from the same tribe as Ishi?" and Zero replies, "We are both tribal artists, and that's our identity." Not even aware of the fact that Ishi names not a person but a constructed museum artifact, Zero himself embraces his identity as generic invented Indian, what Vizenor called a "colonial enactment" in "Ishi Obscura." When he touches the false burial urn, Zero chants, "Ishi is with me, his spirit is coming through my fingers." "What does it feel like," the reporter queries, to which Zero answers, "The greatest power of my life, the spirit of my people." After Ashe asks if Zero means that his "people" are indigenous Northern Californians like Ishi's, the dialogue continues to the detriment of the "native" sculptor:

> ZERO: We are one as tribal people.
> Zero trembles, and he smiles as the camera comes closer. Trope moves closer to be sure he does not drop the pot.
> ASHE: Which one?
> ANGEL: He means a universal tribal spirit.
> ASHE (ironically): That explains it.

Act Two ends with Boots chanting, "Zero, zero and the cemetery liars," and Ishi asking, "Do you think they could hear my duck stories?"

The third act of *Ishi and the Wood Ducks* features a meeting of the Committee on Names and Spaces in Kroeber Hall at the University of California. We are told that "[t]he faculty is seated at a conference table to consider a proposal to rename the building Ishi Hall." In this act, Angel Day has mutated into a professor of anthropology, Trope Browne, a history professor, Ashe Miller appropriately a professor in mass communication, and Prince Chamber in visual arts. Professor Alfred Kroeber, the distinguished anthropologist, is present as sponsor of the proposal to rename his own hall in honor of Ishi.

"Why would he want to change his own name?" Trope Browne asks just before Kroeber appears on stage. When questioned, Kroeber says simply, "Ishi made my name . . ." and adds, "Ishi's name is not genuine." Angel Day says, "Several years ago, as you know, we received a proposal from an errant faculty member to change the name of Kroeber Hall to Big Chiep Hall (*pause*). Naturally, and in honor of your distinction as an anthropologist, we chose not to discuss the proposal." Kroeber replies, "I supported that proposal." Kroeber goes on to explain that "The Big Chiep is one of his [Ishi's] name stories. . . . Ishi honored me with a nickname, in the same sense that we gave him his name (*pause*); the contradiction, of course, is that our name for him is romantic, while his name for me is a story."

Throughout this act, Ishi and Boots stand at the edge of the stage and comment upon the proceedings. "Kroeber said it," Boots tells Ishi, "you are his anthropologist." "Not a chance," Ishi replies, "he's the subject not the object." When Boots says, "Who are you then?" Ishi's answer is "The last object of their stone age." When the committee, just like the "real" committee that buried Vizenor's proposals for Ishi Hall in 1985 and 1992, decides that Kroeber's proposal is a "sad romantic visitation" and denies the request, Ishi and Boots—still invisible—begin to address the faculty members directly, with Ishi saying, "Doctor Ishi Hearst[8] proposes that no building on campus would bear the same name for more than two years at a time." The buildings, Ishi suggests, "would be known by their nicknames and stories, and no building would hold even a nickname for more than two years."

Ishi and the Wood Ducks concludes with Act Four set in the Federal Courtroom outside of which Ishi and Boots waited in the Prologue. Ishi, it turns out, has been brought to court on charges of violating the Indian Arts and Crafts Act of 1990, the charge being that "[h]e sold objects as tribal made, and could not prove that he was in fact a member of a tribe or recognized by a reservation government." In this final act, Kroeber is the presiding federal judge, Ashe Miller the prosecutor, Saxton Pope the defense attorney. Other characters from the first three acts are court functionaries or witnesses (and a kind of chorus), including Boots Story. The act opens with Ishi placing "several bows, arrows, arrowheads, and fire sticks on the defense table."

Ishi, we learn, has been arrested at the Santa Fe Indian Market because "other artists complained that he was not a real Indian." The crux of the matter is that like many contemporary Native Americans Ishi belongs to a tribe that is not federally recognized (in his case because his tribe has been ruled extinct). Clearly, the other "real" Indian artists saw greater profit for themselves in barring Ishi from the lucrative native arts and crafts market and are exploiting the colonial definition of Indian identity to their advantage.[9] Not only has Ishi violated the Indian Arts and Crafts Act, he is also charged with purchasing a false certificate of Indianness, an enrollment form from the "Dedicednu Indians of California" based in Laguna Beach, a charge that brings great laughter from the courtroom.

Judge Kroeber declares that "Ishi names a very remote tribe with no immediate evidence of his descent and that, clearly, is a burden under the provisions of the new law." In Ishi's defense, Saxton Pope argues that "my client is more tribal than anyone in the country" despite the fact that Ishi makes arrowheads out of broken bottles. For support, Pope points out the spurious (and romantically racist) evidence that Ishi has wide feet, "would rather not wear shoes," and has leather thongs in his ears, none of which counts for much in court. Pope then turns to absence in a typical Euramerican definition of Indianness, saying, "Ishi never heard of Christmas," but Ashe as prosecutor replies in Vizenoresque language that "[t]he absence is not a presence of character." Finally, Pope introduces Ishi's wood duck stories as the ultimate evidence of his client's tribal identity, arguing "[O]ral stories are none other than a real character, the character of tribal remembrance, the character that heard and remembered the wood duck stories." As Ishi sings "Winotay, winotay, wintotay," Pope begins the wood duck stories that (the actual) Ishi liked to tell in his museum home, stories that took seven hours in the telling and could be told only after dark.

Clearly, Judge Kroeber has a humanitarian and philosophical bent. This Kroeber is not the anthropologist who once labeled Ishi "unspeakably ignorant," but rather the man who, at the time of Ishi's death, wrote, "As to disposal of the body, I must ask you . . . to yield nothing at all under any circumstances. If there is any talk about the interests of science, say for me that science can go to hell. We propose to stand by our friends." This philosophical judge, who bears the name of Ishi's inventor, asks rhetorically, "What is criminal in the imagination of a tribal artist?" before adding, "Colonial inventions are criminal, not tribal survivance." A few lines later, the judge ponders, "Consumer fraud? Or is this a case of cultural romance?" to which the court clerk Prince Chambers replies, "Who knows the difference in Santa Fe?" When the prosecutor says, "The government protects the true Indian," Kroeber reponds with, "Then the Indian, not the buyer, must beware."

Forced to make a ruling, Judge Kroeber finds that "[c]learly the performance of wood duck stories, no matter how great the audience response, does not establish tribal character or identity under the provisions of the Indian Arts and Crafts Act of 1990." He then turns directly to the audience to ask, "What would you do under the circumstances?"

Act Four and the play both end with Kroeber ruling that "Ishi is real and the law is not. Therefore, my decision is to declare that the accused is his own tribe. Ishi is his own sovereign tribal nation. . . . Ishi, the man so named, has established a tribal character in a museum and in his endless wood duck stories. . . . Ishi is an artist, he is our remembrance of justice, and that is his natural character."

In this brief and fast-moving play, within vivid and superbly paced dialogue, Vizenor is able to embed with a deft hand nearly all of the major issues found in his large body of published work: the colonial invention of Indianness; the "word wars" that characterize the five-hundred-year-old Euramerican program to fix the Indian within what, in *Bearheart,* Vizenor calls a "terminal creed"; and the posturing of those Natives who (like Zero Larkin) would pose within the dominant culture's constructed definition of universal Indianness. In foregrounding the issue of Ishi's undocumentable identity, Vizenor illustrates sharply his contention in *Manifest Manners* that "[t]he Indian is the simulation of the absence, an unreal name; however, the misnomer has a curious sense of legal standing. Some of the definitions are ethnological, racial, literary, and juristic sanctions." Vizenor concludes this discussion of Indian identity in *Manifest Manners* with the observations, "Clearly, the simulations of tribal names, the absence of a presence in a mere tribal misnomer, cannot be sustained by legislation or legal maneuvers." And "Postindian autobiographies, the averments of tribal descent, and the assertions of crossblood identities, are simulations in literature; that names, nicknames, and the shadows of ancestors are stories is an invitation to new theories of tribal interpretation." Finally, he argues that "[t]he sources of natural reason and tribal consciousness are doubt and wonder, not nostalgia or liberal melancholy for the lost wilderness; comic not tragic, because melancholy is cultural boredom, and the tragic is causal, the closure of natural reason" (MM 14). In Ishi's defense counsel's argument that "oral stories are none other than a real character, the character of tribal remembrance," Vizenor echoes his position in "Ishi Obscura" that "[t]he natural development of the oral tradition is not a written language. The notion, in the literature of dominance, that the oral advances to the written, is a colonial reduction of natural sound, heard stories, and the tease of shadows in tribal remembrance" (MM 72). In *Ishi and the Wood Ducks,* the written advances to the oral, and the co-constructive audience—brought immediately onto the stage by both Ishi and Judge Kroeber—becomes the active jury and is challenged to deconstruct the Indian to find the lonesome survivor who, in good humor, honored his sacred name and simply called himself "one of the people."

Notes

1. The full text is published in Gerald Vizenor, *Native American Literature: A Brief Introduction and Anthology* (New York: HarperCollins, 1995).

2. Gerald Vizenor, *Manifest Manners: Postindian Warriors of Survivance* (Hanover and London: Wesleyan UP, 1994), 15. Further references will be cited in the text by MM and page number.

3. Vizenor defines trickster as a "comic holotrope: the whole figuration; an unbroken interior landscape that beams various points of view in temporal reveries." *The Trickster of Liberty: Tribal Heirs to a Wild Baronage* (Minneapolis: U of Minnesota P, 1988), x.

4. *The Daily Californian,* 25 Oct. 1985: 1.

5. Ibid.

6. Gerald Vizenor, *Ishi and the Wood Ducks* 301. Unpublished manuscript 3.

7. Vizenor to Chancellor Chang-Lin Tien, January 9, 1992, author's personal papers.

8. In "Ishi Obscura," Vizenor describes Phoebe Apperson Hearst as the creator of the Department and Museum of Anthropology at the University of California (MM 131).

9. The Indian Arts and Crafts Act of 1990 decrees that it is "unlawful to offer or display for sale any good, with or without a Government trademark, in a manner that falsely suggests it is Indian produced, an Indian product, or the product of a particular Indian or Indian tribe or Indian arts and crafts organization, resident within the United States." The Act stipulates that "[f]or a first criminal offense, an individual is fined not more than $250,000 and/or jailed not more than 5 years; subsequent violations are not more than $1,000,000 and/or 15 years." This information is taken directly from U.S. Department of the Interior—Indian Arts and Crafts Board, "Summary and Text of Title I, Public Law 101-644 [104 Stat. 4662], Act of 11,29/90."

Clearly, as Vizenor has pointed out, the "occidental invention" of Indianness has become a very lucrative "bankable simulation" in essentialist and ethnostalgic America. Were Judge Kroeber to find him guilty of criminal offense, Ishi would be in serious trouble indeed. Ishi's difficulty arises out of the Act's definition of an Indian as someone who is "a member of a federally-recognized or state-recognized tribe, or a person who is certified as an Indian artisan by such a tribe." Ishi's extinct tribe is both unrecognized and quite obviously incapable of certifying Ishi.

15

VIZENORIAN JURISPRUDENCE:
LEGAL INTERVENTIONS, NARRATIVE STRATEGIES,
AND THE INTERPRETATIVE POSSIBILITIES OF SHADOWS

Juana María Rodríguez

[T]here is a plurality of resistances, each of them a special case: resistances that are possible, necessary, improbable; others that are spontaneous, savage, solitary, concerted, rampant, or violent; still others that are quick to compromise, interested, or sacrificial; by definition, they can only exist in the strategic field of power relations.
—Michel Foucault, *The History of Sexuality*

I hear the push of the wind in the late summer, in the winter birch, and see the shadows hie over the shore in silence; and my shadows move with the light, the sources of remembrance. We are shadows, silence, stones, stories, never that simulation of light in the distance. Trickster stones and postindian stories are my shadows, the natural traces of liberation and survivance in the ruins of representation.
—Gerald Vizenor, *Manifest Manners*

It is my deep belief that theoretical legal understanding and social transformation need not be oxymoronic.
—Patricia Williams, *The Alchemy of Race and Rights*

I

In the past decade, the field of critical legal theory has emerged as a site where the interpretive practices of discursive analysis interface with the narrative possibilities of courtroom dramas. Much of the emphasis of this work falls upon the relationship between subject position, social-political context, and the limitations of the foundational intentions of the Constitution.[1] For Native Americans, these newly articulated legal themes have particular resonance. Historically, almost every aspect of tribal life has been delineated by U.S. law. From the strictly defined legalities of tribal identity, to water rights, peyote, and bingo parlors, U.S. courts seem to have written more on Native American legal issues than on any other legally constructed category. And, not surprisingly, Native Americans have written back.

In literature, legal themes have served as bountiful sources of metaphor and intrigue in Native American fiction. Writers from D'Arcy McNickle in *The Surrounded* to Leslie Marmon Silko in "The Storyteller" develop the theme of indigenous versus colonial law as metaphors for distinct and oftentimes irreconcilable world views. In "The Storyteller," the female protagonist admits to killing a white man, because in her mind she had wanted him dead. "I will not change the story, not even to escape this place and go home. I intended that he die" (31). In *The Surrounded,* Archilde, the returning son, accepts responsibility for a murder that his mother has committed, and does not reveal her guilt, even after her death and at whatever expense to his own freedom.[2] In both instances, questions of innocence or guilt become complicated by the flurry of narratives revolving around the events themselves.

Gerald Vizenor enters these legal landscapes of contradiction armed with a unique discursive repertoire: novelist, journalist, haiku poet, Anishinabe trickster, cultural critic and theorist. Legal themes, and the narratives that surround them, circulate in his works, appearing and reappearing in different guises, different contexts. I want, here, to examine three key reference points in the expansive body of Vizenor's textual production: "bones," a young Dakota crossblood named White Hawk, and the historic figure of Ishi. These each illustrate Vizenor's unique view of jurisprudence while employing distinct discursive strategies to achieve narrative intervention.

In "Bone Courts: The Natural Rights of Tribal Bones," an essay in the collection *Crossbloods: Bone Courts, Bingo and Other Reports,* Vizenor advocates sovereign rights for the tribal dead and takes up a stance against the museumization of Native American culture. He presents powerful arguments on the racialization of Native Americans that makes the collection of sacred remains so acceptable to many prestigious universities, museums, and cultural centers. His solution, a Bone Court,

This is a contentious discourse on the prima facie rights of human remains, sovereign tribal bones, to be their own narrators, and a modest proposal to establish a Bone Court. This new forum would have federal judicial power to hear and decide disputes over burial sites, research on bones, reburial, and to protect the rights of tribal bones to be represented in court. (63)

He uses an eclectic combination of sources to support his arguments. Included in the forty footnotes that follow are citations from literary theory, legal doctrine, law reviews, newspapers and anthropological texts. He uses these to construct a three-fold argument citing first the difference between the ways in which tribal and non-tribal bones are regarded legally. "White bones are reburied, tribal bones are studied in racist institutions" (67). Then, he argues that, if inanimate, bones represent certain associations and interests, and like other non-speaking entities such as universities, corporations or infants, they have the right to have others represent them in courts of law. Finally, he argues for the narrative possibilities of bones:

Tribal bones as narrators could be considered the real authors of their time and place on the earth; the representation of their voices in a court would overturn the neocolonial perspectives, written and invented tribal cultures. (65)

While at no time does he fall into romanticism about the mystical powers of talking bones, the idea of bones as the source for both old and new tribal narratives is truly inviting. Certainly, these new bone narratives could reveal much about the archaeologists and anthropologists who rob tribal graves, the collectors and institutions that purchase these stolen goods, and the curious scrutiny of social science students who are taught to regard these skeletal remains as evidence of "extinct cultures." These are but a few of the many stories these bones might tell.

This essay is accompanied by two photographs, reversing the narrative ironies Vizenor delineates in the text. The first is presented with the caption "Traditional Anishinabe grave houses near Lake Andrusia, Minnesota" and shows peaceful snow-covered A-framed wood structures. The second photograph depicts a human skull capriciously decorated with a beaded headband sitting on a plain wooded shelf; the caption reads "Caucasian cranium in South Dakota." Vizenor is not about to participate in the further desecration of tribal cultures by illustrating his essay with photographs of the many tribal skeletons irreverently housed in museums, or repositioned in anthropological photographs. Aside from adding further insult, to do so would only fuel the narratives of "victimage" that he detests. Instead, he subverts the journalistic (voyeuristic) expectations of his readers. The images he chooses illustrate both the "civility" and elegance of Anishinabe burial traditions and the inane significance of skulls as mere curios.

The essay is unequivocal in establishing the moral obligation of institutions to return their bone collections to their respective tribes, and cites Stanford and the University of Minnesota as examples of universities that have already done that. He also points to the University of California at Berkeley, and the Smithsonian Institution as two major cultural centers that continue to house and exhibit the remains of thousands of tribal peoples. The essay ends with a brief postscript, which may speak to the limits of irony as an effective vehicle for legal intervention or activism. It reads:

I proposed the Bone Court, and the rights of bones to be represented, at the School of American Research in Santa Fe, New Mexico. The response from other resident scholars, archaeologists and anthropologists, was tolerant; the idea invited some humor as critical abatement, but a discourse never matured at the seminars. (78)

While Vizenor uses his wry humor throughout the essay, his arguments are spurred more by rage rather than by mere whimsical or discursive play. The inclination of his peers in academia to dismiss his arguments with a collegial chuckle, however, may very well be indicative of their own investments in the anthropologisms that Vizenor is critiquing.

The narrative shadows of bones, and the fictional possibilities they suggest, have not escaped Vizenor the novelist. Bones, and the narratives that surround them, have become a recurring theme in Vizenor's fiction, a running metaphor for untold stories. Eva Feder Kittay writes of metaphors as "displaced signs" that possess the power to challenge existing world views:

Metaphor or, at least, metaphor shaped through the imagination, does not record pre-existing similarities in things; rather, it is the linguistic means by which we bring together and fuse into a unity diverse thoughts and thereby re-form our perceptions of the world. (6)

In the years surrounding the quincentenary, the figure of Columbus has become a popular symbol of narrative contestation. In *The Heirs of Columbus,* the bones of both Columbus and Pocahontas become bargaining chips in a new kind of discursive colonial-tribal warfare. Both of these characters, having been stripped of any "real" meaning by centuries of romantic speculation, become empty signifiers, "displaced signs," that Vizenor is free to inhabit as a means to speak back to dominant colonial narratives and to create new metaphorical possibilities.

In *Griever: An American Monkey King in China,* the campus pond that emanates a blue light is discovered to be the burial home of the blue bones of unwanted children and the corpse of Griever's translator/lover, Hester Hua Dan. After their discovery, those in attendance minister to these bones in quiet recognition of their intrinsic value:

Shitou raised the bones of babies from the blue muck. He washed the bones, five small heads, and placed them on the tiers, others fitted the little bones to the shapes of bodies on the terrace. (225)

The passage ends with the arrival of the police, and the end of reverence: "The police ordered the students back to their dormitories, closed the drains in the pond, and pitched the blue bones back into the cold dead water" (226). Bones, like the real stories behind them, are always silent witnesses.

If the ironies of bone collectors and untold stories have failed to reach an audience of social scientists, the political significance of his fictional bones has not been lost on Vizenor's audience of literary scholars. Kimberly Blaeser writes,

In a scene in *Harold of Orange*, Harold implies that the bones in a museum case may actually be, not those of an Indian, but those of a white anthropologist lost in a snow storm, and later mistaken for a dead Indian. In his novel *The Heirs of Columbus*, the characters struggle for possession of the remains of both Pocahontas and Columbus. Vizenor's playful reversals in these stories challenge readers to reconsider the readily accepted treatment of the remains of "primitive" cultures as museum objects and the implied hierarchy that allows or endorses such a practice. (354)

Tribal bones become metaphors for the lost, stolen, appropriated, displaced and disemboweled narratives of indigenous peoples. The strength and elegance of Anishinabe grave houses can also be read as metaphors for the growing body of Native American literary work that houses tribal stories of love, beauty and tragic wisdom. Yet, if bones are metaphors for silent witnesses, then the legal arguments for Bone Courts also reveal a larger claim to all forms of tribal justice.

II

The case of Thomas White Hawk presents a provocative case history of the world view embodied in the U.S. legal system. In 1967, Thomas James White Hawk, a Dakota Indian, was indicted, charged and plead guilty to the murder of James Yeado, a white jeweler, and to the rape of his wife. He was sentenced, without trial, to death by electrocution. In the aftermath of these events, Vizenor, working as a journalist, wrote and distributed thousands of pamphlets publicizing the details of the case and mobilizing support for repeal of the death sentence.[4] Two years later, White Hawk's sentence was commuted to life imprisonment without parole. It was suggested that the controversy surrounding the case had hurt the state's tourism during hunting season.

At first read, "Thomas White Hawk" is a straightforward narrative of murder in post colonial America.[5] Another Bigger Thomas caught in the web of someone else's nightmare. Gerald Vizenor enters in the role of narrative mediator, who, acting through the authority of the text, intervenes to effect communication and renegotiate the terms of the discourse. There is a life at stake. The immediate goal is having White Hawk's death sentence changed to one of life imprisonment. Through the publication and dissemination of the story, this goal is attained: White Hawk's sentence is commuted to life imprisonment without parole. Both the life of Thomas White Hawk and the right of white men to hunt other game in South Dakota, free of Indian protests and controversy, are preserved. But the story and the storyteller remain to unravel the fabric of relations that constitute power.

This is a story about power, and the relations of power that compete within pre-existing narratives. Foucault challenges the paradigm that defines power as a "general system of domination exerted by one group over another." Instead, he writes,

Power is not an institution, and not a structure; neither is it a certain strength we are endowed with; it is the name one attributes to a complex strategical situation in a particular society. (*History* 92-93)

The texts which comprise this case are a study in the ways in which the multiple subject of White Hawk acts, reacts and is acted upon within an interwoven system of power relations and a multitude of discursive systems including psychiatry, law, feminism, and an American Indian national liberation movement. Power within this context consists of both individual and institutional power. In this case, institutional power extends to encompass the reservation, the courts, fosterage and guardian systems, educational systems, prisons, churches, families, and psychiatric institutions.

The story of Thomas White Hawk is made compelling, not because White Hawk did not commit the crime, but because he did. Vizenor begins his essay with the last details of James Yeado's life. It is an intimate portrait; the narrator tells us that Yeado was a Virgo, a gardener, the father of two children, and a member of the Vermillion Chamber of Commerce. On the opposite page is a copy of a handwritten note with the words "Notes Pertaining to My Case" scribbled across the top. Its author is not identified, but we know it is Yeado's murderer.

Vizenor first introduces us to Thomas James White Hawk a few paragraphs later, identified as a freshman pre-med student. He writes: "Yeado had sold a good many engagement rings to University students, but this one was different. He knew them both. They were Indians" (102). The last two lines are short and deliberate, and the sequence seems noteworthy. The narrator does not refer to these Indians by tribe or speculate as to the nature of Yeado's knowledge. The sentences seem somewhat connected, yet the connection is never stated. By beginning from the perspective of Yeado, the narrator creates a sense of textual distance and neutrality from White Hawk, and compassion for the murder victim.

Vizenor's construction of White Hawk develops slowly and deliberately. Bits and pieces of his life are interspersed between vivid details of the crime and the ensuing events of the trial. White Hawk the murderer, the rapist, the Indian becomes layered with other vestments of identity. He is revealed to be a Dakota crossblood born on the Rosebud reservation, an orphan who had lived under the care of white people for most of his life, a football player and track star who had suffered an injury to the head many years back, a young man who dreams of being a doctor.

The omniscient narrator never hints at the source of his construction. Some of the details are mundane, others more profound. Many incidents are only suggested in the text, yet the suggestions are revealing, beginning with the possible murder of his mother. "Friends have told him that his mother died in childbirth, but he has dreams that she died some other way" (111). Later, White Hawk's guardian is introduced with the portentous line "*Phil Zoubek . . .* is Tom's guardian and *a lot more.* Each of these two men is half of a warm human adventure" (115). Zoubek's name and the words "a lot more" are italicized in the text, as if to make explicit the homosexual relationship they shared. The source of this knowledge is again kept hidden, creating a textual silence and raising further questions as to the *actual* nature of this relationship between a white foster father and his teenage Indian son.

Throughout the text, Vizenor amplifies the discursive excesses of journalism. So while the text seems to fulfill the reader's demands for the "facts" of who, what, where, when and why, the meaning of the "facts" is continually being destabilized by references to other narrative shadows. The illusion of distance, and the authorial objectivity associated with journalism, are constantly undercut through dream sequences, italicized texts, authorial speculation and tangential narratives. The text itself reads as a simulation of the journalistic enterprise. Jean Baudrillard defines simulation as the absence rather than the presence of the real; to simulate is to call into question the difference between "true" and "false," in this case journalism and fiction.[6] Instances of italicized text point the reader to discursive contradictions, phrases such as "*cultural norms,*" "*uncontrolled discretion,*" or Judge Bandy's euphemism for capital punishment, "*I am removing him from the world.*" This selective glossing visually marks the text with authorial intention and disrupts the illusion of journalistic objectivity and distance. Vizenor exercises his authorial power through the coded text and its dissemination. It is ultimately this power which "saves" White Hawk from the death sentence.

Already these relationships of power have begun to breed. White Hawk's power over James Yeado and his wife, Zoubek's power over White Hawk, the power of the fosterage system, the courts, the educational system, and of course the authorial power of the text. A Foucaultian nightmare of competing discourses acted out on the body of Thomas White Hawk. In much of his writings, Foucault demonstrates the interdependence of the penal and medical systems in terms of creating mutually supportive discourses on criminality, deviance, and delinquency. In *Discipline and Punish: The Birth of the Prison,* Foucault delineates the history of the penal system in the West. He argues that it is the person, not the crime, that is judged and punished. He writes:

Certainly the "crimes" and "offenses" on which judgement is passed are judicial objects defined by the code, but judgement is also passed on the passions, instincts, anomalies, infirmities, maladjustments, effects of environment or heredity; acts of aggression are punished, so also, through them is aggressivity, rape, but at the same time perversions; murders, but also drives and desires. . . . *For it is these shadows lurking behind the case itself that are judged and punished. . . .* [A]nd which, behind the pretext of explaining an action, are ways of defining an individual. (17-18, emphasis added)

It is these shadows that Vizenor seeks to flesh out in his narratives. Like the courts, he shifts the focus of judgement onto the individual rather than the crime, while providing a social and cultural context for understanding the life of this young Dakota man.

White Hawk's trial inevitably turns on the sanity of the defendant. The judico-psychiatric discourse surrounding the trial was perhaps the most verbose in its depiction of him. Terms such as "psychoneurotic," "sociopathic," *"passive-aggressive,"* and "personality defect" with a *"poor prognosis in treatment"* were all used to describe and define White Hawk. The legally imposed binary of guilty or innocent becomes dependent on the psychiatric binary of sane or insane. Psychiatry helps to create the narrative of victim turned victimizer, "the result of *environmental contacts.*" A "personality disturbance [which] appears to be his ambivalence concerning his psychosexual development." This White Hawk, constructed through a psychiatric discourse, seems to take on the characteristics of an odd sort of Oedipus, murdering the figure of the white paternal father and sleeping with the forbidden mother.

Other preexisting narratives have already circumscribed White Hawk's story.[7] Each represses aspects of the subject's positionality, and tries to reinscribe the story within a specific narrative which is always already written in binary opposites. These arguments are in turn instrumental in reconstructing the binary of victimization and agency, innocence or guilt. They include:

1. The colonial narrative which inscribes the story in terms of civilization/ savagery, christian/heathen. Within this narrative, White Hawk's crime is etched into the dominant psyche as an act of treason against the purity of a white social order and must be punishable by death. How would the trial and the sentence have been different if the Yeados were Chinese, African American, Indian?

2. The cultural nationalist narrative which reads White Hawk as a victim of the hegemonic powers that seek to destroy him. This anti-colonial narrative challenges the occupying state's authority to define criminality, sanity, and jurisdiction. His act is thus inscribed as an act of rebellion against the dominant culture. However, in this narrative the male nationalist fantasy of ultimate revenge thus becomes coded as murdering the white man and sleeping with his wife. Indian vs. White Man.

3. An unwritten radical Anglo feminist narrative which would write White Hawk as a victimizer of women. The act of rape is written as purely an act of male violence, the ultimate expression of patriarchal power. White Hawk is thus written as an agent of male power. The white woman is then revealed as a pawn between the Native man and the white man. Man vs. Woman. However, these terms are already racialized: Native Man, white woman, obfuscating the figure of the white man. In both this and previous scenarios, the Native woman is totally written out of the story.

Vizenor draws on these competing discourses to construct the complexity of social forces impacting the fate of the multiple subject. The origins of these narratives are as old and as new as the binary of "us" and "them." They circulate like viruses, infiltrating the body politic. In contrast, Vizenor deconstructs the tyranny of these preexisting binaries by presenting a multiplicity of voices and power relations. Nowhere in the text is it suggested White Hawk views *himself* as a colonialized subject, or as an agent against cultural hegemony, or white womanhood. These narratives have been constructed by others for their own ends, and White Hawk functions as the unwitting protagonist.

White Hawk's participation in the crime is never contested; instead the text attempts to challenge absolute definitions of agency and victimization. In order to do so, the multiple subject must be repositioned within a legion of oppressive localities. White Hawk as colonized male subject, childhood victim, murderer, rapist, is already racialized and gendered within existing systems of power. These factors exist simultaneously, even as they contradict and contest each other's power to define. This is where Foucault's theories of power as omnipresent and capillary are most productive. Rather than seeing power as something that is held by a centralized force (state or patriarchy), it is something which is fluid and dynamic, something that is exercised rather than possessed.

The omnipresence of power: not because it has the privilege of consolidating everything under its invincible unity, but because it is produced from one moment to the next, at every point. Power is everywhere; not because it embraces everything, but because it comes from everywhere. (*History* 93)

Foucault's work does not deny or minimize the power of the state and its institutions; however, he sees this as only one form of power. By recognizing the fluidity of power he is also able to acknowledge the swarm of power relations that operate on the microlevel of society.

By presenting the case in its fullest complexity, Vizenor is able to capture these subtleties of power and use them to mediate between the several narratives that I have delineated. Vizenor puts flesh on the multiple subject and attempts to reposition White Hawk as a Dakota Indian within post-colonial occupied America. He gives us pictures of White Hawk, of downtown Vermillion, photographs of each of the central characters in the trial in an attempt to make them something more than the individual roles they play. There are no photos of Yeado and his wife. They are incidental characters, whose actions appear offstage and are only alluded to in the text; they have no agency and no voice in this new story of crime and punishment.

Instead, Vizenor's narrative remains focused on White Hawk. His discursive power lies in his ability to reframe judicial and psychiatric discourses in terms of colonialism and power. This would include the diagnosis of White Hawk as suffering from cultural schizophrenia and the coding of Zoubek as homosexual. Throughout the court transcripts, Vizenor again inserts italicized text that is at times White Hawk's memories, dreams and thoughts and at other times, the thoughts of Judge Bandy and others. These glossed phrases suggest a discursive excess which cannot be expressed within the prefigured legal or psychiatric framework.

Vizenor's investment and fascination with White Hawk, beyond the goal of commutation, hints at motives within the shadows of the lines. The question mark that is intent curves ambiguously around each sentence and textual silence. Each time the story is told it becomes transformed. The story becomes multiple, radiating out to encompass the other stories circulating around White Hawk. With each new telling, the position of the narrator shifts.

Vizenor is first and foremost a storyteller. In his writings, the man slips in and out of the shadows he projects. In *Manifest Manners: Postindian Warriors of Survivance,* Vizenor uses the term "shadow survivance" as a means to understand tribal consciousness and stories. He writes,

The shadows are the silence in heard stories, the silence that bears a referent of tribal memories and experience. The shadow words are active memories, and the memories of heard stories. The shadows are intransitive, an animate action in the silence of stories. (72)

It is these shadows that inhabit his own texts. These are the significant silences that weigh on the consciousness of his readers.

In the case of Thomas White Hawk, these shadows of survivance contains stories about other unfathomable acts of violence on tribal lands. In this seemingly nonfictional piece of journalism, Vizenor withholds the political intent of his text, which is clearly the commutation of White Hawk's death sentence. Intent is also related to Vizenor's masking his own subject position. Like White Hawk, Vizenor is a tribal mixed blood survivor of cultural schizophrenia, the foster care system and childhood abuse and neglect. Vizenor's naming himself as a survivor would have further implicated White Hawk's own agency: Good Indian vs. Bad Indian. By cloaking his role as writer and investigator, as well as his connection and insight to White Hawk's past, he veils a vital source of his knowledge. After the immediate goal of commutation has been achieved, other stories can be told.

In the collection *Crossbloods* this first telling is directly followed by the short piece entitled "Commutation of Death," a polemic on the limits of justice in occupied territories. In this piece, Vizenor writes:

[T]he story will not end because White Hawk has become a symbol of the conflicts and injustices of many dakota people living in a white-dominated state. And the dominant white people on the plains will not forget the savage demon who twice raped a white woman while her husband was dying of gunshot wounds in the next room. (152)

In this addendum, the narrator is unrestrained by the simulations of advocacy journalism, and the subsequent problems of audience and authorial motivation. He is able to point directly to the intent of the text, without the concern of alienating many of the white liberals it was intended to sway. Once the immediacy of commuting White Hawk's sentence has been achieved, the narrator is free to move outside the specificities of the case and address larger issues of justice and white domination.

Like the bones that bear witness in Bone Courts, only to appear later in fiction, the stories of Thomas White Hawk reach out to seek new narrative possibilities. In *Wordarrows: Indians and Whites in the New Fur Trade,* the story is retold in a series of veiled fictionalized accounts which allow for details, previously considered too marginal, unspeakable, unsubstantiated or libelous to be told under the guise of fiction. As the story moves farther away from the scene of White Hawk's crime, the image of the author and his own investment and attraction to the stories become clearer.

In the series of stories in *Wordarrows,* Vizenor inserts himself in the text under the name of Clement Beaulieu, a "liberal tribal writer." Clement Beaulieu is the name of Vizenor's grandfather; Clement is also the name of his father, who was himself the victim of a seemingly senseless murder. The intertextuality that exists between these stories adds credence and depth to the original story of the trial as they explicate the complexities of Indian identity.

By creating himself through the character Beaulieu, Vizenor gives voice to the tribal identity that he shares with White Hawk. Vizenor transforms himself through this character to escape representations of the author. Fiction allows for the articulation of this Native voice which would have further complicated the initial narrative of White Hawk's trail. Yet, even here, Beaulieu is one character, one voice, among many. The position of both the narrator and the author remain shadowed.

The stories in *Wordarrows* have as much to do with the writer's search for a way to understand White Hawk's story, as with the case itself. Here, Vizenor delves even deeper into the micro-level of power relations circulating around the trial. Among the stories woven around the figure of White Hawk is the illicit affair between the minister's wife and the condemned man through the bars of a prison cell, a Pine Ridge Indian law student who testifies for the prosecution as an expert on tribal justice in support of capital punishment,[8] and Beaulieu's invisibility as a tribal person which allows others to speak uncensored about the Indians in their midst. The characters he invokes are marginal at best to the narratives I have delineated, yet they reveal the many ways in which Native peoples are made savage, exotic, invisible, insane within the dominant culture.

In a third, and as yet unfinished future telling of the story, Vizenor plans to reinsert himself through the use of first person narration. Yet, even from within this posture, the "real" author remains in the shadows. Even within the genre of personal testimony through autobiography, the author remains the fictive construction of authorial imagination, as evidenced by the subtitle of Vizenor's own autobiography, *Interior Landscapes: Autobiographical Myths and Metaphors*. Again, the lines between true and false, myth and science, reality and fiction, are blurred rather than clarified.

In *Manifest Manners,* Vizenor delves deeper into the interpretive possibilities of critical theory without the burdens of journalistic simulations. His capacity for irony, word play, and theoretical imaginings are unleashed in this text. His prolific body of essays, critical theory and literature combine with the countless eclectic sources for his authorial imagination and insights to create mind-boggling potential for intertextual possibilities, possibilities that he manipulates at every turn.

III

In the essay "Ishi Obscura," published in *Manifest Manners,* Vizenor begins the narrative of Ishi with the sentence: "Ishi was never his real name." This figure who has come to represent either the "last true American Indian" or the epitome of indigenous victimage at the hands of "civilization" and "anthropology" has other stories to tell. In this essay, Vizenor articulates the difference between the simulations of Indian identity that Ishi has come to represent and the possibilities of a man with his own stories to tell. Vizenor creates a story, not of victimage but of survivance. Like the mantra "This portrait is not an Indian" that is repeated in "Postindian Warriors," we are reminded that Ishi is more than a simulation of Indian identity.

The Ishi Vizenor presents is a man of gentle humor, with a voracious appetite for storytelling, and profound intellectual insights. Vizenor also creates a story of polite but unequivocal resistance. Ishi refused to remove his overalls to satisfy the dioramic colonial fantasies of photographers interested in capturing the vanishing race on film as the constructed simulations of Indian identity. More importantly, he never revealed his name,

His survivance, that sense of mediation in tribal stories, is heard in a word that means "one of the people," and that word became his name. So much the better, and he never told the anthropologists, reporters, and curious practitioners his sacred tribal name, not even his nicknames. The other tribal pronoun ended in silence. He might have said, "The ghosts were generous in the silence of the museum, and now these men pretend to know me in their name." Trickster hermeneutics is the silence of his nicknames. (128)

Ishi's stories of museum life become acts of survivance, a means of retaining tribal dignity by his selective silences, and the speed with which he told his stories, frustrating anthropological efforts at translation and transcription. These subtle acts of resistance are his legacy, not stories of victimization or portraits of "wild" Indians living in museums.

Toward the end of the essay, in an unexpected and almost imperceptible narrative transition, Vizenor shifts from third to second person. He writes,

You hear his name now in the isolation of his photographs. You must imagine the lonesome humor in the poses that pleased the curators in the natural light near the museum at the University of California. Their dead voices haunt the margins of our photographs. You were not the last to dream in his stories. You were not the last memories of the tribes, but you were the last to land in a museum as the simulations of a vanishing pose in photographs. (133)[9]

Even within this paragraph the referent for the "you" changes, from the reader to Ishi, himself, as the unnamed referent. This temporary blurring of Ishi's "you" and the reader's "I" further unsettles Vizenor's essay. The personal possessive of "his photographs" that begins the paragraph shifts to the collective "our" of "our photographs," insinuating the reader's responsibility as the recipient of tribal simulations. As a narrative ploy it succeeds in destabilizing the reader and momentarily erasing the distinction between the other and the self.

Ishi appears previously in at least two of Vizenor's essays. As the opening reference in "Bone Courts," he functions as a reminder of the spirit that once inhabited the bones that now serve as scientific inquiry. Vizenor begins the essay with Kroeber's arguments to defend the sanctity of his tribal friend's last remains. This opening move seems to suggest that the friendship that developed between Alfred Kroeber, the Berkeley anthropologist, and Ishi, the Yahi Indian, may hold a glimmer of promise for greater understanding between social scientists and native communities. As mentioned earlier, in the final note that ends the essay, the unwillingness of contemporary academics to take up in earnest the repatriation of tribal remains may foreclose any such reconciliations between the morbid interests of science and the rights of bones.

In the essay "Socioacupuncture: Mythic Reversals and the Striptease in Four Scenes," a genre-bending critical piece that fuses elements of history, fiction and cultural theory, Ishi functions as the narrative foil to Tune Browne, a postindian warrior lost within his own simulation of tribal identity. "[Tune] and Ishi lived together and worked at the museum to protect the anthropologist, for a time, from vanishing" (93). Kroeber is also present in this narrative refiguration of simulation and academic colonization. When Ishi and Tune are awarded honorary doctorates from the University of California, Phoebe Apperson Hearst, Robert Sproul, Benjamin Ide Wheeler and other scholarly luminaries are all in attendance to witness the festivities. Ironically, it has been these names that have been etched on the architectural history of the University of California, at Berkeley, Ishi's presence has remained a silent shadow until very recently. In 1993, Vizenor succeeded in getting a courtyard on the Berkeley campus named for Ishi, the first formal recognition of his academic and scholarly contributions.

IV

Vizenor creates new narratives to liberate the stories of tribal bones, jailed young men, and Indians living in museums. The narratives he employs can also be seen as three examples of successful strategic interventions. While to date, a federal bone court has not been established, Vizenor was instrumental in persuading the University of Minnesota to return their bone collections. And he continues to advocate for the rights of tribal dead in each classroom seminar, and in his many public appearances. In the case of White Hawk, Vizenor's textual maneuvers saved a young man from the death penalty. And Ishi, while not awarded a doctorate, has finally been honored as the first tribal person to make his mark on Berkeley's campus map.

These examples illustrate the many ways that Vizenor advocates for the rights of tribal peoples; in fiction, in theory, in classrooms, and in boardrooms, he uses interpretation and metaphor to challenge the perspectives, world views and beliefs of his multiple audiences. Law, like literature, gains meaning only through interpretation. Vizenorian textual interpretations embody elements of journalism, law, and fiction, spiced with the narrative shadows of haiku and the political insights of social commentary, to deconstruct binaries of innocence and guilt, tragic victims and romantic heros, fact and fiction. In the process he creates new landscapes of interpretive possibilities, new narratives of liberation, in the service of tribal justice.

Notes

1. See specifically Patricia J. Williams, *The Alchemy of Race and Rights: Diary of a Law Professor.*

2. Given the way in which the novel is framed, the linear cause-and-effect narrative style, and the original ending as it appeared in *The Hungry Generation,* it could easily be argued that this entire text is a legal presentation with a judge as the unnamed narratee of the novel. For more on narratees see Gerald Price, "Introduction to the Study of the Narratee," in *Essentials of the Theory of Fiction.*

3. For a thoughtful essay on the ethical implications of anthropological collection practices see James Clifford, "On Collecting Art and Culture."

4. This pamphlet, edited as an article and entitled "Thomas White Hawk" was reprinted with the addendum "Commutation of Death," in Gerald Vizenor's collection *Crossbloods: Bone Courts, Bingo and Other Reports.*

5. I use post colonial here in the sense of after the onset of colonialism. See *The Empire Writes Back: Theory and Practice in Post-Colonial Literatures.*

6. See Baudrillard 5. For Vizenor's uses of simulations see also *Manifest Manners.*

7. For an example of how preexisting narratives frame political arguments see Lata Mani, "Multiple Mediations: Feminist Scholarship in the Age of Multinational Reception."

8. In another example of thematic re-circulation, in "Post Indian Warriors" in *Manifest Manners,* Vizenor reveals more details about this person, Ed McGaa and the specific nature, circumstances and consequences of his testimony.

9. *Dead Voices* is also the title of a 1992 novel by Vizenor.

Works Cited

Ashcroft, Bill, Gareth Griffiths, and Helen Tiffin, eds. *The Empire Writes Back: Theory and Practice in Post-Colonial Literatures.* London: Routledge, 1989.

Baudrillard, Jean. *Simulations.* Trans. Paul Foss, Paul Patton, and Phillip Beitchman. New York: Semiotext(e), 1983.

Blaeser, Kimberly. "The New 'Frontier' of Native American Literature: Dis-Arming History with Tribal Humor." *Genre: Forms of Discourse and Culture* 25 (1992): 351-64.

Clifford, James. "On Collecting Art and Culture." *Out There: Marginalization and Contemporary Cultures.* Ed. Russell Ferguson, Martha Gever, Trinh T. Minh-ha and Cornel West. New York: New Museum of Contemporary Art, 1990.

Foucault, Michel. *Discipline and Punish: Birth of the Prison.* Trans. Alan Sheridan. New York: Vintage, 1979.

———. *The History of Sexuality: Volume I, An Introduction.* Trans. Robert Hurley. New York: Vintage, 1990.

Fusco, Coco. "The Other History of Intercultural Performance." *English Is Broken Here: Notes on Cultural Fusion in the Americas.* New York: New P, 1995.

Kittay, Eva Feder. *Metaphor: Its Cognitive Force and Linguistic Structure.* Oxford: Clarendon P, 1987.

Mani, Lata. "Multiple Mediations: Feminist Scholarship in the Age of Multinational Reception." *Feminist Review* 35 (Summer 1990): 24-39.

McNickle, D'Arcy. *The Surrounded.* 1936. Albuquerque: U of New Mexico P, 1993.

Price, Gerald. "Introduction to the Study of the Narratee." *Essentials of the Theory of Fiction.* Ed. Michael Hoffman and Patrick Murphy. Durham: Duke UP, 1988.

Silko, Leslie Marmon. "The Storyteller." *The Storyteller.* New York: Seaver, 1981.

Vizenor, Gerald. *Crossbloods: Bone Courts, Bingo and Other Reports.* Minneapolis: U of Minnesota P, 1990.

———. *Dead Voices: Natural Agonies in the New World.* Norman: U of Oklahoma P, 1992.

———. *Griever: An American Monkey King in China.* Normal: Illinois State U/Fiction Collective, 1987.

———. *The Heirs of Columbus.* Hanover, NH: Wesleyan UP, 1991.

———. *Interior Landscapes: Autobiographical Myths and Metaphors.* Minneapolis: U of Minnesota P, 1990.

———. *Manifest Manners: Postindian Warriors of Survivance.* Hanover, NH: Wesleyan UP, 1994.

———. "Socioacupuncture: Mythic Reversals and the Striptease in Four Scenes." *Out There: Marginalization and Contemporary Cultures.* Ed. Russell Ferguson, Martha Gever, Trinh T. Minh-ha, and Cornel West. New York: New Museum of Contemporary Art, 1990.

———. *Wordarrows: Indians and Whites in the New Fur Trade.* Minneapolis: U of Minnesota P, 1978.

Williams, Patricia J. *The Alchemy of Race and Rights: Diary of a Law Professor.* Boston: Harvard UP, 1991.

16

THE ONLY GOOD INDIAN IS A POSTINDIAN?
CONTROVERSIALIST VIZENOR AND *MANIFEST MANNERS*

A. Robert Lee

> Bound with mixedblood memories, urban and reservation disharmonies, imagination cruises with the verbs and adverbs now, overturns calendar nouns in wild histories where there are no toeholds in material time . . .
>
> —"Crows Written on the Poplars:
> Autocritical Autobiographies" in *I Tell You Now:*
> *Autobiographical Essays by Native American Writers* (1987)

> The Anishinaabe are my ancestors. I am a crossblood descendant of these families and, by chance, and vision, bear the narratives of native reason and the associations of both colonial and national dominance.
>
> —"Visions, Scares, and Stories," in Contemporary
> Authors Autobiography Series (1995)

I

"My pen was raised to terminal creeds." In an author rightly celebrated for his obliquity, his tease, this line from "Avengers at Wounded Knee" offers a rare moment of near manifesto (235). But much as the piece leaves little doubt as to its focus—the warrior bravura, the posturings, of Dennis Banks and his American Indian Movement (AIM) cadre of "new tribal totalitarians," it also loses nothing in the way of Vizenor's customary ironic skirmish. Furthermore, though it can stand perfectly well in its own right, it serves as but one of twenty-nine interfoliations, each strategically gapped yet full of linkage and continuity, in his crossblood life story, *Interior Landscapes: Autobiographical Myths and Metaphors.*

Of necessity "Avengers" assumes a historical reference—back to the Seventh U.S. Cavalry's destruction of Big Foot and the Minneconjou Sioux at Wounded Knee Creek in 1890. Vizenor has left no doubt of how he views that event in the light of its onetime status as frontier triumphalism, an assumed last or decisive chapter in the Winning of the West. He has often spoken, and written, of it as a prior My Lai, the brute "pacification" of encamped indigenous tribespeople seventy years or so before Vietnam by soldiery also in U.S. army uniform.

But, typically, and in the light of the Wounded Knee march and occupation in March 1973, "Wounded Knee" also for Vizenor involved another false face, another, however less dire, transformation. To what, initially, had been his *Minneapolis Tribune* reporter's eye, the 1973 happenings in a number of key respects became less a wholly deserved memorial protest than *kitsch,* a colluded-in media confection.

To the one side mainstream TV and press had exhibited an uncertain mix of stereotype ("Indians on the Warpath") and liberal guilt ("Indians as Victims"), not to say an often selective, even sloppy, use of the known facts. To the other side Dennis Banks, Russell Means and, in train, Vernon and Clyde Bellecourt and their cohorts, had reciprocally behaved as tribal mimic-men, "kitschymen" Vizenor calls them, each duly costumed in a mix of "feathers and braid," and, a nice turnabout, "cowboy clothes." They had also taken to a symbolic show of horsemanship, anachronistic though not out of keeping with a "revolutionary tribal caravan." Here, for Vizenor, was a double charade, literally out of time Indians and Cowboys.

As to the actual AIM leadership of Banks and his fellow luminaries, such, he argued, had come about only by an act of self-arrogation. They blithely ignored all prior and ongoing tribal-white negotiations with Mayor Donald Barnett of Rapid City. Several, if not Banks himself, booked into an air-conditioned motel, and travelled by quite unrevolutionary limousine to Wounded Knee. The plentiful drugs, especially marijuana, left about, borrowed, likely sold, Vizenor also underscores as yet another deficit. For however full of dexterity or wit, this unyielding smack at shadow over substance was also scrupulous reportage.

The evident impiety, or at any rate the unwillingness to go along with the hype, was not calculated to put Vizenor in the running for AIM's "man of the year" award. AIM, in fact, placed his name on their enemies list—both for his original *Minneapolis Tribune* articles on Wounded Knee and the reworked book pieces in its wake, a disesteem which has continued to the present time. The gesture, despite itself, paid unintended tribute to some of Vizenor's liveliest powers ("Dennis Banks"). Then, as now, these reside in an unblinkingly polemical (though never less than tricksterishly playful) eagerness to call time on bad faith fakery or, to invoke one of his favored terms from Baudrillard, on bad faith simulation.

Vizenor's long held notion, too, of "terminal" would come into play, a trope, a figuration, for signalling utter impatience with any or all pantribal reductionism, each static or essentializing version of "the Indian." If, as his writings have emphasized throughout, the process has most of all arisen in Euro-America's multiple travesties, not a few Native-born counterparts have colluded in the responsibility.

Mimeshows of the Banks-Means variety, however, Vizenor takes to offer but the one instance. He includes in his sweep all wannabe Indians (in this respect his shot at the literary scholar Hertha Wong became another controversy).[1] "Ethnic transvestites" have equally come under his ironic purview, from Forrest Carter in (as it has turned out) his mock "true story" of a Cherokee childhood in *The Education of Little Tree* (1976) to Jamake Highwater purveying "Indian" (would-be Blackfoot and Cherokee) spirituality in *Shadow Story: An Autobiographical Insinuation* (1986). Nor does an "all one under the mask" anthropological savant like Joseph Campbell escape his censure in his frequent treatment of Native myths and animisms as somehow shared variations on a single theme.

Almost two decades on from when Vizenor first lowered his ironic gaze upon the Avengers of Wounded Knee, his *Manifest Manners: Postindian Warriors of Survivance* (1994), then, offers a yet further rumination on the identifyings and misidentifyings of "Indianness," or on what, innovatingly, he has called postindianness.[2]

II

Much as it confirms controversialist Vizenor, *Manifest Manners* wholly, and in equal part, also gives a vintage show of all his best compositional arts and tactics. For a start, and tricksterish as ever, it dissolves any fixed line between essay and story, each more borderland than boundary and always readily given to overlap, reversibility, a working interplay of the one with the other. For if Vizenor has been singular enough in his polemical stances towards America both Native and non-Native, so his textual chameleonism serves alongside as quite his identifying signature.

Manifest Manners takes up many of the issues which have concerned him from the outset, above all the always vexed alchemy of representation. The early journalism in the *Minneapolis Tribune* and *Twin Citian Magazine,* of which "Avengers" offers so lively an instance, in fact can be seen merely to have inaugurated the process.

A symptomatic circuit of interests includes his different takes on Columbus, the whole ethos of "Vanishing Americans," the Federal policies of removal and allotment from the Dawes Act of 1887 onwards, the role of the Bureau of Indian Affairs (BIA) since its establishment in 1824 and the first "Removal" bill in 1830, the land claim controversies which have arisen in Taos and Maine, Minnesota and Alcatraz, the recent casino wars in Mohawk and other Indian Country, pop culture "Indian" iconography and, perhaps above all, the pervasive, and anything but concluded, implications of *métis* and *mestizo* history. Figures, too, like Ishi, Thomas White Hawk or Dane Michael White, to whom he has been recurrently and intimately drawn, each help personalize these concerns. Dead or alive, as he deploys them, they serve as key evidentiary and nothing if not multifaceted sentinels.

When, however, in a 1981 interview, he observed in respect of static versions of "Indian identity" that "some upsetting is necessary," he clearly had in mind also the kind of textuality best suited to his needs (Bowers and Silet 47). For Vizenor as textual shapeshifter has from the outset equally assumed rights of transgression against virtually every fixed literary kind. Native America's ranking postmodern author (a label, even so, whose own fixity paradoxically leaves him uneasy), could it ever be doubted that his has been a lifetime's writing done as much against the grain of received literary genre as subject?

The novels have been a renowned instance, full of controlled discontinuity and inhabited by a gallery of baroque or virtual reality prime players. *Darkness in Saint Louis Bearheart* (1978), subsequently retitled *Bearheart: The Heirship Chronicles* (1990), offers its own eddying story of the quest for spiritual hope within a hyper-consumerist, phantasmagoric America; *Griever: An American Monkey King in China* (1987) plays Native and Chinese "mind-monkey" tricksterisms into each other, and then against, both American and Chinese cultural orthodoxy; *The Trickster of Liberty: Tribal Heirs to a Wild Baronage* (1988) makes its "detection" as much the plot of American history as purloined relics; *The Heirs of Columbus* (1991) inverts, or rather turns inside out, 1492, as if to give a latter-day twist to Columbus's own misnomered belief that he had discovered India; *Dead Voices: Natural Agonies in the New World* (1992) gives an Anishinaabe-tribal variation to *Waiting for Godot;* and *Hotline Healers: An Almost Browne Novel* (1997) puts "Indians" under Naanabozho comic-trickster rules not least in Almost's Blank Book business.

A crossblood signature in textuality to match that in life: what could be more fitting? It would surely have been out of keeping had Vizenor's flair for mixed genre not also carried over into his equally voluminous discursive writing.

III

The "exploration of the myths and representations of Native Americans" runs Vizenor's own gloss for *Manifest Manners* (cover note). It could as well hold for the three volumes which supply a series of antecedent links: *Wordarrows: Indians and Whites in the New Fur Trade* (1978, 1989), *Earthdivers: Tribal Narratives on Mixed Descent* (1981) and *Crossbloods: Bone Courts, Bingo, and Other Reports* (1990). Each offers a pointer to Vizenor's presiding notion of "postindian," the play of representational guises and identity to have emerged from Euro-American and tribal encounter. This process whereby all native cultures (each themselves richly heterodox) have been pressed into the unitary phenomenon of "The Indian" he has again returned to, and with startling bravura, in *Fugitive Poses: Native American Indian Scenes of Absence and Presence* (1998).

Who, by now, can afford *not* to be familiar with the double helix of good and bad Indian, whether Rousseau's Noble Savage and Shakespeare's Caliban or Chateaubriand's heroic Atala and Mary Rowlandson's "murderous wretches" as she describes them in her *Narrative of the Captivity and Restauration of Mrs. Mary Rowlandson* (1682)? Does not, too, the view of John Winthrop and other Anglo-American Puritans that Indians were given to speaking some diasporic (not to say debased) Lost Tribe's Hebrew link directly to the view of them as impediments to American modernity?

Screen visualizations, as Vizenor has always been quick to point out, have especially compounded the problem, from D. W. Griffith's two-reeler "redskins" through to Jay Silverheels's Tonto, Jeff Chandler as muscled warchief in *Broken Arrow* (1950) through to Richard Harris as white sundancer in *A Man Called Horse* (1970) and, latterly, from Kevin Costner's Vanishing American Sioux (Comanches in Michael Blake's original, actually highly unoriginal, novel) in *Dances with Wolves* (1990) through to Disney's Hollywood "mother of the nation" animation replete in pastoral and lovesong in *Pocahontas* (1995). Which, or more to the point whose, Indians, Vizenor persists in asking, exactly are these?

The double take for him has been as extensive as it has been carnivalesque, whether Indian dimestore manikins, the Indian Head nickel, the casually debasing nomenclature of a Washington Redskins or Atlanta Braves, or the commodification by the auto industry of names like Pontiac and Winnebago. The *faux* "Indians," too, of counterculture 1960s Hippyism, or of the drug circuits of campus and suburb, or of New Age shamanism with its crystals and channeling, he sees as but latest styles of silhouette. Perhaps the phenomenon of Iron Eyes Cody as "TV Indian" (aired first in 1971 as part of the "Keep America Beautiful" campaign), tearful and clad in buckskin as he canoes his way along a polluted river, acts as summary. The supposed icon of an ecologically purer America he may be, but if so, in despite of the military and related "pollution" visited on the tribes themselves.

How, thus, for Vizenor, or any other Native writer, to locate anything like real-time historic tribal and crossblood life, pre- or post-Columbian? How to re-create the sumptuous oral heritage of irony, humor, drama, performance, "survivance," yet within scriptural storytelling? How to make "Indians" as contrary as anyone else? When the Paiutes of Pyramid Lake, Nevada, or the Mescalero Apache of New Mexico offer to site nuclear waste on their reservations in the form of Monitored Retrieval Storage (MRS) facilities, are they conforming to "good" or "bad" ecological role models?

How, in fact, to *write* Native America at all? Vizenor's argument would be that since so-called Discovery, all "Indians" have been hedged about with, pre-textualized, in fantasy, and in ways as improbable as anything in his own best devising. His, one imagines him ironically likely to suggest, has been no more than a matchingly "postindian" inscribing of the process. In all three of these earlier volumes these different sleights of hand call upon a style as double as their subject. Sportive yet continuingly serious in target, a trickster interaction of first and third person, they again conjure with each assumed boundary of fact and fiction. Report shades into oral-performative story, journalism into parable. If, at times, this has irritated, indeed angered, some Vizenor detractors like Ward Churchill ("cliquish obscurantism," "puerile impulses"), it has also by admirers been taken to exert quite the opposite effect: one of challenge, exhilaration (Churchill).

Wordarrows, told in part in the crossblood persona of Clement Beaulieu (the name of a family relative), sets the pace as a kind of fact-fiction playfield. "Indians" living on and around Franklin Avenue, Minneapolis, give rise for him to an "urban reservation," new "Indian Country." Their survival, he suggests, lies in adaptation and a remaking of "tribal skills." The BIA transforms into an updated "fur trade" bearing latter-day bureaucratic legalisms and snares. Even his meditation on the life and sentence for murder of Thomas White Hawk in Vermillion, South Dakota, moves into a Vizenorian fiction of fact, a way to map, to enter, the "cultural schizophrenia" he believes has always underwritten the young crossblood Sioux's undoubted violence and crime.

The preface supplies working rules of engagement, an invitation to the text's ludic, yet typically benign, protocols. The voice in play,

Vizenor's yet that of Vizenor's persona, amounts to a textual elision of the "traditional tribal arrowmaker" (or traditional author) with the latter-day "wordmaker" (or post-traditional author) who is pledged to enter the "war words . . . outside the allegorical tipi" and through a cast of "real and imagined characters" (vii-xii).

Earthdivers, its span running from University Departments of Indian Studies to "terminal creeds," the Sand Creek Massacre of 1864 in Colorado to the suicide and funeral of Dane Michael White in 1968, sets out its own magic realist credentials in the preface. Where better to indicate a terrain as factual as White Earth, Minneapolis, or San Francisco and Berkeley, yet whose presiding spirits lie in a trickster cast of Mouse Proof Martin, Captain Shammer, Doc Fountain or Father Bearald? Not inappropriately, too, it is a preface conceived as a reflexive turn in its own imaginative right:

The names of the characters in these . . . narratives are real and imagined, but it will be difficult to know the differences. Real characters seem fictional, at times, more imagined; the text identities of several fictional characters seem real in imagined places. The real worlds are not unlike imagined mythic worlds. Differences in realities are never clear because the differences between tribal dreams, earthdiver myths, comedies and metaphors, and familiar places float free from time to time in some conversations. (xviii)

In *Crossbloods,* apparently reportage more than storytelling, the same genre bending operates. From an opening analysis of bingo and gaming among the White Earth Chippewa to a closing analysis of the firewater myth and tribal alcoholism, Vizenor's tribal-cum-postmodern stylings again work at one with their subject matter. Typical of the pieces would be his *legerdemain* put downs of social science Indians in "Socioacupuncture: Mythic Reversals and the Striptease in Four Acts" and of fake tribal appropriations of sun and ghost dance ritual in "Speaking For Mother Earth."

As likely, too, and at any turn, to invoke a French Michel Foucault as a Sioux Vine Deloria, an American John Rawls as a Chippewa Harold Goodsky, each contributing piece might best be thought the expression of what Vizenor calls "new survivance." Why not, he unapologetically assumes, avail yourself of both postmodern western theory and cross-blood "stories in the blood"? Why not, once again, subject text as much as ethnicity or race to a "loosening of the seams" ("Crows")?

Nor should the cues and pathways Vizenor gives in his collection *Narrative Chance: Postmodern Discourse on Native American Indian Literatures* be overlooked. Its introduction speaks of Native American literatures having been "pressed into cultural categories, transmuted by reductionism, animadversions and the hyper-realities of neocolonial consumerism." No hostage here, notice is invited, to mainstream complacencies about the single or unitary accounting of Native American life or literary voice. Even the title phrase "narrative chance" does good service, a decategorizing prompt to both the writerly and readerly challenge in play.

That challenge, or rather series of challenges, Vizenor has sought to inscribe from the outset and in each of his own literary fashionings right through to *Manifest Manners*. For it has been none other, in all its unique and massive tribal-white, Old World-New World *métissage,* than Native America's historic step, sought or otherwise, from ancient to modern to postmodern. Given in but one word, in Vizenor's own but one word, it has been the challenge of Native America's postindianness, and, as in keeping, of finding and using a literary idiom to match.

IV

Ceci n'est pas une pipe. Magritte's celebrated jugglery of a title, a text, which undermines its own accompanying visual image, gives Vizenor his opening cue for *Manifest Manners*. With a yet additional nod to Michel Foucault's study *This Is Not a Pipe,* he makes over the phrase into "This portrait is not an Indian." The disclaimer does immediate, and almost literally and appropriately eye catching, good service, a simultaneous yes and no to the ironies of being endlessly imaged, and multiplied, as shadow, harlequin, hologram, manikin, travesty, chimera, other, or rather, in Vizenor's greatly purposive own coining, "double other."

The ironies, in fact, begin with the volume's cover, a studio reproduction of Andy Warhol's silk screen acrylic Russell Means. Braided, in a bone choker, apparently silent-wise in demeanor, a pastel brown-red daubed from his forehead to chest, Means looks to be the perfect brave, except that, in fact, he is out of time, posed, painterly, a simulation from a New York studio, in every kind of way "not an Indian." As title-phrase, too, "manifest manners," another of Vizenor's revamps, contributes its own working gloss; this is "manifest destiny" detriumphalized, guyed, for its damage of privileging the one version, the one language, of American history over another.

"Postindian Warriors," as opening chapter, confirms how the book will operate overall, a collage of observation and example rather than some single line of chronological argument. Even so a very precise two-way exchange of journeys is invoked, Meriwether Lewis and Captain William Clark stepping westward in 1804-05 hoping, benignly, uncooptively, to be *seen* by tribal people, and Luther Standing Bear stepping eastward in 1879 (according to *My People, the Sioux,* 1928) as a first enrollee in the Federal Indian School at Carlisle, Pennsylvania. The juxtaposition supplies a necessary set of bearings: white explorers wanting to be seen by Indians, Indians, in their turn, seeing whites (1-4). This exchange of view, at once so exact in time and place, and yet so emblematic, Vizenor makes his paradigm throughout, the seeing and being seen (and, later, the not being seen), or put another way, the sign as against the signal, which at the outset, and ongoingly, has inhered in almost all Native-white encounter.

Two further seeings, or rather not seeings, ensue. Lieutenant William Reynolds, on a U.S. Navy expedition in 1841 and in contrast with Lewis and Clark, is invoked as being "disgusted with all naked Indians and primitive people" (3). The tribes could not be more dae-monic, infantile, uncivil. As for Standing Bear, teacher, himself to become a writer, he contracts into playing "invented Indian" (4) as a Buffalo Bill circus "redskin"; he also witnesses a similar (if this time uncontracted) fate when, appropriately in a Philadelphia theater, he hears Sitting Bull being mistranslated in his mission of greeting to Congress. Words meant as diplomacy, Native America's salute, metamorphose through their white interlocutor into the sensationalist, and so bankable, drama of the "massacre of General Custer at the Little Big Horn." Sitting Bull, in fact, did not participate. Whose is the true, the truer, *simulation?* Which "theater of tribal consciousness" (5), a notion he will amplify in *Fugitive Poses,* best obtains?

The spectrum to follow puts each further irony into a similar run of appositions. *Dances with Wolves* as "postindian simulation," "the absence of the tribes," and by implication "an obituary" (6-8), allows a theory perspective to enter through Jean Baudrillard's *Simulares et Simulations* and Umberto Eco's *Travels in Hyperreality.* Scott Momaday on "tribal imagination" (10) and self-imagined identity allows Vizenor his own observation that "the Indian was an occidental invention . . . the word has no referent in tribal languages or cultures" (11). Tricksterism becomes a countervailing force, a way for tribal culture, and Vizenor himself, to deliver respectively a spoken and a writerly ironic riposte to "unreal names," "absences," "lies," "simulations," all, in turn, supremely, farcically, sometimes dangerously, "manifest manners."

The text so sets about the task of de-encrypting each of these simu-lations. Means is opened to Vizenorian parodic scepticism as respec-tively Warhol figurine, Chingachgook in Michael Mann's film-version of *The Last of the Mohicans,* and oratorical guardian of "Indian values." Paula Gunn Allen is teased for her "gynocratic" (21) pose as having channeled to the Crystal Skull, likely more a Tiffany's than Aztec artifact. He lowers an ironic eye upon Lynn Andrews for her New Age birthing of "Agnes Whistling Elk" (22). Both the latter serve Vizenor as perpetrators of "ersatz spiritualism" (23). The voice is play, Vizenor in trickster guise, acts simultaneously as one of both play and seriousness, a lightly worn dark laughter.

Nor is this anything like the full roster. William Least Heat-Moon takes his shot for the "Indian silhouettes" of *PrairyErth* (24). Ed McGaa, author of *Rainbow Tribe,* proves especially egregious; Vizenor reports him, despite all the "tribal brotherhood" talk, as having acted as a secret prosecution witness in the Thomas White Hawk trial. Louise Erdrich and Michael Dorris, America's then-reigning Native writer-spouse duo, offend by their untribal call for the imprisonment, even obligatory abortion, for Fetal Alcohol Syndrome (FAS) tribal mothers with all its past firewater demonization. Literary "missionaries of manifest manners" (31), from James Fenimore Cooper to Frederick Manfred to Karl May, are teased for their adventure book Indians, a savagery noble or fiendish according to taste. The 1988 Gaming Regulatory Act is pursued as an update of allotment policy and keeping Indians in their uncapitalist place. Each, again, becomes as much a feat of authorial voice as argument, Vizenor's telling as matchingly "double" as the double-standards it seeks to unmask.

Other mistranslations of tribal life, equally willful or at best careless, add to the mosaic. Garrison Keillor fails to discern in his Lake Wobegon an Anishinaabe comic irreverence toward the white settler progenitors, however smalltown quaint, of his Chatterbox Café and Pretty Good Grocery world. Robert Bly, in the search for an American masculinist lineage, gets wrong most of his tribal citations in *Iron John.* Longfellow, the debt to Henry Rowe Schoolcraft's *Algic Researches* more traduced than translated, bequeaths a celebratedly erroneous Anishinaabe-Iroquois congruence in "Hiawatha."

And, likewise, the *Encyclopaedia Britannica* ("the encyclopedia of dominance") literally miscostumes its supposed Indian Chiefs— "tribal simulations" right to the point of design fault yet given the most scholarly imprimatur. He recalls a white, ex-military superintendent of a North Dakota Indian School calling upon one of its children to dance, a-historically and touristically, a "tribal" dance in chicken feathers. As a USIA visitor in Germany, Vizenor hears a member of a Native troupe almost by rote addressed as "Chief" and asked if he will be doing a war dance. These "facts of fiction" Vizenor at once shadows, and countermands, by his own "fictions of fact."

They also circle back to AIM's Clyde Bellecourt, Banks and Means, and to their collaborationist fakery. As a defamiliarization of the familiar, a working through of "this portrait is not an Indian" within the nice ambivalence of the essay-cum-story, "Postindian Warriors" positively triumphs. Vizenor's own command of equivocation both exorcises and rehabilitates.

V

"Double Others," which follows, could easily be thought a *Who's Who* in small within Vizenor's diorama of simulations. The continuum of inversion, edge and irreverence, again becomes the working principle. Against shaman chic, for instance, the issue is put of how best to recover a truer shamanism. Vizenor's examples are those of the Santo Domingo Pueblo healer, Santiago, who showed a white doctor how dancing was a route to recuperation, and the Santee Sioux medical doctor, Charles Alexander Eastman, tribally named Ohiyesa, who in the light of his attendance on the Wounded Knee survivors, and then in its wake, "endured the treacherous turns and transvaluations of tribal identities" (50).

In this light, and by a time-jump whose initial improbability becomes utterly probable, if a Vietnam Veterans Memorial for the one "modern" war then why not, precisely, a Wounded Knee Memorial to honor not the "last major battle of the Indian Wars" but a "massacre of tribal women and children" (50)? Did not that "war," too, cause "even more posttraumatic burdens than other horrors of war because the stories of the survivors were seldom honored" (48)? This, indeed, inverts steplock history, Wounded Knee as Vietnam, history-then as history-now, both in Vizenor's telling an eerily transhistorical or shared one American story.

"Shadow Survivance," the third general chapter, works similarly, a disquisition on "the postindian turns in literature" (63) and, as its two predecessors, itself the very thing it thematizes. With a smack at the levelling of anthropological Indian studies, and then an invocation of Derrida on *différance* and of the tensile, performative nature of haiku, Vizenor invokes a line of Native authorship from William Apess, mixedblood Pequot, through to Louis Owens, mixedblood Choctaw-Cherokee. Severally, and together, and like the literary crossblood Vizenor who summons them, theirs has been the composite making of postindian identity.

No one regime, furthermore, he suggests, need hold, a literary variety to embrace a novelist of tribal survival like Elizabeth Cook-Lynn (Crow Creek Sioux) in *From the River's Edge* (1991), or Thomas King (Cherokee) as the author of so lightly comic-wry a portrait as *Medicine River* (1990), or Diane Glancy (Cherokee), the short story ironist of *Firesticks* (1993), or each and all of the first-person contributors to *I Tell You*

Now: Autobiographical Essays by Native American Writers (1987). Controversy, too, and as ever, enters the reckoning: whether a teasing of Paula Gunn Allen as this time "lesbian spiritualist" (86), or a scepticism at the literary scholar Charles R. Larson in his *American Indian Fiction* (1978) as having applied to Native writing quite the "wrong categories" (80).

But as much as anything there has to be Vizenor's insistence on taking over, or rather taking back, the English (the American?) language which *ab initio* has pre-empted Indianness, and whether in spoken or written script. "We must represent our own pronoun poses in autobiographies," Vizenor argues, and be about the "imagining of ourselves" (97). This, thereby, will be to counter the English language's dispossession and appropriation starting, he implies, with the very word "Indian." The span, again, can, or rather should, be as various as need be, running from oral-aural invention to script, from music and the visual arts to dance, from high seriousness to humor, from a voicing of the Natives in the city as much as on the reservation. In this Vizenor joins James Baldwin, writing in 1964, in his call for the operative language to be "made my own," to "bear the burden of my experience" (Baldwin).

As in all of *Manifest Manners,* "Shadow Survivance" does more, however, than simply exhort. Its endemic reflexivity actually embodies, or textualizes, Vizenor's credo, or whatever could be said to run close to his credo. If, indeed, the call is for a new "ghost dance literature," a new "shadow literature of liberation" (106), the essay offers no less in and of itself; a call to remedy and, at the same time, the very embodiment of remedy.

VI

Although they work in shorter scale the five essays which follow in *Manifest Manners* show the same continuing chameleon play of voice. "Eternal Havens" develops its own riff on Columbus as the "Admiral of the Ocean Sea" yet "wounded adventurer" (107). Vizenor's touch is everywhere again playful, disruptive, a counterpoint, another contradance, of the historic pluses and minuses of Columbianism and so much more to the point than mere by-rote partisanship.

Why not, by way of an opener for this "miraculous representation of the nation" (110), a mischievous analogy in Renaldus Columbus, Padua's self-proclaimed discoverer of the clitoris? Why not a querying of the Columbus name for the 1893 Exposition in Chicago where, three years on from Wounded Knee, bronze sculptures of "The Indian" would further help dehistoricize the tribes? How to disensnare actual Columbus from the Dominican Republic's *Faro a Colón,* or from a parsing of names which include "Cristóbal Colón, Colombo, Colom, Colomb, or

Christopher Columbus" (112), or from a Jewish or *marrano* Columbus, or from the Columbus written into the uncertainly passed down Las Casas account, or from a Columbus (like Shakespeare) without a single credible canvas? Given each, too, Vizenor can affect to turn teasingly un-pc to a fault: how, even as an "Indian," to feel himself oppressed by a Columbus as much *figura* as fact?

If, as an addendum, Columbus needs to be seen in all these different competing versions, so, in like manner, does the cult of "Mother Earth" as attributed to the New World he traversed. Vizenor moves into story mode, an imagined colloquium, to make the point, the pastiche "black flies" parable of a trickster called "Mother Earth." Eco-sentimentality is thus also put under satiric rules, the supposed "Indian" maternal or gyno-centric cycle of land, nature, season, the elements and animals. Mother Earth, Vizenor offers himself as saying, sidesteps quite how few tribes held to this mythology or how it became lore as much through non-Native anthropology as anything else. A better, fuller, view would insist upon the quite unsentimental working process of birth and death, "natural reason" or "fetor," than bogus theocentric maternalism. He so again, controversially, seeks to lay to rest another simulation in story terms to match, his own counter parable.

"Ishi Obscura," Vizenorian acuity at its best, pursues a yet further bead on the Vanishing American mythology. "Ishi was never his real name" (126) offers but an opening strike in a deconstruction of the Yahi survivor as "captured portrait," "simulation," the California "man of stone," and "racial photograph" (127-29). Vizenor's feat is to show how Ishi, simply Yahi/Yana for "man," became a perfect simulation, a figure of romance and Stone Age primitivism within an America of accelerating industrialization and the cities.

Tables get turned exquisitely. Who is to be thought "the savage," Ishi or the mining prospectors who found him (127)? Who constitutes "the other," the Yahi world or "the lonesome and melancholy civilization" (137) that brought on its demise? Who, in fact, lives on which side of "the scratch line of savagism and civilization" (127)? Who, finally, speculates a Vizenor himself the highwire performer with language, proved the subtler linguist, Ishi, or "Big Chiep [Chief] Kroeber" (130) as the anthropologist and who helped arrange for him to live out his days making "Indian heritage" at the University of California Anthropology Museum in San Francisco, or the Chicago philologist Edward Sapir, brought in to "translate"? Each query cannily undercuts this "museumization," Vizenor, textual Vizenor at least, self-positioned as savvy innocent.

"Casino Coups" offers another two-way seeing: Luther Standing Bear, Lakota activist, observing coins thrown at him by whites on the train-journey east, and Vizenor himself observing "white people throwing money at the tribes" in contemporary tribal casinos. It affords a classic double reflection, a frame, in which to consider "the new wampum" (139) and, followingly, the divides brought on by the 1988 Indian Gaming Regulatory Act, the State as against Tribal contestations over tax and sovereignty, and the contrast of "moccasin games" of chance and "casino avarice" whether in Mohawk country, Mystic Lake Sioux country or White Earth. Vizenor's essay again carries the impress of insider and outrider, his own postindian co-witness for prosecution and defence.

"Radical Durance," the pun in its title a marker, again makes AIM its target: a leadership "more kitsch and tired simulation than menace or moral tribal visions" (154), "the simulation of tribal chiefs" (149), with Clyde Bellecourt "one of the most contumacious crossblood radical simulations in the nation" (154). AIM, then, becomes absence rather than presence, an occlusion which gives him the opportunity to do some added dictionary definition of his own. *Kitsch,* in its tribal implication, yields "banal spiritualism," "consumer sun dances" (154). Vizenor's efficacy lies exactly in his manner of making the stock parlance of a Banks, Means or Bellecourt into the satiric currency of the essay itself.

Vizenor's "Epilogue" to *Manifest Manners* does a last double duty, tricksterism as at once "survivance hermeneutics" (167) and, precisely, as an acting out of tricksterism in its own textual right. As he invokes a spectacle varying literal and mythic, whether Emerson's seeing "Sacs & Foxes" at the Boston statehouse, Lewis and Clark seeking Natives from along the Oregon Trail, Luther Standing Bear viewing the Carlisle Indian School, or America at large faced with the "Indians" of its own pop culture from the romance-novel's Chingachgook to TV's Tonto, he has every grounds to reinvoke his notion of "double others."

Little wonder, thus, that for him the postindian author "renounce[s] the inventions and final vocabularies of manifest manners" (167). It is a formulation as precise, and as self-referring, as any with which to move towards a close; however provisional that might always prove in Vizenor's case. Indeed, the publication of *Fugitive Poses: Native American Indian Scenes of Absence and Presence* (1998) gives further emphasis to the point—"Indians" freed from "the archive of victimry" and rendered in their own full, ever ongoing, and affirmative diversity.

Seeing, unseeing. Single vision, double vision. Vizenor has throughout negotiated a discursive style in kind with the massive contradance which he believes has been the story of Native America since Columbus first registered his "gentle" Arawak/Guanahani in 1492. His own writings, accordingly, and one can concede sometimes elusively, have indeed not hesitated to mix metaphors, tease boundaries, assume contrary voices, or avail themselves of an authorial—a literary-cross-blood—irony both gentle and fierce, general and local. Controversialism was rarely so adept.

Manifest Manners offers confirmation, one more in Vizenor's ongoing postindian texts for postindian times.

Notes

1. Hertha Dawn Wong, *Sending My Heart Back Across the Years: Tradition and Innovation in Native American Autobiography* (New York: Oxford UP, 1992). Vizenor has in mind the following from the preface: "When I began writing this book in 1984, I had little idea that I was part Native American, one of the unidentified mixed-bloods whose forbears wandered away from their fractured communities . . . Like many urban mixed-blood Indians, I am not a member of a native community, but much of what my mother taught me reflects values long associated with Native American cultures (although she did not label her teachings "Indian").

2. *Manifest Manners: Postindian Warriors of Survivance* (Hanover and London: Wesleyan UP, 1994). All page references given in the essay are to this edition.

Works Cited

Baldwin, James. "Why I Stopped Hating Shakespeare." *Sunday Observer* [London] 19 Apr. 1964.

Bowers, Neal, and Charles L. Silet. "An Interview with Gerald Vizenor." *MELUS* 8.1 (1981): 41-49.

Churchill, Ward. Review of *Manifest Manners: Postindian Warriors of Survivance. American Indian Culture and Research Journal* 18.3 (1994): 313-18.

Vizenor, Gerald. "Avengers at Wounded Knee." *Interior Landscapes: Autobiographical Myths and Metaphors.* Minneapolis: U of Minnesota P, 1990. 229-41.

——. *Bearheart: The Heirship Chronicles.* Minneapolis: U of Minnesota P, 1990.

——. "Crows Written on the Poplars: Autocritical Autobiographies." *I Tell You Now: Autobiographical Essays by Native American Writers.* Ed. Brian Swann and Arnold Krupat. Lincoln: U of Nebraska P, 1987.

——. *Dead Voices: Natural Agonies in the New World.* Norman and London: U of Oklahoma P, 1992.

——. "Dennis Banks: What Sort of Hero?" *Minneapolis Tribune* 22 July 1978: A4.

——. *Fugitive Poses: Native American Indian Scenes of Absence and Presence.* The Abraham Lincoln Series. Lincoln: U of Nebraska P, 1998.

——. *Griever: An American Monkey King in China*, 1987. Minneapolis: U of Minnesota P, 1990.

——. *The Heirs of Columbus.* Hanover, NH: Wesleyan UP, 1991.

——. *Hotline Healers: An Almost Browne Novel.* Hanover and London: Wesleyan UP, 1997.

——. *Interior Landscapes: Autobiographical Myths and Metaphors.* Minneapolis: U of Minnesota P, 1990.

——. *Manifest Manners: Postindian Warriors of Survivance.* Hanover and London: Wesleyan UP, 1994.

——. *Narrative Chance: Postmodern Discourse on Native American Indian Literatures.* 1989. Paperbound edition, U of Oklahoma P, 1993.

——. *Tribal Scenes and Ceremonies.* Minneapolis: Nodin P, 1976.

——. *Tribal Scenes and Ceremonies.* Rev. ed. Minneapolis: U of Minnesota P, 1990.

——. *The Trickster of Liberty: Tribal Heirs to a Wild Baronage.* Minneapolis: U of Minnesota P, 1988.

——. *Wordarrows: Indians and Whites in the New Fur Trade.* Minneapolis: U of Minnesota P, 1978.

Wong, Hertha Dawn. *Sending My Heart Back Across the Years: Tradition and Innovation in Native American Autobiography.* New York: Oxford UP, 1992.

17

OVERTURNING THE BURDENS OF THE *REAL:* NATIONALISM AND THE SOCIAL SCIENCES IN GERALD VIZENOR'S RECENT WORKS

Colin Samson

Most photographers of *indians* focused on the fugitive warrior pose and decorative costumes as traditional, the occidental simulations of the *indian*; these interimage closures of presence would be mimicked several generations later by postindian leaders as the actual sources of traditions and identities.

—Fugitive Poses

Gerald Vizenor's most recent books, the novel *Hotline Healers* and the essay *Fugitive Poses,* contain some of his most forceful commentaries on the politics and aesthetics of contemporary Native American predicaments. The sheer playfulness of his writing—toying with words and inventing neologisms while his plot or text meanders, shoots off on trajectories, and doubles back on itself—always subverts the certainties of both social science and pan-Indian nationalism that address the predicaments that concern him. His sympathy is always with the active and dynamic real, rather than the simulation, the sense of a native presence, rather than the markers of its absence which began with the invention of the Indian and continue to be manifest in the objectifications of natives in universities and political movements. This essay addresses some twists of these themes in *Hotline Healers* and *Fugitive Poses.* I begin with a postindian tale.[1]

Postindian Thespians

George "Tink" Tinker, the Osage/Cherokee writer and Professor of Theology at Denver University, performed the Opening Ceremony for the "Translating Native Cultures" conference at Yale University in February 1998. He is a broad man with a long pony tail. Clad in jeans and western garb, he made his way to the podia holding a circular drum and a switch that had been cut from a tree on Church Street a few minutes earlier. Solemnly, he announced that he was going to perform a Lakota Sun Dance song. He was not a Lakota Sun Dancer himself, but, he revealed, he had friends and relatives on a Lakota Reservation. With this he drummed and sang in the Whitney Humanities Center auditorium, thousands of miles away from the lands of the Lakota to which the song refers.

My memories of the five days of conference are dominated by the passionate enunciations of Indian nationalism from several delegates, the contemplative readings of poetry and prose in English and Tohono O'odham by Ofelia Zepeda, vibrant performance pieces of the actress and dramatist Monica Mojica, self-consciously academic presentations, such as Robert Warrior's verbatim reading of a "paper," full of obligatory references to fashionable academicians, and the booming charisma of N. Scott Momaday on time, indigeneity, the Alta Mira caves and the bear.

A tone for the conference was set by the Santee/Yankton Sioux writer Elizabeth Cook-Lynn, whose keynote address was delivered in the style of a political soapbox orator. There were none of the sudden twists, verbal movements of space and time, changes of pitch and emphasis that we later heard from Momaday in the final keynote address. Instead, she denounced and accused, clearly drawing a line between those on the right and wrong sides of American Indian struggles. Because she did not use the language of "diversity," "multiculturalism," "postmodernism," and "post-colonialism," she admitted to being "out of the loop." Sensing a momentum, Cook-Lynn berated the suggestion that "we" were now all "post-Indians," a term that, she maintained, only obfuscates and confuses. "What do these words mean in terms of sovereignty, land and the revitalization of our languages?" she asked before proceeding to denounce colonialism and the "notoriously self-serving" universities, the real "colonial master guardians of western civilization." Her clarion call, however, was to propose a restricted nationalist agenda for Native American Studies. She ended with the rhetorical question that she answered herself in the negative, "Are we satisfied to be 'post'—colonial,—modern,—Indian?" Although not mentioned by name, Gerald Vizenor was clearly one of the objects of her scorn.

On the final day, "Tink" Tinker was called upon to take the stage for a closing ceremony. If the first performance had something of the absurd about it, the second was tragic. This time he mounted the stage with neither drum nor drumstick. With head slightly hanging, he told us that he was not going to perform because a "white person had demonstrated once again that whites know more about us than we do." "Whites," he angrily asserted, need to examine their own minds and purge themselves of their colonial mentalities. After several forceful denunciations in this vein, he moved toward a redemption from what the "white person" had charged him with—that he was performing the song out of its context, that he was unqualified to do it in the first place and that the performance was spiritually negative. In defense, Tinker claimed to be performing not with any sense of self-publicity, but for the sake of Native American unity and the conference. He had been asked to perform, he explained. But now he had been upstaged by a "white" woman, who before the performance had informed him of his errors. With obvious sadness and anger, he left the stage to silence and the hugs of a few delegates in the front row. Finally, Ines Talamantez, an Apache academic at the University of California at Santa Barbara, stepped up to praise Tinker and his performance and to ask the Creator to help the misguided and unrevealed individual who had taken issue with Tinker. I later discovered that the "white" person who had instructed Tinker on the finer points of Sun Dance performance was an administrator at Rutgers University named Nancy Omaha Boy, once herself a resident of Pine Ridge, having been married to a Lakota.

In many ways the performances of both Cook-Lynn and Tinker were postindian. They celebrated the *indian* rather than the native, an absence rather than a presence in their orations. They presented two sides of the same coin: the performance of the invented indian with all its claims of authenticity and racialism and of the victim, retaliating through the rationalist institutions of higher education and racial literalism.

Cook-Lynn's call for a unifying Native American Studies which would, *post facto,* oppose colonization and promote native sovereignty would be "regulated" by Native Americans themselves. Although universities received a great deal of her wrath, they were the institutional supports for her reconfigured "Native American Studies." She denounced native scholars in universities who carried on dialogues furnished for them by Euro-American traditions as "Colonial laureates." Her own political convictions were certainties, and her unifying call was racialist and nationalist. Rather than challenging the ideological grounds of Euro-American dominance over natives, the very concepts which invest power in colonialism—"sovereignty" and "race"—were being advocated as the weapons of Native Americans, or at least a vanguard of Native American scholars. These scholars would "regulate" the academic agenda and stand opposed to "Colonial laureates."

Likewise, Tinker cut a curious figure with his drum, singing a Lakota Sun Dance song in the hallowed halls of that Ivy League university, far away from the people of the Great Plains. His performance recalled Edward Curtis's photographs, replete with the photographer's own props and regalia to frame his "vanishing Indians" of the late nineteenth and early twentieth centuries (see Lyman). The face, the pony tail, the body were framed by the drum and the pan-Indian performance. As a native, he had brought along not his own, but someone else's song that he was singing for the benefit of a university audience. He had composed his own picture. A "white" photographer was not needed. In fact, Tinker's performance was a double simulation. He was simulating the Lakota and at the same time he was simulating a Curtis-like *indian.*

Tinker and Cook-Lynn could be cast as postindian thespians in some of the eight native theaters identified by Gerald Vizenor in *Fugitive Poses.* Vizenor distinguishes between native by concession, native by creation, native by countenance, native by genealogies, native by documentation, native by situations, native by trickster stories, and, "the most wearisome," native by victimry (*Fugitive* 88-94). Both Tinker and Cook-Lynn invoked *genealogy* as a source of native identity, and, perhaps more importantly, native authority. It was genealogically sound natives that would "regulate" Cook-Lynn's academic agenda and it was Tinker's own uncontested native-ness and his lineages with reservations, challenged as somewhat tenuous by a "white" woman, which were produced as badges of authenticity. Tinker's retort to the "white" woman underscored the assumption that genealogy is, contrary to the position Vizenor adopts, the last word. The tetchy denunciations of both Tinker and Cook-Lynn were karaokes in a native theater of victimry. "The natives in this theater," writes Vizenor, "are cast as representations, the racialist tropes of vanishment; the historical measures of dominance, concessions, desistance, and the vectors of durative victimry" (*Fugitive* 91). Like the karaoke, their aesthetics are kitsch.

Teasing the University

Gerald Vizenor's university is not the setting for any political agendas of "Native American Studies." Rather, the university is full of bureaucratic pieties in "departments" and "faculties." Its earnest self-regard and its self-appointed mission to uplift the minds of the population make it ripe for satire. In *Hotline Healers,* Vizenor lets tricksters loose in the university to devastatingly subversive effect. Few academics have had the nerve to tease the university, although many, such as Cook-Lynn, criticize it. Her criticisms, however, served only to provide a rationale for abducting the institution for a particular ethnic mission. The tease is more powerful than the critique, since the critique only seeks to reform, humanize or racialize, while the tease mocks the pretensions which legitimize the university. The tease is a presence, the critique only an absence. The critique is formal and often bureaucratic, while the tease undermines both formality and bureaucracy. The tease can more fully bring out the ironies of university life—the mixtures of expressed pomposity and aesthetic tackiness, libertarianism and puritanism, and, as is noted in *Hotline Healers,* the fact that elite universities such as the University of California at Berkeley were founded on stolen native land.

Vizenor introduces numerous professors into the stories in *Hotline Healers.* Their utterances are often direct quotes from their books or statements in the press. Instead of engaging in formal debate as occurs at academic conferences and in journals, Almost Browne, the trickster figure in the book, dialogues with them, playfully mocking the self-important poses of the academics. His effectiveness lies in his trickery. Almost Browne entertains no privileged logic of argumentation or rationalist one-upmanship. In one adventure, Almost attends the lectures of Berkeley philosopher John Searle. After hearing several expositions on metaphor, language and logic, Almost teases Searle on his statement, in another context in opposition to affirmative action, that he was "part Cherokee." He does this through using the arguments Searle himself presents in his lecture to expose the fact that Searle's claim to be part Cherokee must be "irony or a metaphor " (Vizenor, *Hotline* 45).

Similarly, more "politically correct" factions are also teased for their attachments to the tired tropes of modernism. The Ethnic Studies Department at Berkeley is rendered as the Transethnic Studies Department. The department is founded on the fictional concept of "race" and proceeds by adopting the objectivist epistemology of the social sciences. Vizenor's Transethnic Studies is "an ironic creation of academic extremes, no less than the angry politics of peace. The diverse faculty was driven by chance, doubts, suspicion, envy and aesthetic vengeance, for more than two decades of ethnic poses and politics" (*Hotline* 51).

One of the opening sequences of *Fugitive Poses* is an anecdote about censure and censorship at the Department of Ethnic Studies at the University of California at Berkeley. It is a story that many people familiar with academic sensibilities would recognize. Such events are usually allowed to be lost in the bustle of the semester cycles, the demands of word productivity and the exchange of memoranda. Yet, the tale is a telling reminder of the deadening humorlessness and repressive realism of university life. Vizenor's head of department removed the cover of his book *Shadow Distance,* which was mounted in the departmental display case along with a photograph of the author. She did this in response to student complaints, claiming the naked androgynous trickster figure was "offensive," despite the lack of anatomical orifices, pubic hair or sexual protuberances (*Fugitive* 9-10).

We gratefully acknowledge permission of the artist, Dick Görtler, to reproduce this cover illustration.

Like the performances of Cook-Lynn and Tinker, the chair, Elaine Kim, lacked humor and irony. The trickster figure, which, after all, was a reproduction of a work of art on a book cover, was literalized as sexually offensive; Vizenor compares it to various acts of censorship he had witnessed while a Visiting Professor at the University of Tianjin in China. The androgynous figure is subversive of the starkly sober realism which holds sway over many of those in "faculties" of humanities and social science in universities. Censorship, "politically correct" or otherwise, merely reasserts the dominance of reason over the transgressive crossings of the invented modernist animal-human and male-female boundaries. In opposition to modernism, Almost's "natural ties" are chance, anything but the treason of absolutes and victimry. The native stories that overturn the burdens of the *real* are his natural beam (*Hotline* 78).

Sciences of the Real

For Vizenor and his trickster heroes, natives can avoid the yoke that is Euro-American domination through overturning the *real,* while in the theatrics of Cook-Lynn and Tinker, respectively, it is the enunciation or enactment of a *real* world of *real* Indians that is the rallying call of Native American Studies and political struggle. The reality to which Vizenor refers is that of European Enlightenment thought. That is, the *real* is that which is demonstrated through the inventions and conventions of empirical methodologies, such as those found in the natural and social sciences. This is why the *real* is italicized. "It" is always made up. As Michel Foucault observes, "[t]ruth is a thing of this world. It is produced only by virtue of multiple forms of constraint, and it induces regular effects of power" (13). The notion that there is one irreducible truth which will resolve all debate as to what exists or what caused what to occur is itself the very instrument of dominance.

The most important creation of science, both a crutch and cliché, has been the concept of objectivity. Objectivity has given science a "desperate privilege" (Wright 23-42) predicated on the fantastic notion that the world is one "thing" which can be divided between the objective and the subjective, and that the division itself is somehow not a subjective one. The methods of science or social science, conceived of as measuring "reality," are represented in the dominant philosophy of science, positivism, as beyond human bias. In its most imperial claim, science advances the laboratory, experimental, survey, ethnographic, photographic and other methods as capturing and explaining reality, independent of individual human perception. As such, scientific methods are considered superior, not only because they purport to neuter human senses, passions and interests, but because science positioned itself within a linear and temporal hierarchy of knowledge in which it stood at the apex, throwing into relief "prior" systems of explanation such as religion, and non-European ideas. Because of their alleged "rigor," "reliability," and "validity," scientific methods are endorsed as—and this is perhaps the least imperial claim—better and truer explanations of nature. This nature is thought to be "out there," a reality ready to be captured and explained.

Hence, many social and natural scientists believe themselves to be "realists" because, in contrast to the superstitiousness that they believe to have triumphed over, they are engaged in the professional pursuit of the "real" world with all the excitement of discovery and finality that it entails. As such, the doctrine of *real*ism is always encased in an aesthetics of chauvinism and boorishness. It consigns that which cannot be apprehended by its own empirical methods variously as subjectivity, nonsense, superstition, myth and legend. The Scottish psychiatrist R. D. Laing provided a long list including, ". . . love and hate, joy and sorrow, misery and happiness, pleasure and pain, right and wrong, purpose, meaning, hope, courage, despair, God, heaven and hell . . ." which science disregards because to contemplate these aspects of life, the scientist would have to enter into the subjective world and abandon his or her empirical methods (34). Hence, what science accomplishes is not "enlightenment," but an obscuring of the most intense and meaningful human experiences.

In this vein, both science and literature execute a closure of the rich imaginative life of animals in native stories and memories. In *Fugitive Poses,* Vizenor contrasts animals as literal similes or anthropomorphic creations with imputed human characteristics with metaphorical animals, which he believes are, "closer to nature and animal consciousness than a literal simile. The authors are animals, the readers are animals, the animals are humans, and the authored hunters are the animals in their own novels" (142). In science, the simile was given full scientific legitimacy in *The Expression of Emotions in Man and Animals,* the pioneering work of Charles Darwin, published in 1872. In it, Darwin universalizes emotions, creates nouns for feelings and obliterates any playfulness, uncertainty or spectacular feats of which animals might be capable. But, even Darwin's notion of evolution, as Vizenor points out, "is more chance than closure" (*Fugitive* 143).[2] Hence, it is possible in *Hotline Healers* for mongrels to take a short evolutionary leap, learn to drive and become chauffeurs.

But these remarks on science only highlight part of the trouble with the *real.* The real as an "it" is a simulation, something *real.* What is labeled as "real," what is concluded to be "fact," what is produced as the trump card over all other forms of making sense of the world, simulates the real experience of people, or in the case of natives, groups of people who become configured as *indians*. A simulation purports to represent some reality, but, like the *indian*, it takes on a life of its own, it becomes a free-floating signifier, disconnected from that which it is supposed to represent. As such, and Vizenor tells us this many times in *Fugitive Poses,* simulations like the *indian* celebrate the absence of people, not their presence. People—Vizenor's natives—which are a moving and dynamic presence, are mute and silent beside the simulation. In North America, it is the *indian* as a simulation that has informed racist cultural representations and repressive public policies.

What breathes life into the simulation—and invests it with power— is social science. Ironically, social science, an intellectual surface for Ethnic Studies and Native American Studies, represents itself as an emancipatory and "progressive" undertaking, often in opposition to what is sometimes depicted as the technocratic conservatism of the natural sciences. In many ways, however, the social sciences are themselves embodiments of a deep conservatism. As carriers of modernist epistemologies, they are the conduits for modes of defining reality which legitimize European or Euro-American dominance over natives and other colonized peoples. For example, fundamental social science assumptions such as causality infer an ultimate origin to all events. This not only conflicts with the native sense of overlapping realities and the reluctance to draw definitive causal conclusions, but it positions native reality variously as primitive, a type of superstition, "functional" to certain modes of social organization or simply "wrong." Similarly, as Vizenor tells us, the social sciences are predicated on objectification. Their reference is to "things" which are fixed and describable. By contrast, "native hands and hearts are traces of sound and stone, the tease of nature, not science" (*Fugitive* 95).

The social sciences of anthropology and sociology are heirs to the Enlightenment quest for certainty. Their very birth expressed the desire to discover laws of cause and effect over human social, mental and cultural life. Social sciences have been parties to the idea of progress. Their twentieth-century emissaries, social theorists, have exerted great efforts, similar to mock military exercises, contriving duels between the various "founding fathers," who spar over the precise "mechanisms" of social change, cultural refinement, progress and development. The chief distinction between sociology and anthropology has been that the one concentrated on urban, Western societies, while the other was granted domain over the "Other," the atavistic peoples of the European colonial imagination. Fixing sights on the description and explanation of the primitive, the numerous empirical studies and theoretical tracts in the discipline of anthropology have had the effect of transforming natives into *indians*. Within anthropology, natives have become objectified entities which can be described in terms of their myths, legends, social functions, kinship structures, as well as their bones, which were collected.[3] In Vizenor's film, *Harold of Orange,* the trickster-figure Harold performs an oration to liberal philanthropists atop a vitrine filled with native bones.

In 1911, A. L. Kroeber of the anthropology department at the University of California at Berkeley even collected a live Yahi specimen, Ishi, the "last of his tribe." Ishi lived in a museum and became a live exhibit. The meanings of the connections between Ishi and the University of California were explored in Vizenor's essay "Ishi Obscura" in *Manifest Manners,* as well as works of fiction such as *The Trickster of Liberty* and *Ishi and the Wood Ducks,* but the events are teased out again in both *Hotline Healers* and *Fugitive Poses.* Vizenor petitioned the university authorities for part of a building to be named after Ishi in honor of his service to the university. Although this was unsuccessful, an interior space in a building called Dwinelle Hall, the former location of Ethnic Studies, was named Ishi Court in 1993.

Because social science methods fix, objectify and, in the case of Ishi, literally "capture," they are a drag on the sense of movement, what Vizenor calls *transmotion,* which is integral to native life and history. In Vizenor's interpretations, anthropology produces "narrative closures." It privileges the "seen over the heard, the simulation of icons over chance, emblems over totemic names, manners over native tease, and the desire of the scriptural over the performance of oral narratives" (Vizenor, *Fugitive* 148). It is not hard to understand why this is the case. Social science discourse is both academic- and policy-directed, and what is produced is by nature a *confined* and *confining* knowledge. It is *confined* in that it is almost exclusively produced for a professional and student audience. But, ironically, the confinement itself grants a wider cultural authority to academic doctrines. Most of it—one only need think of the musty volumes of obscure journals, hard-bound and shelved in university libraries —never emerges for public consumption and increasingly serves as a vector of professional power, a measure of academic productivity and guide to the protocols of advancement and demotion. Social science that is used for public policy purposes in relation to "natives" is *confining* in that it presents a reified and still-life picture which policymakers can easily discern and act upon. Although anthropologists have confessed to the service anthropology provided to colonial administrations in producing images of "otherness," the ethnographic method and the concept of "culture" are still employed to compose stills of natives around the world.[4] Without the method, anthropology would almost certainly cease to exist.

Cultural evolutionist theories, popular until the 1970s in anthropology, fixed the native in the distant European past. Movement in evolutionary thought was planted on a "material" foundation, catalogued by "stage," and arrayed along an incremental line according to modes of subsistence from hunting to agriculture to industry. These "stages" and the "material" realities to which they are supposed to refer are, likewise, simulations since they are abstracted from the real activities of people and the meanings individuals derive from them. Likewise, the discipline of sociology, following the doctrines of various "founding fathers," created the idea of an autonomous "social" sphere. Perpetuated by generations of professional sociologists, people are represented in batches, conducting their affairs under the ubiquitous causality of unseen social forces. People rarely speak except through the voice of academic interpreters, some of whom labor under the conceit that they are "giving voice" to their subjects. As masses, they are frozen and filed into class, "race," and gender groupings. These abstract groupings are then constituted as "things"—social facts in "founding father" Emile Durkheim's words—having real cause and effect power.

It is these kinds of doctrines which comprise a target of tease in Vizenor's recent writings. In the commencement address sequence in *Hotline Healers,* Almost Browne spars with the social scientists and their dogmas. Addressing Transethnic Studies graduates at the Ishi Auditorium at the University of California at Berkeley, Almost points out that the alliance between transethnic studies and the social sciences "is another statement of that dominance." This provokes the dissension of the anthropologist, Macbeth, who interrupts Almost's orations to defend the good work of anthropology in preserving "native traditions and the standards of research" (Vizenor, *Hotline* 89). After demanding that Almost be silenced, their altercations end with the anthropologist walking off the graduation stage as a mark of protest for Almost's jocular jabs at the politics of his "discipline."

Sovereignty and Nationalism

Like one of Vizenor's frequently cited authorities, Jean Baudrillard, the real is not avoided, but actually embraced.[5] When, all around, one finds New Age posers and postindian warriors of tragic victimry, Vizenor tenaciously defends the real. This is the reality of transmotion, tricksterism, sovenance, survivance, the tease and humor, rather than the *real* of the invented blood taxonomies, pan-Indian nationalism and categorical certainties of Euro-American scientific modernism.

There are many similarities between pan-Indian nationalism and the political aesthetics of modernism. In the writings of Ward Churchill, perhaps the most eminent native nationalist in the United States, "Indians" are frequently depicted as racially real, grouped by blood quantum into long-suffering "nations." Churchill, whom Vizenor recently referred to as "an ideologue of *indian* victimry" (Lee and Vizenor 160), has become a tenacious documentarian of Nazi-like genocide on the part of Aryan Euro-Americans against native "nations."

In her essay on Wallace Stegner, Cook-Lynn lambasts the "half-breed" as being a cultural and biological threat to Plains Indians. According to Cook-Lynn, "for the most part, native populations continue to view intermarriage as one of the risks to cultural and political survival, and there is plenty of evidence in contemporary tribal life to indicate that the Plains Indians have always regarded it with suspicion" (36). For Vizenor on the other hand, the invoking of racial purity signifies a native absence. Its referent is primarily to the European concept of "race" as a biological entity which confers physical and cultural characteristics upon arbitrarily bounded groups of people. The real in Vizenor's writings is never signified by bloodlines. Blood quantum and "race" are "kitschy" European political fictions which have no connection to the ways of life or sensibility of a people. "Exclusion by natives is not resistance," writes Vizenor in *Fugitive Poses*. Invoking the lineage of racialism is to trace one's authority to a native absence. By contrast, Vizenor tells us, leaders such as Tecumseh, Sitting Bull, Crazy Horse, Chief Joseph, Geronimo and Wovoka traced their sense of union to a native presence.

The biological notions and "nations" of the nationalists are constituted as political mirror images of European concepts. While there are obvious political advantages to the invention of natives as "nations," these are always simulations. In fact, in Vizenor's sense they are double simulations. The original representation was a European one which helped to legitimate dispossession—if natives were separate and distinct, "nations," then acts of theft made legal by "treaties" could be rationalized in terms of contracts between equals. Indian nationalism, which Vizenor characterizes as "the ideology of banality," transfigures natives into the forms invented by their colonists. Natives may receive certain benefits from this double simulation in terms of assistance with land returns, reparations, tribal administrations, the marketing of arts and crafts and the casino economy, but nationhood or pan-nationhood, as it has evolved, again harks back only to the native absence. Even the treaties, which numerous scholars and activists are now poring over as a means to secure various advantages for natives, fixes natives as *indians*. It constitutes them as bona fide members of invented and contrived groupings.

As Vizenor tells us in *Fugitive Poses,* treaties are a "perversion of native transmotion" (148).

Nationalism tethers sovereignty to land and nationhood. Yet, for Vizenor, sovereignty is much more. It must "embrace more than mere reservation territory." Native sovereignty is:

[T]he right of motion, and transmotion is personal, reciprocal, the source of survivance, but not territorial . . . in the visions of transformation: the humor of motion as survivance over dominance; the communal movement to traditional food sources; dreams and memories as sources of shared consciousness; the stories of reincarnation, out of body travel; the myths and metaphors of flying; communal nicknames and memories of migration; the spiritual and herbal powers to heal lost souls. (*Fugitive* 182, 184)

Vizenor's vision of sovereignty, what he usually terms sovenance or survivance, does not operate on the same epistemological playing field as the European concept of sovereignty. It is here that we can once again contrast the real with the *real.* Sovereignty is a quality which Europeans conferred upon themselves in territories that they colonized. Following a long tradition of European philosophy, the state and civil society were thought to be the products of various social contracts or "covenants" that bound individuals into a larger unit of organization for mutual protection. According to the seventeenth-century English philosopher Thomas Hobbes, the sovereign is one man or an assembly of men in whom authority has been invested by a populace in exchange for protection against each other and "outsiders." The absolute condition of this arrangement, or "covenant," is that the subjects forego authority over themselves and submit completely to the will of the sovereign within a defined territory. Sovereignty can be attained through the establishment of political institutions or by conquest. Either way, covenants are made to bind both subjects and sovereigns (Hobbes 139-70).

The colonization and settlement of North America must be assumed to fall under Hobbes's notion of sovereignty by conquest. While certain conventions, such as treaties or exchanges, were sometimes followed in order to assume authority and ownership, sovereignty itself generally stands alone. The treaty merely provided some formal legitimacy when it was necessary. The European concept of sovereignty is an irreducible absolute which powers the workings of the state. It over-rides all treaties and other agreements, demonstrating that these too were double simulations. They not only simulated native groups as *indians,* but they simulated sincerity and authority. As such, European sovereignty ranks, like the "invisible hand" of the market, as one of the most fantastic creations of the European imagination. Hobbes's covenants, as Michael Taussig has pointed out, are not covenants in any real sense of an exchange between people. Rather, they are "not agreement so much as the agreement to agree, not belief so much as make-believe which, in retrospect, is but a formula of infinite regress checked by mythic power (of the covenant)" (Taussig 125-26).

Thus, the European idea of sovereignty, embraced by nationalism, is a simulation, a real abstraction, removed from the histories and experiences of *all* people. It is the experiences of native people in their humor, motion, survival, and memories that is real for Gerald Vizenor, and it is to this realism, and not the burdens of the *real* world of science, nations and victimhood, that he upholds. Although some may see Vizenor's writings as nihilist or "obscurantist," as Ward Churchill once remarked, there is clearly a positive, affirmative message of native survivance which comes through. The affirmation is always to the autonomous ways of thinking and being of native people. If a political platform were to be advanced, it would involve whatever promotes these native realities in contrast to the contrived, and entirely self-defeating *real*ism of racialism, nationalism, and social science.

Notes

1. Vizenor combines the words "post" and "Indian" to avoid capitalizing "Indian." The postindian refers to the manifold representations of natives that have been created since Columbus. Its nuances are explored more fully in *Manifest Manners: Postindian Warriors of Survivance* (Wesleyan UP/UP of New England, 1994) and *Hotline Healers: An Almost Browne Novel* (Hanover, NH: Wesleyan UP/UP of New England, 1997).

2. This is presumably because of the enormously open, contingent, random and flexible nature of the "environment" within which Darwinian natural selection occurs.

3. After the bones of 23 natives were discovered in a campus laboratory, the University of Nebraska recently announced that it would return the bones of 1,702 natives to tribal authorities. See "Nebraska University to Give Indian Bones to Tribes for Reburial" (*San Francisco Chronicle* 3 Sept. 1998: A10). It has been estimated that the number of natives whose bones are held at the Smithsonian Institution is 18,500, while there are another 5,000 at Harvard's Peabody Museum, and 20,000 with the National Park Service. See Pemina Yellow Bird and Kathryn Milun, "Interrupted Journeys: The Cultural Politics of Indian Reburial," in *Displacements: Cultural Identities in Question,* ed. Angelika Bammer (Bloomington and Indianapolis: Indiana UP, 1994), 3-24.

4. See the excellent discussions in James Clifford, *The Predicament of Culture* (Cambridge: Harvard UP, 1986), and Johannes Fabian, *Time and the Other: How Anthropology Makes Its Object* (New York: Columbia UP, 1983).
5. A commentary along these lines is provided by Rex Butler, "Jean Baudrillard's Defence of the Real," in *Jean Baudrillard: Art and Artefact*, ed. Nicholas Zurbrugg (London: Sage, 1997), 51-63.

Works Cited

Butler, Rex. "Jean Baudrillard's Defence of the Real." *Jean Baudrillard: Art and Artefact*. Ed. Nicholas Zurbrugg. London: Sage, 1997. 51-63.

Clifford, James. *The Predicament of Culture*. Cambridge: Harvard UP, 1986.

Cook-Lynn, Elizabeth. *Why I Can't Read Wallace Stegner and Other Essays*. Madison: U of Wisconsin P, 1996.

Durkheim, Emile. *The Rules of the Sociological Method*. Trans. Sarah Solovay and John Mueller. Chicago: U of Chicago P, 1938.

Fabian, Johannes. *Time and the Other: How Anthropology Makes Its Object*. New York: Columbia UP, 1983.

Foucault, Michel. *Power/Knowledge: Selected Interviews and Other Writings 1972-1977*. Trans. Colin Gordon. Brighton: Harvester P, 1980.

Hobbes, Thomas. *Leviathan Parts I and II*. Indianapolis: Bobbs-Merrill, 1980 [1631].

Laing, R. D. *The Voice of Experience*. New York: Pantheon, 1982.

Lyman, Christopher. *The Vanishing Race and Other Illusions*. New York: Pantheon, 1982.

"Nebraska University to Give Indian Bones to Tribes for Reburial." *San Francisco Chronicle* 3 Sept. 1988: A10.

Taussig, Michael. *The Magic of the State*. New York: Routledge, 1997.

Vizenor, Gerald. *Fugitive Poses: Native American Indian Scenes of Absence and Presence*. Lincoln: U of Nebraska P, 1998.

——. *Hotline Healers: An Almost Browne Novel*. Hanover, NH: Wesleyan UP/UP of New England, 1997.

Vizenor, Gerald, and A. Robert Lee. *Postindian Conversations*. Lincoln: U of Nebraska P, 1999.

Wright, Will. *Wild Knowledge: Science, Language, and Social Life in a Fragile Environment*. Minneapolis: U of Minnesota P, 1992.

Yellow Bird, Pemina, and Kathryn Milun. "Interrupted Journeys: The Cultural Politics of Indian Reburial." *Displacements: Cultural Identities in Question*. Ed. Angelika Bammer. Bloomington and Indianapolis: Indiana UP, 1994. 3-24.

GERALD VIZENOR:
A BIBLIOGRAPHY

Books

Cranes Arise. Minneapolis: Nodin P, 1999.

Postindian Conversations, Gerald Vizenor and A. Robert Lee. Lincoln: U of Nebraska P, 1999.

Fugitive Poses: Native American Indian Scenes of Absence and Presence. The Abraham Lincoln Series. Lincoln: U of Nebraska P, 1998.

Hotline Healers: An Almost Browne Novel. Hanover, NH: Wesleyan UP/UP of New England, 1997.

ed., *Native American Literature: A Brief Introduction and Anthology.* Literary Mosaic Series. New York: HarperCollins, 1995.

Harold of Orange/Harold Von Orangen. Trans. Wolfgang Hochbruck. Osnabrück Bilingual Editions of Marginalized Authors, Eggingen, Germany: Editions Klaus Isele, 1994.

Manifest Manners: Postindian Warriors of Survivance. Hanover, NH: Wesleyan UP/UP of New England, 1994.

Shadow Distance: A Gerald Vizenor Reader. Edited and introduced by A. Robert Lee. Hanover, NH: Wesleyan UP/UP of New England, 1994.

ed., *Narrative Chance: Postmodern Discourse on Native American Indian Literatures.* Albuquerque: U of New Mexico P, 1989. Reprinted Norman: U of Oklahoma P, 1993.

Summer in the Spring: Anishinaabe Lyric Poems and Stories. Norman: U of Oklahoma P, 1993. New edition of *Summer in the Spring: Ojibwe Lyric Poems and Tribal Stories.* Minneapolis: Nodin P, 1981—rev. ed. of writings published in *Summer in the Spring* (1965), *anishinabe adisokan* (1970) and *anishinabe nagamon* (1965).

Dead Voices: Natural Agonies in the New World. Norman: U of Oklahoma P, 1992.

The Heirs of Columbus. Hanover, NH: Wesleyan UP/UP of New England, 1991.

Landfill Meditation: Crossblood Stories. Hanover, NH: Wesleyan UP/UP of New England, 1991.

Crossbloods: Bone Courts, Bingo, and Other Reports. Minneapolis: U of Minnesota P, 1990.

Interior Landscapes: Autobiographical Myths and Metaphors. Minneapolis: U of Minnesota P, 1990.

Water Striders. Porter Broadside Series. Santa Cruz, CA: Moving Parts, P, 1989.

The Trickster of Liberty: Tribal Heirs to a Wild Baronage at Petronia. Minneapolis: U of Minnesota P, 1988.

Griever: An American Monkey King in China. Normal: Illinois State U/Fiction Collective, 1987. Reprinted U of Minnesota P, 1990.

ed. *Touchwood: A Collection of Ojibway Prose.* New York: New Rivers P, 1987.

Matsushima: Pine Islands. Minneapolis: Nodin P, 1984.

The People Named the Chippewa: Narrative Histories. Minneapolis: U of Minnesota P, 1984.

Beaulieu and Vizenor Families: Genealogies. Minneapolis: privately printed, 1983.

Earthdivers: Tribal Narratives on Mixed Descent. Minneapolis: U of Minnesota P, 1981.

Darkness in Saint Louis Bearheart. Minneapolis: Truck P, 1978. Reprinted as *Bearheart: The Heirship Chronicles.* Minneapolis: U of Minnesota P, 1990.

Wordarrows: Indians and Whites in the New Fur Trade. Minneapolis: U of Minnesota P, 1978. Italian trans.: *Parolefrecce.* Trans. Maria Vitotoria D'Amico. Series Indiamericana. Ed. Laura Coltelli, U of Pisa, 1992.

Tribal Scenes and Ceremonies. Minneapolis: Nodin P, 1976. Rev. Minneapolis: U of Minnesota P, 1990.

The Everlasting Sky: New Voices from the People Named the Chippewa. New York: Crowell-Collier P, 1972.

anishinabe adisokan: Tales of the People. Minneapolis: Nodin P, 1970.

Escorts to White Earth, 1868-1968: 100 Years on a Reservation. Minneapolis: Four Winds, 1968.

Thomas James White Hawk. Mound, MN: Four Winds, 1968.

Empty Swings: Haiku in English. Minneapolis: Nodin P, 1967.

Slight Abrasions: A Dialogue in Haiku. With Jerome Downes. Minneapolis: Nodin P, 1966.

anishinabe nagamon: Songs of the People. Minneapolis: Nodin P, 1965.

Raising the Moon Vines: Original Haiku in English. Minneapolis: Nodin P, 1964.

Seventeen Chirps: Haiku in English. Minneapolis: Nodin P, 1964.

Two Wings the Butterfly: Haiku Poems in English. St. Cloud, MN. Privately printed, 1962.

Born in the Wind. St. Cloud, MN. Privately printed, 1960.

Excerpted Short Fiction, Stories and Essays

"Feral Lasers." *Postmodern American Fiction: A Norton Anthology.* Ed. Paula Geyh, Fred Leebron, and Andrew Levy. New York: Norton, 1998. 548-54.

"Oshkiwiinag: Heartlines on the Trickster Express." *The Year's Best Fantasy and Horror.* Ed. Ellen Datlow and Terri Windling. Tenth Annual Collection, New York: St. Martin's P, 1997. 480-94. Also published in *Blue Dawn, Red Earth,* ed. Clifford Trafzer (New York: Doubleday/Anchor, 1996), 231-54; and *Native American Literature,* ed. Gerald Vizenor (New York: HarperCollins, 1995), 142-57. First published in *Religion and Difference,* The U of Notre Dame 26.1 (Spring 1994): 89-106.

"Transethnic Anthropologism." *Margins in British and American Literature, Film and Culture.* Ed. Marita Nadal and Dolores Herreto. Departmento de Filologia Inglesa y Alemana, Universidad de Zaragoza, Spain, 1997. 181-84.

"Bone Courts: The Rights and Narrative Representations of Tribal Bones." *Contemporary Archaeology in Theory.* Ed. Robert Preucel and Ian Hodder. New York and Oxford: Blackwell, 1996. 652-63. First published in *American Indian Quarterly* 10.4 (Fall 1986): 319-31. Revised and reprinted in *The Interrupted Life* (New York: Museum of Contemporary Art, 1991), 58-67.

"Gambling." *Encyclopaedia of the American Indian.* Ed. Frederick Hoxie. Boston: Houghton Mifflin, 1996. 212-14.

"Postindian Autoinscriptions: The Origins of Essentialism and Pluralism in Descriptive Tribal Names." *Cultural Difference and the Literary Text.* Ed. Winfried Siemerling and Katrin Schwenk. Iowa City: U of Iowa P, 1996. 29-39.

"Authored Animals: Creature Tropes in Native American Fiction." *Social Research. New School for Social Research* 2.3 (Fall 1995): 661-83.

"Gerald Vizenor: Notes and Commentary." *Writer's Notebook.* Ed. Howard Junker. New York: HarperCollins, 1995. First published in *Zyzzyva* 8 (Winter 1992): 126-43.

"Hotline Healers: Virtual Animals on Panda Radio." *Caliban* 15 (1995): 17-28.

"Indian Identities." *A Companion to American Thought.* Ed. Richard Wightman Fox and James Kloppenberg. New York and Oxford: Blackwell, 1995. 331-33.

"Native American Indian Identities: Autoinscriptions and the Culture of Names." *Native American Perspectives on Literature and History.* Ed. Alan Velie. Norman: U of Oklahoma P, 1995. 117-26. First published in *Genre: Forms of Discourse and Culture* Special Issue 25.4 (Winter 1992): 431-40.

"Stone Columbus: Talk Radio from the Santa Maria Casino." *After Yesterday's Crash: The Avant-Pop Anthology.* Ed. Larry McCaffery. New York: Viking Penguin, 1995. 220-31.

Ishi and the Wood Ducks. Native American Literature: An Introduction and Anthology. Ed. Gerald Vizenor. New York: HarperCollins, 1995. 299-336.

"Almost Browne: The Twice Told Tribal Trickster." *Listening to Ourselves: More Stories from "The Sound of Writing."* Ed. Alan Cheuse and Caroline

Marshall. New York: Doubleday/Anchor, 1994. 233-41. Also published in *The Harper American Literature Anthology*, vol. 2, 2nd ed., ed. Donald McQuade (New York: HarperCollins, 1994). 2199-2206.

"Monte Cassino Curiosa: Heart Dancers at the Headwaters." *Caliban* 14 (1994): 60-70.

"Reversals of Fortune." *Shadow Distance: A Gerald Vizenor Reader*. Hanover, NH: Wesleyan UP/UP of New England, 1994. 219-26. Previously published as "Reversals of Fortune: Tribalism in the Nick of Time." *Caliban* 13 (1993): 22-28.

"The Ruins of Representation: Shadow Survivance and the Literature of Dominance." *An Other Tongue*. Ed. Alfred Arteaga. Durham: Duke UP, 1994. 139-67. Previously published in *American Indian Quarterly* 17.1 (Winter 1993): 7-30.

"The Tragic Wisdom of Salamanders." *Shadow Distance: A Gerald Vizenor Reader*. Hanover, NH: Wesleyan UP/UP of New England, 1994. 194-209. Previously published in *Caliban* 12 (1993): 16-27 and *Sacred Trusts: Essays on Stewardship and Responsibility*, ed. Michael Katakis (San Francisco: Mercury House), 161-76.

"The Envoy to Haiku." *Chicago Review* 39.3 (1993): 55-62.

"The Power of Names." *News from Native California* 7.3 (Summer 1993): 38-41.

"Trickster Discourse: Comic and Tragic Themes in Native American Literature." *Buried Roots and Indestructible Seeds: The Survival of American Indian Life in Story, History, and Spirit*. Ed. Mark Lindquist and Martin Zanger. 1993. Madison: U of Wisconsin P, 1994. 33-41.

"Trickster Photography: Simulations in the Ethnographic Present." *Exposure* 29.1 (Fall 1993): 4-5.

"Wings on the Santa Maria." *Avante-Pop: Fiction for a Daydream Nation*. Ed. Larry McCaffery. Boulder, CO: Black Ice, 1993. 199-206.

"Christopher Columbus: Lost Havens in the Ruins of Representation." *American Indian Quarterly* 16.4 (Fall 1992): 521-32.

"Gambling on Sovereignty." *American Indian Quarterly* 16.3 (Summer 1992): 411-13. Republished in [Tokyo] *Japan Times Weekly* Summer 1992.

"Introduction." *Genre* 25.4 (Winter 1992): 315-19.

"Ishi Bares His Chest: Tribal Simulations and Survivance." *Partial Recall: Photographs of Native North Americans*. Ed. Lucy R. Lippard. New York: New P, 1992. 65-71.

"Manifest Manners: The Long Gaze of Christopher Columbus." *Boundary 2* 19.2 (Fall 1992): 223-35.

"The Moccasin Game." *Earth Song, Sky Spirit: Short Stories of the Contemporary Native American Experience*. Ed. Clifford E. Trafzer. New York: Doubleday, 1992. 37-62.

"Moccasin Games." *Without Discovery*. Ed. Ray Gonzales. Seattle: Broken

Moon P, 1992. 73-89. Previously published in *Caliban* 9 (Spring 1990): 96-109.

"Native American Indian Literature: Critical Metaphors of the Ghost Dance." *World Literature Today* 66.2 (Spring 1992): 223-27.

"Bad Breath." *Landfill Meditation: Crossblood Stories* by Gerald Vizenor. Hanover, NH: Wesleyan UP/UP of New England, 1991. 68-97. Previously published in *An Illuminated History of the Future*, ed. Curtis White (Normal: Illinois State U/Fiction Collective Two, 1989), 135-64.

"The Baron of Patronia." *Talking Leaves:Contemporary Native American Short Stories*. Ed. Craig Lesley. New York: Dell, 1991. 284-93. Previously published in *The Trickster of Liberty: Tribal Heirs to a Wild Baronage at Petronia* (Minneapolis: U of Minnesota P, 1988), 3-19.

"China Browne." *Talking Leaves: Contemporary Native American Short Stories*. Ed. Craig Lesley. New York: Dell, 1991. 284-93. Reprinted from *The Trickster of Liberty: Tribal Heirs to a Wild Baronage at Petronia* (Minneapolis: U of Minnesota P, 1988), 21-42.

"Confrontation or Negotiation." *Native American Testimony: A Chronicle of Indian-White Relations from Prophesy to the Present, 1492-1992*. Ed. Peter Nabokov. New York: Viking Penguin, 1991. 376-80.

"Episodes in Mythic Verism, from *Monsignor Missalwait's Interstate*." *Landfill Meditation: Crossblood Stories* by Gerald Vizenor. Hanover, NH: Wesleyan UP/UP of New England, 1991. 116-35. Previously published in *The New American Novel: Works in Progress*, ed. Mary Dougherty Bartlett (Albuquerque: U of New Mexico P, 1986), 109-26.

"Feral Lasers." *Landfill Meditation: Crossblood Stories* by Gerald Vizenor. Hanover, NH: Wesleyan UP/UP of New England, 1991. 11-21. Previously published in *Caliban* 6 (Fall 1989): 16-23.

"Four Skin Documents." *Landfill Meditation: Crossblood Stories* by Gerald Vizenor. Hanover, NH: Wesleyan UP/UP of New England, 1991. 162-79. Previously published as "Word Cinemas," *Book Forum*, ed. Elaine Jahner, Special Issue: *American Indians Today: Thought, Literature, Art* 5.3 (Summer 1981): 389-95. Reprinted in revised version as "Four Skin," *Tamaqua* 2 (Winter 1991): 89-104.

"Heirs of Columbus." *Fiction International* 20 (Fall 1991): 182-92. Vol. republished as *Looking Glass*, ed. Clifford Trafzer (San Diego: San Diego State UP, 1992).

"Ice Tricksters." *Landfill Meditation: Crossblood Stories* by Gerald Vizenor. Hanover, NH: Wesleyan UP/UP of New Engand, 1991. 22-34. Previously published in *A Gathering of Flowers*, ed. Joyce Carol Thomas (New York: Harper and Row, 1990), 3-20.

"Land Fill Meditation." *Landfill Meditation: Crossblood Stories* by Gerald Vizenor. Hanover, NH: Wesleyan UP/UP of New England, 1991. 98-115.

Previously published in *Minneapolis Star Saturday Magazine* 10 Feb. 1979: 8-12, and in *Words in the Blood: Contemporary Indian Writers of North and South America,* ed. Jamake Highwater (New York: New American Library, 1984) 89-104.

"The Last Lecture." *American Indian Literature.* Ed. Alan Velie. Norman: U of Oklahoma P, 1991. 339-47.

"Luminous Thighs: Mythic Tropisms." *Landfill Meditation: Crossblood Stories* by Gerald Vizenor. Hanover, NH: Wesleyan UP/UP of New England, 1991. 180-201. Published as "Luminous Thighs," *The Lightning Within,* ed. Alan Velie (Norman: U of Oklahoma P, 1991), 67-89. Previously published in *Genre* 18.2 (Summer 1985): 131-49.

"The Psychotaxidermist." *Landfill Meditation:Crossblood Stories* by Gerald Vizenor. Hanover, NH: Wesleyan UP/UP of New England, 1991. 136-46. Previously published in *Minneapolis Star Saturday Magazine* 29 July 1978: 8-11; *The Minnesota Experience,* ed. Jean Ervin (Minneapolis: Adams, 1979), 220-28; and *Words in the Blood: Contemporary Indian Writers of North and South America,* ed. Jamake Highwater (New York: New American Library, 1984), 124-31.

"Rattling Hail Ceremonial." *Landfill Meditation: Crossblood Stories* by Gerald Vizenor. Hanover, NH: Wesleyan UP/UP of New England, 1991. 147-54. Previously published in *Minnesota Star Saturday Magazine,* 2 Apr. 1978: 8-9; and reprinted in *Words in the Blood: Contemporary Indian Writers of North and South America,* ed. Jamake Highwater (New York: New American Library, 1984), 131-36.

"Reservation Café: The Origins of American Indian Instant Coffee." *Landfill Meditation: Crossblood Stories* by Gerald Vizenor. Hanover, NH: WesleyanUP/UP of New England, 1991. 155-61. Previously published in *Earth Power Coming: Short Fiction in Native American Literature,* ed. Simon J. Ortiz (Tsaile, AZ: Navajo Community College P, 1983), 31-36. Revised version of "Anishinabica: Instant Tribal Coffee," *Minnesota Star* 1981. French translation: "Café ou les origins du café instante." Trans. Manuel Van Thienen, *Sur le dosde la litérature amerindienne,* 1991.

"Stone Trickster." *Northeast Indian Quarterly* 8 (Fall 1991): 26-27.

"Bone Courts: The Rights and Narrative Representation of Tribal Bones." *Crossbloods: Bone Courts, Bingo, and Other Reports* by Gerald Vizenor. Minneapolis: U of Minnesota P, 1990. 62-82. Also published in *American Indian Quarterly* 10.4 (1986): 319-31. Reprinted and revised as "Bone Courts: The Natural Rights of Tribal Remains," *The Interrupted Life* (New York: The Museum of Contemporary Art, 1991), 58-67.

"Native American Dissolve." *Oshkaabewis Native Journal* 1.1 (1990): 63-65.

"Socioacupuncture: Mythic Reversals and the Striptease in Four Scenes." *Out There: Marginalization and Contemporary Cultures.* New York: New

Museum of Contemporary Art/MIT P, 1990. Previously published in *The American Indian and the Problem of History*, ed. Calvin Martin (New York: Oxford UP, 1987).

"Trickster Discourse." *American Indian Quarterly* 16.3 (Summer 1990): 277-87.

"Trickster Discourse: Comic Holotropes and Language Games." *Narrative Chance: Postmodern Discourse on Native American Indian Literatures.* Ed. Gerald Vizenor. Albuquerque: U of New Mexico P, 1989. 187-211. Reprinted Norman: U of Oklahoma P, 1993.

"Trickster Discourse." *Wicazo Sa Review* 5.1 (Spring 1989): 2-7.

"Laurel Hole in the Day." *Touchwood: A Collection of Ojibway Prose* by Gerald Vizenor. New York: New Rivers P, 1987. 138-41. Previously published in Gerald Vizenor, *Wordarrows: Indians and Whites in the New Fur Trade* (Minneapolis: U of Minnesota P, 1978) 47-53; and *On the Reservation* 14.3 (Spring 1986): 30-32.

"Wampum to Pictures of Presidents." *Different Shores: Perspectives on Race and Ethnicity in America.* Ed. Ronald Takaki. New York: Oxford UP, 1987. 126-28.

"Mystic Warrior Speaks with Tongue Forked and a Vision Flawed." *Minneapolis Star and Tribune* 18 May 1984: C16.

"Indian Alcoholics Are Individuals, Not White Mice." *Minneapolis Tribune* 23 Apr. 1982: A15.

"Buffalo Bill: An Emblem of Ersatz History." *Minneapolis Tribune* 29 Nov. 1981: A19.

"Indian Manikins with a Few References." *Minneapolis Tribune* 23 Apr. 1981: A10.

"Paraday Chicken Pluck." *Earthdivers: Tribal Narratives on Mixed Descent* by Gerald Vizenor. Minneapolis: U of Minnesota P, 1981. 95-104. Previously published as "Paraday at the Berkeley Chicken Center," *Metropolis Magazine* 12 Apr. 1977: 23.

"Tribal Trickster Dissolves: White 'Word' Piles with a Red Man's Brew." *Minneapolis Star* 31 Aug. 1981: A4.

"Smallpox and the River Are Dead." *Minneapolis Tribune Sunday Picture Magazine* 30 Dec. 1979: 12.

"Dennis Banks: What Sort of Hero?" *Minneapolis Tribune* 22 July 1978: A4.

"Fruit Juice and Tribal Tricksters." *Wordarrows: Indian and Whites in the New Fur Trade* by Gerald Vizenor. Minneapolis: U of Minnesota P, 1978. 75-81. Previously published as "MacChurbbs and the Celibate Juicer: Winter Quarter Lecture Notes," *Metropolis Magazine* 15 Feb. 1977: 27.

"Migration Tricks from Tribalness: Five Stories." *Minnesota Monthly* Jan. 1978: 8-9.

"Preserving Trivial Tattle in California." *Minneapolis Tribune* 5 Feb. 1978: A13.

"Tribal People and the Poetic Image: Visions of Eyes and Hands." *American Indian Art: Form and Tradition.* Minneapolis: Walker Art Center, 1972. 15-22.

"Thomas James White Hawk: Wrap-Up?" *New Twin Citian* 1.1 (Jan. 1970): 39-44.

"'This Is Good for the People': Indian Education and Senator Mondale at Rough Rock." *Twin Citian* July 1969: 17-20.

"We Rarely Turn Anyone Down." *Twin Citian* 6 Oct. 1969: 35-38.

"Why Must Thomas White Hawk Die?" *Twin Citian* 10 June 1968: 17-32.

"How Sly Sees It." *Twin Citian* 10 Oct. 1967: 60-62.

"Job Center at Lydick Lake: For Some a Wager, for Others a Chance." *Twin Citian* 9 (Aug. 1966): 15-21.

"1966: Plymouth Avenue Is Going to Burn." *Twin Citian* 9 (Oct. 1966): 20-21.

"The Ojibway." *Twin Citian* 8 (10 May 1966): 18-19.

"The Urban Indian." *Twin Citian* 8 (June 1966): 13.

Autobiographical Essays

"Gerald Vizenor: Visions, Scares, and Stories." *Contemporary Authors Autobiography Series* 22. Detroit, MI: Gale, 1995. 255-77.

"July 1947: Many Point Camp." *Inheriting the Land.* Ed. Mark Vintz and Thom Tammaro. Minneapolis: U of Minnesota P, 1993. 313-18.

"Crows Written on the Poplars: Autocritical Autobiographies." *I Tell You Now: Autobiographical Essays by Native Writers.* Ed. Arnold Krupat and Brian Swann. Lincoln: U of Nebraska P, 1987. 99-110.

"Gerald Vizenor, Ojibway/Chippewa Writer." *This Song Remembers: Self-Portraits of Native Americans in the Arts.* Ed. Jane B. Katz. Boston: Houghton Mifflin 1980. 163-69.

"I Know What You Mean, Erdupps MacChurbbs." *Growing Up in Minnesota: Ten Writers Remember Their Childhoods.* Ed. Chester Anderson. Minneapolis: U of Minnesota P, 1976. 79-111.

Selected Interviews

"Postindian Comments: Gerald Vizenor in Dialogue with A. Robert Lee." *Third Text* 43 (Summer 1998): 69-79.

"On Thin Ice, You Might as Well Dance." Interview by Larry McCaffery. *Some Other Frequency: Interviews with Innovative American Authors.* Philadelphia: U of Pennsylvania P, 1996. 287-309.

"Gerald Vizenor." Interview by Helmbrecht Breinig and Klaus Losch. *American Contradictions: Interviews with Nine American Writers.* Ed. Wolfgang Binder and Helmbrecht Breinig. Hanover, NH: Wesleyan UP, 1995. 143-65.

"Mythic Rage and Laughter: An Interview with Gerald Vizenor" by Dallas Miller. *Studies in American Indian Literatures* 7.1 (Spring 1995): 77-96.

"Head Water: An Interview with Gerald Vizenor" by Larry McCaffery and Tom Marshall. *Chicago Review* 39.3/4 (1993): 50-62.

"'I Defy Analysis': A Conversation with Gerald Vizenor" by Rodney Simard. *Studies in American Indian Literatures* 5.3 (Fall 1993): 43-51.

"Gerald Vizenor." Interview in *Winged Words: American Indian Writers Speak.* Ed. Laura Coltelli. Lincoln: U of Nebraska P, 1990. 287-310.

"Follow the Trickroutes: An Interview with Gerald Vizenor." *Survival This Way: Interviews with American Indian Poets.* Ed. Joseph Bruchac. Tucson: U of Arizona P, 1987. 287-310.

"An Interview with Gerald Vizenor" by Neal Bowers and Charles Silet. *MELUS* 8.1 (1981): 41-49.

Book Reviews

Review of Brian Swann, ed., *On the Translation of Native American Literatures* in *World Literature Today* Spring 1993.

"Christopher Columbus: Lost Havens in the Ruins of Representation." Review of thirteen new books on Columbus. *American Indian Quarterly* Fall 1992.

Review of William Least Heat-Moon, *PrairyErth,* in *San Francisco Chronicle* 6 Oct. 1991. Expanded review in *World Literature Today* 1992.

Review of Maxine Hong Kingston, *Tripmaster Monkey,* in *American Book Review* Jan. 1990.

Review of Tom McNab, *The Fast Men,* in *Los Angeles Times* 23 Apr. 1989.

Review of W. P. Kinsella, *The Fencepost Chronicles,* in *Los Angeles Times* 20 Dec. 1987.

Selected Criticism about Gerald Vizenor

Allen, Paula Gunn, ed. *Studies in American Indian Literature: Critical Essays and Course Designs.* New York: Modern Language Association P, 1983.

Bell, Betty Louise, "Almost the Whole Truth: Gerald Vizenor's Shadow Working and Native American Autobiography." *A/B Auto/Biography* 2.2 (Fall 1992): 180-95.

Blaeser, Kimberly M. *Gerald Vizenor: Writing in the Oral Tradition.* Norman: U of Oklahoma P, 1996.

Boyarin, Jonathan. "Europe's Indian, America's Jew: Modiano and Vizenor." *Storm from Paradise: The Politics of Jewish Memory.* Minneapolis: U of Minnesota P, 1992. 9-31.

Fleck, Richard, ed. *Critical Perspectives on Native American Fiction.* Three Continents P, 1993.

Jahner, Elaine. "Allies in the Word Wars: Vizenor's Uses of Contemporary Critical Theory." *Studies in American Indian Literatures* 9.2 (1985): 64-69.

Krupat, Arnold. *The Turn to the Native: Studies in Criticism and Culture.* Lincoln: U of Nebraska P, 1996.

Krupat, Arnold, ed. *New Voices in Native American Literary Criticism.* Washington, DC: Smithsonian Institution P, 1993.

——. *The Voice in the Margin: Native American Literature and the Canon.* Berkeley and Los Angeles: U of California P, 1989.

Krupat, Arnold, and Brian Swann, eds. *I Tell You Now: Autobiographical Essays by Native American Writers.* Lincoln: U of Nebraska P, 1987.

——. *Recovering the Word: Essays on Native American Literature.* Berkeley and Los Angeles: U of California P, 1987.

——. *For Those Who Come After: A Study of Native American Autobiography.* Berkeley and Los Angeles: U of California P, 1985.

Lee, A. Robert. Introduction. *Postindian Conversations.* Gerald Vizenor and A. Robert Lee. Lincoln: U of Nebraska P, 1999. 9-29.

——. "Towards America's Ethnic Postmodern: The Novels of Ishmael Reed, Maxine Hong Kingston, Ana Castillo and Gerald Vizenor." *Roman Contemporain et Identité Culturelle en Amerique du Nord/Contemporary Fiction and Cultural Identity in North America.* Ed. Jaap Lindvelt, Richard Saint Gelais, Will Verhoeven, and Cathérine Raffi-Beroud. Québec, Canada: Nota Bene, 1998. 189-208.

——. "'I Am Your Worst Nightmare': I Am an Indian with a Pen': Native Identity and the Novels of Thomas King, Linda Hogan, Louis Owens and Betty Louise Bell." *Beyond Pug's Tour: National and Ethnic Stereotyping in Theory and Literary Practice.* Ed. C. C. Barfoot. Amsterdam and Atlanta, GA: Rodopi P, 1996. 445-67.

——. "Afro-America, the Before Columbus Foundation and the Literary Multiculturalization of America." *Journal of American Studies* 28.3 (Dec. 1994): 433-50.

——. Introduction. *Shadow Distance: A Gerald Vizenor Reader.* Hanover, NH: Wesleyan UP/UP of New England, 1994. 9-29.

——. "Self-Inscriptions: James Baldwin, Tomás Rivera, Gerald Vizenor and Amy Tan and the Writing-in of America's Non-European Ethnicities." *A Permanent Etcetera: Cross-Cultural Perspectives on Post-war America.* Ed. A. Robert Lee. London and Boulder: Pluto P, 1993. 20-42 and 170-78.

Murray, David. *Forked Tongues: Speech, Writing, and Representation in North American Indian Texts.* Bloomington: Indiana UP, 1980.

Owens, Louis. *Mixedblood Messages: Literature, Film, Family, Place.* Norman: U of Oklahoma P, 1998.

——. "'Grinning Aboriginal Demons': Gerald Vizenor's *Bearheart* and the Indian's Escape from Gothic." *Frontier Gothic: Terror and Wonder at the*

Frontier in American Literature. Ed. Joanne B. Karpinski, David Mogen, and Scott P. Sanders. Rutherford, NJ: Fairleigh Dickinson UP, 1993. 71-83.

——. *Other Destinies: Understanding the American Indian Novel.* Norman: U of Oklahoma P, 1992.

——. " 'Ecstatic Strategies': Gerald Vizenor's *Darkness in Saint Louis Bearheart.*" *Narrative Chance: Postmodern Discourse on Native American Indian Literatures.* Ed. Gerald Vizenor. Albuquerque: U of New Mexico P, 1989. 141-53.

Owens, Louis, issue ed. Gerald Vizenor, special ed. *Studies in American Indian Literatures* 1 (Spring 1997).

Ruoff, A. Lavonne Brown. *American Indian Literatures: An Introduction, Bibliographic Review, and Selected Bibliography.* New York: The Modern Language Association of America, 1990.

——. "Woodland Word Warrior: An Introduction to the Works of Gerald Vizenor." *MELUS* 13.1-2 (Spring-Summer 1986): 130-43.

Ruppert, James. *Mediation in Contemporary Native American Fiction.* Norman: U of Oklahoma P, 1995.

Simard, Rodney, issue ed. Gerald Vizenor special ed. *Studies in American Indian Literatures* 5.3 (Fall 1993).

Velie, Alan, ed. *Native Perspectives on Literature and History.* Norman: U of Oklahoma P, 1994.

——. "The Trickster Novel." *Narrative Chance: Postmodern Discourse on Native American Indian Literatures.* Ed. Gerald Vizenor. Albuquerque: U of New Mexico P, 1989. 121-37.

——. *Four American Indian Literary Masters: N. Scott Momaday, James Welch Leslie Marmon Silko, and Gerald Vizenor.* Norman: U of Oklahoma P, 1982.

Weaver, Jace. *That the People Might Live: Native American Literatures and Native American Community.* New York: Oxford UP, 1997.

Wiget, Andrew O. *Native American Literature.* Twayne's United States Authors 467. Philadelphia: Hall, 1985.

Wiget, Andrew O., ed. *Critical Essays on Native American Literature.* Philadelphia: Hall, 1985.

Wilson, Terry P., and Robert Black, eds. Gerald Vizenor Issue. *American Indian Quarterly* 9.1 (1985): 1-78.

CONTRIBUTORS

Elizabeth Blair received her doctorate in poetry from the University of Illinois at Chicago. She writes articles about Native American Literature and is currently an Assistant Professor at Southwest State University in Marshall, Minnesota.

Douglas Dix, Institute for Advanced Cultural Studies, Brno, The Czech Republic; **Wolfgang Hochbruck,** University of Stuttgart, Germany; **Kirstie McAlpine,** University of Newcastle, England; **Dallas Miller,** University of Freiburg, Germany; and **Mary Tyne,** University of Leiden, Holland, were members of the Third Annual "Stuttgart Seminar in Cultural Studies" in which Gerald Vizenor was a featured speaker and which led to this collective essay.

Amy J. Elias is Associate Professor of English at the University of Alabama at Birmingham. Her articles have appeared in *Contemporary Literature, Modern Fiction Studies, Critique* and *Postmodern Studies.* She recently completed a book on postmodern fiction and historiography and is now working on a study of contemporary literature and historical trauma.

Linda Lizut Helstern is an adjunct lecturer in English and Assistant to the Dean for External Affairs, College of Engineering, Southern Illinois University, Carbondale. Her critical studies of Gerald Vizenor and Louis Owens have appeared in *Studies in American Indian Literatures,* and her poems have appeared in a number of journals and little magazines.

Richard Hutson is Associate Professor in the English Department of the University of California, Berkeley, where he teaches American literature and cultural history. He is co-director of the American Studies Program.

Elaine A. Jahner is Professor of English at Dartmouth College. She has published widely, both in the United States and Europe, on the cross-cultural relationships between literary analysis and anthropology and sociology. Her essays have appeared in Paula Gunn Allen, ed., *Studies in American Indian Literatures* (1983), *American Indian Quarterly* (1983), *Narrative Chance* (1989), *Feminist Measures* (1994) and elsewhere.

Arnold Krupat is the author of *For Those Who Come After: A Study of Native American Autobiography* (1985), *The Voice in the Margin: Native American Literature and the Canon* (1989), *Ethnocriticism: Ethnography, History, Literature* (1992) and *The Turn to the Native: Studies in Criticism and Culture* (1996) and editor (with Brian Swann) of *I Tell You Now: Autobiographical Essays by Native American Writers* (1987). He teaches at Sarah Lawrence College.

A. Robert Lee is Professor of American Literature at Nihon University, Tokyo, having previously taught at the University of Kent at Canterbury, England. His publications include *Designs of Blackness: Mappings in the Literature and Culture of Afro-America* (1998); eleven volumes in the Vision Press Critical Studies Series from *Black Fiction: New Studies in the Afro-American Novel Since 1945* (1980) to *William Faulkner: The Yoknapatawpha Fiction* (1990); the essay-collections *A Permanent Etcetera: Cross-Cultural Perspectives on Post-War America* (1993), *Other Britain, Other British: Contemporary Multicultural Fiction* (1995), with W. M. Verhoeven, *Making America/Making American Literature: Franklin to Cooper* (1995), and *The Beat Generation Writers* (1996). He is the editor of *Shadow Distance: A Gerald Vizenor Reader* (1994) and the co-maker, with Gerald Vizenor, of *Postindian Conversations* (1999).

Tom Lynch wrote his Ph.D. dissertation (University of Oregon, 1989) on American haiku and has published articles on both haiku and Native American literature. He is adjunct professor at New Mexico State University, where he teaches Southwestern literature and nature writing. Currently he is researching and writing an ecocritical study of Southwestern writers and compiling an anthology of works on the Chihuahuan desert.

David Mogen (B.A. Columbia University; Ph.D. University of Colorado, Boulder) teaches American frontier literature, Native American literature, and interdisciplinary courses integrating the arts and sciences in the English Department at Colorado State University. His publications include *Wilderness Visions: The Western Theme in Science Fiction Literature* (1985; 1993), *Ray Bradbury* (1986), and two co-edited anthologies of original essays: *The Frontier Experience and the American Dream* (1989) and *Frontier Gothic* (1993).

David Murray teaches American Studies at the University of Nottingham, England, and includes among his publications the essay-collection *Literary Theory and Poetry: Extending the Canon* (1989) and *Forked Tongues: Speech, Writing and Representation in North American Indian Texts* (1991).

Barry O'Connell is Professor of English at Amherst College. He has published essays on country music, the history of Appalachian coalminers, and American literature. *On Our Own Ground: The Complete Writings of William Apess, a Pequot,* which he edited and introduced, is his most recent publication. He co-edits, with Colin Calloway, a series for the University of Massachusetts Press: Native Americans in the Northeast: History, Culture, and the Contemporary.

Louis Owens is currently Professor of English at the University of New Mexico. Of Choctaw, Cherokee, and Irish-American descent, Owens is a widely published author of both fiction and critical works. Among his full-length works are the novels *Bone Game* (1994), *The Sharpest Sight* (1992), *Wolfsong* (1990), *Nightland* (1996), *Dark River* (1999), and the critical studies *John Steinbeck's Re-Vision of America* (1985), *American Indian Novelists: An Annotated Critical Bibliography* (1985), *The Grapes of Wrath: Trouble in the Promised Land* (1989), *Other Destinies: Understanding the American Indian Novel* (1992), and *Mixedblood Messages: Literature, Film, Family, Place* (1998).

Joe Rigert has been a friend and colleague of Gerald Vizenor for most of the thirty-three years that Rigert has been a reporter, editor and editorial writer for the Minneapolis newspaper now known as the *Star Tribune.*

Juana María Rodríguez recently obtained her doctorate in Ethnic Studies at the University of California at Berkeley and is currently Assistant Professor in the English Department at Bryn Mawr College. Her research explores the intersections and interstices of discourses on ethnicity, gender, sexuality, and subjectivity.

James Ruppert holds a joint appointment in English and Alaska Native Studies at the University of Alaska, Fairbanks. He is a past president of ASAIL and a frequent contributor of articles on Native American literatures. His most recent book is *Mediation in Contemporary Native American Fiction* (1995), published by the University of Oklahoma Press.

Colin Samson is a lecturer in the Department of Sociology at the University of Essex, England, where he is also Director of Native American Studies. He is currently researching the effects of forced settlement on the nomadic Innu people of Northern Labrador, Canada.

Index

1 6/09